MW00639895

This collection of essays by some of the leading scholars in the field sheds new light on the verb in English. The central concern of the volume is to illustrate that verbs can only be adequately and properly understood if studied from both a theoretical and descriptive perspective. In part one, theoretical topics are explored: terminological problems of classifying verbs and verb-related elements, the 'determining' properties of verbs, verb complementation, the semantics and pragmatics of verbs and verbal combinations, and the notions of tense, aspect, voice and modality.
In part two, computer corpora are used to study various types of verb complements and collocations, to trace the development in English of certain verb forms, and to detail the usage of verbs in different varieties and genres of English.

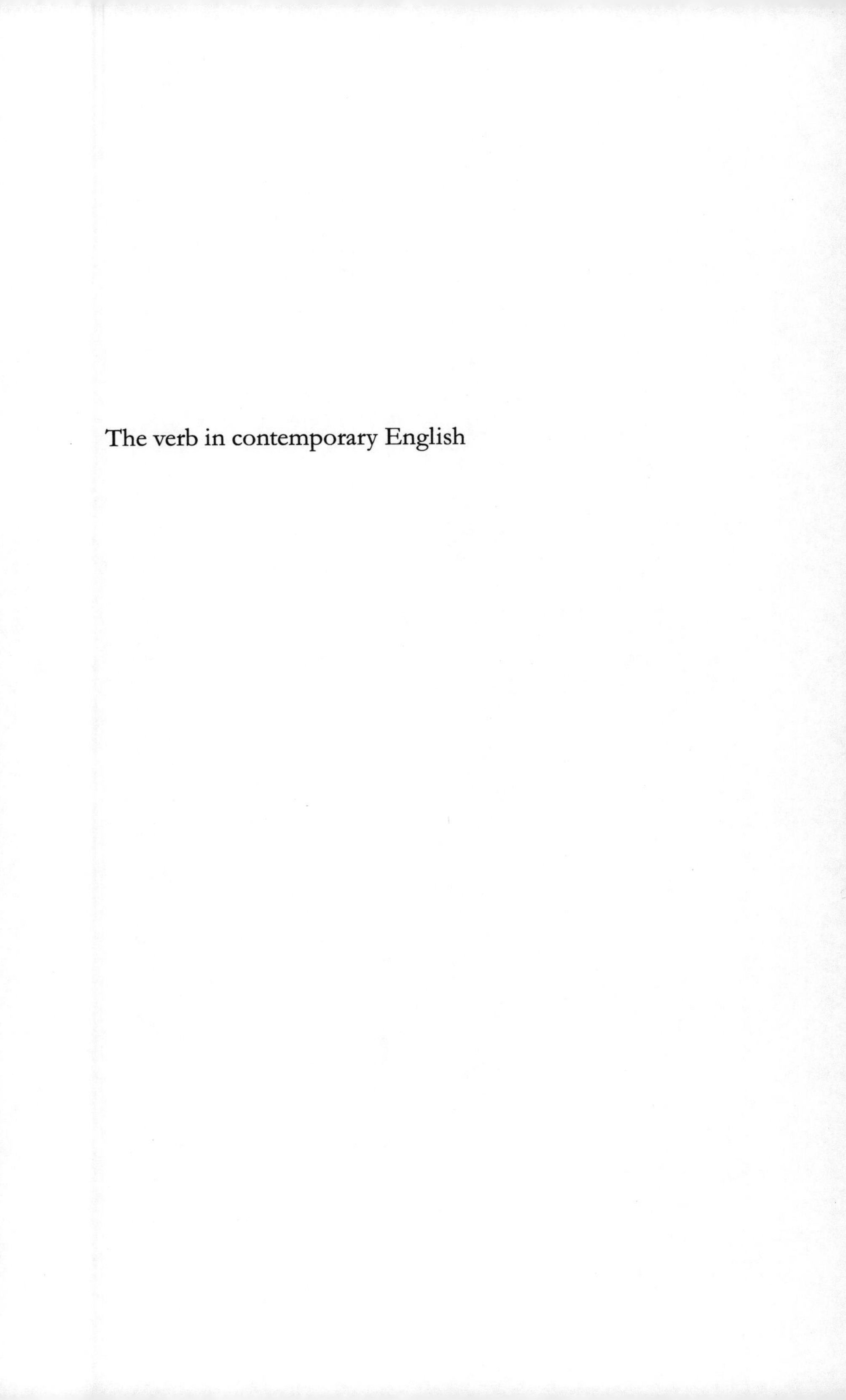

The verb in contemporary English

The verb in contemporary English

Theory and description

Edited by

BAS AARTS
Department of English Language and Literature,
University College London

and

CHARLES F. MEYER
Department of English,
The University of Massachusetts at Boston

Published by the Press Syndicate of the University of Cambridge
The Pitt Building, Trumpington Street, Cambridge CB2 1RP
40 West 20th Street, New York, NY10011-4211, USA
10 Stamford Road, Oakleigh, Melbourne 3166, Australia

First published 1995

Printed in Great Britain at the University Press, Cambridge

A catalogue record for this book is available from the British Library

Library of Congress cataloguing in publication data

The verb in contemporary English / [edited by] Bas Aarts and Charles F. Meyer
p. cm.
Includes index.
ISBN 0 521 46039 5 (hardback)
1. English language – Verb I. Aarts, Bas, 1961– . II. Meyer, Charles F.
PE1271.V46 1995
425 – dc20 95–5277 CIP

ISBN 0521 46039 5 hardback

TS

Dedicated to SIDNEY GREENBAUM
by the editors and contributors

Contents

Contributors

Bas Aarts, Department of English Language and Literature, University College London, UK
Flor Aarts, Department of English, University of Nijmegen, The Netherlands
Jan Aarts, Department of English, University of Nijmegen, The Netherlands
John Algeo, Department of English, University of Georgia, USA
Douglas Biber, Department of English, Northern Arizona University, USA
Jennifer Coates, Department of English, Roehampton Institute, London, UK
Olof Ekedahl, Department of English, University of Lund, Sweden
Edward Finegan, Department of Linguistics, University of Southern California, USA
Rodney Huddleston, Department of English, The University of Queensland, Australia
Richard Hudson, Department of Phonetics and Linguistics, University College London, UK
Stig Johansson, Department of British and American Studies, University of Oslo, Norway
Geoffrey Leech, Department of Linguistics and Modern Languages, University of Lancaster, UK
Lu Li, Institute of Linguistics, Beijing Foreign Studies University, China
Christian Mair, Department of English, University of Freiburg, Germany
Charles F. Meyer, Department of English, The University of Massachusetts at Boston, USA
Andrew Rosta, Department of English, Roehampton Institute, London, UK
I. M. Schlesinger, Department of Psychology, The Hebrew University, Jerusalem, Israel
Anna-Brita Stenström, Department of English, University of Bergen, Norway
Jan Svartvik, Department of English, University of Lund, Sweden

Preface

It is with great pleasure that we dedicate this book to Sidney Greenbaum. In all his work, Sid has stressed the importance not only of understanding the theory behind English grammar, but also the importance of investigating how English is actually used. As a tribute to these interests we have brought together a collection of papers that provide theoretical and descriptive insights into the study of the verb in English.

Sid's work on modern English grammar throughout his career has contributed significantly to the understanding of the structure of the English language. As former students of his, we have benefited from his knowledge of the English language, his instilling in us an appreciation for the complexity of language, and his expert guidance of our work. We hope that this book adequately expresses our gratitude to him.

We would like to offer special thanks to Libby Fay and Laura Melo without whose support this book would not have been possible, and also to Judith Ayling, Kay McKechnie and Joanna West of Cambridge University Press.

August 1994
London and Boston

Bas Aarts
Charles Meyer

1 Introduction: theoretical and descriptive approaches to the study of the verb in English[1]

BAS AARTS and CHARLES F. MEYER

A verb is a power in all speech,
Rings through prose and verse.
It brings to birth.
Elizabeth Jennings,
Parts of Speech, in *Times and Seasons*

1 Introduction

Verbs are found in virtually all the languages of the world (Lyons 1977: 429, Allerton 1982: 1), and throughout history their semantic and syntactic properties have interested philosophers and grammarians alike. As early as *c.* 100 BC Dionysius Thrax stressed the importance of the verb (*rhema*) which he defined in his *Téchne grammatiké* as 'a part of speech without case inflection, but inflected for tense, person, and number, signifying an activity or process performed or undergone'. This definition brings out that the very earliest grammarians were interested in both formal and semantic, or 'notional', characterisations of the word classes. Later grammarians, such as Apollonius Dyscolus in the second century AD, became more interested in the distributional (i.e. syntactic) properties of the word classes.[2] Linguists of all later centuries have been much influenced by the works of these early grammarians, to the extent that, while there might still be disagreement as to whether, for example, pronouns form a separate word class or are simply to be regarded as nouns, no grammarian today would deny that verbs constitute a relatively easily delimitable word class.

While it is true that contemporary linguists and grammarians agree upon the existence of the grammatical class of verb, their approaches to the study of the verb are nevertheless quite varied. Linguists with theoretical orientations have studied the verb from the perspective of X-Bar Theory (Jackendoff 1977), while linguists with both theoretical and descriptive orientations have focussed more on the role of the verb in grammar of English (Huddleston 1976a, 1984, Matthews 1981, Hudson 1990). Descriptive linguists have provided general descriptions of the English verb (Palmer 1987, 1990), as well as specific descriptions of particular complementation patterns (van Ek 1966) or verb forms, such as the infinitive (Andersson 1985, Mair 1990, Duffley 1992). Finally, semantically oriented linguists have been concerned with topics such as the valency of verbs (Allerton 1982), the particular semantic roles that verbs determine in a clause (Fillmore 1968, Schlesinger 1994 and this volume), and the manner in which verbs express tense and aspect (Comrie 1976, 1985, Declerck 1991).

We take the view in this book that an adequate understanding of the verb in contemporary English is best achieved if theoretical treatments of the verb are accompanied by studies that describe its usage. To provide this view of the English verb, we have divided the book into two parts. Part 1, 'Theoretical approaches to the study of the English verb', contains chapters that provide differing theoretical perspectives on the syntax and semantics of the English verb. Part 2, 'Descriptive approaches to the study of the English verb', contains chapters in which analyses of computer corpora are conducted to trace the development of certain verb forms in English, to study various types of verb complementation, and to detail the usage of verbs in different varieties and genres of English. In the remainder of this chapter, we provide an overview of issues that have played a role in theoretical and descriptive treatments of the verb, and detail how these studies relate to the topics explored in this book.

2 Theoretical approaches to the study of the English verb

In this section we deal with a number of issues that have been important in theoretical work dealing with the verb. More specifically, we discuss the terminological problems of classifying verbs and verb-related elements, the 'determining' properties of verbs, verb complementation, the semantics and pragmatics of verbs and verbal combinations, and the notions of tense, aspect, voice and modality.

2.1 Problems in the classification of verbs and verb-related elements

Because the verb has been so widely discussed, its treatment within the grammar of English has raised a number of questions about classifications of the verb and verb-related elements. These questions range from whether the function of verb complementation ought to be kept distinct from the function of verbs as predicators within the clause, to whether the categories of *complementiser* and *Comp* really exist.

In X-BarTheory, a distinction is made between *complements* and *adjuncts* in the Verb Phrase (Jackendoff 1977). Complements are more closely related to the verb than adjuncts. More specifically, complements are obligatory and analysed as sisters of the head verb, while adjuncts are optional and analysed as sisters of V'. Matthews (1981: 123–141) uses the term adjunct in a different sense. He distinguishes adjuncts from *peripheral elements*. The former are more closely related to the verb than the latter, but less closely than complements. Yet another approach is found in the work of Huddleston who subdivides adjuncts into *modifiers* and *peripheral dependents* (1984: 223–225). We encounter terminological confusion in the area of complementation as well. As Ransom (1986: 29, note) observes, the term *complement* has been used in many different senses to indicate not just constituents that are regarded as complements of verbs, such as direct objects, but nominal clauses functioning as the subject of a clause as well.

To clarify the confusion of how verbs and verb complements ought to be classified within the grammar of English, Charles F. Meyer ('Grammatical relations in English') argues that there need to be two distinct levels of grammatical relations: *general* functions and *clause* functions. Individual verbs, for instance, impose syntactic and semantic constraints on the constituents they can take, a general function of verbs characterised by the notion of 'verb complementation'. In addition, independent of the constraints it imposes on other constituents in the clause, the verb has the function of 'predicator', a clause function indicating a particular relationship between the verb and other clause functions, such as subject, object, adverbial, and complement.

Most contemporary theories of syntax maintain that there is a word class called *complementiser* containing words such as *that*, *if*, *whether*, and *for* and that these words are included within an abstract functional category called *Comp*. This category introduces clauses that complement a preceding verb. However, as Richard Hudson argues in 'Competence without Comp?', the existence of this category has never been satisfactorily established. The class of complementisers is very heterogenous, with some complementisers behaving like interrogative pronouns while others behave like subordinating conjunctions or prepositions. Because complementisers do not form a unified word class, it is questionable whether the abstract category Comp is warranted.

2.2 The 'determining' properties of verbs

For linguists of all persuasions, verbs, more than any other word class, can generally be characterised as 'determining' elements. There are a number of ways in which this can be said to be the case.

Firstly, verbs are said to 'govern' the dependent elements that follow them (or precede them, depending on whether we are dealing with a head-first language or a head-last language). This government relation is morphologically visible in many languages, for example on Noun Phrases through different case forms (e.g. German direct objects require a special form of the Noun Phrase: e.g. *Ich sah den Mann*, 'I saw the man', with objective case on the definite article of the direct object, but not **Ich sah der Mann*, with nominative case on the definite article). In English the reflex of verb-government is visible only on pronouns.

Secondly, and this really concerns a two-way dependency, verbs agree with their subjects (and in some languages with their objects) in one or more features such as number, person and gender. It should be borne in mind, however, that neither agreement nor government are notions that exclusively concern verbs. Other elements, such as for example nouns, can also trigger agreement (with adjectives), and prepositions, like verbs, are also said to govern their objects.

The third way in which verbs can be said to be determining elements is also not exclusively, but nevertheless most markedly, a verbal property, and that is that they are instrumental in licensing the presence of what Tesnière (1953, 1959) (working in the field of dependency grammar) has called the *actants* ('performers') of a proposition.[3] By analogy to chemistry the term *valency* has been used to refer to the number of performers (*valents*) a verb takes (cf. Allerton 1982: 2). Consider in this connexion a simple sentence such as (1) below, the performers of which are *Sandra*, *Martin* and *a joke*:

(1) Sandra told Martin a joke.

In valency theory terms the verb *give* is *trivalent* in that it takes three dependents, corresponding to the functional categories of subject, indirect object and direct object respectively.

The relationship between the verb and its performers in a sentence like (1) is not viewed in the same way by all linguists. Thus, while for dependency grammarians (and some others, e.g. Huddleston 1984: 180) the subject is one of the verb's complements, this is not the case for many other linguists. For those working in the generative tradition a distinction is made between *subcategorisation* and *selectional restriction* to characterise the relationships the verb enters into with other elements. Subcategorisation refers to the idea that a head (noun, verb, adjective or preposition) syntactically requires the presence of a constituent of a particular type (e.g. the adjective *fond* requires a following *of*-phrase). Selectional restrictions (in Chomsky 1965) concern the compatibility of semantic features. For example, in English sentences containing the verb *dream* both the subject and the verb must share the feature [+animate]. If the subject lacks this feature unacceptability results (**The CD was dreaming*). Where Verb Phrases are involved, subcategorisation operates only on postverbal arguments (the so-called *internal arguments*), whereas selectional restrictions operate on both internal and *external arguments* (i.e. subjects). As noted, the syntactic treatment of selectional restrictions in terms of features outlined here is that of Chomsky (1965). Anomalous sentences like the one with the dreaming CD cited above are now sometimes argued to be pragmatically, not grammatically, deviant (Horrocks 1987: 36). Alternatively, selectional restrictions can be handled in terms of thematic roles (agent, patient, experiencer etc.), as will be explained presently.

Chomsky has recently replaced the term subcategorisation and now uses *c-selection* (categorial selection; Chomsky 1986a: 86). A further notion, *s-selection* (semantic selection), has also gained currency and concerns the idea that verbs are lexically marked with regard to the thematic roles they assign to their internal and external arguments. The earlier selectional restrictions on arguments can then be handled in terms of a combination of the meaning of their predicates and the s-selectional properties of those predicates (for example if an argument has the thematic role of experiencer it must be [+animate]). It has also been proposed that we can dispense with c-selection because the c-selectional properties of lexical items can be predicted from their s-selectional properties. (See Chomsky and Lasnik 1993; for textbook discussion see Radford 1988: 378ff, Cowper 1992: 57ff.) Thematic roles are relevant to the generativists' view that subjects are not complements of verbs. The reason for this is that it is thought that it is not the verb alone that determines the thematic properties of its subject, but the Verb Phrase of which it is a part (see Marantz 1984, Chomsky 1986a: 59f; and Rothstein 1983 for a diverging view).[4]

To define grammatical functions (GFs) such as subject or object, it has been customary to associate particular thematic (or semantic) roles with particular GFs. For instance, subjects are typically agents, direct objects patients, indirect objects benefactives, and so forth. In the case of the object, however, this type of analysis is problematic. As I. M. Schlesinger demonstrates in 'On the semantics of the object', because objects in English can take almost any semantic role, it is not possible to discuss constraints on objects in terms of semantic roles. Instead, Schlesinger argues that other semantic considerations must be taken into account to distinguish direct objects from indirect objects and objects of prepositions. For instance, while direct objects express the semantic notions of 'Completion' or 'Feat', objects of prepositions do not. In addition, indirect objects are subject to processing constraints, such as the 'Recoverability Constraint', which stipulates that prepositions associated with indirect objects must be immediately recoverable or a verb is blocked from being ditransitive, and the 'Garden-path Constraint' which accounts for the unacceptability of the double-object construction in certain cases.

2.3 Verb complementation

Of the different types of relationships between verbs and their arguments those between the verb and its internal arguments have always received the most attention. These relationships are studied under the general heading of *verb complementation*, a notion which is closely related to the concept of subcategorisation which was discussed in the previous section. Verb complementation is a term that should be used with some caution because, as Matthews (1981: 142–143) notes, there is considerable variance in how this notion is applied. In transformational-generative grammar, as we have seen, verb complements are obligatory constituents following verbs and are distinct from adjuncts, which are optional. In more descriptively-oriented grammars verb complements are given a more semantically based characterisation as elements that are 'required to complete the meaning of the verb' (Quirk et al. 1985: 65). Verb complementation is part of the more general notion of complementation, a grammatical relation that stands in opposition to other grammatical relations, such as e.g. apposition, modification, parataxis and coordination. For general discussion see Matthews (1981: 223f), and for a discussion of the complementation-apposition gradient see Meyer (1992: 51f).

The differences between grammarians in approaches to verb complementation concern a number of areas which we will now briefly review.

Consider first the Verb Phrase. For descriptive grammarians Verb Phrases often consist only of verbs (cf. Quirk et al. 1985: 61–62). A sentence like (2) below, is analysed as in (3) by Quirk et al.:

(2) They have devoured all the Belgian chocolates.

(3)

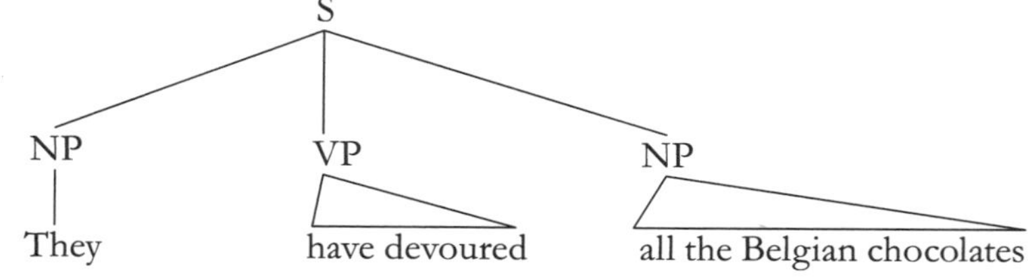

Within the VP a distinction is made between auxiliary verbs (*have*) and main verbs (*devour*), but no further structure is assigned. Notice that the direct object NP is immediately dominated by the S-node. Despite the lack of structure inside the VP, Quirk et al. do suggest that in VPs containing auxiliary verbs the various verb sequences are 'telescoped' into each other (1985: 151). This notion is not made precise, but the suggestion is that the verbs in some sense select each other from left-to-right. Nevertheless, the overall picture is one in which 'the verb phrase operates as the V element in a clause' (1985: 61). The rationale behind Quirk et al.'s treatment seems to be the same as that advocated in Palmer (1987), namely the idea that a complex verb sequence like *may have been devoured* is a 'form' of the verbal paradigm in much the same way as the different elements of the Latin and Greek conjugation classes.

Since the early days of transformational grammar the VP has been a phrase which not only contains verbs, but also verbal complements. (2) is analysed as in (4) in Chomsky (1957: 26, 39).

(4)

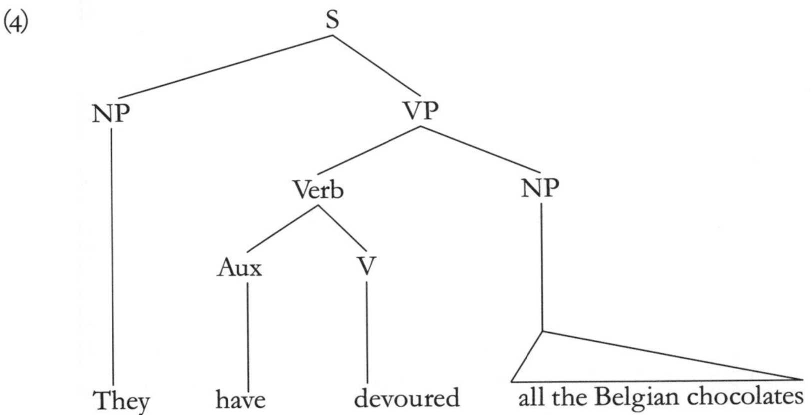

Notice that (4) is similar to (3) in regarding the verb sequence *have devoured* as a verb form.[5] The reason for taking complements to be part of VP is that there is a close relationship between the head verb and its complements, as we have seen. Further reasons are discussed in Aarts (1993). In current versions of generative theory verbal complements are generally still analysed as sister constituents of the verb inside VP (though see Chomsky and Lasnik 1993 for some recent discussion of this issue).

A position which is intermediate between that of Quirk et al. and generative linguists is Huddleston's. He would analyse (2) as in (5) (1984: 112):

(5)

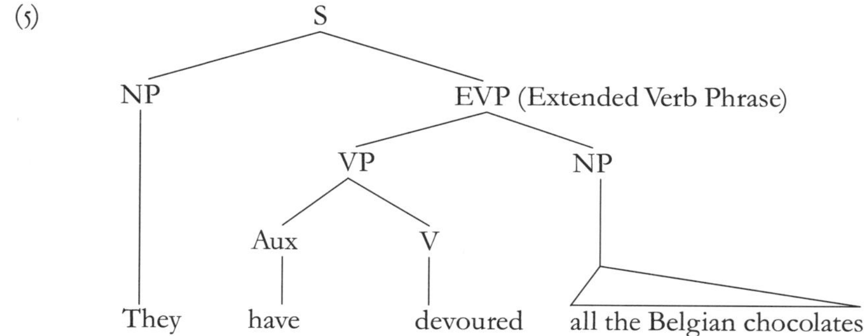

The VP is treated essentially as a verb form, as in the Quirk et al. framework, whereas the posited EVP-node is reminiscent of the Chomskyan VP.

The problem of how to treat auxiliary verbs in English is a complex matter. There seems never to have been agreement among grammarians on their analysis. The *Syntactic structures* analysis in (4) above was modified in the *Aspects* model and has undergone various changes in the course of time. In the recent literature, (2) and structures involving the progressive auxiliary *be* have the D-Structure in (6a) and the S-Structure in (6b).

(6)

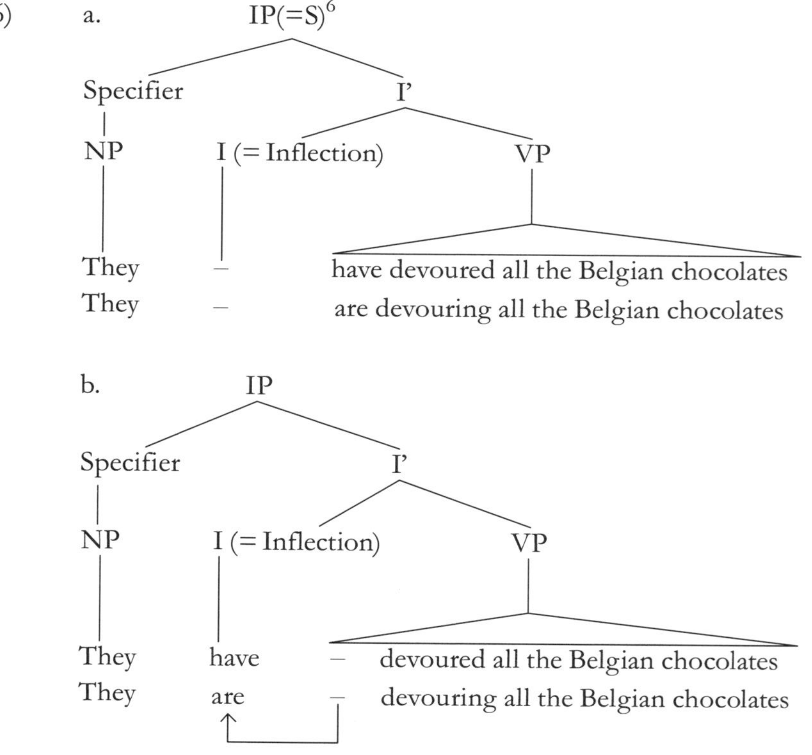

Under this view the aspectual auxiliaries originate in VP and are moved into the I-node to acquire tense features. This movement does not take place (and possible aspectual auxiliaries therefore remain inside VP) if the sentence contains a modal verb. Modals are base-generated in the I-position preventing possible aspectual verbs from moving up.[7] Under the so-called *Split INFL Hypothesis* there have been proposals to 'open up' the inflectional node into a Tense Phrase (TP), Agreement Phrase (AgrP, possibly itself split up) and a Negative Phrase (NegP). For discussion, see Pollock (1989) and Chomsky (1991, 1992).

Space limitations prevent us from outlining all the different approaches to the analysis of constructions involving auxiliary verbs. However, we can give an idea of the complexity of the areas of controversy by listing some of the questions that have been investigated:

- Is there a separate Aux-node, as in Chomsky (1957, 1965)? And, if so, is this node dominated by a 'Verb' (Chomsky 1957: 26, 39; see (4) above) or by 'S' (Chomsky 1965: 68)?
- Are modal auxiliaries to be treated as essentially the same as all the other auxiliaries (i.e. are they all dominated by Aux), or should we regard modals as different and posit a separate node 'M', as in e.g. Jackendoff (1972: 106)?
- Alternatively, if we do treat the modals as different from other auxiliaries, are they perhaps dominated, not by 'M', but by an inflectional category 'INFL' (or 'I' for short), as in Chomsky (1986b: 72; see (6) above)?
- Are auxiliaries main verbs, as in Ross (1969), Huddleston (1974, 1976a, 1976b), Emonds (1976), Pullum and Wilson (1977) and Warner (1993)?
- Alternatively, do we regard auxiliaries as in some sense modifying the main verb + complement sequence, as in Jackendoff (1977), i.e. are auxiliaries to be treated as Specifiers of the VP in the X'-theoretical sense?
- Or are auxiliary + main verb sequences perhaps to be analysed as complex verb forms, as in Palmer (1979, 1987, 1990) and Quirk et al. (1985); see (3) above?
- Do auxiliary verbs, or a subset of them, move from VP to another position in the sentence in which they occur in order to acquire tense features (cf. (6) above), or, conversely, does tense 'hop' onto the auxiliaries? See Pollock (1989), Chomsky (1986b, 1991, 1992).

The representations in (3), (4) and (5) concerned straightforward direct object NPs. There has also been a great deal of debate over the question how we should treat such sentences as (7) below:

(7) Oswald believed the outcome to be a disaster.

The problem concerns the functional status of the postverbal NP. Is it to be regarded as a direct object or as the subject of a complement clause? In a spirited debate on this issue in the early seventies the main protagonists were Chomsky, who favoured the latter position (Chomsky 1973), and Postal who upheld the former (Postal 1974). Postal defended a rule of Raising-to-Object in which the subject of a Deep Structure complement clause was raised to the matrix clause object position. This rule accounted for the intuition that the postverbal NP in sentences like (7) functions at the same time as the direct object of *believe* in the matrix clause and as the subject of *to be* in the subordinate clause. Numerous papers have been published both for and against the rule. Among these the most important are Bresnan (1976), Lightfoot (1976) and Bach (1977).

In the eighties attention turned to structures like (8), which is semantically closely related to (7):

(8) Oswald believed the outcome a disaster.

Again the problem is the status of the postverbal NP. Traditionally it is analysed as a direct object and the predicative phrase following it as a complement or attribute of the object. (See Matthews 1981: 184f, Aarts and Aarts 1982: 141–142, Huddleston 1984: 194f; Wekker and Haegeman 1985: 79; Quirk et al. 1985: 1195f, Burton-Roberts 1986: 81f, and Brown and Miller 1991: 333. See also the theoretical proposals of Williams 1980 which are very much in line with this view.) More recent analyses, foreshadowed by Otto Jespersen in the early part of the century, treat the string *the outcome a disaster* as a clausal unit, a so-called *Small Clause*. (See Stowell 1981, Chomsky 1981. For a discussion of the properties of Small Clauses and the reasons for positing their existence, see Aarts 1992.) The chief rationale behind this analysis is the view that the postverbal NP in (8) is not thematically related to the preceding verb. (Oswald did not believe 'the outcome', he believed 'that the outcome was a disaster'.)

Related to what we have in (8) are constructions like (9) and (10):

(9) He drank the beer cold.
(10) She burnished the gold smooth.

The sentences in (9) and (10) differ from (8) in that the NPs *the beer* and *the gold* clearly *do* have a thematic relationship with the preceding verb. APs such as *cold* and *smooth* have been analysed in various ways in the literature: as object attributes, as complements of the matrix verb or as predicates of adjunct Small Clauses with an empty subject.

Consider also (11):

(11) He cycled home delighted with the progress he had made that day.

This sentence involves an Adjective Phrase that is predicated, not of a direct object, but of a subject, namely *he*. Constructions like (9), (10) and (11) are discussed in the chapter by Bas Aarts ('Secondary predicates in English').

The domain of verb complementation is vast. Areas we have not touched upon are ditransitive complementation (Larson 1988, 1990, Jackendoff 1990), and the analysis of constructions involving multi-word verbs (Bolinger 1971, Fraser 1974, Dixon 1982, Kayne 1984, Aarts 1989).

2.4 The semantics and pragmatics of verbs and verbal constructions

In the previous section, we mainly discussed distributional (i.e. syntactic) aspects of the English verbal system. We might equally well explore the semantic and pragmatic aspects of verbs and verbal constructions. There have been a number of recent books that have approached the study of verbs from a functional or semantic perspective. Among these are Mair (1990), Dixon (1991) and Duffley (1992). In these works the view taken is that if we want to fully understand the behaviour and usage of verbs and verbal combinations we must first and foremost study the relevant functional and semantic properties of the constructions in question. To give a concrete example, consider the following pair of sentences quoted in Duffley (1992: 48):

(12) '. . . suffering as usual', but hoped, he told Arthur, 'to *find* this place *agree* with me better than Naples'.

(13) I measured the tail of the dead rat, and *found* it *to be* two yards long.

In his book Duffley's concern is explaining the differences between the use of the bare infinitive and the use of the *to*-infinitive in the various structures in which one or the other type (or both) may occur. His general hypothesis is that in constructions with the bare infinitive the time stretch denoted by it is always coextensive with that denoted by the verb that precedes it, whereas in structures containing a *to*-infinitive this verb form always signals a time period which is subsequent to that of the main verb. Thus, the difference between the two verbs *find* in (9) and (10) can be explained as follows: in (9) the combination of *find* with the bare infinitive *agree* denotes direct experience and because the agreeing takes place at the same time as the finding the bare infinitive is appropriate. In (10) *find*, used with *to be*, signals the discovery of a fact. 'Knowledge of this fact being the result of the finding, the *to* infinitive is required in order to evoke it in the subsequence of the event of discovering denoted by the main verb' (ibid.). Theoretically minded linguists subscribing to the notion of autonomous syntax would be content to observe that the lexicon lists two verbs (or senses of the verb) *find*, one taking a complement containing a bare infinitive, the other taking a complement with a *to*-infinitive. The semantics of the two different constructions would be mostly neglected by these linguists.

For a lexical semantic approach to the study of the verb in English see Levin (1993).

2.5 Tense, aspect, voice and modality

Straddling the fields of syntax, semantics and morphology are the grammatical categories of tense, aspect, voice and modality. Grammarians have concerned themselves with such questions as 'Are the present perfect and the simple past semantically (i.e. truth-conditionally) equivalent and do they differ only pragmatically?' (Smith 1981), and, similarly, 'Do expressions involving *be going to* and *will* differ in meaning only at the pragmatic level?' (Haegeman 1989). Also: 'How many tenses are there in English?' (Lyons 1977: 677f), 'Is the English present perfect best regarded as an aspectual phenomenon or is it a manifestation of the category of tense?' (ibid.: 715–716). Rodney Huddleston addresses this last question in 'The English perfect as a secondary past tense'. In this chapter, Huddleston argues that English has two past tenses: a primary past tense and a secondary past tense. He then provides evidence demonstrating that the perfect in English should be regarded as a secondary past tense rather than an aspect. To defend this analysis, he points to problems in Comrie's (1976) analysis of the perfective as an aspect and to Declerck's (1991) claim that the perfective is a simple tense.

English has been traditionally thought to contain two voices: the active and the passive. However, there are certain constructions that appear to have characteristics of both voices. One such construction, the *mediopassive*, is the topic of Andrew Rosta's '"How does this sentence interpret?" The semantics of English mediopassives'. Working within the theoretical framework of Word Grammar, Rosta discusses the semantic characteristics of mediopassives exemplified by verbs such as *read* in the construction *The book reads well.* He discusses the semantic roles of subjects of mediopassives, the words that tend to collocate with mediopassives, and the aspect of verbs that are mediopassives.

The topics of mood and modality have spawned a vast literature in recent years. In particular, the meaning of modal verbs in English has been extensively discussed in terms of their 'Root' and 'Epistemic' senses (see Coates 1983, Palmer 1986, 1990). However, for certain modals in English, the Root/Epistemic distinction is problematic. As Jennifer Coates demonstrates in 'The expression of Root and Epistemic Possibility in English', the distinction is particularly problematic when applied to modals such as *must*, *may*, and *can* when they express possibility. For these modals, the distinction is not only weaker but often involves merger and in the case of modals expressing Root Possibility, Epistemic meanings can often develop.

3 Descriptive approaches to the study of the English verb

Descriptive approaches to the study of English grammar have a long tradition, a tradition that includes the works of nineteenth and early twentieth century grammarians such as Sweet (1891–1898), Jespersen (1909–1949), Poutsma (1926–1929), Curme (1931) and Kruisinga (1931–1932). Each of these authors based their discussions of English grammar on (primarily) literary texts of English, and the information and examples that they obtained from these texts were the result of years of detailed and time-consuming analysis. This tradition gave way in the middle part of the twentieth century to more theoretically oriented studies of language, but has seen a resurgence in recent years as a result of increased interest in corpus linguistics.

Corpus linguistics has grown in prominence because of advances in computer technology, and these advances have affected descriptive approaches to the study of English in two regards. First of all, the computer has made it easier to create computer corpora: large collections of spoken and written English made available in computer-readable form. The first computer corpus, the Brown Corpus (Kučera and Francis 1967), was created in 1961 and contains various types of edited written American English, such as journalistic English, fiction, government documents, and technical English. This corpus spawned the creation of a number of other corpora, including the Lancaster–Oslo–Bergen Corpus of edited written British English (Garside, Leech, and Sampson 1987) and the London–Lund Corpus of spoken British English (Svartvik and Quirk 1980, Svartvik 1990. See Edwards and Lampert 1993: 263–306 for a discussion of the many corpora that are currently available, also Aijmer and Altenberg 1991, Svartvik 1992, and Oostdijk and de Haan 1994 for current research in corpus linguistics). The analysis of these corpora has been made easier by the development of sophisticated taggers, parsers, and text analysis programs. The tagger and parser developed at the University of Nijmegen, for instance, can automatically assign a range of sophisticated word-class and syntactic tags to a corpus (see Oostdijk 1988), and text analysis programs such as the ICE Corpus Utility Program can automate the analysis of tagged and parsed corpora (see Quinn 1993).

Although not based on a particular corpus, Quirk et al.'s (1985) *A Comprehensive Grammar of the English Language* is the first descriptive grammar of English to have drawn on the analyses of computer corpora, and the approach to the description of English taken in this grammar has greatly influenced current research in corpus linguistics. Specifically, Quirk et al. (1985) have demonstrated that it is important to base one's description of English on real linguistic examples taken from actual usage; to study both speech and writing, as well as the differing genres occurring in each, because language usage varies by mode and genre; and to consider the frequency of particular grammatical constructions as an important way of determining which constructions are central to English and which are peripheral. These assumptions are embodied in all the chapters in this part of the book, which use various corpora to study verb complements, verb collocations, historical aspects of the use of zero and *that* complementisers, the development of certain verb complements, and the use in speech of particular types of verbs and comment clauses.

3.1 Verb complementation

Because verb complementation is such a wide-ranging topic in English, a linguistic corpus is an excellent resource for studying the various kinds of verb complements that exist. And indeed, many studies have taken this approach. Andersson (1985) analysed verb complements in two kinds of written prose in American and British English: imaginative prose and informative prose. He found a continuum of dependency in this corpus, ranging from verb complements that were not heavily dependent on the verb to those that were. More recently, Mair (1990) and Altenberg (1993) have investigated verb complements in different corpora of British English. Mair studied infinitival complements in the Survey of English Usage Corpus of spoken and written British English, while Altenberg analysed verb complements in the London–Lund Corpus of spoken British English.

While corpora have enabled the description of the many constructions that realise the relation of verb complementation, a more traditional issue within descriptive linguistics has been the general classification of these realisations. Jespersen (1969: 20–22), for instance, posits three types of verb complements: *direct objects, indirect objects*, and *predicatives*. Quirk et al. (1985: 54) maintain Jespersen's categories of direct and indirect object but posit two types of predicatives: *subject complements* and *object complements*. In addition, Quirk et al. (1985: 56) classify verbs in terms of the complements that they take: a *monotransitive* verb, for instance, takes a single complement (a direct object); a *ditransitive* verb takes two objects (a direct and indirect object), while a *complex transitive* verb takes a direct object and an object complement. *Copular* verbs link subjects with subject complements, while *intransitive* verbs take no complements at all. Matthews (1981: 114–117) takes issue with Quirk et al.'s (1985) notion that the verb is solely responsible for determining the type of predicative a clause contains. He notes, for instance, that in clauses containing a subject predicative (subject complement in Quirk et al.'s terminology), the subject rather than the verb determines the predicative. In one of the examples that he cites, *All animals are equal*, the subject *animals* determines the predicative *equal*, not the copula *are*. In '*Find* and *want*: a corpus-based case study in verb complementation' Jan Aarts and Flor Aarts discuss further limitations of classifying verbs as monotransitive, ditransitive etc. In this chapter, Aarts and Aarts demonstrate how *microscopic* and *macroscopic* analyses of corpora are necessary in order to obtain significant generalisations about language. Microscopic analyses, they contend, allow one to deal with the nuances of language use; macroscopic analyses involve a more general and abstract analysis of corpora. They combine both of these approaches to study two verbs in English: *find* and *want*. Their analysis leads them to conclude that while syntactic notions such as monotransitive, ditransitive etc. are useful for general statements about *find* and *want*, for more accurate information about these verbs the actual categories realizing the complements of these verbs must be studied.

A further problem with categories such as monotransitive, ditransitive, object, and complement is that some constituents cannot be clearly classified into only one of the categories. For instance, certain verbs, as Matthews (1981: 125–126) notes, permit 'latent' objects. Consequently, it is difficult to determine whether the verb *finish* ought to be simply classified as monotransitive in (14), even though no object appears in (14a), or whether it ought to be considered intransitive in (14a) and monotransitive in (14b).

(14) a. I didn't finish.
b. I didn't finish the job. (adapted from Matthews 1981: 126)

While Quirk et al. (1985) in general restrict subject and object complements to the form classes of Adjective Phrase, Noun Phrase and clause, they acknowledge that many Prepositional Phrases, such as *in good health* in example (15), are semantically similar to complements.

(15) She is young and *in good health*. (Quirk et al. 1985: 732, emphasis in original)

To explain instances of indeterminacy in examples such as (14) and (15), Quirk et al. (1985: 90–91) draw upon the notions of 'gradience' and 'multiple analysis', concepts which have been posited to explain the fact that grammatical categories do not always have clear boundaries (for more on this notion, see Bolinger 1961 and Matthews 1981: 17–21). The notion of gradience as applied to subject and object complements is discussed in detail by Geoffrey Leech and Lu Li in 'Indeterminacy between Noun Phrases and Adjective Phrases as complements of the English verb'. Leech and Li note that while both subject and object complements can be either Noun Phrases or Adjective Phrases, there is a gradient between the two form classes, with some nominal complements having adjectival characteristics.

3.2 Verb collocations

Closely related to verb complements are verb collocations: particular verbs that tend to cooccur regularly with other types of constituents (including complements).

Firth (1957) posited the notion of collocation to account for the general fact that there are numerous groups of words that regularly cooccur, and this notion has been used to study the cooccurrence of many different types of constituents. Greenbaum (1970, 1974) employed elicitation tests to investigate the collocation of intensifiers and verbs in constructions of the type *I badly need a drink*. Kjellmer (1990, 1991) has written on the problem of defining collocations, and on the general patterns of collocations existing in various computer corpora of English. Others have investigated more specific patterns of collocations. Kennedy (1991) investigated the words that cooccurred with the prepositions *between* and *through* in the Lancaster–Oslo–Bergen Corpus. Renouf and Sinclair (1991) used sections of the Birmingham Corpus (Renouf 1984) to study the types of nouns that occurred in constructions of the type *an* + ? + *of* or *be* + ? + *to*.

An important issue in the study of collocations is how they ought to be defined. Kjellmer (1991: 112–115) classifies collocations according to the degree to which the two units of the collocation are 'fixed'. Some collocations, such as *bubonic plague*, are highly fixed because one of the units is highly suggestive of the other. Other collocations, by contrast, are less fixed. For instance, while the units in the phrase *classical music* quite frequently cooccur, both also occur individually and 'enjoy lexemic status' (Kjellmer 1991: 114). In 'Having a look at the expanded predicate', John Algeo discusses constructions of various fixity ('expanded predicates'), idiomatic units such as *have a look* that contain a general verb followed by a relatively more specific Noun Phrase. He demonstrates that these straddle the boundary between grammar and lexis in the sense that they contain a verb – a central element of the English clause – in a construction whose units combine to yield a specific lexical meaning.

Despite the fact that verbs and adverbs are frequently occurring, very closely related, form classes in English, there have been relatively few studies attempting to describe verb-adverb collocations in English. The most detailed treatment of the topic can be found in Greenbaum (1970, 1974). In Greenbaum (1974), for instance, speakers of American English were given incomplete sentences such as *I badly* . . . and *I entirely* . . . and were asked to complete them with words of their choice. Greenbaum compared the results of these experiments with results of experiments he had conducted earlier with British informants (Greenbaum 1970), and found remarkable similarities. When asked to supply the missing words in a sequence such as *I badly* . . . , both British and American informants chose verbs in the semantic categories of wanting and needing.

Because Greenbaum used only elicitation tests to study verb-adverb collocations, his results are limited to informant preferences. Stig Johansson in '"This scheme is badly needed": some aspects of verb-adverb combinations' focusses on actual occurrences of verb-adverb combinations. He makes general observations about them, noting, for instance, that the positioning of the adverb in relation to the verb depends very much on the individual adverb. To illustrate this general point in detail, he analyses the occurrence of the adverb *badly* in the Lancaster–Oslo–Bergen Corpus and in quotations from the *Oxford English Dictionary*.

3.3 Historical studies of verbs

Reference grammars of English such as Jespersen (1909–1949) provide a wealth of information on the historical development of English. However, such grammars are not based on corpora that have been systematically compiled to include equal proportions of a range of different text types representing various periods of English. Consequently, it is possible to obtain only an approximate sense of how particular grammatical categories have evolved over the history of the English language.

With the compilation of historical corpora such as the Helsinki Corpus, it is now possible to systematically study the development of English. The Helsinki Corpus is approximately 1.5 million words in length and is comprised of samples of various types of English (such as sermons, private letters, and biographies) from Old English through the early eighteenth century. (For more information on the Helsinki Corpus, see Rissanen 1992 and Kytö 1993.) This corpus has enabled the diachronic study of various grammatical categories in English. Kytö (1991), for instance, studied the development of modal auxiliaries such as *can* and *could* in the Helsinki Corpus and in a corpus of colonial American English that she compiled. These corpora contained texts from various periods of English in different registers, as well as ethnographic information about writers. Consequently, she was able to study what she terms 'socio-historical variation', i.e. the effects of sociolinguistic variables on the development of English. For instance, to study the ways in which participant relationships influence language change, Kytö studied texts in the genre of private correspondence. She found that more colloquial uses of *can* in early British and American English predominated in 'intimate down' situations, situations in which the person to whom a letter is written is in an 'inferior position' to the author of the letter (Kytö 1991: 233).

Because the Helsinki Corpus contains text samples extending only to the early eighteenth century, it is not possible to study grammatical categories from Old English through the present. To enable such studies to be conducted, Biber et al. (1993) discuss the development of a historical corpus called ARCHER (A Representative Corpus of English Historical Registers) representing three periods from 1750–1990. To illustrate the kind of comprehensive study that ARCHER permits, Edward Finegan and Douglas Biber describe the evolution of complementisers in '*That* and zero complementisers in Late Modern English: exploring ARCHER from 1650–1990'. In particular, they are interested in the alternation of *that* with zero (*I believe that/ϕ the instructor is wrong*), and demonstrate that certain genres (such as sermons and medicine) have since the mid-seventeenth century favoured *that* over zero, while other genres (such as letters) which formerly favoured zero have now reversed and also prefer *that* over zero.

While the Helsinki Corpus and ARCHER cover the periods of Old, Middle, Early Modern, and Contemporary English, it is also possible to study the evolution of English over a shorter period of time. This is precisely the tack taken by Christian Mair in 'Changing patterns of complementation, and concomitant grammaticalisation, of the verb *help* in present-day British English'. Mair compares the Lancaster–Oslo–Bergen Corpus, containing samples of British English published in 1961, with a comparable modern corpus that he is compiling to demonstrate that the verb *help* has undergone a process of grammaticalisation in the last thirty years. That is, *help* has changed from a distinct lexical item to a grammaticalised semi-auxiliary or infinitival conjunction.

3.4 Verbs in speech

Although speech (rather than writing) has always been regarded as the primary mode of communication, linguists have only recently begun to conduct empirical analyses of spoken language. Most of the early research in this area has been conducted within the paradigm of 'conversation analysis'. This research has focussed on such topics as turn-taking in face-to-face-conversations (Sacks, Schegloff, and Jefferson 1974), speech repairs (Schegloff, Jefferson, and Sacks 1977), and the structure of various types of conversations, such as the openings of telephone calls (Schegloff 1979). While work in the area of conversation analysis has provided important insights into the structure of conversational exchanges, it has not focussed in any great detail, as Levinson (1983: 366) observes, on 'ways in which conversational organisation interacts with sentence and utterance structure'.

The linguistic structure of speech has been treated in greater detail by studies based on computer corpora of spoken language: the London–Lund Corpus of spoken British English (Svartvik 1990) and the Lancaster/IBM Spoken English Corpus (Knowles 1993).[8] These corpora have been compared with written corpora to study the differences between speech and writing, and they have been analysed individually to isolate specific linguistic characteristics of spoken language.

The most comprehensive study of corpora to describe the differences between speech and writing is Biber's 1988 comparison of the spoken London–Lund Corpus with the written Lancaster–Oslo–Bergen Corpus and a separate collection of personal and professional letters. To compare speech and writing, Biber (1988: 121–169) posited various dimensions (e.g. 'narrative versus non-narrative concerns', 'abstract versus non-abstract information') and concluded that 'there is no linguistic or situational characterisation of speech and writing that is true of all spoken and written genres' (Biber 1988: 36). For instance, even though romantic fiction is a written genre and face-to-face conversation a spoken one, both 'deal with active, human participants and concrete topics' (Biber 1988: 154) and therefore contain a high proportion of information that is non-abstract.

Biber's 1988 study is important because it demonstrates that the spoken/written dichotomy is misleading, and that it is more important to study the linguistic structures that typify different spoken and written genres than to posit an absolute difference between speech and writing. This line of inquiry is pursued by Jan Svartvik and Olof Ekedahl in 'Verbs in public and private speaking'. They analyse the usage of verbs in various corpora of speech and writing to ultimately arrive at an understanding of the differences between two very different genres of spoken English: public speaking, which consists of planned monologues that are informative and presented by professionals, and private speaking, which consists of unplanned dialogues involving many different types of speakers. Svartvik and Ekedahl confirm Biber's 1988 notion that the spoken/written dichotomy is misleading: they found that public speaking and private speaking are linguistically more different than public speaking and writing.

One striking characteristic of private speaking that Svartvik and Ekedahl observed was the high frequency of verbs such as *know*, *think*, and *mean*. The high frequency of these verbs in speech has also been noted by Anna-Brita Stenström (1990), who in addition observes that certain high frequency lexical items in speech either do not appear, or appear quite infrequently in written corpora, such as the Lancaster–Oslo–Bergen Corpus. In 'Some remarks on comment clauses' Stenström follows up on this research by investigating 'comment clauses' in the London–Lund Corpus – constructions of the form *you know, I think, I mean* and *you see* which contain the frequently occurring words mentioned above. She demonstrates the difficulty of describing comment clauses in purely grammatical and semantic terms, and provides a detailed description of their functions in speech.

Notes

1. We thank And Rosta for comments.
2. The historical facts are derived from Robins (1990: 34f.).
3. Matthews (1981: 124) translates Tesnière's term as *participant*.
4. We observed above that the nature of the third 'determining property' of verbs is also not exclusively verbal. In many frameworks (especially X-bar theory; cf. Chomsky 1970, Jackendoff 1977) the determining properties of lexical elements are generalised cross-categorially.
5. In *Lectures on government and binding* Chomsky still entertains the possibility that the Aux-V sequence is a verbal complex. See Chomsky (1981: 140 fn. 28).
6. The sentential node is regarded in current GB-theory as the maximal projection of the functional category 'I' (=Inflection). The I'(I-bar)-level is intermediate between IP and I.
7. It has been argued that subjects too originate from inside VP at D-Structure (from the VP-Specifier position) and are then moved to the Specifier-of-IP position.
8. Other corpora of spoken English are currently under development. The International Corpus of English (Greenbaum 1992) will contain samples of spoken English from numerous regional varieties of English, such as American English, Australian English, and Indian English. The Corpus of Spoken American English (Chafe, Du Bois and Thompson 1991) will consist of various kinds of spoken American English, such as face-to-face conversations, speeches, and broadcast discussions and interviews.

References

Aarts, B. (1989) Verb-preposition constructions and small clauses in English. *Journal of Linguistics* **25**. 277–290.

(1992) *Small clauses in English: the nonverbal types*. Topics in English Linguistics **8**. Berlin and New York: Mouton de Gruyter.

(1993) Descriptive linguistics and theoretical linguistics: some thoughts on a (still) uneasy relationship. *Moderne Sprachen* **37**. 197–208.

Aarts, F. and Aarts, J. (1982) *English syntactic structures*. Oxford: Pergamon Press.

Aijmer, K. and Altenberg, B. (eds.) (1991) *English corpus linguistics: studies in honour of Jan Svartvik*. London: Longman.

Allerton, D. J. (1982) *Valency and the English verb*. London: Academic Press.

Altenberg, B. (1993) Recurrent verb-complement constructions in the London–Lund Corpus. In Aarts, J., de Haan, P. and Oostdijk, N. (eds.), *English language corpora: design, analysis and exploitation*. Amsterdam: Rodopi. 227–245.

Andersson, E. (1985) *On verb complementation in written English*. Lund Studies in English **71**. Lund: Gleerup/Liber.

Bach, E. (1977) Review article of Postal (1974). *Language* **53**. 621–654.

Biber, D. (1988) *Variation across speech and writing*. Cambridge University Press.

Biber, D., Finegan, E., Atkinson, D., Beck, A., Burges, D. and Burges, J. (1993) The design and analysis of the ARCHER corpus. In Kytö, M., Rissanen, M. and Wright, S. (eds.), *Corpora across the centuries. Proceedings of the First International Colloquium on English Diachronic Corpora*. Amsterdam: Rodopi.

Bolinger, D. (1961) *Generality, gradience and the all-or-none*. The Hague: Mouton.

(1971) *The phrasal verb in English*. Cambridge, MA: Harvard University Press.

Bresnan, J. (1976) Nonarguments for raising. *Linguistic Inquiry* **7**. 485–501.

Brown, K. and Miller, J. (1991) *Syntax: A linguistic introduction to sentence structure*. 2nd edition. London: Routledge.

Burton-Roberts, N. (1986) *Analysing sentences: an introduction to English syntax*. London and New York: Longman.

Chafe, W., Du Bois, J. and Thompson, S. (1991) Towards a new corpus of American English. In Aijmer, K. and Altenberg, B. (eds.), *English corpus linguistics: studies in honour of Jan Svartvik*. London: Longman. 64–91.

Chomsky, N. (1955) MS of *The logical structure of linguistic theory*. Published as Chomsky (1975).

(1957) *Syntactic structures*. The Hague: Mouton.

(1965) *Aspects of the theory of syntax*. Cambridge, MA: MIT Press.

(1970) Remarks on nominalisation. In Jacobs, R. A. and Rosenbaum, P. S. (eds.), *Readings in English transformational grammar*. Waltham, MA: Ginn and Co. 184–221.

(1972) *Studies on semantics in generative grammar*. The Hague: Mouton.

(1973) Conditions on transformations. In Anderson, S. and Kiparsky, P. (eds.), *A Festschrift for Morris Halle*. New York: Holt, Rinehart and Winston. 232–286.

(1975) *The logical structure of linguistic theory*. New York: Plenum.

(1981) *Lectures on government and binding*. Foris: Dordrecht.

(1986a) *Knowledge of language: its nature origin and use*. New York: Praeger.

(1986b) *Barriers*. Cambridge MA: MIT Press.

(1991) Some notes on economy of derivation and representation. In Freidin, R. (ed.), *Principles and parameters in comparative grammar*. Cambridge, MA: MIT Press. 417–454.

(1992) A minimalist program for linguistic theory. In Hale, K. and Keyser, S. J. (eds.), *The view from building 20: essays in linguistics in honor of Sylvain Bromberger*. Cambridge MA: MIT Press. 1–52.

Chomsky, N. and Lasnik, H. (1993) The theory of principles and parameters. In Jacobs, J., von Stechow, A., Sternefeld, W. and Vennemann, T. (eds.), *Syntax: an international handbook of contemporary research*. Berlin: Walter de Gruyter.

Coates, J. (1983) *The semantics of the modal auxiliaries*. London: Croom Helm.

Comrie, B. (1976) *Aspect*. Cambridge University Press.

(1985) *Tense*. Cambridge University Press.

Cowper, E. (1992) *A concise introduction to syntactic theory.* Chicago and London: Chicago University Press.

Curme, G. (1931) *A grammar of the English language.* Boston: Heath.

Declerck, R. (1991) *Tense in English: its structure and use in discourse.* London: Routledge.

Dixon, R. M. W. (1982) The grammar of English phrasal verbs. *Australian Journal of Linguistics* **2**. 142

(1991) *A new approach to English grammar on semantic principles.* Oxford: Clarendon Press.

Duffley, P. J. (1992) *The English infinitive.* London: Longman.

Edwards, J. and Lampert, M. (eds.) (1993) *Talking data.* Hillside, NJ: Lawrence Erlbaum.

Ek, J. A. van (1966) *Four complementary structures of predication in contemporary English.* Groningen: Wolters.

Emonds, J. (1976) *A transformational approach to English syntax.* New York: Academic Press.

Fillmore, C. (1968) The case for case. In Bach, E. and Harms, R. T. (eds.), *Universals in linguistic theory.* New York: North Holland. 1–88.

Firth, J. R. (1957) Modes of meaning. In *Papers in linguistics 1934–1951.* London: Oxford University Press. 190–214.

Fraser, B. (1974) *The verb-particle combination in English.* Tokyo: Taishukan Publishing Company.

Garside, R., Leech, G. and Sampson, G. (1987) *The computational analysis of English.* London: Longman.

Greenbaum, S. (1970) *Verb-intensifier collocations in English.* The Hague: Mouton.

(1974) Some verb-intensifier collocations in American and British English. *American Speech* **49**. 79–89.

(1992) A new corpus of English: ICE. In Svartvik, J. (ed.), *Directions in corpus linguistics.* Berlin: Mouton de Gruyter. 171–179.

Haegeman, L. (1989) *Be going to* and *will*: a pragmatic account. *Journal of Linguistics* **25**. 291–317.

Horrocks, G. (1987) *Generative grammar.* London: Longman.

Huddleston R. D. (1974) Further remarks on the analysis of auxiliaries as main verbs. *Foundations of language*, **11**. 215–229.

(1976a) Some theoretical issues in the description of the English verb. *Lingua* **40**. 331–383.

(1976b) *An introduction to English transformational syntax.* London: Longman.

(1984) *Introduction to the grammar of English.* Cambridge University Press.

Hudson, R. (1990) *English word grammar.* Oxford: Blackwell.

Jackendoff, R. (1972) *Semantic interpretation in generative grammar.* Cambridge, MA: MIT Press.

(1977) *X'-syntax: a study of phrase structure.* Cambridge, MA: MIT Press.

(1990) On Larson's treatment of the double object construction. *Linguistic Inquiry* **21**. 427–456.

Jennings, E. (1992) *Times and seasons.* Manchester: Carcanet.

Jespersen, O. (1909–1949) *A modern English grammar on historical principles.* Copenhagen: Munksgaard.

(1969) *Analytic syntax.* New York: Holt, Rinehart and Winston.

Kayne, R. S. (1984) Principles of particle constructions. In Guéron, J., Obenauer, H.-G. and Pollock, J.-Y. (eds.), *Grammatical representation*. Dordrecht: Foris. 101–140.

Kennedy, G. (1991) *Between* and *through*: the company they keep and the functions they serve. In Aijmer, K. and Altenberg, B. (eds.), *English corpus linguistics: studies in honour of Jan Svartvik*. London: Longman. 95–110.

Kjellmer, G. (1990) Patterns of collocability. In Aarts, J. and Meijs, W. (eds.), *Theory and practice in corpus linguistics*. Amsterdam: Rodopi. 163–178.

(1991) A mint of phrases. In Aijmer, K. and Altenberg, B. (eds.), *English corpus linguistics: studies in honour of Jan Svartvik*. London: Longman. 111–127.

Knowles, G. (1993) The machine-readable Spoken English Corpus. In Aarts, J., de Haan, P. and Oostdijk, N. (eds.), 107–119.

Kruisinga, E. (1931–1932) *A handbook of present-day English*. Groningen: Noordhoff.

Kučera, H. and Francis, W. N. (1967) *Computational analysis of present-day American English*. Providence, RI: Department of Linguistics.

Kytö, M. (1991) *Variation and diachrony, with early American English in focus*. Frankfurt: Peter Lang.

(1993) *Manual to the diachronic part of The Helsinki Corpus of English Texts: coding conventions and lists of source texts*, 2nd edition. Helsinki: Department of English, University of Helsinki.

Larson, R. K. (1988) On the double object construction. *Linguistic Inquiry* **19**. 335–391.

(1990) Double objects revisited: reply to Jackendoff. *Linguistic Inquiry* **21**. 589–632.

Levin, B. (1993) *English verb classes and alternations: a preliminary investigation*. Chicago University Press.

Levinson, S. (1983) *Pragmatics*. Cambridge University Press.

Lightfoot, D. W. (1976) The theoretical implications of subject raising. *Foundations of Language* **14**. 257–286.

Lyons, J. (1977) *Semantics*. 2 volumes. Cambridge University Press.

Mair, C. (1990) *Infinitival complement clauses in English: a study of syntax in discourse*. Cambridge University Press.

Marantz, A. (1984) *On the nature of grammatical relations*. Cambridge, MA: MIT Press.

Matthews, P. H. (1981) *Syntax*. Cambridge University Press.

Meyer, C. F. (1992) *Apposition in contemporary English*. Studies in English Language. Cambridge University Press.

Oostdijk, N. (1988) A corpus for studying linguistic variation. *ICAME Journal* **12**. 3–14.

Oostdijk, N. and de Haan, P. (eds.) (1994) *Corpus-based research into language: in honour of Jan Aarts*. Amsterdam: Rodopi.

Palmer, F. (1979) Why auxiliaries are not main verbs. *Lingua* **47**. 1–25.

(1986) *Mood and modality*. Cambridge University Press.

(1987) *The English verb*. 2nd edition. London: Longman.

(1990) *Modality and the English modals*. 2nd edition. London: Longman.

Pollock, J.-Y. (1989) Verb movement, Universal Grammar, and the structure of IP. *Linguistic Inquiry* **20**. 365–424.

Postal, P. (1974) *On raising*. Cambridge, MA: MIT Press.

Poutsma, H. (1926–1929) *A grammar of late modern English*. Groningen: Noordhoff.

Pullum, G. and Wilson, D. (1977) Autonomous syntax and the analysis of auxiliaries. *Language* **53**. 741–788.

Quinn, A. (1993) An object-oriented design for a Corpus Utility Program. In Aarts, J., de Haan, P. and Oostdijk, N. (eds.), *English language corpora: design, analysis and exploitation*. Amsterdam: Rodopi. 215–225.

Quirk, R., Greenbaum, S., Leech, G. and Svartvik, J. (1985) *A comprehensive grammar of the English language*. London: Longman.

Radford, A. (1988) *Transformational grammar: a first course*. Cambridge University Press.

Ransom, E. (1986) *Complementation: its meanings and forms*. Typological studies in language **10**. Amsterdam: John Benjamins.

Renouf, A. (1984) Corpus design at Birmingham University. In Aarts, J. and Meijs, W. (eds.), *Corpus linguistics*. Amsterdam: Rodopi. 3–39.

Renouf, A. and Sinclair, J. (1991) Collocational frameworks in English. In Aijmer, K. and Altenberg, B. (eds.), *English corpus linguistics: studies in honour of Jan Svartvik*. London: Longman. 128–143.

Rissanen, M. (1992) The diachronic corpus as a window to the history of English. In Svartvik, J. (ed.), *Directions in corpus linguistics*. Berlin and New York: Mouton de Gruyter. 185–205.

Robins, R. H. (1990) *A short history of linguistics*. 3rd edition. London: Longman.

Ross, J. (1969) Auxiliaries as main verbs. In Todd, W. (ed.), *Studies in philosophical linguistics*. Series 1. Evanstown IL.: Great Expectations Press. 77–102.

Rothstein, S. (1983) The syntactic forms of predication. Dissertation MIT, distributed in 1985 by the Indiana University Linguistics Club.

Sacks, H., Schegloff, E. A. and Jefferson, G. (1974) A simplest systematics for the organization of turn-taking in conversation. *Language* **50**. 696–735.

Schegloff, E. A. (1979) Identification and recognition in telephone conversation openings. In Psathas, G. (ed.), *Everyday language: studies in ethnomethodology*. New York: Irvington. 23–78.

Schegloff, E. A., Jefferson, G. and Sacks, H. (1977) The preference for self-correction in the organization of repair in conversation. *Language* **53**. 361–82.

Schlesinger, I. M. (1994) *Cognitive space and linguistic case*. Cambridge University Press.

Smith, N. V. (1981) Grammaticality, time and tense. *Philological transactions of the Royal Society London* **259**. 253–265.

Stenström, A.-B. (1990) Lexical items peculiar to spoken discourse. In Svartvik, J. (ed.), *The London–Lund Corpus of spoken English*. Lund University Press. 137–175.

Stowell, T. (1981) Origins of phrase structure. Unpublished doctoral dissertation MIT.

Svartvik, J. (ed.) (1992) *Directions in corpus linguistics*. Berlin: Mouton de Gruyter.

Svartvik, J. and Quirk, R. (eds.) (1980) *A corpus of English conversation*. Lund University Press.

Sweet, H. (1891–1898) *A new English grammar*. Oxford: Clarendon Press.

Tesnière, L. (1953) *Esquisse d'une syntaxe structurale*. Paris: Klincksieck.

(1959) *Eléments de syntaxe structurale*. Paris: Klincksieck.

Warner, A. R. (1993) *English auxiliaries: structure and history*. Cambridge University Press.

Wekker, H. and Haegeman, L. (1985) *A modern course in English syntax*. London: Croom Helm.

Williams, E. (1980) Predication. *Linguistics Inquiry* **11**. 203–238.

PART 1

Theoretical approaches to the study of the English verb

2 Grammatical relations in English[1]

CHARLES F. MEYER

1 Introduction

In their discussions of the verb in English, linguists and grammarians have introduced numerous terminological distinctions to capture the various characteristics of the English verb. For instance, the verb *fired* in example (1) has the 'form' of a *Verb Phrase* and the 'function' of *predicator*. In turn, *his executive staff* has an additional 'function': namely *complement* of the verb *fired*.

(1) The president of the company fired his executive staff.

Functional notions like 'predicator' and 'complement' are commonly known as *grammatical relations* because they refer, as Matthews (1981: 2) notes, to 'a unit's internal connections': *fired* is predicator of sentence (1) precisely because it stands in a particular relationship to the subject of the sentence. If, for instance, example (1) is made into an interrogative sentence, the predicator *fire* will be placed following the operator *did* and the subject *the president of the company*:

(2) Did the president of the company *fire* his executive staff?

Grammatical relations have been widely discussed in the literature and as a result they have been subject to a number of different interpretations. Because functions like subject or modifier 'are inherently relational', Huddleston (1984: 7) classifies all grammatical relations as 'syntactic functions'. Quirk et al. (1985), on the other hand, distinguish clause functions from phrase functions, and posit different functional relationships for each level of structure. To distinguish the types of relationships existing in a clause, Quirk et al. (1985: 49) posit five functions: subject, verb, object, complement, and adverbial. To depict the relationships between constituents in a phrase, Quirk et al. (1985: 64) posit only three functions: determination, modification, and complementation.[2] A survey of other sources reveals a similar trend: considerable variation both in the types of relations proposed and in the definitions that they are assigned.

While it is common for linguists and grammarians to differ in their systems of classification, the classification of grammatical relations is so inconsistent that there is a fundamental misunderstanding of the role that these relations play in the grammar of English. To clarify this misunderstanding, I argue in this chapter that it is necessary to distinguish two levels of relations: one level containing clause functions such as subject and complement and a second containing more general functions such as complementation and modification. To support this view, I focus on the grammatical relations 'complement' and 'complementation', which have been subject to widely different interpretations. I demonstrate that inconsistencies in the various uses of the terms 'complement' and 'complementation' result from failing to distinguish the clause function 'complement' from the more general function of 'complementation'. I then argue that while all of the grammatical relations have, as Huddleston (1984) claims, similarities, relations such as complement and complementation are fundamentally different, but not, as Quirk et al. (1985) claim, at the level of structure (clause as opposed to phrase) at which they operate. I conclude by proposing criteria that distinguish the general function of complementation from both the clause function complement and the other general functions (such as modification).

2 The necessity of distinguishing two levels of grammatical relations

In her discussion of complementation, Ransom (1986: 29, note) remarks that the term *complement* has been applied to a wide array of postverbal constructions: not just predicative Noun Phrases and Adjective Phrases but subjects and direct objects as well. The confusion over the use of the term complement that Ransom (1986) documents results mainly from there being three different interpretations of the relation of complement. Some sources regard the relation as only a clause function; other sources distinguish the clause function complement from the more general function of complementation; still other sources view the relation of complement as only a general function.

A number of sources consider complements only as a type of clause function, and use the notion to capture the relationship between the italicised Noun Phrases in examples (3) and (4) and, respectively, the subject and object of the clauses in which the Noun Phrases occur.

(3) Dr Joan Smith is *the president of the company.*

(4) President Clinton appointed Mayor Flynn *Ambassador to the Vatican.*

The terms used to depict these relationships, however, are quite varied. Curme (1947) labels the italicised construction in (3) a *predicate complement* (110f.) and the construction in (4) an *objective predicate* (138f.). Fries (1952) labels the same constructions *predicate nominatives* (187–188) and *object complements* (185–186). While Jespersen (1964: 124f.) considers the construction in (3) a type of *predicative*, he claims that the construction in (4) is not a separate clause function. Instead, the entire postverbal sequence of Noun Phrases is an object, with *Ambassador to the Vatican* an 'adnex' (p. 309) of *Mayor Flynn*, a construction that in modern syntactic theory is referred to as a *small clause* (see Chomsky 1981, Stowell 1981, and Aarts 1992).

Because the italicised NPs in examples (3) and (4) have certain similarities (e.g. they both stand in a copular relationship with the Noun Phrases that they complement), Quirk et al. (1985) label them *subject complement* and *object complement*, respectively. In addition, Quirk et al. (1985: 66) posit the relation of complementation to depict the relationship between the direct object and verb in example (5) and the infinitive clause and adjective in example (6).

(5) He deceived *his father.* (emphasis in original)
(6) Mr Gould is likely *to resign.* (emphasis in original)

To distinguish complements from complementation, Quirk et al. (1985) state that the relations operate at different levels of structure: functions such as subject complement at the level of the clause (pp. 49f.) and functions such as complementation at the level of the phrase or the clause (p. 65).

A number of sources do not limit complements to the constructions in (3) and (4) or distinguish clause functions from phrase functions. Instead, they posit a more general function for complement that would include all or some of the constructions in (3)–(6). Sweet (1891) uses the term complement to identify the requirement that a direct object occur after a transitive verb (sec. 248) and that a Noun Phrase or Adjective Phrase (i.e. an object complement in Quirk et al.'s 1985 terms) occur after a direct object (sec. 267). Matthews (1981: 146) expands the notion of complementation even further, regarding complementation as a type of 'dependency' relation between verbs, nouns, or prepositions and the obligatory constituents that must occur with them. Huddleston (1984: 177f.) posits a general class of 'complements' of which objects and predicative complements (i.e. subject and object complements in Quirk et al.'s 1985 terms) are specific members. For Huddleston (1984: 177–181), the defining characteristic of complements is that they are 'nuclear elements' in the clause: the type of object a clause will contain, for instance, is determined by the specific verb in the clause; moreover, the object will generally be obligatory rather than optional.

In general, Huddleston (1984: 7) does not draw a sharp distinction between functions like complement and subject, classifying them simply as 'grammatical relations'.

While it is certainly true that notions such as complement and complementation are grammatical relations, I wish to argue that there are enough differences between the relations to posit two different levels of grammatical relations. It is too restrictive to only recognise the clause function of complement: this ignores, for instance, the obligatory nature of objects after certain verbs that the more general relation of complementation attempts to capture. On the other hand, considering only the general function of complementation fails to capture the fact that while the functions of complement and complementation are grammatical relations, they differ in enough respects to warrant the positing of two different levels of grammatical relations.

3 Differences between the clause function complement and the general function complementation

A general sense of the difference between the relations of complement and complementation can be obtained by examining Huddleston's (1984: 181) definition of complement. Although Huddleston does not explicitly distinguish levels of function, he does posit 'two . . . kinds of complement, objects and predicative complements'. The category of complement, according to this view, is superordinate to the specific functions of object and predicative complement, and it is posited to capture the obligatory nature of a range of postverbal constituents.

Huddleston's (1984) notion of complement is very similar to the general function of complementation that I am advancing because it points to the broader and more abstract nature of complementation: it recognises, for instance, the fact that the clause function complement would be among the group of constituents standing in the relation of complementation to the verb of the clause in which this relation occurs. To illustrate this conception of the relationship between clause function and general function, I will compare one type of complement – subject complement – with one type of complementation – verb complementation. As I will demonstrate, the main difference between these functions is that while subject complements have a rather narrow and clearly defined function within the clause, the relation of verb complementation has a broader, more abstract function.

3.1 Realisations

Subject complements not only have a more limited range of realisations than verb complements but form one part of the group of realisations that make up the relation of verb complementation.

As Quirk et al. (1985: 728) observe, a subject complement can be a Noun Phrase (example 7), an Adjective Phrase (example 8), or a nominal clause (example 9).

(7) John Sculley is *the former CEO of Apple Computers.*
(8) Punk rock is *loud and obnoxious.*
(9) The man's greatest virtue is *that he is hardworking and understanding.*

The relation of verb complementation, on the other hand, has a greater range of realisations. These realisations include not only the clause function subject complement but other clause functions as well (Quirk et al. 1985: 722–723), such as direct object (example 10) and adverbial (example 11):

(10) The publisher rejected *the final draft of the book.*
(11) The sweater is *in the bedroom.*

In addition, clause functions such as object, as Andersson (1985: 9) observes, can be realised by various non-finite clauses, such as a *to*-infinitive clause (example 12) or *-ing* clause (example 13), also entering into the relation of complementation with the verb.

(12) I wanted *him to go.*
(13) George watched *me baking a cake.*

3.2 General semantic and syntactic differences between subject complements and verb complementation

Subject complements have very specific semantic and syntactic functions within the clause. Semantically, subject complements have one primary function: to describe or identify the subject of the sentence. Syntactically, subject complements are restricted (usually) to occurring after a linking verb.

The relation of verb complementation, however, is characterised by much broader and more general semantic and syntactic considerations. Specifically, verb complementation can be described as a 'dependency' relation (Matthews 1981: 78–84 and Hudson 1990: 105f.), i.e. a relation in which certain constituents must occur together. And, as Huddleston (1984: 181f.) observes, for verbs this dependency is both semantic and syntactic. Semantically, a verb 'is analysable into a **semantic predicate**' (Huddleston 1984: 182, emphasis in original) and can be described in terms of the number of 'arguments' that the predicate must take. The verb *give*, for instance, requires three arguments: someone doing the giving, something being given, and someone being given something. Semantic predicates, as Huddleston (1984) further points out, can be specified syntactically as well: a verb such as *give* is ditransitive, and requires two objects, unless one of the objects is 'latent' (Matthews 1981: 125–126).[3]

In addition to having general semantic and syntactic differences, the relations of subject complement and verb complementation have a number of specific syntactic differences as well – differences that serve to further distinguish clause functions from general functions.

3.3 Specific syntactic differences between the relations of subject complement and verb complementation

While Quirk et al. (1985: 49) regard subject complements as part of clause structure, they are less clear about the level of structure at which the relation of complementation operates.

If constructions that Quirk et al. (1985) admit into the relations of subject complement and verb complementation are compared, the constructions appear to operate at similar levels of structure. For instance, Quirk et al. (1985) regard *ugly* in (14) as a subject complement, and *a respite* in (15) as a verb complement:

(14) The painting is *ugly*. (p. 403)
(15) He allowed me *a respite*. (p. 66)

In (14), there is clearly a relation among clause elements: *ugly* serving as complement to the subject of the sentence, *the painting*. However, in (15), the relation of verb complementation also involves two clause elements: a verb, *allowed*, and a direct object, *a respite*. Therefore, in (14) and (15) the relations of subject complement and verb complementation occur at the level of clause.[4]

But while the relations of subject complement and verb complementation appear to operate at the same level of structure, a survey of other clause functions and general functions reveals that the functions have quite different syntactic distributions. Functions such as complement and subject will always depict relationships between constituents at the level of clause because such functions are necessary for defining the clause. Functions such as modification and complementation, however, occur across a wide range of structures. Because modification usually involves a relation between a noun or an adverb and a modifier (Quirk et al. 1985: 65), this relationship typically occurs in phrases. Complementation, in contrast, involves relations either within phrase boundaries (in the case of adjective complementation) or across phrase boundaries (in the case of verb complementation). And if one regards apposition as a general function (as Meyer 1992 does), one can find clauses in apposition, as the marker of apposition *that is* in example (16) indicates.

(16) The senate rejected the amendment; that is, they sent it back to committee.

In short, while clause functions always occur at the level of clause, general functions have more varied syntactic distributions and can occur at any level of structure.

Clause functions like subject complement and subject are closely interrelated. However, general functions like verb complementation and modification are not. To define a subject complement, close reference must be made to two other clause functions: the verb (or predicator) and the subject. Indeed, the defining characteristic of all of the clause functions is their close interrelationships: to define the subject or object of a sentence, one must make reference to the verb; to define an indirect object, one must make reference to the direct object; and so forth.

Functions like verb complementation and modification, on the other hand, are not closely interrelated. The relation of verb complementation, for instance, can occur totally independently of the relation of modification, and the definition of each of these relations does not depend on the definition of the other.

4 The difference between verb complementation and other general relations

Having established some differences between the clause function of subject complement and the general function of verb complementation, I now turn to describing how the relation of verb complementation differs from two other relatively different general relations: modification, and what I term *disassimilation*.

Because relations such as complementation and modification depict general and relatively abstract grammatical relationships, it is appropriate that these relations be named with abstract nouns. Other general relations, however, are not named with terms that accurately reflect their functions. For instance, to characterise constructions that stand in various degrees of dependency, Matthews (1981: 140–141) introduces the terms *adjunct* and *peripheral element* to describe the different degrees of integration in the clause exhibited by, for instance, the words *clearly* and *yesterday* in a sentence such as *I saw him clearly yesterday*.[5] The adverb *clearly* is an adjunct because it exhibits 'direct dependency within a predicative construction . . .' (Matthews 1981: 141). On the other hand, because *yesterday* could be removed from the sentence without seriously changing the meaning, it is a peripheral element that is not dependent on the verb. While the terms *adjunct* and *peripheral element* quite accurately reflect different degrees of integration in the clause, the terms unfortunately suggest particular grammatical constructions rather than relations between constituents. Therefore, to more accurately capture the relationship between adjuncts and peripheral elements and the clauses in which they occur, I will analyse these constructions as realisations of the relation of *disassimilation*, a relation in which there are varying degrees of integration between constituents.

Like verb complementation (and indeed all grammatical relations), modification and disassimilation will be characterised by realisations with particular semantic and syntactic characteristics. Modification, for instance, can be a relation between an adjective and noun, disassimilation a relation between a conjunct such as *however* and the clause in which it occurs. A key semantic and syntactic difference between these relations and verb complementation involves the notion of dependency.

4.1 Dependency and general relations

If the relations of complementation, modification, and disassimilation are compared, a continuum of dependency (as schematised in Figure 2.1) can be discerned. The relation of complementation exhibits the highest degree of dependency, followed by modification, and then disassimilation. Within the relation of disassimilation, there are two types of realisations – adjuncts and peripheral elements – demonstrating varying degrees of dependency and pointing to the heterogenous nature of the relation of disassimilation.

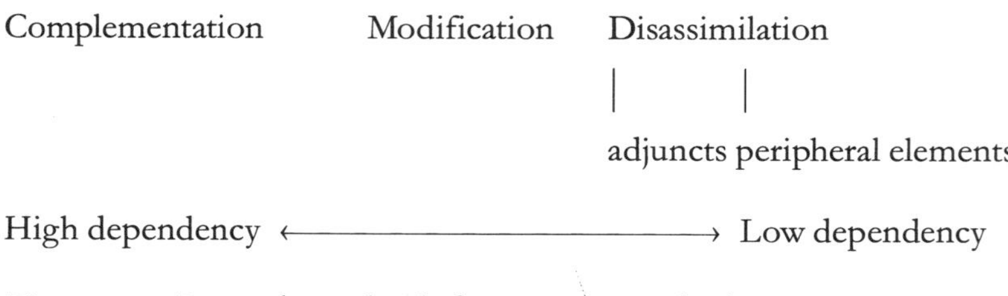

Figure 2.1 Dependency levels for grammatical relations

Although discussions of dependency relations focus on a variety of criteria for indicating dependency, three criteria stand out as key markers of dependency between two units:[6]

(a) Both of the units in the relation are obligatory;
(b) If one of the units is optional, its meaning upon omission can be inferred from the context;
(c) One of the units determines the form and meaning of the other unit.

Figure 2.2 applies these criteria to the relations specified in Figure 2.1 and reveals the gradient between relations such as complementation that have high dependency to those such as disassimilation that have lower dependency.

	(a)	(b)	(c)
Complementation	?	+	+
Modification	?	–	?
Disassimilation			
– adjuncts	?	–	?
– peripheral elements	–	?	–

Figure 2.2 The gradient of high to low dependency

4.1.1 Criterion (a): the obligatory or optional nature of the units

Because units in the relation of complementation are so highly dependent on each other, they tend to be much more obligatory than units in the relations of modification and disassimilation.

While modifiers are semantically obligatory, they are syntactically optional. In example (17a), the premodifier *wealthy* can be omitted and the resultant sentence (17b) will be syntactically well-formed but semantically different in meaning. Hence, modifiers only questionably satisfy criterion (a).

(17) a. The woman is a wealthy executive.
b. The woman is an executive.

Constructions in the relation of disassimilation, however, will vary in satisfying criterion (a). Many adjuncts are like modifiers in the sense that if they are omitted, the resultant construction (18b) will be grammatical but different in meaning.

(18) a. The woman drove the car dangerously.
b. The woman drove the car.

Other adjuncts, however, are semantically and syntactically obligatory. As Matthews (1981: 136) notes, a verb such as *last* requires an obligatory adjunct (19a), and without the adjunct a questionable sentence (19b) results:

(19) a. It lasted for three hours.
b. ?It lasted.

Peripheral elements, in contrast, are truly optional; their omission (20b) has no syntactic effect on the clause in which they occur and has a marginal effect (at most) on the meaning of the clause.

(20) a. Apples taste good. Moreover, they are healthy.
b. Apples taste good. They are healthy.

4.1.2 Criterion (b): latency

Complementation is a relation of high dependency: the verb of a sentence, for instance, typically places very strong semantic and syntactic restrictions on the object. In some cases, the verb so strongly determines the object that even if the object is missing, it can be 'latent' (criterion b). As Matthews (1981: 125) notes, in a sentence such as *I was reading*, the object (*a novel*, for instance) is implied.

Latency, however, tends not to be a possibility for constructions in the relations of modification or disassimilation. For instance, as Huddleston (1984: 224) points out, if the adjunct *in 1942* is removed from example (21a), the resultant sentence (21b) has a different meaning. This difference in meaning is a strong indication of the lack of potential for latency with adjuncts: the inability of the verb *died*, for instance, to indicate the date of someone's death.

(21) a. She died in 1942.
b. She died.

With peripheral elements, however, latency is less clear. It might be argued that the contrast between the sentences in example (22) below, expressed by the peripheral element *however*, could be inferred from the linguistic context in which the sentences occur.

(22) John did quite well on his college entrance exams. However, he still wasn't admitted to Harvard.

Other peripheral elements, on the other hand, are far less latent. For instance, the disjunct *unfortunately* in (23a) could not be inferred if it were omitted (23b).

(23) a. Unfortunately, the rains in the midwest have not diminished.
b. The rains in the midwest have not diminished.

4.1.3 Criterion (c): the effects of one unit on the form and meaning of the other unit

A major difference between complementation and the other relations is specified in criterion (c). While verbs play a major role in restricting the semantic and syntactic characteristics of the complements that they take, such restrictions are either limited or non-existent for the relations of modification and disassimilation.

Although modifiers are optional, there are both semantic and syntactic constraints on their occurrence. The meaning of the head noun in a Noun Phrase limits the modifiers that can occur with it. The adjective *tall*, for instance, can only modify nouns capable of having height (24a but not 24b):

(24) a. the *tall* child
b. *the *tall* canyon

In addition, there are complex semantic and syntactic constraints on whether certain Adjective Phrases can occur attributively as modifiers. While *faint* can be a modifier in some contexts (25a), in other contexts (25b), as Quirk et al. (1985: 432) note, it cannot, its occurrence restricted to predicative positions (25c) instead:

(25) a. the *faint* murmurings of a dying man
b. *the *faint* man
c. The man felt *faint*

Peripheral elements, however, are completely independent: an adverbial such as *however* can occur in any clause, and its acceptability in the clause is not determined by any constituent in the clause, including the verb.

5 Conclusion

I have argued in this chapter that there are enough differences between relations such as complement and complementation to posit two levels of grammatical relations: clause functions and general functions. However, while I have demonstrated the necessity for two levels of relations, I have not dealt with the issue of what particular relations need to be posited at each level in order to yield a satisfactory description of English and other languages.

Presently, there is some consensus on the kinds of relations needed to describe clause functions. While terms do vary (e.g. predicator is sometimes used instead of verb), functions such as object and complement are commonly agreed upon. With the general functions, however, disagreement is much more common. For instance, while Quirk et al. (1985: 64–67) propose only three general functions – determination, modification, and complementation – Matthews (1981: 223) posits six: two – modification and complementation – that Quirk et al. propose, and four – coordination, juxtaposition, peripheral elements, and parataxis – that Quirk et al. do not consider. Differences as great as this suggest that future research needs to carefully examine the phenomenon of general functions and to determine precisely which relations are needed.

Notes

1. I wish to thank Bas Aarts for comments on this chapter.
2. Even though Quirk et al.'s (1985: 646) discussion of determination, modification, and complemention appears in a section entitled 'Form and function in phrase structure', they seem to suggest that the relation of complementation can occur at the level of the clause as well: functions such as object and adverbial, they remark, involve 'complemention in clause structure' (Quirk et al. 1985: 85). In 3.3, I discuss the types of structures in which relations such as modification and complementation commonly occur.
3. The semantic and syntactic characteristics I discuss in this section correspond, respectively, to the notions in generative grammar of *selectional* and *subcategorisation* restrictions (see Aarts and Meyer this volume).
4. Unlike other grammarians, Quirk et al. (1985: 61) do not consider objects to be part of the Verb Phrase. Instead, the Verb Phrase consists only of main verbs and auxiliaries (see Aarts and Meyer this volume).
5. Matthews (1981: 123–136) proposes various criteria to distinguish *complements*, *peripheral elements*, and *adjuncts*. Some of these criteria (such as latency) are discussed in 4.1.
6. For a discussion of various criteria for dependency, cf. Matthews (1981: 78f.), Huddleston (1984: 108f.), and Hudson (1990: 189f.).

References

Aarts, B. (1992) *Small clauses in English: the nonverbal types*. Topics in English Linguistics **8**. Berlin and New York: Mouton de Gruyter.

Andersson, E. (1985) *On verb complementation in written English*. Malmo, Sweden: GWK Gleerup.

Chomsky, N. (1981) *Lectures on government and binding.* Foris: Dordrecht.
Curme, G. (1947) *English grammar*. New York: Harper and Row.
Fries, C. C. (1952) *The structure of English*. New York: Harcourt.
Huddleston, R. (1984) *Introduction to the grammar of English*. Cambridge University Press.
Hudson, R. (1990) *English word grammar*. Oxford: Blackwell.
Jespersen, O. (1964) *Essentials of English grammar*. University AL: University of Alabama Press.
Matthews, P. H. (1981) *Syntax*. Cambridge University Press.
Meyer, C. F. (1992) *Apposition in contemporary English*. Cambridge University Press.
Quirk, R., Greenbaum, S., Leech, G. and Svartvik, J. (1985) *A comprehensive grammar of the English language*. London: Longman.
Radford, A. (1988) *Transformational grammar*. Cambridge University Press.
Ransom, E. N. (1986) *Complementation: its meanings and forms*. Amsterdam: John Benjamins.
Stowell, T. (1981) Origins of phrase structure. Unpublished doctoral dissertation MIT.
Sweet, H. (1891) *A new English grammar*. Oxford: Clarendon Press.

3 Competence without Comp?

RICHARD HUDSON

1 Introduction

Over the last two decades the category 'complementiser', often abbreviated to 'Comp' or 'C', has become part of a widely accepted canon of grammatical categories not only for English but for all languages, via 'Universal Grammar'. Like so many other categories it has a double identity, as a word-class and as a position in abstract sentence-structure. It is the class to which words such as *that, if, whether* and *for* (the *for* which precedes an infinitive) are said to belong. I shall reserve the name 'complementiser' for this word-class. It is also the position at the head of the sentence (in both senses of 'head'), otherwise described as the abstract functional category which heads the 'CP' (alias 'sentence') and which may be phonologically empty. The structure in (1) illustrates this analysis. In the text I shall call this abstract position 'Comp'. These assumptions are standard in Chomskyan syntax (e.g. Haegeman 1991: 111), but the belief in the word-class 'complementiser' goes much further (e.g. Gazdar et al. 1985: 112).

In this chapter I shall question both these assumed categories. I shall argue that *that, if, whether* and *for* do not all belong to the same word-class; specifically, I shall suggest that *whether* is an interrogative pronoun, whereas either the others are syncategorematic – belonging to no general word-class – or they belong to the much bigger class that Quirk et al. call 'subordinators' (1985: 998). As for Comp, there is evidence against the reality of this assumed abstract position. Whatever structural similarities the supposed complementisers share, they also share with relative and interrogative pronouns, subordinating conjunctions and even prepositions; and in the absence of an overt complementiser, there are reasons for doubting the existence of an empty Comp slot.

(1)

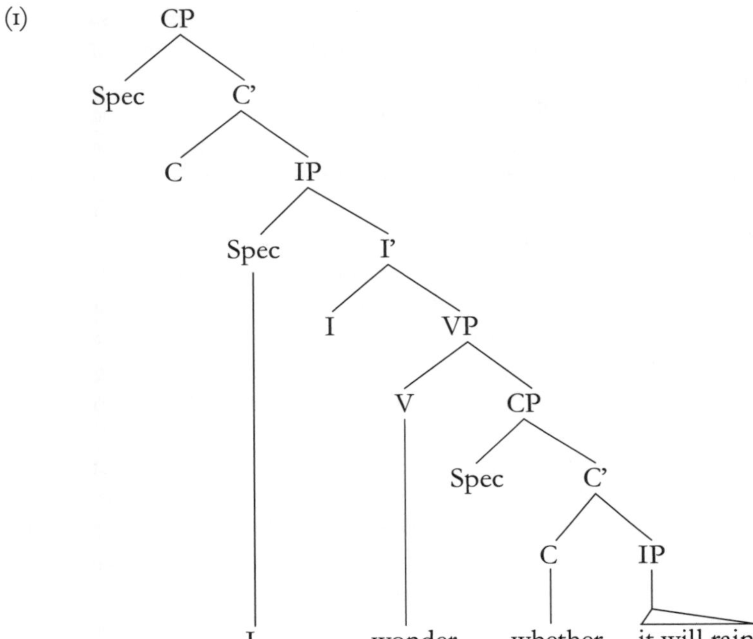

2 Classification of *that, if, whether* and *for*

I could call these four words 'the so-called complementisers', but for brevity I shall call them just 'the linkers'. The motivation for grouping them together in the first place was the fact that they can all introduce a clause which is the complement of a higher verb – hence the name 'complementiser' (Rosenbaum 1967). Relevant examples follow:

(2)
a. I think *that* it's going to stop raining.
b. I wonder *if* it's going to stop raining.
c. I wonder *whether* it's going to stop raining.
d. I'm waiting *for* it to stop raining.

This similarity in itself does not prove that they all belong to the same word-class, because there are many other words that can be used in the same way (i.e. to link a verb to a complement clause) – most obviously *to* (infinitival *to*), but also words like *when* and *on*:

(3)
a. I want *to* go home.
b. I wonder *when* it's going to stop raining.
c. He insisted *on* going out.

It is true that *on* could have introduced an ordinary Noun Phrase instead of a gerundive clause, but it qualifies as a linker because it links *insisted* to this clause in the same way as the other words.

To was one of the original complementiser list, as part of the compound complementiser *for-to*, but these two words have now been firmly separated into the complementiser *for* and the non-complementiser *to*. No one has ever suggested (so far as I know) that interrogative pronouns like *when* and prepositions like *on* should be reclassified as complementisers.

We can conclude that this class has never been designed to include all and only the words which link a subordinate clause to the verb of a higher clause. In fact, it looks suspiciously like a dustbin for the words which can introduce a complement-clause but which do not seem to belong to any other word-class such as 'pronoun' or 'preposition', rather than a word-class which plays an essential role in the grammar.

This impression is confirmed when we consider the facts. The most important facts that involve the linkers are matters of valency – the valency of the higher verb, and the valency of the linkers themselves. In both cases, the facts tend to refer to specific words or inflectional categories, leaving little room for generalisations in terms of word-classes.

2.1 The valency of the higher verb

Most verbs that allow a linker only allow one or two linkers; and I do not know of a single verb that allows all four linkers. Here are some typical examples:

(4) a. I believe *that* it's going to stop. (*whether, if, for)
b. I wonder *whether* / *if* it's going to stop. (*that, for)
c. I'm longing *for* it to stop. (*that, whether, if)
d. I'm hoping *that* it's going to stop / *for* it to stop. (*whether, if)
e. I know *that* / *whether* / *if* it's going to stop. (*for)

This simple observation suggests that all the generalisations that need to be made can and should be expressed in terms of individual words (relating individual verbs to individual linkers), and none will refer to the class 'linker' (alias 'complementiser'). We need to relate *believe* to *that*, and *long* to *for*, but there are no verbs that are allowed to take simply 'a complementiser'.

It is true that all verbs that allow *whether* also allow *if*, and vice versa; but this mini-generalisation does not justify lumping all four words together. Furthermore, in almost every case[1] where these words are possible, it is also possible to use an interrogative pronoun such as *what* or *when* instead, so the generalisation that needs to be expressed has nothing to do with the classification of *whether* and *if* as linkers.

Incidentally, it is these valency facts that show beyond reasonable doubt that a linker is the head of the subordinate clause; in other words, the rest of the subordinate clause, including its verb, is subordinate to the linker, and not the other way round as in traditional analyses. The argument is simple, and rests on a widely accepted principle: the only part of a word's complement which is 'visible' to valency restrictions is its head word. It is clearly the linkers that these restrictions apply to, and not some other part of the subordinate clause such as its verb. (The minor exception of 'subjunctives' will be considered below.) Therefore the linker must be the subordinate clause's head. This conclusion is generally accepted in generative grammar, and I have no quarrel with it.

2.2 The valency of the linkers themselves

The linkers are related 'upwards' to the higher verb for the reasons just stated, but they are also related 'downwards' to the verb of the subordinate clause for rather similar reasons. Each linker restricts the kind of verb that is possible after it, as shown in Table 3.1 and illustrated in (5).

(5)
a. I know *that* it *has* stopped raining. (tensed)
b. I insist *that* the council *reconsider* its decision.
(subjunctive; example from Quirk et al. 1985: 155)
c. I wonder *if* it *has* stopped raining. (tensed)
d. I wonder *whether* it *has* stopped raining. (tensed)
e. I'm wondering *whether to* take an umbrella. (to)
f. *I'm wondering *if to* take an umbrella. (*to)
g. I'm longing *for* it *to* stop raining. (to)
h. *I'm longing *for* it *stops* raining. (*tensed)

Table 3.1 *Linkers and the subordinate verb*

'linker'	following 'verb'
that	tensed verb (or 'subjunctive'[2])
if	tensed verb
whether	tensed verb or *to*[3]
for	*to*

The main point about the facts in Table 3.1 is that each of the linkers is unique. Each one allows a different range of words as the root of the rest of the subordinate clause. This again suggests strongly that the category 'complementiser' cannot justify itself in terms of generalisations about the following verb. All the relevant facts are facts about individual words such as *that*, and not about all the linkers together.

Furthermore, with the exception of the marginal 'subjunctive', the range of 'verbs' that is allowed with the various linkers is precisely the same as we find with other kinds of subordinating words, notably interrogative pronouns. Most interrogative pronouns allow either a tensed verb or *to*, though *why* is a lexical exception:

(6) a. I'm wondering *when* I *should* go. (tensed)
b. I'm wondering *when to* go. (to)
c. I'm wondering *why* I *should* go. (tensed)
d. *I'm wondering *why to* go.

Thus if there is any generalisation to be made, it applies to most interrogative pronouns and to *whether*, but not to *that*, *if* or *for*.

This difference between *whether* and *if* is quite well known, and similar conclusions have been drawn by Chomskyan linguists as well, notably Kayne, following Larson (quoted in Henry 1992). It is true that Henry reports data from Belfast English that appear to show the opposite. In Belfast, interrogative pronouns can combine with *that*:

(7) I don't know when that he's going.

But *that* is impossible after *whether*, which Henry takes as support for the analysis of *whether* as a complementiser. The objection to this conclusion is that it leaves our differences between *whether* and *if* unexplained. The alternative is to recognise *whether* as an interrogative pronoun, and seek another explanation for its incompatibility with *that*.

This regrouping of *whether* (but not *if*) with the interrogative pronouns is supported by another well-known fact (as well as by the obvious fact that it starts with Wh-). Like all the interrogative pronouns (including *why*), it can occur in all the positions which allow nouns or Noun Phrases.[4] In this respect it differs from both *that* and *if*. Most obviously, it can occur as the object of a preposition:

(8) a. I'm thinking *about when* I should go.
b. I'm thinking *about whether* I should go.
c. *I'm thinking *about if* I should go.
d. *I'm thinking *about that* I should go.

It can also occur as the object of verbs like *discuss* which in general have to be Noun Phrases rather than subordinate clauses:

(9) a. We were discussing *linguistics*.
b. We were discussing *what* we should wear.

c. We were discussing *why* we should go.
d. We were discussing *whether* we should go.
e. *We were discussing *if* we should go.
f. *We were discussing *that* we should go.

Slightly less obviously, it can occur as an inverted subject:

(10) What you wear matters a great deal.
a. So does *when* you arrive.
b. So does *whether* you come with someone famous.
c. *So does *if* you come with someone famous.
d. *So does *that* you behave well.

And of course it can occur as an ordinary subject as well, though this is also possible for *that*:

(11) a. *When* you arrive matters a great deal.
b. *Whether* you come alone matters a great deal.
c. **If* you come alone matters a great deal.
d. *That* you behave well matters a great deal.

The facts reviewed so far suggest strongly that *whether* should be classified as an interrogative pronoun, but that *if* and the other linkers should not (Hudson 1990: 375). What can we say about the classification of the other linkers? The easiest one to deal with is *for*, which is explicitly claimed to be a preposition[5] in Chomskyan analyses (e.g. Haegeman 1991: 155). This classification explains why a noun follows *for*, and it may well be correct. Admittedly it does not in itself explain why there should also be a following *to*, which is not part of the normal valency for a preposition, but there are other prepositions which allow a second complement – *from* and *with* are examples. Thus, '*from* NP *to* NP' can[6] be a single phrase, as witness (12a) where *from London to Edinburgh* is the focus of an it-cleft, a sure sign of a single phrase.

(12) a. It was *from* London to Edinburgh that he walked.
b. It was only *with* him away that we managed to get any work done.

In (12a) *from* has two complements, *London* and *to* (Edinburgh), and likewise in (12b), where the complements of *with* are *him* and *away*.[7] The two-complement pattern thus cannot be taken as evidence against treating *for* as a preposition, so this analysis must remain on the agenda. Admittedly it is hard to produce clearer evidence for this analysis, because there are very few clear tests for prepositionhood,[8] and none which are relevant here. But no other classification seems obviously superior, so let's assume, with GB, that *for* is a preposition. The trouble with the Chomskyan analysis is that it does not address the obvious questions: How can a single word be simultaneously a preposition and a complementiser? And if a phrase headed by a preposition is a PP rather than a CP, why is not this also true of one headed by *for*?

What about the remaining linkers? The only words left on our list are *that* and *if*, but there is another word(-pair) which could have been included (though it is not generally recognised as a complementiser), *as though*. This is used to introduce a complement clause after verbs like *sound* (Gisborne, in preparation), instead of the expected *that*.

(13) a. It seems *as though* / *that* it's going to rain.
b. It looks *as though* / **that* it's going to rain.

So what can we say about the classification of *that*, *if* and *as though*?

The most obvious fact about these words is that none of them is limited to introducing the complement (or subject) of a higher verb.

(14) a. So many people came *that* we had to turn some away.
b. We'll get wet *if* it rains.
c. He's behaving *as though* he's got a pain.

Admittedly *if* and *as though* have different meanings in these other uses, so it may be that we should recognise them as distinct homonyms. The same cannot be said, however, of *that*, because its meaning seems to remain constant (at zero); so at least this word seems to recur outside the strict 'complementiser' position.

If our linkers are the same words as we find in sentences like (14), then their classification ought to reflect this fact. But how? The distribution of *that* is simply unique: there is no other word, for example, which can be used as the complement of *so* as in (14a). In contrast, *if* and *as though* are used in (14) as adjuncts of verbs, in much the same way as adverbs or prepositions. But this does not in fact help with their classification because the classification of 'adverbs' is notoriously messy, and remains one of the major challenges for syntactic research, with Greenbaum's contributions summarised in Quirk et al. (1985) as one of the main starting-points. In particular, we cannot be sure that a word is an adverb (or preposition) just because it can occur as an adjunct of a verb.

However, it is important to bear in mind as background to this debate the possibility that there is no word-class of 'adverbs'. There is no reason to believe that every word belongs to a major word-class; some words (e.g. *hello, ah*) are obvious candidates for classification simply as 'words', or as members of minor word-classes, with their own unique properties. It is possible that words like *that*, *if*, *for*, *as though, because, before* and so on are also like this – in contrast with the word-classes 'noun', 'verb' and 'adjective' which strike me as beyond reasonable doubt. The obvious candidate for classifying these words is the traditional class 'subordinating conjunction', but this is virtually the only one of the traditional word-classes which generative linguists have generally not used. It is hard to think of relevant generalisations that could only be made in terms of this class, so we cannot assume that it is a safe place for us to pop our words into. In conclusion, it seems premature to try to classify our linkers (other than *whether* and *for*), so the most conservative position is to leave them unclassified.

3 The structural 'position'

The second question is about the abstract position which has been called 'Comp' since Bresnan (1970). This position may be occupied by the linker, but in the absence of a linker it is assumed still to be present, as an abstract structural slot. This leaves two possibilities: either it is empty, or it is filled by some word other than a linker. Both of these possibilities are exploited in recent Chomskyan analyses.

3.1 Empty Comp

The standard assumption is that initial Wh-phrases are specifiers of Comp, i.e. they are just before it, with Comp empty.

(15)

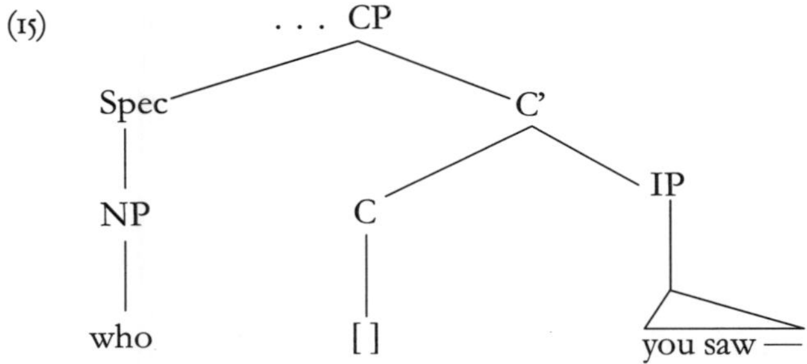

This analysis raises some problems. First, why should the specifier of Comp influence the selection of the complement of Comp, i.e. the IP?[9] As we noted in (6), most of the interrogative pronouns allow either a tensed verb or *to*, but *why* allows only the former. This is odd, considering how indirect the relation is between the specifier and complement positions.

Second, why should *where* and *whether* both have the same effect on extraction, if they are in different positions (specifier of Comp and Comp)? The following judgements are Radford's (1981: 220):

(16) a. *What might he ask where I hid?
b. *What might he ask whether I hid?

It would be much easier to explain this similarity if *where* and *whether* were related in the same way to the rest of the sentence; but such an analysis is incompatible with one in which *where* and *whether* occupy distinct positions.

And third, why are preposed adjuncts possible at the start of a Wh-interrogative main clause whereas they have to follow an overt *that* in a subordinate clause?

(17) a. Tomorrow what [$_C$] are you going to wear?
b. ?What [$_C$] tomorrow are you going to wear?
c. He told me [$_C$ that] tomorrow he's going to wear a suit.
d. *He told me tomorrow [$_C$ that] he's going to wear a suit.

There is no reason to expect preposed adjuncts to stand in different positions relative to Comp according to whether the clause concerned is embedded or not. So if we make the standard assumptions about Comp and Wh-pronouns, we can locate Comp after *what* in (17a), which means in turn that Comp follows the preposed adjunct *tomorrow*, and it is doubtful whether this order can be reversed, as in (17b). But if we try to repeat this pattern in a subordinate clause, where Comp is overtly filled by *that*, we get the ungrammatical sentence in (17d).[10] To be grammatical, in this case the reverse order is required: Comp followed by preposed adjunct.

The evidence suggests that the standard assumptions about Comp may be wrong. The problem arises only because we assume an empty Comp, marking the position where *that* would supposedly have been. If we abandon that assumption, then the problem disappears: whatever rules or principles are responsible for the position of a preposed adjunct must simply ensure that it follows *that*, and precedes a Wh-pronoun.

3.2 Filled Comp

Since Chomsky (1986) the otherwise empty Comp node has been available for the 'operators' of Quirk et al. (1985) – i.e. tensed auxiliary verbs. This has provided an apparently explanatory account of subject-auxiliary inversion, which is now seen as the result of 'inverting' the auxiliary round the subject and into the empty Comp position.

(18) a. [$_C$] He is ready.
b. [$_C$ Is] he [ ] ready?

One of the attractions of this analysis is said to be that it explains why inverted auxiliaries never cooccur with overt complementisers.

A number of serious problems arise. First, is an inverted auxiliary an auxiliary or a complementiser? Put another way, if a tensed verb projects to a phrase which reflects this classification (e.g. to Tense-P or IP), why doesn't an inverted tensed verb also project to such a phrase, instead of to CP? This is the same problem as the one we noted above in connection with *for*: how can a word belong to two otherwise incompatible word-classes at the same time?

Second, why is inversion impossible in subordinate clauses without overt *that*?

(19) a. *I know [$_C$ that] is he ready.
b. *I know [$_C$] is he ready.
c. *I know [$_C$ is] he ready.

If the explanation is that Comp is actually filled, though inaudibly, then why does this filler not block extraction out of subject position in 'Comp-trace' examples? For instance, the standard GB explanation for the difference between the sentences in (20) is that the Comp filled by overt *that* is fundamentally different from the unfilled one, to the extent that only the filled one acts as a barrier to government. If Comp in (20a) is genuinely empty, it is hard to see why it could not, in principle, have been filled by raising the tensed auxiliary into it.

(20) a. Who do you think [$_C$] will come?
b. *Who do you think [$_C$ that] will come?

Third, why is inversion in fact compatible with an overt *that*, contrary to the original claims?

(21) I admit [$_C$ that] only here *does* it rain every day.

The inversion in this example is triggered by the initial negative *only*, according to very general rules which ignore the initial *that*. The problem is well known to Chomskyan linguists (though not widely publicised in textbooks!), and various solutions have been suggested, but so far without success. For example, Authier (1992) suggests that *only here does it rain every day* is a CP, so *that* is allowed to have either an IP or a CP as its complement. The solution creates as many problems as it solves, because it has to stipulate that a CP complement must have an inversion-trigger like *only* in its specifier, and must not have an overt complementiser.

The last problem is that inversion is triggered by interrogative pronouns in main clauses but not in subordinate clauses. If this is because there is some general mechanism that somehow fills Comp in any subordinate clause, then why are sentences like (22) possible?[11]

(22) Here are the results, none of which *were* we expecting.

Indeed, why should inversion be obligatory in main Wh-interrogatives, given that the inversion is not necessary as a bearer of interrogative semantics? It seems that inversion is triggered by the interrogative pronoun, because there is at least one pronoun that does not allow it, *how come*:[12]

(23) a. How come this is grammatical?
b. *How come is this grammatical?
c. *Why this is grammatical?
d. Why is this grammatical?

These subtleties are very hard to reconcile with the Chomskyan assumption that inversion is simply the result of optionally moving an auxiliary into an empty Comp position.

4 Conclusion

I have suggested that the four words *that*, *if*, *whether* and *for* do not comprise a word-class. Their syntactic behaviour is controlled by rules which refer to them as individual words, not by rules that refer to the category 'complementiser'. I have also argued that assuming the abstract syntactic position called 'Comp', with the properties that are typically assigned to it, creates more problems than it solves. If my arguments are valid, there is no justification for postulating either a word-class 'complementiser', containing just *that*, *if*, *whether*, *for* and (possibly) *as though*, or a syntactic position 'Comp' which is typically filled by a member of this non-class.

Where, then, does this very negative discussion leave us? As far as the list of word-classes is concerned, it returns us to the traditional view, in which 'complementiser' has no place. This is one of the innovations of modern linguistics, but in my view it is an invention rather than a discovery; traditional grammarians were right not to recognise it. (I would say the same about the other major innovative word-class, 'determiner', but that is a different story.[13]) The same is true for the supposed 'position' called 'Comp'; traditional grammarians ignored it and were right to do so.

On the other hand, the view of structure that survives is a definite advance on traditional views, now that we can distinguish 'heads' and 'complements'. In an example like *I know that he came*, we can recognise *know* as the head of *that* (or, changing terminology, as the head of its own phrase, with the phrase headed by *that* as its complement); and we can recognise the same relation repeated between *that* and its complement (the phrase headed by) *came*. It is in this sense that the word *that* is a 'subordinator', marking the following clause as subordinate to the higher verb. But in this respect it is no different from a host of other words, including not only interrogative pronouns but also the traditional subordinating conjunctions like *although*, whose status in modern grammars has always been uncertain. Nor need we restrict the comparison to words that subordinate one verb to another; if we generalise to those which link other word-classes we can bring in all the prepositions as well. In this broader context, the notion 'complementiser' dwindles into insignificance as a very special case of a much more general, and interesting, pattern.

Notes

1. The only exception that I know of is the verb *doubt*, which allows either *if* or *whether* but not an interrogative pronoun; and significantly, of course, it can also take *that* without change of meaning (cf. for example the entry at $doubt_4$ in *Collins Cobuild English Language Dictionary*):

   (i) I doubt that/if/whether/*when it will rain.

2. The so-called 'subjunctive' is at best marginal for most speakers, so it should not be allowed to influence the analysis seriously. It is true that the higher verb determines whether the lower verb is tensed or subjunctive, which suggests a direct link between them rather than the indirect one mediated by *that* which I am assuming. One way to show this link is to distinguish a sub-lexeme for *that*, *that* $_{\text{subjunctive}}$, which is selected by verbs such as *insist* and which in turn selects a subjunctive inflection; but there are other possibilities. This pattern of selection is an exception to the general pattern, in which the subordinate 'verb' is selected by the linker, and *not* by the higher verb; for example, *whether* allows *to* but *if* does not, regardless of the higher verb.
3. I am including *to* among the list of 'verbs', but nothing hangs on the classification of *to*. As in Chomskyan analyses, I assume that *to* takes a bare infinitive as its (optional) complement, so there is no need to mention the infinitive in this table (any more than we need to mention, say, the fact that the tensed verb after *that* has to have an overt subject).
4. I am trying to balance between the majority view of syntax based on phrase-structure and my own view which is based on dependencies between individual words. In the former view the complement of a preposition is a Noun Phrase, but in the latter it is a noun.
5. Actually, *for* is called a 'prepositional complementiser', but this is presumably a subtype of preposition, because it is only if it is a preposition that *for* can assign Case to the following NP. This terminological fudge obscures the logical inconsistency of assigning *for* to two supposedly non-overlapping word-classes at the same time.
6. Admittedly '*to* NP' can also be a separate phrase, as in *From London he walked to Edinburgh*, but that is irrelevant.
7. It is common in GB to analyse the structure after *with* in examples like *with John away* as a small clause – i.e. a single constituent. For a particularly clear presentation of this position see Aarts (1992). There is clearly some kind of subject-predicate relation between *John* and *away*, but the small-clause analysis

is only one way of showing it, and maybe not the best way. A more conservative analysis would relate both *John* and *away* directly to *with*, in which case *with* has two complements. Notice that *away* cannot be treated as a modifier of *John*, because the sequence *John away*, in this semantic relation, is possible only after *with* and various verbs (such as *find*). Nor can we treat *away* as some kind of adverbial modifier of *with*, because it can be replaced by virtually any word or phrase that can express a (stage-level, i.e. temporary) predicate e.g. *with John to sign the cheques*, *with John playing*, *with John ill*.

8. Prepositions are surprisingly hard to identify because the main characteristic of the class is a matter of subcategorisation (i.e. valency), namely the ability to take an NP as complement. In all other word-classes this is a matter for individual lexical items within the class; e.g. some verbs take an object, and others do not, but we do not define verbs as words which can take an object. There are very few rules (if any) which apply to all PPs, and to no other phrasal class. This makes it virtually impossible to decide conclusively whether *for*, or any other word, is a preposition.
9. I am aware that the phrase that I have labelled 'IP' ('Inflection Phrase') is now given a variety of different labels such as Tense-P and Agreement-P; the labelling is not relevant to my argument here, so I have stuck to the relatively simple label, old-fashioned though it is.
10. It is tempting to explain the badness of (17d) by invoking the principle proposed in Chomsky (1986: 6) that bans all adjunction (by movement) to complements. However, the same restriction applies to all subordinate clauses, regardless of their function or position in sentence structure. The following all seem to be equally bad:
    (i) *I wonder tomorrow what will happen
    (ii) *Tomorrow what will happen is unclear
    (iii) *It's unclear tomorrow what will happen.
    (iv) *I'm thinking about tomorrow what will happen.
    (v) *The big question is tomorrow what will happen.
    (vi) *We're considering the question tomorrow what will happen.
11. An example of this type was uttered by one of my colleagues. The style is high, and the relative clause has to be non-restrictive, but native speakers seem to agree that the pattern is possible.
12. The etymology of *how come* is irrelevant, because *that* is no longer possible, *come* shows no agreement, and *come* is not an invertible auxiliary verb.
13. I tell the story in Hudson (1990: 268ff).

References

Aarts, B. (1992) *Small clauses in English.* Topics in English linguistics **8**. Berlin and New York: Mouton de Gruyter.

Authier, J.-M. (1992) Iterated CPs and embedded topicalization. *Linguistic Inquiry* **23**. 329–336.

Bresnan, J. (1970) On complementizers: towards a syntactic theory of complement types. *Foundations of Language* **6**. 297–321.

Chomsky, N. (1986) *Barriers*. Cambridge, MA: MIT Press.

Gazdar, G., Klein, E., Pullum, G. and Sag, I. (1985) *Generalized phrase structure grammar.* Oxford: Blackwell.

Gisborne, N. (in preparation) The syntax and semantics of English perception verbs. PhD Dissertation University of London.

Haegeman, L. (1991) *Introduction to Government and Binding Theory.* Oxford: Blackwell.

Henry, A. (1992) Infinitives in a for-to dialect. *Natural Language and Linguistic Theory* **10**. 279–301.

Hudson, R. (1990) *English word grammar.* Oxford: Blackwell.

Quirk, R., Greenbaum, S., Leech, G. and Svartvik, J. (1985) *A comprehensive grammar of the English language.* London: Longman.

Radford, A. (1981) *Transformational syntax: a student's guide to Chomsky's Extended Standard Theory.* Cambridge University Press.

Rosenbaum, P. (1967) *The grammar of English predicate complement constructions.* Cambridge, MA: MIT Press.

4 On the semantics of the object[1]

I. M. SCHLESINGER

1 Introduction

How does the direct object differ in meaning from the prepositional object? Is there a principled distinction in semantic terms? In this chapter an attempt is made to find such a distinction. Since there is no unanimity regarding the definition of direct object, I will use this term for any Noun Phrase that is a verb complement and is not preceded by a preposition, regardless of whether the sentence can passivise or not and regardless of whether any other tests are passed by it (cf. for instance, Quirk et al. 1972, section 7.19, note b), the only exception being the indirect object in a double-object construction, which will be dealt with in the final section. Clausal complements will not be dealt with here.

2 Can the direct object be defined in terms of semantic roles?

It has often been noted that the most frequent thematic role expressed as direct object is the Patient or the Theme. But not only are these categories difficult to define (Dowty 1991: 577), they by no means exhaust the notions that may be expressed by the direct object, as observed already by Jespersen (1933: 108). Many direct objects are locative, e.g. (1a–b) (Quirk et al. 1985: 749), and in sentences with mental verbs, the Percept or Stimulus (sometimes called Theme) is typically the direct object; see (1c–d). The direct object may also express the Instrument, as in (1e), or the Beneficiary, as in (1f).

(1) a. jumps the fence
b. crosses the square
c. sees the show

d. enjoys the show
e. uses a fork (to eat spaghetti)
f. presents John with a book

It might seem therefore that the direct object may be defined in terms of a disjunction of thematic relations (which may form a hierarchy, as proposed by Givón 1984). There are reasons, however, why this would not lead to an interesting semantic characterisation. First, the number of thematic relations that may be expressed as direct objects is very large. Besides Patient, Theme, Location, Stimulus, Instrument, and Beneficiary, which have already been mentioned, there are a great variety of roles that cannot be assigned to any one of the customary semantic roles. The examples in (2) are only a sample of a much wider range of verbs and their objects.

(2)

beware the Jabberwock!	explains the theorem
indicates approval	equals fourteen
imitates the speaker	studies Latin
avoids the question	reports the incident
resembles a lion	reflects the light
misses the train	calculates the cost
owns a house	computes the costs
denies the charges	wears clothes
describes the picture	admits the charge
keeps the secret	proves sb's guilt
touches the wall	paints the clouds
examines the outcome	costs a fortune
forgives the insult	joins the group
measures the width of	resists temptation
finds the pencil	deserves a rest
precedes the procession	lacks funds
follows the guidelines	needs food
discovers the island	derives some benefit
regrets the mistake	grants permission
revenges the murder	

Examples like these lend support to Jespersen's (1961: 230) claim that 'on account of the infinite variety of meanings inherent in verbs the notional (or logical) relations of the verbs and their objects are so manifold that they defy any attempt at analysis or classification'.

Not only are there many semantic roles that can be expressed as direct objects, but the same roles may also be expressed by other constructions. Semantically, there is a large overlap between direct and prepositional objects, and to some extent even between direct objects and subjects.

The only definite statement in terms of semantic roles that can be made concerning the direct object is negative: a Noun Phrase that is an Agent cannot be a direct object.

In the following list, the italicised Noun Phrase is direct object in the first sentence in each set, prepositional object in the second sentence, and subject in the third sentence (when there is one). (The semantic roles are those widely used in the current literature, but nothing hinges on the classification of every single Noun Phrase in (3) being correct.)

(3)	Patient:	He boiled *the milk*.
		He cooked the pie with *milk*.
		The milk boiled.
	Theme:	He threw *stones* at the window.
		He pelted the window with *stones*.
		The stones landed right near the window.
	Location:	The helicopter crossed *the road*.
		The helicopter flew across *the road*.
	Source:	The train left *Rome* for Florence.
		The train to Florence left from *Rome*.
	Goal:	The mountaineer reached *the mountain top*.
		The mountaineer climbed to *the mountain top*.
	Experiencer:	The movie pleased *John*.
		The movie was pleasing to *John*.
		John liked the movie.
	Stimulus:	Jean admires *the painter*.
		Jean marvels at *the painter*.
		The painter impresses Jean.
	Instrument:	He used *a knife* to cut the cake.
		He cut the cake with *a knife*.
		The knife cut the cake.
	Beneficiary:	They presented *Jill* with a medal.
		They presented a medal to *Jill*.
		Jill received a medal.

A description of the direct object in terms of semantic roles will be incomplete without an account of what determines whether a given semantic role is expressed as direct object, as prepositional object, or as subject.

A new departure in defining thematic roles for the purpose of argument selection is due to Dowty (1991). Dowty identifies two Proto-Roles – that of the Agent and that of the Patient. The Patient Proto-Role is assigned to that Noun Phrase which has the relatively greater number of the following properties:

a. undergoes change of state
b. Incremental Theme
c. causally affected by another participant
d. stationary relative to movement of another participant
(e. does not exist independently of the event, or not at all)

The parentheses are meant by Dowty to indicate his doubts as to whether this property ought to be included. The term Incremental Theme refers (roughly speaking) to a Theme the state of parts of which is reflected in the parts of the events referred to by the predicate; for a full explanation see Dowty (1991).

Dowty states that the Patient Proto-Role is expressed as direct object. But there are direct objects that do not express the Patient Proto-Role: none of the direct objects in (2) have properties a–d and only the last five (*a rest, funds, food, some benefit* and *permission*) have property e. It appears therefore that, while many direct objects have the Patient Proto-Role, a great variety of direct objects are left unaccounted for by Dowty's proposal.

3 Other approaches

It appears that to characterise the direct objects in (2) in terms of semantic roles one might have to introduce a different role for the direct object of almost every single verb. At best, some verbs of related meanings may form a class and their objects assigned the same semantic role. Such a classification (based not only on the role of the direct object) has been proposed by Dixon (1991). Among the sets he identifies is that of 'speaking' verbs, some subsets of which have the Addressee as direct object and others, the Message; the set of 'giving' verbs requires the roles of Recipient and Gift, both of which may become direct object under certain conditions.

This raises the question of a general principle that predicts what roles will be realised as direct objects. Dixon (1991: 11) holds that the direct object expresses the semantic role that is regarded as most salient for the activity, and there is much material in Dixon's book to bear this out. Saliency, though, is a very slippery concept. What is needed is an independent criterion for what is salient for the activity; without this, Dixon's formulation incurs the risk of circularity.

At any rate, Dixon's proposal contains an important insight, which informs the proposal to be made further on. He talks about what is 'most salient for the *activity*' (emphasis mine), not about the saliency of the Noun Phrase in and by itself. He thus refers to the Verb Phrase as a whole, and in this respect he differs from most previous writers, who in assigning semantic roles focus only on the Noun Phrase.

This focus on the Verb Phrase is already found in Jespersen (1961: 229), for whom the object 'is intimately connected with the verb of a sentence' and in an early formulation by Jakobson (1936/1971: 31), pertaining to the accusative case marking, which in many languages (e.g. Russian) is associated with the direct object: 'Der Akkusativ besagt stets, dass irgend eine Handlung auf den bezeichneten Gegenstand gewissermassen gerichtet ist, an ihm sich äussert, ihn ergreift' ('The accusative always indicates that some action is directed at the thing referred to, manifests itself through it, involves it'). Jakobson talks here about the relation between the 'action' and the 'thing', that is, what is referred to by the verb and the noun. However, like saliency, the notion of 'directed at' remains vague. The proposal made in the following, like those of Jespersen, Jakobson, and Dixon, focusses on the Verb Phrase as a whole. To characterise the direct object semantically, three properties will be referred to; the first of these is dealt with in the following section.

4 Defining participants

The lexical entry of a verb will comprise various participants in the activity, event or state referred to by the verb (its arguments). Now, for practically all verbs there will be one or more participants that are inherently implicated in the event or state expressed by the verb; that is, for the event or state to occur it is necessary that there be such a participant. One of these will end up as the sentence subject. When water is boiled, there is typically someone who instigates the activity of boiling, and this someone will be expressed as subject.

(4) He boiled the water.

The other participant in (4), expressed by water, is also inherently implicated in the event: it is totally inconceivable that boiling might proceed without some stuff (normally liquid) that is being heated. Such a participant that is inherently implicated in the event described by the verb and is not expressed as the underlying subject will be called *Defining Participant* (DP). The subject, then, has to be determined first; the direct object refers to a participant that is part of the mental definition of the verb and does not become the subject. The treatment of direct objects in Schlesinger (1995) is similar in most respects to the present one, but is embedded in a different theoretical framework.

The DP will typically be salient and the activity will be directed at it (note also the term 'direct object'), and here the present characterisation overlaps with those of Jakobson and Dixon. The concept of a DP has the advantage of being less vague than the notions proposed by those writers. This does not mean, of course, that there will be no borderline instances where doubts will remain as to whether a participant is defining or not.

The thesis that direct objects usually express DPs takes care of affected objects. Take the verb *push*: pushing requires, by definition, something that is pushed, and this something is a DP and is expressed by a direct object. Likewise, effected objects are DPs: the lexical entry for *build*, for instance, will refer to the resultant of the activity, since whenever the activity of building occurs there is something that is built, be it only a castle of sand. In the entry for mental verbs, the Percept or Stimulus are DPs: it is inconceivable that seeing occurs without something to see (though it might be no more material than a fata morgana), or that someone envies without there being someone he envies. The reader can satisfy himself that the notion of DP also accommodates all the direct objects in (2).[2]

The notion of DP is obviously related to that of an obligatory argument. However, I refrain from characterising the direct object in terms of syntactic concepts like this and like valency or subcategorisation, because what is at issue here is a semantic description of the direct object.

A caveat is in order here. Our definition of a DP is unrelated to the possibility of ellipsis of the direct object. Omission of the direct object is very common. Eating, for instance, is inconceivable without some stuff that is eaten, but it is perfectly normal to say *He has eaten* without mentioning the food consumed. The substance taken into the mouth and swallowed is a DP, but it need not be mentioned in a sentence with *eat* as the main verb.

The direct objects in (1)–(3) are all DPs, and so are direct objects in general.[3] However, being a DP is neither a necessary nor a sufficient condition for being realised as a direct object, as will become clear in the following sections.

5 Multiple DPs

When a verb has more than one DP, one of them may be expressed by a Noun Phrase in a Prepositional Phrase. Hitting, for instance, requires an instrument with which one hits (possibly, one's hand) and an object that is hit; these are its two DPs. The verb *beg* also has two DPs: the person one begs from, and the thing one begs. Any one of the two DPs may become direct object, and the other then becomes the prepositional object; and similarly for the verb *blame*.

(5) He hit the stick [DP_1] against the fence.
He hit the fence [DP_2] with the stick.

He begged the governor [DP_1] for mercy.
He begged a favour [DP_2] of the governor.

She blamed the secretary [DP_1] for the delay.
She blamed the delay [DP_2] on the secretary.

Jespersen (1961: 240–242) gives examples of additional verbs that can take two different DPs as objects, like *entrust*, *present*, *provide*, and *wrap*.

A further example is the locative alternation. The verb *load*, for instance, has two DPs: one is the material that changes place, and the other, the place to which it is transferred. Either one may be direct object, while the other ends up in a Prepositional Phrase:

(6) They loaded the wagon [DP_1] (with hay).
They loaded the hay [DP_2] on the wagon.

Recent analyses of the locative alternation are to be found in Pinker (1989) and Dowty (1991). The determinants of the choice between the alternatives in (6) will be discussed later on; the determinants of choice in respect to (5) remain to be investigated.

Some verbs require that one of their DPs remain unexpressed, for instance:

(7) The pupil answered the teacher.
The pupil answered the question.

Which of the two DPs is expressed will depend on the speaker's decision as to the relative importance of the respective items of information.

There is one type of DP that is never expressed as direct object when it competes with another DP: the instrument with which an activity is performed. In (8) there are two Noun Phrases realising DPs: *water* and *a coal fire*; the former is the direct object and the latter is the instrument and appears in a Prepositional Phrase:

(8) He boiled the water with/by means of a coal fire.

The Prepositional Phrase headed by *with* or *by means of* is reserved for the expression of the instrument, and this is how the instrument is realised even when the other DP is left unexpressed.[4] Thus, although the stuff that is cooked (a DP of the verb *cook*) is not mentioned in (9), the instrument is not 'promoted' to direct object position but remains in the Prepositional Phrase.

(9) He cooks with a pressure cooker.

Locative DPs are also often not realised as direct objects:

(10) She put the book on the table.

The lexical entry for *put* includes a DP for the thing that is moved and one for the place where it is put; it is inconceivable for putting to occur without any such 'destination'. The competition between these two DPs for direct object position is always decided in favour of the thing that is moved, the 'destination' never being expressed as direct object. We will presently see why this should be so.

6 The Recoverability Constraint

As we have just seen, a locative DP may be expressed as object of a preposition rather than as direct object. This is because there are many possible spatial relations between a thing and a location, and each such relation requires a different preposition. Thus, instead of (10) one might say

(11) She put the book under/near/at the side of the table.

Locative prepositions are typically not redundant, and if the 'destination' of putting would be realised as direct object, i.e. without a preposition, the message might be ambiguous. There is, then, a *Recoverability Constraint* which may block the assignment of a Noun Phrase to direct object position (cf. Larson, 1988: 371, on a 'prohibition on nonrecoverable deletion'). The preposition of a Locative tends to be less recoverable than that of Noun Phrases with other semantic roles because of the large number of possible locative relations: there are over fifty locative prepositions, and only a handful of other prepositions that subserve other roles (see Hill 1968).

Consider now the Noun Phrases *the Channel* and *the mountain* in (12). These describe locations, and are presumably part of the mental definition of the verb. The idea of swimming presupposes a body of water that can be swum in and that of climbing an object that is climbed on. These are therefore DPs, but in (12) they are not direct objects. It might be thought that, because the prepositions in (12) can be replaced by others, as in (13), the Recoverability Constraint obviates their omission.

(12) a. swim across the Channel
b. climb up the mountain

(13) a. swim in/near/at the edge of the Channel
b. climb down the mountain

But here we run into a problem, because *swim* and *climb* may also take direct objects, as in (14):

(14) a. swim the Channel
b. climb the mountain

That the Recoverability Constraint does not bar (14) is probably due to the fact that the hearer or reader supplies the most frequently occurring and most obviously applicable preposition in construing (14). Thus, *swim the Channel* means 'swim across the Channel' and not 'swim in the Channel/near the Channel shore' or the like, and climb the mountain means 'climb up the mountain' and not 'climb down the mountain'.

But why should there be alternative formulations like (12) and (14)? The locative expressions in (14) are DPs; the missing prepositions appear to be the most obviously applicable ones, which is why (14) is not barred by the Recoverability Constraint. But if so, there is no need for the longer expressions in (12). The same question arises with several other verbs that can have either a direct object or an object of a preposition:

(15)		
	a. flee the country	flee from the country
	b. ride a horse	ride on a horse
	c. cross the square	cross over the square
	d. turn the corner	turn round the corner
	e. pass the statue	pass by the statue
	f. walk the streets	walk in the streets
	g. approach the highway	

In spite of the lack of prepositions, the expressions in the left-hand column of (15) are likely to be construed like those in the right-hand column. *Flee the country* is most plausibly construed as 'flee from the country' (although there is a somewhat less plausible alternative: 'flee to the country'). Our knowledge of the world leads us to construe *ride a horse* as 'ride on a horse'. The notion expressed by *over* is contained in the verb *cross*, and hence *cross the square* can be construed only as 'cross over the square'; no other preposition will fit. *Turn the corner* can mean only 'turn round the corner'. Passing something can mean only passing by it; similarly for *walk the streets*. All these phrases are hardly more ambiguous than the last, *approach the highway*, for which there is no alternative with a preposition (**approach to/toward the highway*). Observe that in all these phrases the locative expression realises a DP: the notion of riding implies something that is ridden on, that of crossing requires a place that is crossed, and so on. The direct object construction is therefore indicated, and the constructions in the right-hand column of (15) are in need of explaining.

Part of the explanation is that recoverability is not an all-or-none affair. Speakers may opt for the prepositional object construction when this makes the meaning clearer or more easily accessible. We return to this issue in the following section.

Summarizing the results of our investigation so far, it may be said that a DP is normally expressed as a direct object. However, when more than one DP is expressed, only one of the DPs becomes direct object – see (5), (6) and (8) – and to the extent that the relevant preposition is not recoverable, a prepositional object may be chosen.[5]

7 Direct object versus Prepositional Phrase

In this section I discuss two additional semantic determinants that decide whether the verb takes a direct object or one with a preposition.

7.1 Completion

Let us return first to (12) and (14). The reader will note that the direct object implies that the activity has been successful and has been brought to its completion, whereas the corresponding sentence with a prepositional object does not have this implication (cf. Quirk et al. 1985: 685). Thus, *swim the lake* means that the lake has been successfully crossed by swimming, whereas *swim in the lake* can also be said of an event in which the other shore has not been reached. Similarly, *climb the mountain* implies that the top of the mountain has been reached, but this does not follow from *climb up the mountain* (Moravcsik 1978: 256). The same distinction applies to (15a): one who *fled the country* has actually succeeded in leaving it, whereas one who *fled from the country* might have been caught before leaving it.

This property, which distinguishes some direct objects from prepositional objects, will be called *Completion*. This notion is roughly the same as that of the Vendlerian *Accomplishment* (Dowty 1979). Similar differences in meaning between objects with and without prepositions are found in several other languages (Moravcsik 1978: 256–261). The choice between direct and prepositional object in (16) is also determined by this factor. Pushing away at something means that one does not quite succeed at the job, and knowing of somebody implies less complete knowledge than knowing somebody.

(16) a. push the table — push (away) at the table
b. know the boy — know of the boy

Completion is also a determinant of the choice between the two constructions of the locative alternation (see (6) above). It has often been pointed out that sentences like (17a) and (18a) require 'wholistic' interpretations. Thus, (17a) says that the wagon ended up being fully loaded, whereas (17b) is neutral on this point; and similarly for (18b).[6]

(17) a. They loaded the wagon with hay.
b. They loaded the hay on the wagon.

(18) a. Susan sprayed the wall with paint.
b. Susan sprayed the paint on the wall.

In all the above examples the direct object expresses a DP. These DPs may have either a direct object or a prepositional one, depending on the presence or absence of Completion. Now, this property also licenses the direct object construction when the verb does not have a DP. It may be argued that the transitive verbs *grasp*, *kick*, and *shoot* do not involve DPs: one can shoot in the air and not at any target, and one can make grasping and kicking movements in the absence of anything to be grasped or kicked. But as shown in (19), these verbs take a direct object when Completion is involved; otherwise an oblique Noun Phrase is required, as in the right-hand column.

(19)	a. shot the fox	shot at the fox
	b. grasp the rope	grasp at the rope
	c. kick the table	kick at the table

When you have *shot* the fox, it is necessarily hit; when you have *shot at* it, you may have missed; and similarly for the other two verbs.[7]

In these examples, unlike those in (15), the prepositions apparently do not remove ambiguity; instead, they indicate the *lack* of Completion. Completion also accounts for several other verbs that can appear with or without prepositions: *stab* (*at*), *catch* (*at*), *clutch* (*at*), and *strike* (*at*). For some verbs, though, there seems to be no such difference in meaning: *improve* (*on*), *check* (*on*), and *forget* (*about*) (Moravcsik 1978: 256).

Note that Completion is a property of the Verb Phrase as a whole. In this it is like the notion of a DP, which applies to the activity denoted by the verb, rather than to the argument expressed by the Noun Phrase in isolation.

7.2 Feat

Use of the direct object for the verbs *swim* and *climb* is subject to an additional condition. With these verbs, the direct object tends to be chosen when the activity leads to a not quite usual achievement, a 'feat', so to speak. Compare the sentences in the following pairs:

(20) John swam the lake.
??John swam the pond.

(21) Jack climbed the mountain/the pyramids.
*Jack climbed the bed.

It is only when the swim or the climb present some difficulty that we use the verb with a direct object. We will call this property *Feat*. When the activity does not have this property, the locative Noun Phrase will appear as a prepositional object, even when the activity has the property Completion:

(22) a. John swam in the pond.
b. Jack climbed into/onto the bed.

Even riding a horse, (15b), may be viewed as something of a Feat, not being merely 'sitting on top of it, but "controlling", "mastering" it' (Givón 1984: 99).

Feat in conjunction with Completion may license the direct object construction even where the Noun Phrase does not express a DP. For instance, the verb *jump* presumably has no DP, because one can jump without jumping over anything.[8] In (23a) *jump* describes a Feat, and accordingly takes a direct object. No such Feat is involved in (23b), and a preposition is therefore mandatory, as in (23c).[9]

(23) a. Jill jumped the fence.
b. *Jill jumped the stool/the gutter.
c. Jill jumped over the stool/the gutter.

When the activity has a strongly accentuated characteristic of Completion, however, even (23b) may be acceptable. Completion is context dependent. Out of context the sentences in (24) will be exceedingly odd, because of the absence of Feat, but when the notion of Completion is focussed on, they might be appropriate (Richard Hudson p.c.). Thus, (24a) might be said by someone who has made a bet that he will jump every gutter in the neighbourhood, and (24b) by someone who has betted that he will climb on every seat in the cinema.

(24) a. I have already jumped this gutter.
b. I have already climbed this seat.

Consider now (25), due to And Rosta (p.c.):

(25) John is a promising young violinist; he has already played the Albert Hall.

The DP of *play* is a piece of music, and not the place where it is played. However, when one intends to express the notion of Feat, as in (25), the place becomes the direct object. When there is no such Feat, the direct object construction is odd in spite of the presence of Completion:

(26) ??John has already played the market place.

Like Completion, Feat is a property of the event as a whole and applies to the Verb Phrase rather than to the Noun Phrase by itself.

The properties Completion and Feat thus explain the direct object/prepositional object alternation of some verbs. Those in (15c–f) and the following examples, given in Jespersen (1933: 110), however, are not accounted for by these properties:

(27) confess a crime — confess to a liking of something
believe the story — believe in God
meet a person — meet with him

The direct objects here, like those in (15), express DPs, and it is therefore the phrases in the right-hand column that stand in need of explanation. Further examples are given in Jespersen (1961: 252–272). Also unaccounted for are *permit/permit of*, *approve/approve of*, and *ponder/ponder over*.[10]

7.3 Why Completion and Feat?

That the two properties Completion and Feat are associated with the direct object is probably due to their being intimately related to affectedness. A large proportion of DPs which are expressed as direct objects are affected by the activity denoted by the verb; they are Patients. This may lead to an effect in the reverse direction: participants that are not DPs but are in some sense affected will tend to be expressed by direct objects. Now, other things being equal, a participant will be more affected when the action has been successfully completed. Completion may therefore result in a Noun Phrase becoming direct object even when it does not realise a DP, as shown by (24).[11] Further, it is often the case that the more the object is affected, the greater and the more spectacular will be the achievement; compare for instance:

(28) a. He broke the plank with his bare hands.
b. He smashed the plank with his bare hands.

While there are many activities where this relationship does not hold, it is instantiated often enough to establish an association in our minds between affectedness and the notion of Feat. And, again, the property Feat results in the participant being realised as direct object even where it is not a DP, as shown by (24) and (25).

It appears, then, that a direct object either expresses a DP, or else the Verb Phrase is characterised by Completion or Feat. The disjunction of these three characteristics is a necessary condition for the direct object.[12] Being a DP, however, is not a sufficient condition for realisation as direct object, see (5), (6), and (9). Neither is Completion a sufficient condition, as shown by (29), where prepositions are mandatory before the Noun Phrases; and the same holds true for Feat, as shown by (30).

(29) a. She dismounted from her horse.
b. He did away with his opponents.
c. They escaped from the drizzle.

(30) a. Michelangelo exceeded in productivity.
b. Cassandra peered into the future.
c. Hercules succeeded in the seven tasks.

8 The indirect object

We have postponed so far treatment of double-object constructions, like those in (31). As will presently become apparent, the first of the two objects in such a construction – the indirect object – differs in its semantic characterisation from the objects discussed so far.[13]

(31) a. She gave Bill a book.
b. He told John the news.
c. The policeman fined the driver five Pounds.
d. They envied Mary her new car.
e. The student asked the teacher a question.
f. The new car cost us a fortune.
g. We wished John success.
h. The guard denied us access to the private rooms.

8.1 Characteristics of the indirect object

Like the direct object, the indirect object cannot be economically characterised by semantic relations. Some indirect objects are Beneficiary or Recipient – e.g. (31a–b) – but those in (31e–g) are not. Now, the indirect objects in (31) are like direct objects in that they express DPs. The two DPs of the verb *give* are the thing that is transferred and the person or animal it is transferred to. The verb *tell* implies the existence of an Addressee and a

Message. The two DPs of the verb *fine* are the person fined and a certain amount of money constituting the fine; and the verbs in (31d–h) also have two DPs each. As shown in (31), both DPs may in each case be realised as Noun Phrases without prepositions.

We have seen that some indirect objects in (31) express DPs but not the Beneficiary or Recipient; the indirect objects in (32), by contrast, express the Beneficiary or Recipient, but not DPs (cf. Hudson 1992: 260):

(32) a. He peeled me an orange.
b. She sang me a song.
c. They found us a hotel.
d. We built them an igloo.
e. I bought her a villa.
f. You cooked her some potatoes.

Completion is present only in (32c–f), and none of the activities in (32) has the property Feat. The indirect object, then, differs from the direct object in that it occurs also when the Noun Phrase is not a DP and in the absence of such features as Completion and Feat; in these instances the indirect object expresses either a Beneficiary or Recipient.

8.2 The Garden-path Constraint

For (31a), (31b), and (31e) there exist the alternative realisations in (33): only one of the Noun Phrases is a direct object, and the other is expressed by a prepositional object.

(33) a. She gave a book to Bill.
b. He told the news to John.
c. The student asked a question of the teacher.

No such alternative exists for the other examples in (31), however. The indirect objects of these sentences do not express the Beneficiary or Recipient, as those in (31a–b), but this cannot account for the difference, since (31e) also does not express these roles.

We come now to a problem that has recently been investigated by various writers (see e.g. Pinker 1989), namely the eligibility of verbs to the double object construction. There are many verbs which, unlike those in (31), do not take double objects:

(34) a. *She pushed Bill a chair.
b. *John shot his girl-friend a tiger.
c. *John mentioned Paul the incident.

What determines whether a verb can be used with double objects – as in (35) – or not, as in (34)?

(35) a. She gave Bill a chair.
b. John bought his girl friend a tiger.
c. John told Paul the news.

Note, first, that the Recoverability Constraint cannot account for the difference between (34) and (35). In the case of (35) the prepositions are fairly easily recoverable, considering that double objects usually occur with the Beneficiary; but so are the prepositions omitted in the quite similar sentences in (34).

It has been hypothesised that the unacceptability of the double-object construction with some verbs is due, at least in part, to another processing constraint (Schlesinger 1977). Suppose one hears (34a) and processes it from left to right. At the instant the hearer reaches *Bill*, he has the option of an incorrect construal: *She pushed Bill*, with *Bill* as the person pushed. When the initial part of the sentence is so construed, the hearer will subsequently have to backtrack. This increases processing difficulty, and therefore double objects are avoided with this verb. The preposition is thus *temporarily* irrecoverable, and so are those in (34b–c). This variant of the Recoverability Constraint may be called the *Garden-path Constraint*. (35a), by contrast, is acceptable, because the erroneous construal *She gave Bill*, with *Bill* as direct object, does not arise because of its extreme implausibility. Nor does one buy a girl friend – (35b). Finally, *John told Paul* can be understood only with *Paul* as indirect object – *Paul* as the person *John* tells something to; a construal with *Paul* as direct object would be completely meaningless. In other words, one may expect an inverse relation to hold between the plausibility of an incorrect construal of the first words of a double-object construction (i.e. as subject–verb–direct object) and the acceptability of the whole sentence: the more likely the incorrect construal, the lower the acceptability.

Empirical evidence for the Garden-path Constraint has been obtained in a study with native speakers of English (see Schlesinger 1977 for details). In that study, passive sentences of the following two types were used:

(36) a. Paul was mentioned the incident by John.
b. Paul was mentioned by John.

Observe that (36a) is the passive of the unacceptable (34c). (The passive voice was used because a pilot study suggested that this form would accentuate the differences in acceptability.) *Paul was mentioned* in (36a) can be incorrectly construed in the same way as *Paul was mentioned* in (36b) – namely with Paul as direct object rather than as indirect object – thus requiring backtracking and reorganizing the structure of (36a). The Garden-path Constraint predicts therefore that (36a) will be rated as unacceptable. When such a construal is implausible – as for instance in (37a), where *Paul was given* makes little sense – no incorrect construal will be engaged in and no backtracking will be required; (37a) will therefore be acceptable.

(37) a. Paul was given a drink by John.
b. Paul was given by John.

In short, the hypothesis of the study was that the greater the plausibility of a passive sentence without a direct object (as in (36b)), the lower the acceptability of the corresponding sentence with a direct object (as in (36a)).

Two rating scales were prepared. One was a plausibility scale, comprising sentences of the form of (36b) and (37b), and the other was an acceptability scale, comprising sentences like (36a) and (37a).

For each of the scales two versions were prepared, differing only in the sequence in which the sentences appeared. Each of the two scales, and each of the two versions, was given to a different group of subjects.

Table 4.1 gives some illustrative examples (from one of the two versions) of how the various sentences in this study scored on plausibility and acceptability.

Table 4.1 *Plausibility and acceptability of passive sentence*

	plausibility	acceptability
Paul was mentioned by John.	1.06	
Paul was mentioned the incident by John.		1.12
Paul was taken by John.	1.40	
Paul was taken the check by John.		1.27
Paul was sold by John.	3.13	
Paul was sold a book by John.		3.17
Paul was offered by John.	4.25	
Paul was offered a candy by John.		5.67
Paul was given by John.	6.54	
Paul was given a drink by John.		6.00

Note: 1 – completely plausible, 7 – completely implausible
1 – completely unacceptable 7 – completely acceptable

The shorter form of the first two sentence pairs in the table was judged to be plausible (a score of 1 means completely plausible) and, as predicted, the double object form was judged to be unacceptable (a score of 1 means completely unacceptable). In the last two sentence pairs, the shorter form was implausible and accordingly the double object form was acceptable. The sentence pair with *sell* was intermediate in plausibility and in acceptability. As stated, these are only illustrative examples, and not all sentence pairs conformed to the prediction as well as these (see Schlesinger 1977 for details). But the Spearman rank-order correlations for implausibility and acceptability were .487 (p=.013) for one of the versions and .447 (p=.022) for the other, thus confirming our hypothesis.

9 Conclusion

In this chapter it has been argued that a semantic characterisation of the direct object cannot be based on thematic roles. Instead, such a characterisation has to based on three kinds of factors:

(i) The semantics of the Verb Phrase, i.e. whether the Noun Phrase expresses what is a DP in the lexical entry. These factors were found also to partially characterise indirect objects.

(ii) The situation referred to, i.e. whether it has the properties Completion or Feat. These account partially for the choice between direct object and object of preposition.

(iii) Performance factors: the Recoverability Constraint and the Garden-path Constraint (that is, the recoverability of the preposition and the extent to which omission of the preposition permits an incorrect construal).

Notes

1. I am indebted to Richard Hudson, And Rosta and Nik Gisborne for insightful discussions. Richard Hudson also made many valuable comments on a previous version of this chapter, as did Bas Aarts, Edit Doron, Charles Meyer, Anita Mittwoch, and Anat Ninio. Many thanks to them, and to Yael Ziv for referring me to relevant publications. Work on this chapter has been conducted in part when I was an Honorary Research Fellow at the Survey of English Usage, University College London, and I am grateful to the director, Sidney Greenbaum, for letting me benefit from the atmosphere prevailing at the Survey, which is so conducive to research.
2. It is also inconceivable for boiling to occur except at a certain time, but then this is true of every activity, event and state. Time of occurrence is what one might call a 'background' participant; it will not be registered separately for each verb in its semantic description and thus is not a defining participant. Location of the event may also be such a background participant, but see the treatment of locatives further on.

3. A cognate object (see the examples below) is redundant, in a sense, but what it expresses is, like a DP, part of the meaning of the verb.

   (i) a. He slept a sound sleep.
   b. He dreamt a disturbing dream.
   c. He laughed a hoarse laugh.

   The complements in the following sentences (which are direct objects according to the foregoing definition: they are not preceded by a preposition) are also DPs. Weighing implies a certain weight, running, a certain distance that is transversed, and so on.

   (ii) a. He weighs 130 pounds.
   b. He ran a mile.
   c. He grew a lot last year.
   d. The book cost £15.

   Further examples of Noun Phrases expressing DPs are:

   (iii) a. purse his lips
   b. nod his head
   c. clap his hands

4. In advertisements one finds expressions like

   (iv) Fly British Airways.

   The analysis of *British Airways* is equivocal: it may be an instrument, but it may also be a Locative (the instrumental meaning being conflated with that of the verb, since flying, for humans, can mean only fly by plane or some similar vehicle), or an adverbial, as in *run bezerk*, *bathe naked*.
5. There are a handful of verbs, notably mental verbs, that have DPs but do not take direct objects, although the prepositions are easily recoverable. These include: *arrive (in/at)*, *aspire (to)*, *belong (to)*, *desist (from)*, *long (for)*, *marvel (at)*, and *wonder about*. In Hebrew, too, these verbs take prepositions. The German translation equivalents of both *belong* and *long* take the dative.
6. The same alternation exists in Hungarian and with the same difference in meaning (Moravcsik 1978: 256–257). In German, there are many verbs that take the prefix *be-* when the construction has a wholistic meaning:

   (i) Er streut Sand auf den Weg. ('He scatters sand on the way')
   (ii) Er bestreut den Weg mit Sand. ('He scatters the way with sand')

   See Wunderlich (1987) and Booij (1992).
7. A similar distinction exists in German. The German translation of (19a–b) is:

(i)	erschoss den Fuch	schoss auf den Fuchs
	('shot the fox'	'shot at the fox')
(ii)	ergreift das Seil	greift nach dem Seil
	('grasps the rope'	'grasps at the rope')

Spanish distinguishes between providing a (definite) answer to the question and giving a (not satisfactory) response to it (Haiman 1983: 790):

(iii) contestar la pregunta/contestar a la pregunta
(both: 'answer the question')

Spanish mental verbs may have a dative or an accusative object, and Hurst (1951) notes 'a leaning toward the dative when the dynamic quality of the verb is weakened'. For instance, *inquietar* ('to worry') takes the accusative when the danger is imminent and the dative when it is remote. That Completion, as used in this chapter, is a broader notion than 'delimiting' (Tenny 1990), can be seen from the discussion of (19).

8. According to the *Oxford English Dictionary*, the transitive sense of *jump* appears somewhat later than the intransitive one. Certain idiomatic uses of *jump* also involve DPs and the notion of Completion: *jump (the) ship*, *jump the rails*, *jump the queue*.
9. The Recoverability Constraint is not violated by (23a). Direct objects of *jump* are restricted to instances where they paraphrase prepositional objects with *over*: *jump the fence* can mean only 'jump over the fence', not 'jump from the fence', 'jump under the fence' or 'jump near the fence'. Here, too, the preposition *over*, carries little information, in the technical sense.
10. For some verbs the preposition involves a change of meaning; cf. *touch/touch on*, *treat/treat of*, *improve/improve on*, *attend/attend to*, and *consult/consult with* (Jespersen 1961: 252–272).
11. Givón (1984) notes that in (18a) the wall is 'most affected' and the paint 'less involved', and vice versa in (18b).
12. Exceptions are a few verbs taking direct objects that neither have Completion or Feat nor have DPs: *protest his innocence*, *nod approval*. (But in *scramble his way through the crowd* Completion seems to be present.)
13. Opinions are divided as to which of the two objects in (31) is the direct object. Here we follow Hudson (1992), who concludes on the basis of an array of syntactic and semantic criteria that the first of the two objects is an indirect object (or an 'indirect', as he proposes to call it) and the second, the direct object. But note that *the driver*, *Mary*, and *the teacher*, in (31c–e) do not exhibit all of Hudson's (1992) characteristics of the indirect.

References

Booij, G. (1992) Morphology, semantics and argument structure. In Roca, I. M. (ed.), *Thematic structure: its role in grammar*. Berlin and New York: Foris. 47–64.

Dixon, R. M. W. (1991) *A new approach to English grammar, on semantic principles*. Oxford: Clarendon Press.

Dowty, D. (1979) *Word meaning and Montague grammar*. Dordrecht: Reidel.

(1991) Thematic proto-roles and argument selection. *Language* **67**. 547–619.

Givón T. (1984) Direct object and dative shifting: Semantic and pragmatic case. In Plank, F. (ed.), *Objects: toward a theory of grammatical relations*. London: Academic Press. 151–182.

Haiman, J. (1983) Iconic and economic motivation. *Language* **59**. 781–819.
Hill, L. A. (1968) *Prepositions and adverbial particles*. London: Oxford University Press.
Hudson, R. (1992) So-called 'double objects' and grammatical relations. *Language* **68**. 251–276.
Hurst, D. A. (1951) Spanish case: influenced subject and connotation of force. *Hispania* **34**. 74–78.
Jakobson, R. (1936) Beitrag zur allgemeinen Kasuslehre: Gesamtbedeutungen des russischen Kasus. Reprinted in Jakobson, R. *Selected writings*. Volume 2: *Word and language*. The Hague: Mouton, 1971. 23–71.
Jespersen, O. (1933) *Essentials of English grammar*. London: Allen and Unwin.
(1961) *A modern English grammar on historical principles*. Part III: *Syntax*. Second volume. London: Allen and Unwin.
Larson, R. (1988) On the double object construction. *Linguistic Inquiry* **19**. 335–391.
Moravcsik, E. A. (1978) On the case marking of objects. In Greenberg, J. H. (ed.), *Universals of human language*. Volume 4: *Syntax*. Stanford, CA: Stanford University Press.
Pinker, S. (1989) *Learning and cognition: the acquisition of argument structure*. Cambridge, MA: MIT Press.
Quirk, R., Greenbaum, S., Leech, G. and Svartvik, J. (1972) *A grammar of contemporary English*. London: Longman.
(1985) *A comprehensive grammar of the English language*. London: Longman.
Schlesinger, I. M. (1977) *Production and comprehension of utterances*. Hillsdale, NJ: Lawrence Erlbaum.
(1995) *Cognitive space and linguistic case*. Cambridge University Press.
Tenny, C. (1990) The role of the internal argument: measuring out events. Unpublished MS, MIT Center for Cognitive Science.
Wunderlich, D. (1987) An investigation of lexical composition: the case of German *be*-verbs. *Linguistics* **25**. 283–331.

5 Secondary predicates in English[1]

BAS AARTS

1 Introduction

Recently there has been an enormous interest in the linguistic literature in so-called secondary predicates.[2] These can be defined as phrases which are predicated of a constituent which stands in a thematic relation to the main verb of the sentence in which the secondary predicate occurs, typically a direct object. The main clause predication is referred to as the primary predication. The stock example of a sentence involving a secondary predicate is (1):

(1) Jim ate the meat raw.

The Adjective Phrase *raw* is a secondary predicate which is predicated of the NP *the meat* which stands in a direct object relation to the verb *eat*. A defining characteristic, then, of secondary predicates is that they take as their subject expression a constituent which is an argument of the verb in the primary predication. Another characteristic is that there is a copular, or 'intensive' (*be*), relationship between the subject expression and the secondary predicate. The aim of this chapter is to examine some of the general properties of constructions involving secondary predicates. The relevance of secondary predicates to the study of the verb is that they are often closely related to verbs, and have been analysed by some linguists as verbal complements.

2 Secondary predicate or not?

The characterisation of secondary predicates I gave earlier makes the issue as to which phrases to admit to the class of secondary predicates a controversial one. The example in (1) is clear-cut: every linguist would agree that the NP *the meat* is an argument of the verb *eat* and therefore a possible subject expression for the predicate *raw*. But what of sentence (2)?

(2) She makes me happy.

Here it is highly debatable whether or not the postverbal NP has a thematic relation with the verb *make*. Traditionally (2) is analysed as involving a direct object *me* and an *object complement* (or *object attribute*) *happy*. Under this traditional approach *happy* could be regarded as a secondary predicate. The view that *me* in a sentence like (2) is an argument of *make* is also found in theoretically oriented work. Williams (1980) has argued for a conceptually similar analysis in his Predication Theory framework. For Williams (2) is an example of *thematically governed predication*, i.e. a relationship in which a phrase is predicated of the theme of a verb. He would analyse (2) as in (3):

(3) She makes me_i $happy_i$

The coindexing here does not indicate coreferentiality, as it usually does, but the fact that *me* and *happy* are in a relation of predication with each other; that is, *me* is the subject of *happy*. Other linguists have taken *me happy* to express a proposition, an analysis which is reflected in taking this string of words to be a clause, more specifically, a Small Clause (SC). (2) is then analysed as in (4):

(4) She makes [$_{SC}$ me happy]

See Aarts (1992) for discussion. It should be noted that Williams' theory is not the only theory of predication and that his analysis of (2) is not followed by all predication theorists. Thus, for example, for Rothstein (1983) the sentence in (2) does not involve a secondary predicate but a Small Clause. In what follows I will be concerned only with structures like that in (1) where the postverbal NP is uncontroversially an argument of the main verb.

3 Four types of secondary predicate

Secondary predicates can be of four types along two dimensions: *resultative* or *depictive* (Halliday 1967) and *subject-related* or *object-related*.

Resultative predicates express a result. This is what we have in a sentence like (5):

(5) They elected her senior treasurer.

Here, as a result of the election process, the person referred to as *her* has become senior treasurer.

An example of a depictive predicate has already been given in (1): the Adjective Phrase *raw* describes the state the meat was in when it was eaten. We can paraphrase this sentence as *I ate the meat while it was raw*. From this we see that the secondary predicate has a temporal adverbial function in the structure of the sentence. Notice that sentences containing a depictive secondary predicate in the form of an Adjective Phrase are near paraphrases of sentences with an attributive phrase inside the postverbal NP, as can be seen in (6) and (7):

(6) Bill drank the coffee cold.
(7) Bill drank the cold coffee.

These are close, but not identical, in meaning: (6) means 'He drank the coffee while it was cold', as we have seen, whereas (7) means 'He drank the coffee which was cold.' Sentences containing resultative secondary predicates do not show alternations of the kind in (6) and (7), as (8) and (9) show:

(8) He rubbed the plate dry.
(9) *He rubbed the dry plate. (* as a paraphrase of (8))

Let us now turn to the two other types of predicate. Subject-related predicates are predicated of the main clause subject. An example is given in (10):

(10) Jim left his house angry.

Here *angry* is predicated of *Jim*; that is, Jim was angry when he left the house. *Angry* cannot be predicated of *his house* as houses are not entities capable of showing emotions, except perhaps in fairy tales.

Object-related predicates have already been instantiated in sentence (1), repeated here for convenience:

(1) Jim ate the meat raw.

In this sentence the property of being raw is predicated of the direct object of the matrix clause.

It is important to point out that I am using the terms subject-related and object-related secondary predicate as terms of convenience. I will for now remain neutral with regard to the question whether or not sentences (1), (5) and (10) contain Small Clauses as in (11–13) such that what we are here calling a secondary predicate is predicated of an implicit PRO subject expression which is coindexed with an element in the main clause, although in fact I do support such an analysis.

(11) Jim ate the $meat_i$ [$_{SC}$ PRO_i raw].
(12) They elected me_i [$_{SC}$ PRO_i senior treasurer].
(13) The $Prime\text{-}Minister_i$ left the house [$_{SC}$ PRO_i angry].

It is possible to set up a grid with the subject and object-related secondary predicates along the horizontal axis, and the depictive and resultative predicates along the vertical axis, as under (14). The example sentences already discussed have been entered:

(14) Secondary predicates

	Subject-related	Object-related
Resultative	*	(5)
Depictive	(10)	(1)

The restriction indicated by the asterisk will be discussed in sections 4 and 5.

Apart from resultative and depictive we should perhaps allow other semantic types of secondary predicates to be part of the system. Halliday (1967) mentions what he calls *conditional attributes* and gives the sentence in (15) as an example

(15) I can carry it empty.

Apart from a depictive reading: 'I can carry it while it is empty', this sentence could be argued to have a conditional interpretation as well: 'I can carry it (only) if it is empty.' (16) can likewise either have the reading 'He drinks his Coca Cola when it is cold' or 'He drinks his Coca Cola (only) if it is cold.' In each case the conditional readings have special intonational patterns.

(16) He drinks his Coca Cola cold.

Conditionals seem to be possible in situations where the main predication has modal meaning as in the example with *carry* in (15), and also in example (17) with the modal verb *will* in the main clause:

(17) I will look at your essay typed.

(17) has the readings 'I will look at your essay when it is typed' or 'only if it is typed.' A conditional reading also seems possible in cases where a general habit is involved as in the *Coca Cola* example in (16) and as in (18):

(18) I eat kiwis ripe.

(18) has the readings 'I eat kiwis when they are ripe' or 'only if they are ripe'. Conditionals seem to be ruled out if a particular situation is being referred to. Thus the sentence in (19)

(19) The next time I will drink my tea cold.

cannot have a conditional reading 'The next time I will drink my tea (only) if it is cold.'

Despite the fact that conditional overtones of meaning are clearly present in some instances, it is not clear whether we should recognise three distinct semantic categories resultative, depictive and conditional. Halliday himself expresses some doubt over this. Certainly the difference between the conditional and non-conditional readings for sentences like *He likes his drink cold* is very subtle. In what follows I will continue to work with the resultative and depictive categories only, treating conditionals as a subtype of depictives. This position can be justified by observing that temporal clauses introduced by the conjunctions *when* or *while* (which are used to paraphrase sentences containing depictive secondary predicates) can carry an element of conditional meaning, as in (20):

(20) I will resign when I feel like it.
'I will resign if/at a time I feel like it'

The conditional conjunction *if*, however, cannot carry temporal meaning. Thus depictive secondary predicates always have an adjunct interpretation and encode *time when*, and may furthermore convey conditional meaning. Resultatives encode only resultative meaning.

Before discussing the various types of secondary predicate shown in the grid in (14) in more detail, I will first turn to the question of their possible syntactic realisations.

4 The categorial status of secondary predicates and their subject expressions

Secondary predicates of either the object-related or subject-related types can be NPs, APs or PPs, though not all of these can express both resultative and depictive meaning. VPs are excluded as secondary predicates. In (21)–(28) I give examples of subject-related and object-related secondary predicates, realised by the various different phrase types. I will be discussing some of the restrictions on the occurrence of secondary predicates which are indicated by the asterisks.

Subject-related Secondary Predicates

(21) *Noun Phrase Secondary Predicate*
a. resultative *
b. depictive Professor Jones retired *a happy man.*

(22) *Adjective Phrase Secondary Predicate*
a. resultative *
b. depictive Jim faxed his newspaper a story *delighted/ill.*

(23) *Prepositional Phrase Secondary Predicate*
a. resultative *
b. depictive Jim left the hospital *on cloud nine.*

(24) *Verb Phrase Secondary Predicate*
a. resultative *
b. depictive *

Object-related Secondary Predicate

(25) *Noun Phrase Secondary Predicate*

a. resultative They appointed her *managing director.*
b. depictive I met her *the same age I met you.*[3]

(26) *Adjective Phrase Secondary Predicate*

a. resultative We sprayed our hair *pink/ *coloured.*
b. depictive He drinks his tea *cold/flavoured.*

(27) *Prepositional Phrase Secondary Predicate*

a. resultative She pushed him *out of the house.*
b. depictive We found him *in tears.*

(28) *Verb Phrase Secondary Predicate*

a. resultative *
b. depictive *

Subject-related secondary predicates may be predicated of the subjects of predicates involving either intransitive verbs (as in (21b)), ditransitive verbs ((22b)) or simple transitive verbs ((23b)), but object-related secondary predicates can obviously only occur if the main predication involves a transitive verb. The subject expression of secondary predicates is always an NP.

There are cases where a secondary predicate can be related to either the subject of the sentence in which it occurs or to its direct object, or even to both, as in the following attested example:

(29) For much of the story we could be anywhere: in the sphere where writers meet their readers naked, and draw them into the free world of their imagination. (*The Independent*, 24 April 1993)

This sentence can be interpreted in such a way that either the writers or the readers are naked, or both.

The restrictions on secondary predicates are the following: firstly, resultative secondary predicates cannot be related to non-derived subjects, i.e. subjects which are subjects both at a deep level of representation and at a surface level of representation (cf. (21a)–(24a)). This restriction will be discussed further in the next section.

Secondly, it has been claimed by linguists (Green 1972: 89; Goldberg 1991: 87; Carrier and Randall 1992: 184) that it is not possible to have deverbal APs as object-related resultative secondary predicates (cf. (26a)). However, there is evidence that the observed restriction on object-related resultative deverbal APs is perhaps too strong because it is possible to say *He pulled the door shut* and *I have to produce the essay typed.* The first of these sentences clearly involves a resultative deverbal AP, and the second[4] arguably does too. Deverbal APs are fine as subject-related or object-related depictives (cf. (22b) and (26b)).

Thirdly, object-related NP depictive secondary predicates of the kind we have in (25b) are severely restricted in occurrence. We get close to an object-related depictive Noun Phrase with something like (30):

(30) *I described Jim a painter.
(* under the reading 'I described Jim while he was a painter')

This sentence is only possible with an intonational break between *Jim* and *a painter* which would, however, turn the second NP into an appositive. (30) is uninterpretable without a break. It cannot mean 'I described Jim, while he was a painter', analogous to *I ate the meat raw* with the meaning 'I ate the meat while it was raw.' There is a construction that gets close to (30), namely (31):

(31) I described Jim as a painter.

This sentence is problematic for theories of Predication which would presumably take *as* to be a preposition and *as a painter* to be a PP. There are, however, indications that *as* is not a preposition; witness the fact that this element can also be followed by an Adjective Phrase, as in *I described Jim as foolish.* For Small Clause proponents *as a painter* is a Small Clause with a PRO subject, as in (32):

(32) I described Jim_i $[_{SC}$ PRO_i as a painter]

For discussion, see Aarts (1992). However we analyse (31), it is not entirely clear whether the string *(PRO) as a painter* expresses depictive meaning. It has the feel of an adjunct of manner to it in that it expresses 'how' we described Jim. At the same time, however, it is also complement-like because *describe* selects *as*. If we allow only depictives and resultatives to be secondary predicates, as is common in the linguistic literature, then sentences like (31) do not involve secondary predication despite the copular relationship between *Jim* and *a painter*. An object control structure, as in (32), would seem more appropriate. That is, the verb *describe* subcategorises for an NP and a Small Clause.

Returning now to (21)–(28), notice that subject-related and object-related secondary predicates in the form of a VP also do not occur. The reason why secondary predicates cannot be VPs is twofold. The first reason is that although the VP-secondary predicate and its subject expression would form a traditional subject-predicate relationship, these two phrases would not be in a copular relationship. Recall that the existence of a copular relationship between two constituents A and B is a precondition for it to be possible for B to have the status of secondary predicate. The second reason why VPs cannot be secondary predicates is a theory-internal one. As we will see later, secondary predicates, both resultative and depictive, are positioned inside VP. Now, if we allowed secondary predicates in the form of VPs, the structure of their containing VP would be as in (33):

(33)

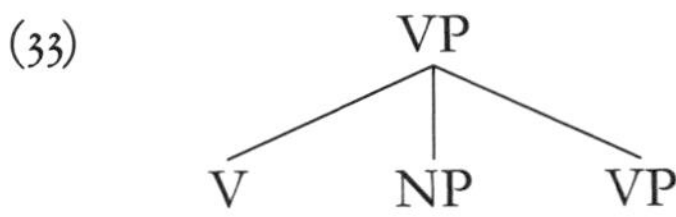

In (33) we have a bare VP inside VP acting as a secondary predicate taking the direct object NP as its subject expression. However, there are strong reasons for disallowing bare VPs, at least in the Government-Binding theory framework (see e.g. Koster and May 1982). The closest we get to something like (33) is a sentence like (34):

(34) Pete forced Lee to leave.

In standard Government-Binding theory the VP of the matrix clause in (33) is analysed as in (35):

(35)

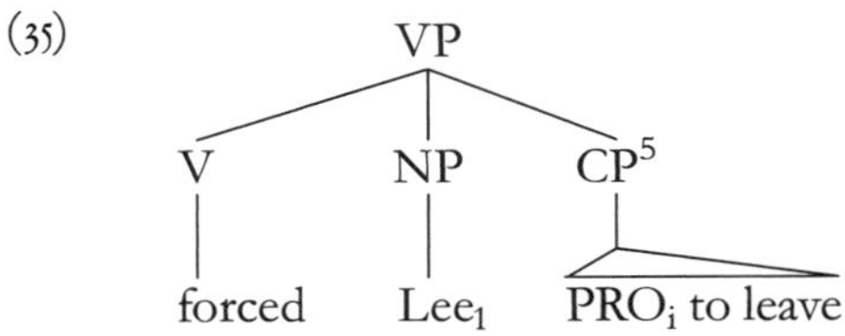

This is an object control structure in which the CP is analysed as a complement of the verb. Although the leaving is predicated of Lee through the mediation of PRO here, we would not want to regard the CP as a secondary predicate in this sentence because there is no copular relationship between the NP and the CP. Notice, though, that the CP does express a result: the result of Pete's forcing Lee was the fact that Lee left. In the same way a CP could express depictive meaning specifically in sentences involving perception verbs, such as (36a), which would be analysed as in (36b):

(36) a. Pete saw Lee leave.
b.

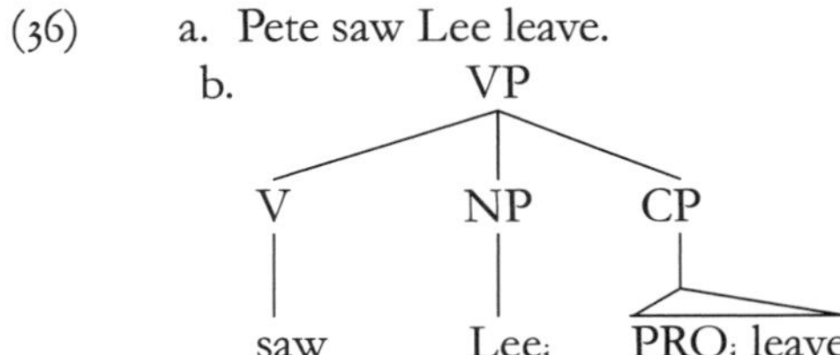

This sentence would then receive the normal paraphrase for depictives: 'Pete saw Lee while Lee was leaving'. Subject-related resultatives are never possible, as we will see, but a possible candidate for a sentence containing a subject-related depictive CP is (37):

(37) I saw Rome sitting on a plane.

where *sitting on a plane* is a CP with a PRO subject that could be regarded as depicting the subject, i.e. 'I saw Rome while I was sitting on a plane.' We would analyse (37) as in (38):

(38) I_i saw Rome [$_{CP}$ PRO_i sitting on a plane]

However, because of the lack of a copular relationship we would not want to say that the CP is a subject-related secondary predicate in (38).

5 Subject-related resultative secondary predicates

Let us now turn to the restriction that I have already mentioned, namely that subject-related resultative secondary predicates are not possible in English. This is demonstrated by sentences (39) and (40), which contain a transitive and an intransitive verb, respectively:

(39) *Jim travelled the world confident.
(40) *Jim was day-dreaming happy.

These are unacceptable with the meanings 'Jim travelled the world resulting in his becoming confident' and 'Jim was day-dreaming and became happy as a result.'

The generalisation regarding the occurrence restrictions of resultative secondary predicates thus seems to be the one in (41) (cf. Simpson 1983: 144–145):

(41) Resultative predicates can only be predicated of direct objects.

This restriction has been called *the direct object restriction* in Levin and Rappaport (1989: 9) and Rothstein (1992: 126). The set of sentences in (42)–(49) further illustrates it:

(42) The committee appointed her senior lecturer.
(43) We named her Catherine.
(44) They baptised him Jim.
(45) The people crowned him King.
(46) *Jim cooks his meals happy.
'Jim cooks his meals and he became happy as a result'
(47) *Phil sold his car rich.
'Phil sold his car and became rich as a result'
(48) *Tom ate too many sausages fat.
'Tom ate too many sausages and became fat as a result'
(49) *Janet missed her train unhappy.
'Janet missed her train and became unhappy as a result'

In (42)–(45) the resultative secondary predicates are predicated of a direct object in each case, whereas in (46)–(49) they are predicated of a subject, leading to ungrammaticality.

I should emphasise here that (46)–(49) are unacceptable only as subject-related *resultatives*. I will discuss the question whether these sentences are acceptable as subject-related *depictive* secondary predicates later.

It appears that (41) may be too strong a claim as it is possible to find examples of sentences which seem to falsify the observation that resultative secondary predicates can only be predicated of objects. Consider (50)–(55):

(50) The door slammed shut.
(51) The river froze solid. (Levin and Rappaport 1989: 9)
(52) She was appointed senior lecturer (by the committee).
(53) She was named Catherine (by us).
(54) He was baptised Jim (by them).
(55) He was crowned King (by the people).

In (50) the door is shut as a result of someone slamming it, and in (51) cold weather has resulted in the river freezing up solid. The resultative predicates *shut* and *solid* seem to be predicated of subjects. However, on closer examination (50) and (51) are not counterexamples to the claim that resultative secondary predicates can only be predicated of objects because they instantiate ergative constructions. This means that *the door* in (50) and *the river* in (51) are deep-structure direct objects.

Consider also (52)–(55): these are also not counterexamples to the generalisation that resultative secondary predicates can only be predicated of objects. In these cases we will also say that the secondary predicates are predicated of phrases that are underlyingly direct objects.

A further possible counterexample to (41) is given in (56):

(56) They became angry.

Here the resultative AP *angry* is predicated of the subject *they*. However, on closer inspection (56) does not constitute a violation of (41) if we regard *angry* not as a secondary, but as a primary predicate. (56) is then derived from (57):

(57) [e] became [$_{SC}$ they angry]

In view of (50)–(55) we ought to perhaps rephrase (41) as in (41'), a descriptively more adequate generalisation:

(41') Resultative predicates can only be predicated of direct objects and derived subjects.

Consider now (58):

(58) a. *He talked hoarse.
b. He talked himself hoarse. (Levin and Rappaport's (12))

For Levin and Rappaport (58b) involves a direct object, namely *himself*, which must be present for the resultative AP *hoarse* to be predicated of it. (58a) is ungrammatical because there is no direct object present. This explanation for the obligatory presence of *himself* is available only for frameworks in which the reflexive NP is analysed as an argument of *talk*. It seems, however, to be much more plausible to assign the structure in (59) to (58b):

(59) He talked [$_{SC}$ himself hoarse]

Under this view the Small Clause, not just the Adjective Phrase, expresses a result. After all, the result of the talking is not just hoarseness, but the fact that *he is hoarse* (see also Hoekstra's 1988 and 1992 papers). In the Small Clause framework the AP *hoarse* is predicated of the subject expression *himself*. It is a primary predicate so that (41) is not violated.

It is interesting that resultative secondary predicates may be predicated of a syntactically non-overt direct object, as in the sentences in (60) (which are sometimes said to involve a so-called *absolute comparative*):

(60) a. Concentrated washing powders wash whiter.
b. These revolutionary new brooms sweep cleaner than ever.

What we have here is implicit direct objects. The resultative secondary predicate *whiter* is predicated in (60a) of whatever it is that is being washed, i.e. the unexpressed direct object of *wash*, i.e. *clothes*, *shirts*, *sheets* or whatever. In (60b) the implicit object is a surface that can be swept. The constructions in (60) are theoretically of interest because null objects of the type found in Romance languages such as Portuguese and Italian have been argued not to be possible in English, for example in Brody and Manzini (1988). Notice that in (60) the subject NPs cannot be regarded as underlying direct objects, because they have an instrumental, rather than a patient/theme, thematic role. The existence of sentences like those in (60) may also throw some light on the controversial question whether verbs like *read* in sentences like *Amy was reading* involve an intransitive lexeme *read* or an implicit direct object. The fact that in (60a) and (60b) the resultatives *must* be predicated of implicit direct objects, and that hence implicit direct objects exist in English, might be taken to be indirect evidence for denying the existence of two lexemes *read*.

Incidentally, *wash* is an interesting verb, because it can also be used ergatively. I came across the following short news item in a local newspaper:

(61) Black wash
Clothes were washing blacker at the Winchester Road, Swiss Cottage launderette on Thursday night after vandals poured black paint into

washing machines and tumble dryers, causing £5,000 worth of damage. (*Camden New Journal*)

Here, clearly, the subject *clothes* is an underlying object and the resultative predicate AP *blacker* is predicated of it.[6]

Returning now to (60), on the basis of these sentences we might be led to surmise that an object can remain implicit in English expressions involving resultative secondary predicates if the context or knowledge of the world make it clear what entity these secondary predicates are predicated of. This hypothesis is confirmed by the example we have in (62) below (from a sun-cream information leaflet) where the direct object is omitted in the italicised reduced adverbial clause:

(62) Sun E45 is long-lasting and water-resistant, so it does not require frequent re-application. Every three hours is usually sufficient, unless rubbed off *while towelling dry*.

Here the most likely implied direct object is the reflexive pronoun *yourself*. The full version of the adverbial clause in (62) would then be *while you are/were towelling yourself dry*. However, the hypothesis is falsified by (63) and (64):

(63) He warmed the milk in a pan. *Then he whipped frothy.
(64) He only dusts the tables most days. *But on Wednesdays he really wipes clean.

Even though it is clear from the context that it is the milk that is being whipped in (63) and the tables that are being wiped in (64), we cannot leave out the direct object in the sentences with the resultative predicates. We might ask, then, why it is possible to leave the object implicit in (60) and (62), but not in (63) and (64)? Flor Aarts (p.c.) suggests the possibility that the object may be suppressed in constructions like (60) if their subject expressions have an instrumental thematic role (cf. also *This brush paints darker*). Another relevant factor may be that we can only leave out direct object NPs which are indefinite non-referring expressions. Thus, someone who utters sentences like (60a/b) can omit the objects because s/he does not have particular washable items or sweepable surfaces in mind. By contrast, in (63) and (64) the elipted objects are definite referring NPs. Omitting them leads to ungrammaticality. The above conjecture could also be said to hold for (62): although the elipted object is definite and grammatically 'referential' (bound) in that it is an anaphor that derives its content from another expression in the sentence, namely the subject, it cannot be said to refer to an entity in the world of discourse directly. A further possible answer to the puzzle posed by (60) and (62)–(64) is suggested in the work of Dixon (1991: 288) who submits that what he calls *AFFECT verbs* (i.e. typically transitive verbs) may omit their direct objects in case the activity denoted by the verb continues over an extended period of time and/or can be construed with a range of objects. In (60) and (62) the verbs can indeed be construed with a variety of objects, and the verbal action continues in time to the extent that we are dealing, at least in (60), with generic statements that hold true over a period of time that stretches into the past and into the future.[7]

6 Subject-related depictive secondary predicates (21b–24b)

Subject-related depictive secondary predicates, like subject-related resultative secondary predicates, are restricted in occurrence. Demonte (1987: 6), writing on Spanish, proposes that secondary predicates can only be predicated of subject expressions that have the thematic role of theme or agent, but not if they have an experiencer role. This would explain the contrasts in (65)–(68):

(65) Las aguas bajan turbias.
'The waters run down muddy(ly)'

(66) El músico nos aburre tan tranquilo.
'The musician bores us so happy(ly)'

(67) *La tormenta hizo estragos ruidosa.
'The storm caused the destruction noisy'

(68) ??Juan oía los ruidos preocupado.
'Juan heard the noises worried'

In (65) and (66) we have subjects with the thematic role of theme and agent respectively, which is permitted, whereas in (67) and (68) the subjects have the role of non-volitional causer and experiencer respectively and this explains their unacceptability.

Demonte's account works for Spanish, but clearly not for English, as the glosses show: with the exception perhaps of the gloss of sentence (65) all the English equivalents of the Spanish sentences are unacceptable (if we disregard the adverb paraphrases for the moment). There is a further problem and that is that whereas some sentences containing an experiencer subject and a depictive predicate at the end of the sentence are indeed ruled out, as in (69), it seems that a secondary predicate predicated of an experiencer subject is not in principle disallowed in English, as (70) shows:

(69) ?*Jim saw the film happy.

(70) Jim saw the film naked.

English clearly requires an alternative account to explain the facts.

Consider also the contrast between (71) and (72):

(71) ?*The waiter smiled naked.
(72) The waiter danced naked.

Before attempting an explanation of these facts a few observations are in order about the syntactic position of subject-related depictive secondary predicates. At a superficial level one might observe that they are positioned either sentence-initially, as in (73), or sentence-finally, as in (74):

(73) Angry, Jim left his house.
(74) Jim left his house angry.

However, we need to be more precise than that. It has been argued by various linguists that subject-related depictive secondary predicates are positioned inside VP (see, for example, Andrews 1982, Roberts 1988, Napoli 1989, Mallén 1991, Aarts 1992). This can easily be demonstrated by using standard tests of constituency. Consider the sentences in (75)–(77):

(75) *VP-Preposing*
a. Jim said he left his house angry and leave his house angry he did.
b. *Jim said he left his house angry and leave his house he did angry.

(76) *Though-Movement*
a. Leave his house angry though Jim did, he was much calmer at lunch-time.
b. *Leave his house though Jim did angry, he was much calmer at lunch-time.

(77) *Pseudoclefting*
What Jim did was leave his house angry.

In (75) VP-Preposing has applied and the result of this process is ungrammatical if the secondary predicate is left stranded. The sentences in (76), in which *Though*-Movement has operated, lead to the same conclusion: the secondary predicate must be pied-piped along with the matrix verb and its direct object. Finally, (77) shows that under Pseudoclefting the main verb, direct object and secondary predicate taken together form a constituent. These three tests therefore show that subject-related depictive secondary predicates are part of the matrix clause VP.

Roberts (1988) offers further evidence based on scope of negation data in English for the claim that subject-related depictive secondary predicates are in VP. Consider the sentences in (78)–(81):

(78) John didn't kiss his wife deliberately.
(79) John deliberately didn't kiss his wife.
(80) John didn't kiss his wife, deliberately.
(81) Deliberately, John didn't kiss his wife.

In (78) (to be read without comma intonation) the adjunct modifies the VP, that is, it is VP-internal, whereas in (79)–(81) it does not; it modifies the proposition as a whole. Now, notice that (78) cannot have a reading in which *deliberately* is outside the scope of negation. That is, (78) cannot mean 'John deliberately did not kiss his wife.' The significance of this is the generalisation that VP-adjuncts are always inside the scope of negation. Consider next (82):

(82) Bill didn't leave [angry at John].

Roberts claims that (82) has two readings only, namely one where the scope of negation extends over the proposition as a whole, as in (83a), or over only the AP, as in (83b), but that it cannot have the reading in (83c), where the AP is outside the scope of negation.

(83) a. not [Bill left angry at John] (. . . he left pleased with John)
b. Bill left [not [angry at John] (. . . he left angry at Pete)
c. [not [Bill left]] angry at John

In view of the scope facts pertaining to sentences (78)–(81), namely that VP-adjuncts cannot be outside the scope of negation, and in view of the fact that the AP *angry at John* cannot be outside the scope of negation in (82), we must conclude that this AP is inside the VP in this sentence.

Now, how can the fact that subject-related depictive secondary predicates are positioned inside VP help us to explain the contrast between sentences like (69) and (70) and (71) and (72)? I would like to claim that by virtue of the fact that sentence-final subject-related secondary predicates occupy a VP-internal position they tell us something about the subject but *at the same time* they also modify the verbal action. The generalisation that we can make seems to be the one in (84):

(84) A subject-related depictive secondary predicate can occur sentence-finally if a semantic/pragmatic relationship can be established between it and the predication expressed by its containing VP.

The connexion would have to be a semantic or pragmatic one as most linguists will agree that depictive secondary predicates have an adjunct reading and the restrictions cannot therefore be explained by positing a lexical relationship between the head of the VP and the secondary predicate, as has been proposed for resultative predicates, which will be discussed later.

The connexion between the Verb Phrase predication and the secondary predicate referred to in (84) can often be made explicit by using a manner adverbial instead of a secondary predicate. If we compare (85)–(87) to (88)–(90) we find that there is very little difference between them.

(85) Tom read his paper absent-minded.
(86) Antoinet sang on public transport unconcerned.
(87) Jerry wrote his essay complacent.
(88) Tom read his paper absent-mindedly.
(89) Antoinet sang on public transport unconcernedly.
(90) Jerry wrote his essay complacently.

In (85)–(87) the secondary predicate performs a dual function: it tells us something about the subject and *at the same time* it modifies the verbal action. Although (85)–(87) are semantically similar to (88)–(90) it is not the case that there are no differences between these two sets of sentences. In this connexion consider the pairs of sentences in (91)/(92) and (93)/(94):

(91) Jim left his house angry.
(92) Jim left his house angrily.
(93) Angry, Jim left his house.
(94) Jim left his house, angry.

(91) and (92) are a minimal pair. They are alike in that both entail that Jim was angry. They differ in that (92) also entails that he left his house in an angry fashion. This can be demonstrated by the sentence in (95):

(95) Jim left his house angrily, but nevertheless showed no outward emotion.

This is a contradiction. In (91) the proposition that he left the house in an angry fashion is only an implicature, witness (96):

(96) Jim left his house angry, but nevertheless showed no outward emotion.

Here the implication that he also left in an angry fashion has been cancelled. In (93) and (94) nothing is said about *how* Jim left the house. These sentences tell us only that he happened to be in a state of anger when he did. (93) and (94) are truth-conditionally equivalent, differing only with regard to where the secondary predicate is positioned in the associated phrase markers. In Aarts (1992) I have argued that subject-related depictive secondary predicates that occur sentence-initially or sentence-finally with comma intonation are adjoined to the maximal sentential projection (CP in the Government-Binding framework) where they have wide scope.

Let us now see how (84) can explain the contrast we have between (71) and (72), repeated here:

(71) ?*The waiter smiled naked.
(72) The waiter danced naked.

(71) is odd because it is hard to envisage, without specifying a context of utterance, how we can link the waiter's nudity to the fact that he was smiling. (72) is fine because it is easier to see how the waiter's being nude can be relevant to the way he was dancing. The contrast between (71) and (72) is also brought out by paraphrasing (71) as (71'), which is odd, and (72) as (72'), which is fine:

(71') ??The waiter smiled while he was naked.
(72') The waiter danced while he was naked.

I should stress the fact that (71) and (72) are isolated sentences and that if we put them in context the results are far better. In (97) I have created a context for (71):

(97) They played a really rather silly game: if you got an answer wrong you had to take off a piece of clothing. The waiter was the first person to be completely undressed, but he wasn't unhappy about it: he stood up unperturbed, he smiled naked and then he proceeded to stand on his head.

(71) is therefore only pragmatically odd.

Napoli in discussing (98) seems to be hinting at something along the lines of (84) when she says that '[nudeness] characterises the arrival' (1989: 154).

(98) The ambassador arrived nude. (ibid. and 1992: 54)

However, her example is somewhat infelicitous as it involves a verb which might be said to be unaccusative (as has been argued in Levin and Rappaport 1989 and 1992), so that really the AP *nude* is predicated of a deep-structure direct object.

Let us now turn to (69) and (70), repeated for convenience:

(69) ?*Jim saw the film happy.
(70) Jim saw the film naked.

This contrast is less obviously explained by (84), but again it seems that in (69), as it stands, happiness does not characterise the seeing of the film. However, as with (71), (69) could be made to be acceptable if we constructed a particular context for it. Such a context is less easy to envisage for (69) than for (70) and this fact accounts for the contrast between these sentences.

7 Object-related resultative and depictive secondary predicates

Object-related resultative secondary predicates and object-related depictive secondary predicates have perhaps been discussed most in the recent theoretical literature. Here are two examples:

(99) Jim rinsed the cups clean. (object-related resultative)
(100) Jim usually drinks his whisky neat. (object-related depictive)

It is uncontroversial to claim that both object-related resultative secondary predicates and object-related depictive secondary predicates are positioned inside VP. The tests in (101)–(103) make this clear:

(101) *VP-Preposing*

a. Jim said he would rinse the cups clean, . . . resultative
. . . and rinse the cups clean he did.
b. Jim said he would rinse the cups clean, . . .
. . . *and rinse the cups he did clean.
c. Jim said he usually drinks his whisky neat, . . . depictive
. . . and drink his whisky neat he usually does.
d. Jim said he usually drinks his whisky neat, . . .
. . . *and drink his whisky he usually does neat.

(102) *Though-Movement*

a. Rinse the cups clean though Jim did, . . . resultative
. . . he didn't bother about washing the plates.
b. *Rinse the cups though Jim did clean, . . .
. . . he didn't bother about washing the plates.
c. Drink his whisky neat though Jim usually does,. . . depictive
. . . he nevertheless sometimes adds a little ice.
d. *Drink his whisky though Jim usually does neat, . . .
. . . he nevertheless sometimes adds a little ice.

(103) *Pseudoclefting*

a. What Jim did was rinse the cups clean. resultative
b. *What Jim did clean was rinse the cups.
c. What Jim usually does is drink his whisky neat. depictive
d. *What Jim usually does neat is drink his whisky.

Three standard constituency tests, VP-Preposing in (101), *Though*-Movement in (102) and Pseudoclefting in (103), clearly show that the secondary predicates are inside VP in these sentences. What is less uncontroversial is the issue of what is the exact syntactic position inside VP of object-related secondary predicates. Researchers working in Predication Theory frameworks have made a number of different proposals: for some of them all object-related secondary predicates are lexically selected, as in the work of for example Roberts (1988) and Mallén (1991, 1992). What this means is that they would adopt a structure like that in (104) for sentences like (99) and (100):

(104) Roberts (1988), Mallén (1991, 1992)

The object-related secondary predicate is taken to be a sister of the main verb in (104), a position normally reserved for complements.

For other researchers only object-related *resultative* secondary predicates are lexically selected, as in Rothstein (1983) and Carrier and Randall (1992). For them (99) and (100) are analysed as in (105a) and (105b) respectively:

(105) Rothstein (1983), Carrier and Randall (1992)

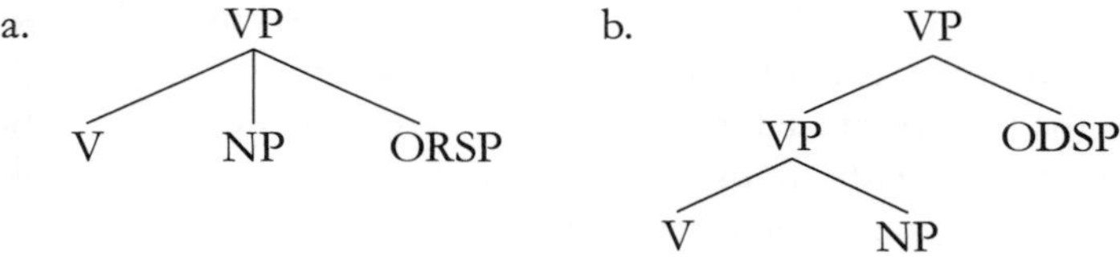

ORSP = object-related resultative secondary predicate
ODSP = object-related depictive secondary predicate

Carrier and Randall also adopt the structure in (105a) for sentences like those in (106), which they refer to as *intransitive resultatives*:

(106) a. He drank his friends under the table.
b. My son always runs his trainers threadbare.
c. We laughed ourselves silly.

Despite the fact that the postverbal NPs in (106) are not analysed as arguments of the matrix verb, they are taken to be sisters of those verbs. The resultative XPs *are* regarded as arguments of the matrix verb. Carrier and Randall do not discuss depictives. Their analysis, and especially the terminology used, are rather unsatisfactory. *Intransitive* in the term *intransitive resultative* suggests that the main verb takes no internal arguments, but in order to have a resultative expression we need a direct object, i.e. an argument. So the term suggests both that the main verb does not take any arguments and at the same time that it does. Another way to put this is to say that these so-called intransitive resultatives violate the direct object restriction.

For Demonte (1987), secondary predicates are reanalysed together with the main verb of the sentences in which they occur as complex verbs, as in (107):

(107) I drink-cold$_i$ my whisky t$_i$

She proposes the structure in (108) for (107) (only the relevant VP is shown):

(108) Demonte (1987)

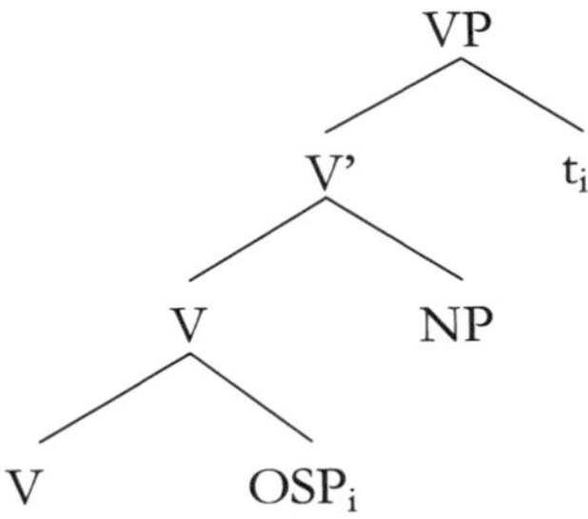

The secondary predicate is a sister of V' in the Deep Structure, but is then reanalysed with the verb forming the complex verb *drink-cold.*

Proponents of Small Clause Theory have made two kinds of proposals. The first, found in the work of Jespersen, and, more recently, Hoekstra, is shown in (110), the tree structure for (109). In (109) Hoekstra takes the resultative predicate to be the predicate of a Small Clause whose subject expression is the postverbal NP. There is no direct object argument for the verb *boil.*

(109) We boiled the rice dry.

(110) Hoekstra (1988, 1992)

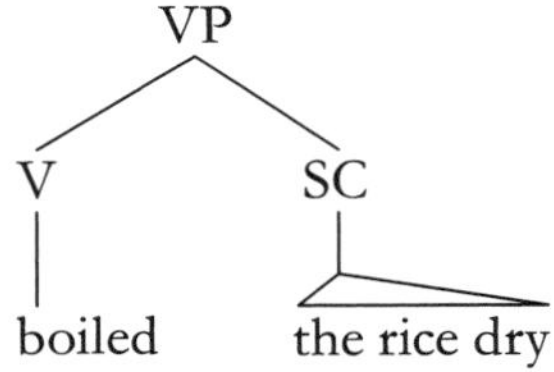

Hoekstra does not discuss depictive secondary predicates.

Other Small Clause proponents have taken object-related secondary predicates (of both the resultative and depictive types) to be adjoined either to V', as in Hornstein and Lightfoot (1987), or to VP, as in Aarts (1992). The structural details of these analyses are shown in (111) and (112):

(111) Hornstein and Lightfoot (1987)

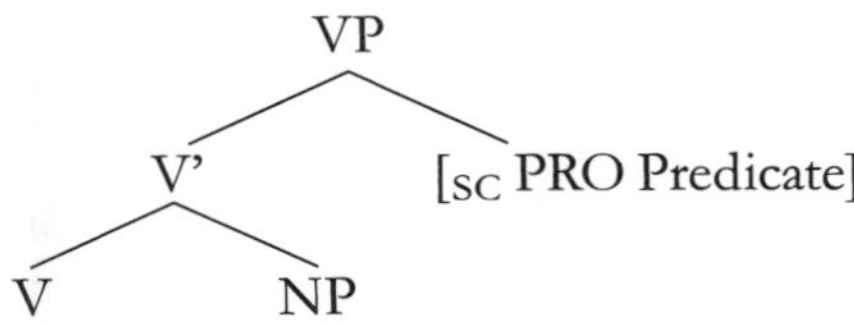

(112) Aarts (1992)

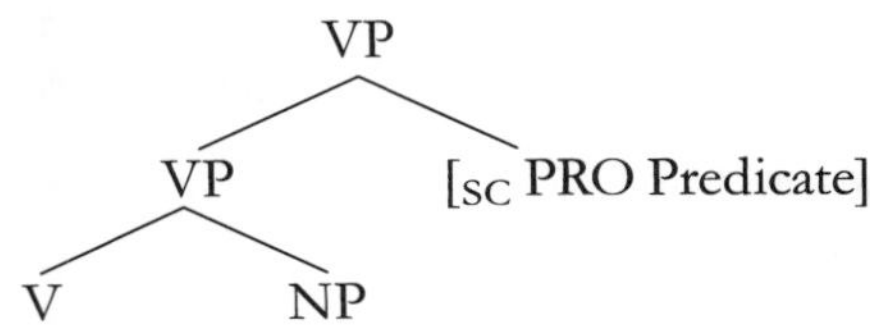

The difference between Hoekstra's analysis, and that of Hornstein and Lightfoot and mine is that for Hoekstra the postverbal NP is not an argument of the main verb, whereas in (111) and (112) the postverbal NP is a direct object, the motivation being that it receives a theta role from the verb (see Carrier and Randall 1992, who discuss this point at great length).

The important point of difference between (104)/(105a)/(108) and (111)/(112) is that in the former proposals it is assumed that there is a lexical relationship of some sort between the head of the main clause VP and the secondary predicate. As Demonte (1987: 27) puts it:

> [Object-related secondary] predicates seem to behave more like elements of the argument structure of the verb than like true adjuncts.

In the proposals in (111) and (112) the secondary predicates are adjuncts.

To support their case proponents of the lexical selection accounts point to certain combinatorial restrictions that have been observed to hold between direct objects and secondary predicates, such as in the so-called *hammer flat*-constructions exemplified in (113):

(113) John hammered the metal flat

*John hammered the metal {beautiful / safe / tubular}

*John wiped the surface {damp / dirty / stained}

*She wrenched the stick {broken / tight}

*She shot him {lame / paranoid / wounded}

(all from Green 1972)

The first sentence of (113) is fine, but the others are not. These data can be taken to demonstrate that the listed verbs lexically select certain predicates, but not others.

Another restriction that has been noted, in Emonds (1976) and Rothstein (1983), among others, is that if a sentence contains both a resultative and a depictive the resultative precedes the depictive, as (114) and (115) show:

(114) I dyed my hair red unwashed.
(115) *I dyed my hair unwashed red.

It is claimed that the resultative is a complement because it must be placed adjacent to the head verb, and that the depictive is an adjunct.

Finally, it has been observed that sentences like (116) are impossible with the AP *worried* construed as a resultative predicate:

(116) *Pete ordered Harry worried to eat his breakfast.

Advocates of a lexical selection account of resultatives would presumably contend that this sentence is ungrammatical because there are too many arguments: the verb *order* subcategorises up to two arguments; here there are three, namely *Harry, worried* and *to eat his breakfast*.

Before discussing these restrictions further let us reflect for a moment on the question of what exactly it means for a secondary predicate to be lexically selected. To my knowledge none of the linguists who have proposed lexical selection for secondary predicates has addressed this question. In grammatical theory there are two related types of lexical selection illustrated by situations in which a head syntactically requires the presence of an argument and this argument has to be of some semantic type or other. These lexical relations are subcategorisation (or c-selection) and selectional restrictions (or s-selection) respectively.[8] Turning now to secondary predicates, first, notice that, at least in GB theory, there would be a problem if we were to allow lexically selected secondary predicates because such predicates would then be *both* arguments *and* predicates. We would then be faced with the anomaly that because they are arguments secondary predicates must get a θ-role from the verb, but because they are predicates they must not. Secondly, it would be hard to envisage exactly what the lexical selection account of secondary predicates would look like. Clearly, the lexical relationship cannot be an instance of either subcategorisation or selectional restriction as these operate on arguments and secondary predicates are *predicates*, not arguments. The drawback of the lexical selection account, then, is that it necessitates an otherwise unmotivated new type of lexical selection, other than subcategorisation or selectional restriction. In view of this, an analysis along the lines of (111) or (112), where the secondary predicate is treated as an adjunct, is to be preferred. These analyses reflect two further related suggestive facts, the first being that the very labels that are used to describe secondary predicates in semantic terms, depictive and resultative, are adverbial notions. Secondly, as we have seen, if we paraphrase sentences containing depictives and resultatives we use adverbial clauses. Thus, a sentence like (1) (*I ate the meat raw*) is paraphrased with a temporal *while*-clause, i.e. 'I ate the meat while it was raw.' And sentences containing resultative predicates can be paraphrased using a *so that*-clause. Thus, *She wiped the blackboard clean* can be paraphrased as 'She wiped the blackboard so that it became clean.'

Let us return now to (113)–(116). With regard to (113) it has been proposed by Dowty, among others, that we can treat the restrictions in terms of pragmatic constraints and that in suitable discourse contexts the sentences in (113) would not be odd. It would take us too far afield to discuss the nature of these restrictions here. I refer those interested in discussions in the literature of the noted restrictions to the work of Green (1970, 1972, 1973), McCawley (1971), Dowty (1976), Rothstein (1983) and Fabb (1984). There is also some discussion in Aarts (1992).

Regarding (114) and (115) two observations can be made. First, it is by no means clear that the requirement that resultative predicates precede depictive predicates is a watertight one. Consider (117) (pointed out to me by Keith Brown):

(117) She pushed him naked out of the house.

Here the resultative predicate *out of the house* is linearly preceded by the depictive predicate *naked*.[9] Secondly, it seems that the ordering restrictions in these sentences need not necessarily be explained by having recourse to selection by the main verb, but can be explained by general semantic constraints. These constraints are difficult to state but it appears that we might regard them as fairly general semantic ordering constraints of the type that we also need for example for modifiers in NP structure. Consider the NPs in (118) and (119):

(118) scarce political know-how
(119) *political scarce know-how

Here the AP *political* must precede the AP *scarce*, but an analysis in which one pre-head constituent is a modifier and another a complement is not possible in (118) as neither of the Adjective Phrases can plausibly be regarded as a complement of the head noun. In other words, neither of the AP modifiers has a privileged syntactic status. (118) and (119) contrast with (120) and (121):

(120) artful sentence analysis
(121) *sentence artful analysis

Here too the order of the two premodifiers cannot be reversed: *artful* must linearly precede *sentence*. In this case, however, the nominal premodifier *sentence* is a complement of the head noun *analysis* (cf. *He artfully analysed the sentence.*). In other words, the NP *sentence* is a sister of the head noun within the NP, and the AP *artful* is a sister of N'. The point I am making with regard to (114)/(115) and (118)/(119) is that if an element appears to be restricted in occurrence to a position closer to the head than some other element, this is necessary, but not sufficient, evidence for taking the first element to be lexically selected.

Finally, with regard to (116), we could also claim that this sentence is bad simply because it is semantically odd to order someone to eat their breakfast with the result that they become worried.

8 Conclusion

To summarise, I have looked at the properties and distribution of both subject-related and object-related depictive and resultative secondary predicates in English, and I have attempted to formulate some of the restrictions that seem to hold in determining the possible structures. I have also discussed the question whether or not object-related resultative predicates should be taken to be lexically selected arguments of main verbs and concluded that the answer should be 'no' and that they are best regarded as adjuncts.

Notes

1. An earlier version of this chapter was presented in the Department of Language and Linguistics at the University of Essex. I would like to thank the audience there (especially Martin Atkinson, Keith Brown, Andrew Radford and Andrew Spencer) for useful comments. Further thanks are due to Flor Aarts, Valerie Adams, Chuck Meyer, and And Rosta.
2. Cf. Simpson (1983), Rothstein (1983, 1990, 1991, 1992), Demonte (1987), Yamada (1987), Sato (1987), Roberts (1988), Napoli (1989, 1992), Levin and Rappaport (1989, 1992), Goldberg (1991), Mallén (1991, 1992), Hasegawa (1991) and Carrier and Randall (1992).

3. This example was pointed out to me by And Rosta. The depictive NP here can also be interpreted as being subject-related.
4. Pointed out to me by Flor Aarts.
5. CP stands for 'Complementiser Phrase', S-bar in previous versions of Chomskian theory. CPs are clausal projections headed by a complementiser 'C'. See also Hudson (this volume).
6. See Rosta (this volume) for discussion of constructions like those in (61).
7. It has been pointed out to me that sentences like (63) and (64) are acceptable if they contain an imperative verb-form:

   (i) Warm the milk in a pan. Then whip frothy.
   (ii) Dust the tables every day. Wipe clean on Wednesdays.

   Imperatives are marked constructions, though, in that in other contexts too they allow direct objects to be left out when this is not normally possible. Contrast (iii) and (iv):

   (iii) He bought a fresh loaf of bread. *He sliced.
   (iv) Buy a fresh loaf of bread. Slice.

8. Selectional restrictions and s-selection are not strictly speaking the same thing. See Aarts and Meyer (this volume).
9. The observation that the AP *naked* can also be a subject-related predicate does not invalidate the point, which is to demonstrate that resultative predicates can follow depictives.

   It might be argued that the resultative predicate has been extraposed in (117), but there would appear to be no grammatical or stylistic motivation for this.

References

Aarts, B. (1992) *Small clauses in English: the nonverbal types*. Topics in English Linguistics **8**. Berlin and New York: Mouton de Gruyter.

Andrews, A. (1982) A note on the constituent structure of adverbials and auxiliaries. *Linguistic Inquiry* **13**. 313–317.

Brody, M. and Manzini, M. R. (1988) On implicit arguments. In Kempson, R. M. (ed.), *Mental representations: the interface between language and reality*. Cambridge University Press. 105–130.

Burzio, L. (1986) *Italian syntax*. Dordrecht: Reidel.

Carrier, J. and Randall, J. H. (1992) The argument structure and syntactic structure of resultatives. *Linguistic Inquiry* **23**. 173–234.

Demonte, V. (1987) Remarks on secondary predicates: c-command, extraction, and reanalysis. *The Linguistic Review* **6**. 1–39.

Dixon, R. M. W. (1991) *A new approach to English grammar on semantic principles*. Oxford: Clarendon Press.

Dowty, D. (1976) Montague grammar and the lexical decomposition of causative verbs. In Partee, B. H. (ed.), *Montague grammar*. New York, San Francisco, London: Academic Press. 201–245.

Emonds, J. (1976) *A transformational approach to English syntax*. New York: Academic Press.

Fabb, N. (1984) *Syntactic affixation*. Published in MIT Working Papers in Linguistics, Cambridge, MA.

Goldberg, A. E. (1991) A semantic account of resultatives. *Linguistic Analysis* **21**. 66–96.

Green, G. M. (1970) How abstract is surface structure?. In Papers from the sixth regional meeting of the Chicago Linguistic Society. *CLS* **6**. 270–281.

(1972) Some observations on the syntax and semantics of instrumental verbs. In Papers from the eighth regional meeting of the Chicago Linguistic Society. *CLS* **8**. 83–97.

(1973) A syntactic syncretism in English and French. In Kachru, B. B., Lees, R. B., Malkiel, Y., Pietrangeli, A. and Saporta, S. (eds.), *Issues in linguistics: papers in honor of Henry and Renée Kahane*. Urbana, Chicago, London: University of Illinois Press. 257–278

Halliday, M. A. K. (1967) Notes on transitivity and theme in English. *Journal of Linguistics* **3**. 37–81.

Hasegawa, H. (1991) Secondary predicates, VP-internal subjects and mutual c-command. *English Linguistics* **8**. 1–15.

Hoekstra, T. (1988) Small clause results, *Lingua* **74**. 101–139.

(1992) Aspect and theta theory. In Roca, I. M. (ed.), *Thematic structure: its role in grammar*. Berlin and New York: Foris. 145–174.

Hornstein, N. and Lightfoot, D. W. (1987) Predication and PRO. *Language* **63**. 23–52.

Koster, J. and May, R. (1982) On the constituency of infinitives. *Language* **58**. 116–143.

Levin, B. and Rappaport, M. (1989) An approach to unaccusative mismatches. *NELS* **19**. 1–16.

Levin, B. and Rappaport Hovav, M. (1992) The lexical semantics of verbs of motion: the perspective from unaccusativity. In Roca, I. M. (ed.), *Thematic structure: its role in grammar*. Berlin and New York: Foris. 247–269.

Mallén, E. (1991) A syntactic analysis of secondary predication in Spanish. *Journal of Linguistics* **27**. 375–403.

(1992) Secondary predicates and lexical identification. *Studia Linguistica* **46**. 1–29.

McCawley, J. D. (1971) Prelexical syntax. In 22nd Annual Round Table, Georgetown University monograph series on language and linguistics **24**. 19–33.

Napoli, D. J. (1989) *Predication theory: a case study for indexing theory*. Cambridge University Press.

(1992) Secondary resultative predicates in Italian. *Journal of Linguistics* **28**. 53–90.

Roberts, I. (1988) Predicative APs. *Linguistic Inquiry* **19**. 703–710.

Rothstein, S. (1983) The syntactic forms of predication. Unpublished doctoral dissertation MIT. Distributed in 1985 by the Indiana University Linguistics Club.

(1990) Review of Napoli 1989. *Language* **63**. 598–606.

(1991) Syntactic predication: a syntactic primitive or a thematic relation. MS Bar-Ilan University.

(1992) Case and NP licensing. *Natural Language and Linguistic Theory* **10**. 119–139.

Sato, H. (1987) Resultative attributes and GB principles. *English Linguistics* **4**. 91–106.

Simpson J. (1983) Resultatives. In Levin, L., Rappaport, M. and Zaenen, A. (eds.), *Papers in lexical-functional grammar*. Distributed by the Indiana University Linguistics Club. Bloomington, Indiana. 143–157.

Williams, E. S. (1980) Predication. *Linguistic Inquiry* **11**. 203–238.

Yamada, Y. (1987) Two types of resultative construction. *English Linguistics* **4**. 73–90.

6 The English perfect as a secondary past tense[1]

RODNEY HUDDLESTON

1 Introduction

This chapter presents an analysis of relevant parts of the English verbal system in which the perfect, marked by *have* + past participle, is treated as a secondary past tense, the primary past tense being of course the inflectionally marked preterite: I use the term 'preterite' for the latter in order to free 'past' for use as a more general term covering both preterite and perfect. I look first at the preterite (section 2), secondly at the perfect itself (section 3), and then take up the implications of the contrast between primary and secondary tense (section 4). The fifth and final section then compares this approach with a number of alternatives, focussing mainly on the classic work of Comrie (1976, 1985).

2 The primary past tense: the inflectional preterite

2.1 Preliminaries

The primary tense system has two terms, preterite and present, as in *took* vs. *takes*. I shall focus here on the preterite, considering the present tense only for purposes of contrast.

In its basic use, tense is relational: it locates one time by its relation to another. I will call the two terms in this relation the *time referred to* (T_r) and the *time of orientation* (T_o). Where the aspectuality is perfective,[2] T_r is simply the *time of the situation* (T_{sit}); but where it is imperfective, T_r is normally a proper subinterval of T_{sit}:

(1)	a. He married his cousin.	[perfective: T_r is whole of T_{sit}]
	b. He already lived here.	[imperfective: T_r is subinterval of T_{sit}]

In (1b) the preterite does not locate the whole of his living here in past time, for a salient contextualisation is one where he still lives here now: what is in the past is not the situation as such but that part of it that I am talking about, referring to.

In the default case, T_o is the time of utterance, which I will call *deictic time* (T_d), and in this default case I will say that the tense is *used deictically*.[3] But tense can also be used non-deictically, for example with a T_o in the future:

(2) a. He *didn't* buy it. [deictic: T_o is T_d]
b. If he doesn't buy it he'll soon regret that he *didn't*. [non-deictic: T_o is not T_d]

It is because of the non-identities illustrated in (1b) and (2b) that we need four temporal concepts, not two, distinguishing T_r and T_{sit} on the one hand, T_o and T_d on the other; for convenience, they are recapitulated in (3):

(3) a. T_{sit} time of situation
b. T_r time referred to (may, but need not, be identified with T_{sit})
c. T_d deictic time
d. T_o time of orientation (identified as T_d in the default case)

The three main relations between T_r and T_o are anteriority, simultaneity and posteriority (or past, present and future)[4] as illustrated in (4):

(4) a. He *died* of lung cancer. [anteriority/past]
b. I *promise* to let you have it back tomorrow. [simultaneity/present]
c. If you *miss* her tomorrow, she'll be back next week. [posteriority/future]

These relations will be symbolised in the standard way, as

(5) a. T_r anterior to T_o $T_r < T_o$
b. T_r simultaneous with T_o $T_r = T_o$
c. T_r posterior to T_o $T_r > T_o$

and I shall use '/' to indicate the identification of one time with another, such as that of T_r with T_{sit} in the case of perfective aspectuality, or of T_o with T_d in deictic uses; the temporal interpretation of (4a) will thus be represented as $T_r/T_{sit} < T_o/T_d$.

2.2 Basic meaning of the preterite

The basic meaning of the preterite involves two components:

(6) a. T_r is anterior to T_o
b. T_o is non-past

(6b) covers the default deictic use and cases like (2b) where T_o is in the future. I see no reason to say that (2a–b) involve different *meanings* of the preterite: they are simply different contextual variants of (6).

2.3 Other uses of the preterite

Clearly (6) does not cover all uses of the preterite. Two other meanings must be recognised:

(a) Modal remoteness

(7) a. I wish they *were* still alive.
b. If they *were* still alive they would be appalled by what has happened.

The preterite here has a modal rather than temporal meaning: their being alive is presented in (7a) as counterfactual, and in (7b) as potentially counterfactual – the remote ('unreal') conditional construction is not used in contexts where the condition is known or assumed to be fulfilled, as in *Well if you're so clever then, why don't you do it yourself?* The time of their being (or not being) still alive is present, simultaneous with T_o/T_d, so that (6a) does not apply.

(b) Backshifted preterite

(8) a. I told Kim that I *was* married.
b. I regret telling Kim that I *was* married.

We are concerned with these in the interpretation – the salient one – where what I said to Kim was *I am married*, or words to that effect, not *I was married*, i.e. an 'original' present tense is backshifted into a preterite. I use this traditional process formulation for expository purposes only: I am not suggesting a syntactic derivation in which a present tense is changed into a preterite. The issue, rather, is what the preterite *means* in examples like (8), and it is less obvious here than in (7) that the preterite does not have the meaning given in (6): one might argue that the T_r for *was* is identical to the time of my telling Kim of my being married and that T_o is the time of my uttering (8), so that both (6a) and (6b) would apply.

There are, however, two reasons for treating a backshifted preterite as different from an ordinary preterite expressing (6). Firstly, a backshifted preterite can appear in the complement of a verb with a preterite tense expressing modal remoteness:

(9) a. I wish he knew that she *had* too many commitments.

b. If he knew she *had* too many commitments, he would do something about it.

The time of her having too many commitments (again in the relevant and salient interpretation) is now, so that there is no anteriority, just as there is none in (7). But the preterite tense of *had* here cannot be subsumed under the modal remoteness meaning attaching to *knew*: the potential or actual counterfactuality applies to his knowing, not to her having too many commitments – on the contrary, both examples at least implicate that she in fact does have too many commitments.

The second point is that such modal verbs as *must* and *ought* which lack preterite forms can appear in a construction that otherwise requires a backshifted preterite, but they cannot appear in place of an ordinary preterite:

(10) a. We knew we *must* leave by noon yesterday to have any chance of catching her.
b. She said he *ought* to invite them both, but he didn't take her advice.

Both *must* and *ought* could here be paraphrased with a preterite form (*We knew we **had** to leave by noon yesterday, She said he **had** an obligation to invite them both*), whereas we could not similarly substitute present tense *must* and *ought* in *We **had** to leave yesterday* and *He **had** an obligation to invite them, so he did.* I will return to this point when comparing the preterite and the perfect.

Backshifting is of course very often optional:

(11) a. I *have* too many commitments. [original utterance]
b. She said she *had* too many commitments. [backshifted report]
c. She said she *has* too many commitments. [non-backshifted report]

We do not need here to discuss in detail the pragmatic factors that favour one or other of the backshifted and non-backshifted versions (for a good recent discussion see Declerck 1991: 182–189): the relevant issue for present purposes is what the contrast between (11b) and (11c) tells us about the meaning of the preterite in (11b). The present tense in (11c) has its basic meaning:

(12) a. T_r is simultaneous with T_o
b. T_o is non-past

In this example T_o is interpreted, more specifically, as having the default identification with T_d.[5] I have argued that a backshifted preterite does not express (6): the difference of meaning between (11b) and (11c) is thus not (6) vs. (12). It is not a matter of the anteriority vs. simultaneity of T_r relative to T_o, but of the identification of T_o; the meaning of the backshifted preterite in (b) is:

(13) T_o is past

The backshifted preterite does not explicitly encode the temporal relation between T_r and T_o (for more on this point see section 3.2 below), but in this example it will be interpreted as simultaneity. The difference between (11b) and (11c) is thus that in (11b) T_r, an interval within the situation of her having too many commitments, is simultaneous with a T_o identified as the original speaker's T_d, whereas in (11c) it is simultaneous with a T_o identified as the reporter's T_d: there are different T_r's, but both can be included within the same T_{sit}. The backshifted version represents the more faithful report since it uses the same T_o as the original speaker, but in a context where it can be assumed that the situation has not changed, the reorientation to the reporter's T_d does not invalidate the report.

(13) does not cover examples like (9), where there is no past time involved at all: it therefore needs to be amended as in (14) to allow for the fact that backshift has been grammaticalised and can apply under conditions where there is no strictly semantic, or certainly no temporal, justification for it:

(14) T_o is past or identified by a superordinate clause with a past tense

The 'or' is of course to be taken inclusively, and normally both disjuncts apply, as in (8a) or (11b), but (8b) illustrates the case where only the first applies and (9) that where only the second does.

A backshifted preterite is thus non-deictic. This is so even for cases like (9), where T_o is in fact present: the tense is non-deictic in the sense that T_o is not identified directly with T_d, but only indirectly via the T_r of the superordinate clause (which is simultaneous with T_o/T_d). The present tense modals in (10) are likewise non-deictic, with a past T_o: it is just that the morphological defectiveness of *must* and *ought* results in the pastness of T_o being left without formal expression. The non-deictic use of primary tense is thus not confined to fairly unusual cases like (2b): it is a common phenomenon. I believe this has significant relevance for an analysis of the perfect.

3 The secondary past tense: the perfect

3.1 The basic use of the perfect

Like the inflectional preterite, the perfect, in its basic meaning, expresses the anteriority of T_r relative to T_o: it is for this reason that they can both be regarded as past tenses. The similarity is seen most clearly in pairs like

(15) a. He *wrote* it last week. [preterite]
b. He is believed to *have written* it last week. [perfect]

There are, however, two respects in which the basic meanings of the two tenses differ. In the first place, with the perfect, T_r may either begin before and extend up to T_o or be wholly before T_o, whereas only the latter possibility exists for the preterite:

(16)	a. He must have lived here ever since the war.	[T_r before and up to T_o: continuative]
	b. He must have told her last week.	[T_r wholly before T_o: non-continuative]
(17)	a. *He lived here ever since the war.	[*T_r before and up to T_o: continuative]
	b. He told her last week.	[T_r wholly before T_o: non-continuative]

The 'before and up to' case I will refer to with the traditional term *continuative*, the 'wholly before' case as *non-continuative*,[6] and I will speak of the perfect as expressing *complex anteriority* (T_r wholly before or before and up to T_o) and the preterite as expressing *simple anteriority* (T_r wholly before T_o). This difference, then, relates to (6a).

The second difference (and again I am concerned here just with the basic meanings) concerns (6b): with the preterite T_o is non-past, whereas with the perfect T_o is determined by the primary tense, as in (18), or (where there is no primary tense) by the superordinate clause, as in (19):

(18)	a. He had written it himself.	[past T_o]
	b. He has written it himself.	[present T_o]
(19)	a. He was believed to have written it himself.	[past T_o]
	b. He seems to have written it himself.	[present T_o]
	c. He intends to have written it by then.	[future T_o]

The T_r of *have written* is anterior to a T_o which is past, present and future, as indicated.

In each of these examples, there are two tense selections, two expressions of a temporal relation between some T_r and its corresponding T_o:

(20)	a. $T_r^1 < T_o^1$; $T_r^2 < T_o^2$	[T_r–T_o relations in (18a), (19a)]
	b. $T_r^1 = T_o^1$; $T_r^2 < T_o^2$	[T_r–T_o relations in (18b), (19b,c)]

Consider first (19a). T_r^1, the time referred to by the preterite of *was believed*, is anterior to T_o^1, which has the default identification with T_d; T_r^2, the time referred to by the perfect tense of *have written* (thus the time of writing, since the aspectuality is perfective), is anterior to T_o^2, which is identified (by virtue of the properties of *believe*) as T_r^1. In (19b) T_r^1 (the time referred to by the tense of *seems*) is simultaneous with T_o^1/T_d, and T_r^2 is anterior to T_o^2, which is again identified as T_r^1. In (19c) the T_r–T_o relations are the same as in the *seems* example: the difference is that (by virtue of the properties of *intend*) T_o^2 is identified not as T_r^1 (the time referred to by the tense of *intends*) but as a time posterior to T_r^1.

(20) holds for the examples where *have* carries primary tense as well as for the nonfinite perfects just discussed: the preterite perfect and present perfect are *compound tenses*. In (18a) T_r^1 is the time referred to by the inflectional preterite, which locates it as anterior to T_o^1/T_d; T_r^2 is the time of writing and is located by the perfect as anterior to T_o^2 – which is identified as T_r^1, just as it is in (19a). (18b) is the same except that the inflectional present tense locates T_r^1 as simultaneous with T_o^1/T_d.[7]

These compound tenses thus involve two T_r's: there are two times being referred to. T_r^2 is the time of the situation expressed by the lexical verb and its dependents (or a subinterval within this time if the aspectuality is imperfective); T_r^1 is the time located by the primary tense and identifies the T_o (T_o^2) to which T_r^2 is anterior. Assuming that the primary tense is being used deictically and considering only the non-continuative perfect, the temporal representations of the preterite perfect, the present perfect and the preterite non-perfect (henceforth the *simple preterite* – it is a simple as opposed to compound tense) will be as follows:

(21) a. preterite perfect: *had written*

T_r^2	$<$	T_o^2/T_r^1	$<$	T_o^1/T_d
writing		intermediate time		now

b. present perfect: *has written*

T_r^2	$<$	$T_o^2/T_r^1 = T_o^1/T_d$
writing		now

c. simple preterite: *wrote*

T_r	$<$	T_o/T_d
writing		now

In a familiar type of example like

(22) When he arrived she *had* already *left* a couple of hours earlier

the temporal adjunct *when he arrived* specifies T_r^1 and *a couple of hours earlier* specifies T_r^2, though there are well-known restrictions on the specification of T_r^2 in the present perfect. The implications of the different temporal schemas of the present perfect and simple preterite shown in (21b–c) will be taken up below.

3.2 Other uses of the perfect

We have seen that the basic use of the primary past tense, the inflectional preterite, is to express the anteriority of T_r relative to a non-past T_o, but that there are two cases where it does not locate T_r anterior to T_o: one where it indicates modal remoteness and one where it indicates that T_o is past (or identified by a superordinate past tense). The expression of the anteriority of T_r relative to T_o in these two cases is achieved by use of the perfect. The modal remoteness case is illustrated in (23d):

(23) **Present time**

a. If they *are* still ill now, they'll be at home. [open]
b. If they *were* still ill now, they'd be at home. [remote]

Past time

c. If they *were* still ill then, they'll have been at home. [open]
d. If they *had* still *been* ill then, they'd have been at home. [remote]

(23a) and (23c) belong to the open ('real') conditional construction, the default one where a preterite has its basic meaning; thus $T_r = T_o/T_d$ with the present tense in (23a) and $T_r < T_o/T_d$ with the preterite in (23c). (23b) and (23d) belong to the marked construction with the preterite expressing modal remoteness and the temporal relations the same as in their open counterparts: the $T_r < T_o$ component in (23d) is thus expressed by the perfect. Notice, moreover, that the T_o in this $T_r < T_o$ relation is identified as T_d: although the perfect is non-deictic in its basic use, there are constructions where it is used deictically.

The backshifted case is seen in (24d):

(24) a. I *love* you. [original: present time]
b. You said you *loved* me. [backshifted report]
c. I *loved* you in those days. [original: past time]
d. You said you *had loved* me in those days. [backshifted report]

In the process formulation of traditional grammars, backshifting changes a simple present into a simple preterite and a simple preterite into a preterite perfect. As far as the meaning is concerned, we can say that in both (24b) and (24d) the preterite expresses just (13), i.e. that T_o is past; the $T_r < T_o$ component in (24d) is expressed by the perfect – and the absence of the perfect in (24b) (and of any factors inducing a posterior relation) results in the default interpretation of the relation between T_r and T_o as simultaneity.

In both the modal remoteness and the backshift cases, then, the perfect assumes the role of expressing the $T_r < T_o$ relation when the primary preterite is not available for this purpose.

A further similarity between the perfect and the preterite is that the former too can be used to express modal remoteness, as in (25c):

(25) a. If they *go* tomorrow they will meet her son. [open]
b. If they *went* tomorrow they would meet her son. [remote]
c. If they *had gone* tomorrow they would have met her son. [doubly remote]

(25a) and (25b) illustrate the familiar contrast between open and remote conditionals: the former presents their coming tomorrow as an open possibility, while the latter presents it as potentially counterfactual, implicating that it is unlikely. In (25c), however, there is a further element of modal remoteness: I refer to this as the 'doubly remote conditional construction'. It presents their coming tomorrow as already counterfactual: it may be that they have gone already or that it has already been arranged that they will not be going tomorrow (perhaps they are going some other day, perhaps they are simply not going at all). This modal use of the perfect is possible only in combination with the modal use of the preterite. And (since there is, as it were, no 'tertiary' past tense) it cannot be used with past-time conditionals as the perfect is needed here to express temporal anteriority: i.e. there is no doubly remote counterpart to (23c–d).[8] Both past tenses can thus be used to express modal remoteness rather than temporal anteriority, though this use is much more restricted with the perfect than with the preterite.

It seems, however, that the perfect does not serve to express (14), to mark T_o as past (or identified by a superordinate past tense), even when the preterite is not available to do so:

(26) a. She said he ought to invite them both. (cf. (10b))
b. She said he ought to have invited them both.

(27) a. She wished he didn't have to leave before the end.
b. She wished he hadn't had to leave before the end.

I observed earlier that present tense *ought*, having no preterite counterpart, can appear in a context which would normally require backshift, as in (26a) when followed by *but he didn't take her advice*: the T_r for *ought* here is simultaneous with a T_o whose location is not expressed but merely inferred. The *have* in (26b) serves to locate the obligation anterior to her speaking: it is not a backshifted counterpart of (26a), but a nonbackshifted report of *He ought to have invited them both*. In (27a) the preterite *didn't* has the modal remoteness sense, and there is again no formal marking of the past location of T_o, though the sentence could be used in a context where backshift would normally be required, one where 'the end' has already occurred. Again (27b) is not a backshifted version: perfect *have* marks the anteriority of T_r relative to T_o, not the past location of T_o. This is evident from the fact that the sentence could not be used in a context where 'the end' was still in the future – a context where backshift is normally possible (as in *She said he didn't have to leave until tomorrow*, where there is no modal remoteness).

4 Primary vs. secondary past tense

The inflectional preterite and the analytic perfect both qualify as past tenses in that they both, in their basic use, express the anteriority of T_r relative to T_o; there are, however, three reasons for distinguishing them as respectively primary and secondary.

Firstly, we have seen that the perfect takes over from the preterite the function of expressing anteriority when the preterite is used to express modal remoteness (as in (23d)) or is backshifted (as in (24d)). Thus the primary past tense does not have its basic meaning here and the secondary one is called into service to locate T_r anterior to T_o.

Secondly, the preterite is prototypically used deictically while the perfect is prototypically used non-deictically – and as a general linguistic category tense is prototypically deictic (cf. Lyons 1977: 678). Moreover, in the most elementary and frequent use of the preterite perfect – that illustrated in (18a), where the preterite and the perfect combine in their basic meanings to express double anteriority with T_o^1 identified deictically – it is the preterite which yields the first move back from T_o/T_d, while the perfect marks the second move back in time.

The third point is that the preterite is more highly grammaticalised than the perfect, where *grammaticalisation*, in Comrie's formulation (1985: 10), involves 'integration into the grammatical system of a language', contrasting with mere *lexicalisation*. He suggests 'that the difference between them can be understood in terms of the interaction of two parameters: that of obligatory expression, and that of morphological boundness', with the clearest instances of grammaticalisation satisfying both criteria. The English preterite and present tenses clearly do satisfy both of Comrie's criteria, whereas the perfect does not.

The primary tenses are morphologically bound in that they are marked inflectionally; the perfect, by contrast, is marked analytically. As for obligatory expression, Comrie in fact uses what I am calling the primary tenses to explain the criterion: 'It is quite impossible to construct an English sentence containing a finite verb that is neutral as between the two poles of this opposition, i.e. *John runs* is clearly non-past, and *John ran* is clearly past, and there is no third term that is neither.' I believe that 'present' is a more appropriate label for *runs* than 'non-past', but whichever term we adopt *runs* is certainly not non-past in the same way that it is non-perfect. Present (or non-past) is a tense, whereas non-perfect is not: it is merely the absence of perfect tense. Thus while *had written* and *has written* are examples of compound tenses (involving two T_r–T_o relations), *wrote* and *writes* are simple tenses (involving just one such relation). That the present tense is not simply a verb form lacking the preterite inflection is evident from third person singular forms, as in Comrie's example, but can be argued for other person/number combinations on the strength of the contrast with the lexeme *be* between present tense *are* and base form *be*. Thus *They are quick* is a tensed construction, whereas *Be quick!*, (*I intend*) *to be quick* and (*I insist*) *that he be quick* are not.

Although the perfect does not satisfy either of the above criteria, it does have a third property that can properly be regarded as an indication of grammaticalisation, namely that its marker, *have*, belongs to a small closed class of words: it is arguable that Comrie's morphological boundness parameter would be better formulated to cover closed class words as well as bound morphemes, though they would still represent a lower degree of grammaticalisation than the latter (cf. the cline of grammaticality, 'content item > grammatical word > clitic > inflectional affix', in Hopper and Traugott 1993: 7). Thus perfect *have* has the well-known properties that define the class of auxiliary verbs in English – special behaviour in negation, the ability to invert with the subject in interrogatives, to be stranded in ellipsis ('code'), carry contrastive stress to mark emphatic polarity, and so on (they are sometimes referred to acronymically as the NIÇE properties – cf. Palmer 1988: 14–25). It is a matter of controversy whether perfect *have* and other members of this class marking aspect, mood and voice are grammaticalised to the extent that they have lost their status as verbs taking nonfinite complements, becoming dependents of the lexical verb with which they are in construction (cf., for example, Palmer 1974, 1979, Huddleston 1976, 1980; see also Aarts and Meyer, this volume). But it is not controversial that they do share a cluster of distinctive properties making them significantly more grammaticalised than such verbs as, say, *begin*, *continue*, *stop* and the like: I would want to say that the degree of grammaticalisation they exhibit is sufficient for them to qualify as auxiliary verbs, and hence for *have* to qualify more specifically as a tense auxiliary.[9] At the same time, the discussion has shown that they are much less grammaticalised than the inflectional tense markers, so that for this and the other reasons given above it makes sense to take the preterite and present as the primary tenses, and the perfect as secondary.

5 Alternatives

In this section of the chapter I defend the above analysis of the perfect as a secondary past tense in comparison with a number of alternatives treating the perfect as an aspect (or some other category distinct from tense) or the present perfect as a simple tense; I also compare it briefly with the 'embedded past' analysis of the perfect. Limitations of space preclude a comprehensive discussion of the literature, and I accordingly focus mainly on the work of Comrie, whose classic textbooks on aspect (1976) and tense (1985) have been so influential.

5.1 Comrie

Comrie distinguishes the categories of aspect and tense in the following way. Aspects are said to be 'different ways of viewing the internal temporal constituency of a situation' (1976: 5), to involve 'the grammaticalisation of internal temporal constituency' (1985: 6), whereas tense is a matter of 'grammaticalised expression of location in time' (1985: 9). He himself deals with the perfect under aspect rather than tense, but with a significant difference between the earlier and later accounts. In the former he in effect acknowledges that the perfect does not fit his definition of aspect. He writes (1976: 52):

(28) Aspect, as we have been concerned with it hitherto, has been concerned with different ways of representing the internal temporal constituency of a situation. The perfect is rather different from these aspects, since it tells us nothing directly about the situation in itself, but rather relates some state to a preceding situation.

(The expression 'as we have been concerned with it hitherto' is somewhat misleading, for expression of internal temporal constituency is not simply a feature of the aspects considered earlier in the book but the *essential* feature of his definition of aspect.) The later discussion begins (1985: 32):

(29) I would claim that the English (present) perfect is not to be analysed simply as a tense, in particular that it differs from other English past tenses in terms of parameters other than tense

– which is non-committal as to whether the difference is one of aspect or of some third kind.

The most important change between the two accounts, however, has to do with the interrelationship between the perfect and tense. In the first book Comrie treats the perfect as an aspect that can combine with any of the tenses:

(30) The present perfect (often simply called the perfect) is only one of the possible tenses of the perfect aspect, the one that expresses a relation between a present state and a past situation. In other tenses we find . . . a past perfect (pluperfect) . . . expressing a relation between a past state and an even earlier situation; and a future perfect . . . expressing a relation between a future state and a situation prior to it.

This implies a parallel treatment of all the perfect forms, all the forms marked by *have* + past participle. Such a uniform treatment is explicitly rejected in the later book. The term 'present perfect' is dropped in favour of 'perfect' *tout court* (as in (29), following the tradition mentioned in (30)), and 'pluperfect' is used in preference to 'past perfect'. The pluperfect and future perfect are now regarded as tenses ('absolute-relative' ones),[10] and the perfect itself is analysed – as indicated in (29) – as a past tense, not a present tense, so that (1985: 78)

(31) the perfect is in fact radically different from the absolute-relative tenses, and should not be given a uniform treatment with them

A major weakness of such a non-uniform treatment, however, is that it fails to account for the property common to all the English perfects, namely that they can all have a continuative interpretation, i.e. they can locate a T_r as beginning before but extending up to T_o:

(32) a. He has lived alone ever since his wife died. [present perfect]
b. He had lived alone ever since his wife died. [preterite perfect]
c. He is believed to have lived alone ever since his wife died. [nonfinite perfect]

This provides a compelling argument for adopting a uniform, compositional treatment at least as a starting-point.

A problem for the uniform treatment is, of course, that the non-present perfects have uses without analogue in the present perfect:

(33) a. *He has told her last week.
b. He had told her last week.
c. He is believed to have told her last week.

In Comrie (1976) this is handled by postulating ambiguity in the non-present perfects between a perfect meaning ('continuing relevance of a previous situation') and a non-perfect meaning:

(34) [I]n English, in certain nonfinite constructions especially (but also in the pluperfect and future perfect), the Perfect form (*have* plus Past Participle) does not necessarily have perfect meaning. (1976: 55)

But there are no grounds for saying that the non-present perfects display a genuine ambiguity as opposed to a neutralisation of a distinction made between the present perfect and the simple preterite – and presumably Comrie himself has abandoned this analysis in the later 1985 account.[11]

The issue that needs to be focussed on is whether the uniform, compositional treatment provides a satisfactory basis for handling the contrast between the present perfect and the simple preterite. Comrie's analysis, while incorporating important modifications and improvements, is strongly influenced by Reichenbach (1947), and in particular he makes use of the concepts symbolised as E (event time), R (reference point), and S (moment of speech).[12] For Comrie the preterite perfect (his 'pluperfect') is an absolute-relative tense, thus involving all three of E, R and S, while the simple preterite is an absolute tense involving just E and S, and hence these would be represented as in (35a–b) below; he argues that if the (present) perfect were treated uniformly with the preterite perfect, its analysis would be as in (35c):

(35) a. $E < R < S$ [preterite perfect]
b. $E < S$ [simple preterite]
c. $E < R = S$ [present perfect]

He then claims, however, that (35c) is not distinct from (35b) in terms of location in time: locating a situation prior to a reference point simultaneous with the present moment (the present perfect) 'would give precisely the same result as . . . (locating) a situation as prior to the present moment' (the simple preterite).

Comrie goes on to draw two conclusions, neither of which I would want to go along with. The first is that 'however (present) perfect differs from preterite, it is not in terms of time location'. One objection to this is the point already emphasised, namely that the present perfect expresses complex anteriority, the preterite simple anteriority – i.e. that the former but not the latter can have a continuative interpretation. More important for present purposes, however, is Comrie's second conclusion – that the (present) perfect is not a present tense; this implies that from a syntactic/semantic point of view the fact that it is marked by the present tense of the auxiliary *have* is of purely historical significance (as arguably it is in such languages as French). A more reasonable conclusion, it seems to me, is that the present tense component of the present perfect does not simply have the function of locating R (which in this case corresponds to my T_o^2). This is where some such concept as current relevance comes in. Adapting Declerck's formulation (1991: 307, 327), which seems to me a good way of putting it, the present perfect (when used deictically) is concerned with the structure of the world at T_d.[13] The focus is not on 'then', the time of the anterior situation, but on 'now'. On this account the interpretation does involve present time – and since the form includes a morphological present tense the default expectation is that it is syntactically a present tense too. This is the account proposed above, where instead of (35) we have (deriving from the earlier (21)):

(36) a. $T_r^2 < T_o^2/T_r^1 < T_o^1/T_d$ [preterite perfect]
b. $T_r < T_o/T_d$ [simple preterite]
c. $T_r^2 < T_o^2/T_r^1 = T_o^1/T_d$ [present perfect]

In the simple preterite (36b) the present moment is involved only 'passively', as T_o/T_d, whereas in the present perfect (36c) it is involved actively since there is reference to a time (T_r^1) located by the present tense as simultaneous with T_o/T_d. In (36b) there is reference just to past time, in (36c) to past and present time, and the current relevance correlates with the fact that there is this reference to present time.

I am not suggesting that the representations (36b–c) fully capture the difference between the simple preterite and the present perfect, only that it provides a better starting-point for a description of the difference than one which treats them as both simple past tenses differing in some other respect than tense. Although I do not accept Comrie's claim that the simple preterite and present perfect do not differ with respect to location in time, it is true that (when the primary tense is used deictically) both refer to a time prior to now and do not involve any third time temporally distinct from now, and in the light of this similarity it is arguably not surprising that they should have become differentiated in a way which is not fully predictable from the different temporal schemas shown in (36b–c). The present perfect expresses complex anteriority by virtue of the perfect component, has present time reference (as well as past time reference) by virtue of the present tense component, but is specialised in such a way that the focus is on 'now' rather than 'then'.

The formal resources of the language do not provide for a contrast matching that between the present perfect and the simple preterite to occur with the non-present perfects. It is therefore not surprising that the latter do not encode a meaning analogous to the continuing relevance/focus on world at T_o/T_d (or rather non-past T_o) that we find with the present perfect. This is not to say that they exclude a pragmatic interpretation of that kind if it is consistent with other features of the sentence and its context, but rather that it is not the meaning of perfect: it is the specialised meaning of the present + perfect combination.

5.2 Neo-Reichenbachian aspect

Comrie, we have seen, distinguishes tense and aspect as involving respectively location in time and internal temporal constituency; an alternative view, which I shall refer to as neo-Reichenbachian, has tense expressing the temporal relation between R and S, and aspect that between R and E (cf. Johnson 1981 and, with different terminology, Klein 1992).

This way of drawing the distinction between tense and aspect, however, does not seem to me as valid or useful as Comrie's. An initial point is that although the inflectional tenses are usually used deictically and the perfect non-deictically, the former are nevertheless often used non-deictically (especially in backshift) and the latter can be used deictically (cf. section 3.2); moreover, I have suggested (section 2.2) that even in its basic meaning the preterite does not express the identification of T_o with T_d (but rather locates T_o as non-past): they are thus not satisfactorily distinguished as relating some time to S (preterite 'tense') and relating some time to R (perfect 'aspect'). A second point is that to distinguish the preterite from the present perfect as $E/R < S$ vs. $E < S/R$ fails to bring out the fact that the present perfect is semantically as well as formally more complex than the preterite: on the analysis of sections 3–4 above, this greater complexity is reflected in the present perfect being a compound tense, the preterite non-perfect a simple one. Thirdly, it is very doubtful whether the range and complexity of aspectual systems can be catered for by treating aspect as essentially concerned with the expression of temporal relations. Take, for example, the English progressive. This is said – e.g. in Klein (1992: 537–538) – to indicate that R is properly included in E (in Klein's terms, that topic time is properly included in the time of the situation). I would argue, however, that the proper inclusion relation is a strong implicature rather than the basic meaning of the progressive. It applies clearly enough in straightforward examples like *When I arrived they were watching TV* but not necessarily in

(37) a. Between 10 and 11 I was working in the library.
b. From after dinner until nearly midnight I was filling in my tax return.

These allow proper inclusion contextualisations – e.g. if (37a) is said in response to *Where were you between 10 and 11?*, when it is consistent with my having worked there all morning, or if (37b) is continued with *I'll have to finish it tonight*. But they also allow interpretations where the adjunct gives the full time of the situation (in my terms, where T_r is co-extensive with T_{sit}): e.g. if (37a) is part of an answer to *What did you do yesterday?* or (37b) is continued with *It took me all that time to do it.*[14] On Comrie's account of imperfectivity (of which progressivity is a special case), it involves taking an internal view of the situation (which is applicable in either contextualisation of (37)); the imperfective does not encode that the situation is presented in its totality – but this is not the same as presenting it as incomplete.

5.3 Declerck

Declerck (1991) rejects the view of the perfect as an aspect, but he does not treat the present perfect uniformly with the preterite, future and conditional perfects in that he includes the former among the absolute tenses (along with the preterite, present and future) while the other three are included among the relative tenses (together with the conditional); this implies that the present perfect is a simple tense, while the three finite non-present perfects are compound tenses.

This is achieved by distinguishing first between past and present 'time-spheres' and then dividing the latter into pre-present, present and post-present 'sectors'; there is no inherent division of the past time-sphere into sectors, so that the whole constitutes a single past sector. These are 'absolute' sectors in that 'they are defined in direct relation to' the zero-point (my T_d) and the four absolute tenses each locate the situation in one of these four absolute sectors: the preterite in the past sector, the present perfect in the pre-present sector, the present in the present sector and the future in the post-present sector (1991: 16–20). However, no adequate explication is given of the distinction between the past sector/time-sphere and the pre-present sector of the present time-sphere, and though Declerck gives an excellent account of the usage difference between the preterite and the present perfect, the distinction between a past sector and a pre-present sector does not play any essential role in accounting for it. For note that the (so-called) future is said to locate the situation in the post-present sector, which makes it the mirror-image of the present perfect as opposed to the preterite, but it does not have the analogue of the special features which characterise the present perfect, namely that 'the speaker is somehow thinking of (T_d) (*now*)' as opposed to *then*. Indeed, Declerck himself observes (1991: 374) that the temporal schemas he provides for examples containing the future 'are mirror images of some of the structures we have argued to hold for either the present perfect or the preterit[e]', which shows 'clearly that the future tense covers the two possibilities which, when the reference is to the past, are distributed over the preterit[e] and the present perfect'. That this can be so while there is no distinction between a post-present and a future sector shows that the distinction between pre-present and past sectors is not crucially involved in the contrast between the present perfect and the preterite. The present perfect involves reference to both present and past time, and there is nothing in Declerck's discussion that requires us to treat it as a simple tense rather than the compound one that its form suggests.

5.4 The perfect as an embedded past

The analysis of section 3 treats the present and preterite perfects as compound tenses and to this extent bears some initial similarity to what is commonly called the embedded past ('EB') theory of the perfect, advanced in McCawley (1971), Huddleston (1969), etc., and criticised in McCoard (1978: chapter 5), Binnick (1991: 103–104, 264–265). It differs in two respects. Firstly, the EB handles the tense recursion in terms of clause embedding, whereas the above analysis is quite neutral as to whether perfect *have* is a head verb taking a nonfinite clause as complement or a dependent of the lexical verb (see note 9).[15] Secondly, while EB theory treats the perfect as a contextual variant of the preterite ('the perfect is treated as a form which conveys the meaning of the [preterite] when that meaning is within the scope of another tense', Binnick 1991: 103), I have been concerned to emphasise the differences as well as the similarities between them. The similarities are that in their basic use both express the anteriority of T_r relative to T_o, and both have a non-basic use in which they express modal remoteness. The differences are: (i) the perfect expresses complex anteriority, the preterite simple anteriority; (ii) the preterite but not the perfect indicates (in its basic use) that T_o is non-past; (iii) the preterite but not the perfect has a backshifted use indicating that T_o is past (or identified by a higher past tense); (iv) the modal use of the perfect is much more restricted than that of the preterite; (v) the present perfect combination has a specialised meaning focussing on the present structure of the world.

Notes

1. This chapter derives from a project on English grammar supported by the Australian Research Council. I am grateful to Jill Bowie for very helpful discussion of the issues dealt with here, and to Bas Aarts and Charles Meyer for useful editorial suggestions.
2. Following Bache (1985), I use 'aspectuality' for meaning, contrasting it with 'aspect' for form (matching the standard distinction between 'time' and 'tense'). We can then talk of perfective and imperfective aspectuality in English although it has no grammatical categories of perfective and imperfective aspect. The distinction also enables us to handle without confusion the fact that, while the basic meaning of progressive aspect is to express progressive aspectuality, it does not always have this meaning, as in (the salient interpretation of) examples like *Will you be going to the shops this afternoon?* Thus the ambiguity of *When the meeting ends we'll be flying to Bonn* is a matter of whether or not it expresses progressive aspectuality: it does in the reading where our flying to Bonn will be (already) in progress at the time in question, but not in the reading where our flying to Bonn takes place after

the meeting. The case is thus similar to that where the preterite does not have its basic past time meaning, as in examples like *It's time he* ***was*** *in bed.*

3. A common alternative to T_d is 'time of utterance/speech' ('S'): I have adopted the former for two reasons. In the first place it allows for the less usual addressee-oriented deixis, not just for speaker-oriented deixis – cf. *You are now leaving West Berlin*, where T_o is identified as the time of decoding, not encoding (Comrie 1985: 16; see also Declerck 1991: 15). Secondly, it correlates conveniently with the distinction between deictic and non-deictic uses of the tenses: a tense is used deictically when its T_o is identified as T_d. The deictic vs. non-deictic distinction is often spoken of as 'absolute' vs. 'relative', but given that tense is relational in either case it is an unfortunate way of drawing the distinction (cf. Comrie 1985: 36) – and it seems to me doubly unfortunate to apply these terms to the tenses themselves rather than to uses of the tenses. (A further term for T_d is 'temporal zero-point', but the abbreviation for this, 'T_0' is too similar to my T_o.)
4. I will use both sets of terms; the former have the advantage of being more transparently relational, the latter that of being simpler. In the absence of indications to the contrary, past, present and future are to be understood deictically.
5. An example with a future T_o for a present tense verb is *If you force her to do the accounts as well she will certainly be able to say she* ***has*** *too many commitments.*
6. Alternative terms applying just to the perfect are 'universal' for 'continuative' and 'existential' or 'indefinite' for non-continuative.
7. In *He will have written it by then* I regard *will* as a modal auxiliary, like *may*, so that the temporal interpretation will be derived in essentially the same way as that of (19c); under an analysis where it is a future tense auxiliary the interpretation will be derived like those for (18), except that the first temporal relation will be $T_r^1 > T_o^1$.
8. With present-time conditionals the doubly remote construction is possible (there being no anteriority for either past tense to express), but the meaning difference between the remote and doubly remote versions is nothing like as sharp as it is with future-time conditionals: compare (23a–b) with *If they had still been ill now, they'd have been at home.*
9. It now seems to me unfortunate to present the controversy as a matter of whether the verbs in question are auxiliaries or main verbs: I would now want to use the term 'auxiliary verb' in such a way that it involves no commitment to one or other position in this controversy. In this chapter I am accordingly using the term auxiliary verb in opposition to lexical verb (not main verb): it applies to a distinct class of grammaticalised verbs whose members are characteristically used to express the verbal categories of tense, aspect, mood or voice.
10. In terms of the framework presented in sections 2–4, an absolute-relative tense is a compound tense where T_o^1 is identified with T_d while T_o^2 is identified with some other time.
11. Convincing arguments against an alleged 'perfect'/'non-perfect' ambiguity are given by Declerck (1991: 356): for him, the only genuine ambiguity, applying potentially to all perfects, is the continuative vs. non-continuative

one, as in *He has/had/will have lived in Paris for four years*, where the four years may (continuative) or may not (non-continuative) be those stretching back from the present, past or future T_o respectively. Palmer (1988: 51) goes further than proposing ambiguity: he goes so far as to say that whereas *have* marks perfect phase in examples like (32b) it marks 'past tense' (preterite) in examples like (33b): this, however, seems to me to confuse form and (alleged) meaning, for preterite and perfect phase are categories of form, not meaning. Consistent application of such an approach would lead us to say that in *If Ed came tomorrow we could play bridge* the inflection in *came* (which expresses modal remoteness, not past time) marks subjunctive mood, not preterite tense, an analysis Palmer himself emphatically rejects (1988: 46).

12. S corresponds to my T_d, and where the aspectuality is perfective, E corresponds to my T_r/T_{sit}; there are problems with R (see Klein 1992: 533–535; also Declerck 1991: 250–251, who points out the danger of equivocation between an interpretation as 'time referred from' and one as 'time referred to') and there is no simple translation in my framework.
13. Declerck is critical of the appeal to current relevance (e.g. 1991: 320), claiming that it is not a necessary condition for the use of the present perfect. This is certainly so if current relevance is interpreted specifically as a matter of current results, but it is surely intended to have a broader interpretation as used by Comrie, Palmer and others. It can be argued that it is too vague (and I do think Declerck's account is an improvement in this regard), but hardly that it does not always apply. If, as Declerck puts it, the speaker using the present perfect is concerned with 'now', with the structure of the world at (what I am calling) T_d, how could the past situation not have current relevance? For observations on the present perfect in terms of relevance theory, see Smith (1981: 260).
14. Another case where the proper inclusion implicature does not go through is illustrated in *When I said 'the boss' I was referring to you.* Neither this nor (37) can be accounted for in the way suggested in note 2 for the relevant interpretation of *When the meeting ends we'll be flying to Bonn*: there is no reason to deny that they do express progressive aspectuality.
15. An account in terms of recursion within the verbal group is found in the work of Halliday, e.g. (1976).

References

Bache, C. (1985) *Verbal aspect: a general theory and its application to present-day English*. Odense University Press.
Binnick, R. I. (1991) *Time and the verb*. Oxford University Press.
Comrie, B. (1976) *Aspect*. Cambridge University Press.
(1985). *Tense*. Cambridge University Press.
Declerck, R. (1991) *Tense in English: its structure and use in discourse*. London: Routledge.
Halliday, M. A. K. (1976) The English verbal group. In Kress, G. (ed.), *Halliday: system and function in language*. London: Oxford University Press.

Hopper, P. J. and Traugott, E. C. (1993) *Grammaticalization*. Cambridge University Press.

Huddleston, R. D. (1969) Some observations on tense and deixis in English. *Language* **45**. 777–806.

(1976) Some theoretical issues in the description of the English verb. *Lingua* **40**. 331–383.

(1980) On Palmer's defence of the distinction between auxiliaries and main verbs. *Lingua* **50**. 101–115.

Johnson, M. R. (1981) A unified temporal theory of tense and aspect. In Tedeschi, P. and Zaenen, A. (eds.), *Tense and aspect. Syntax and Semantics* **14**. New York: Academic Press. 145–175.

Klein, W. (1992) The present perfect puzzle. *Language* **68**. 525–552.

Lyons, J. (1977) *Semantics*. 2 volumes. Cambridge University Press.

McCawley, J. D. (1971) Tense and time reference in English. In Fillmore, C. J. and Langendoen, D. T. (eds.), *Studies in linguistic semantics*. New York: Holt, Rinehart and Winston. 97–113.

McCoard, R. W. (1978) *The English perfect: tense-choice and pragmatic inferences*. Amsterdam: North-Holland.

Palmer, F. R. (1974) *The English verb*. London: Longman.

(1979) Why auxiliaries are not main verbs. *Lingua* **47**. 1–25.

(1988) *The English verb*. 2nd edition. London: Longman.

Reichenbach, H. (1947) *Elements of symbolic logic*. New York: Free Press and London: Collier-Macmillan.

Smith, N. V. (1981) Grammaticality, time and tense. *Phil. Trans. R. Soc. Lond.* B. **259**. 253–265.

7 'How does this sentence interpret?' The semantics of English mediopassives[1]

ANDREW ROSTA

1 Introduction

In the 1946 film of *The Big Sleep*, when Humphrey Bogart is being threatened with being slapped he says: *I don't slap so good this time of the evening.* The *slap* in this utterance is not the normal active version of the verb but, rather, is a mediopassive version. Such verbs are what this article is about. The traditional view of them is that they are 'active in form but passive in sense' (Nesfield 1898); accordingly, Jespersen (1961) calls them *activo-passive* (as do Bresnan 1982b and Levin 1982). Other terms for the construction are *middle voice* (e.g. Andrews 1982), *middle* (e.g. Bresnan 1982a), which is currently the standard term, and *mediopassive* (e.g. Bresnan 1982c), which I have preferred to use on the grounds that the construction is intimately related to passive, and the term middle has so many different meanings in linguistics.[2]

The observations made in this article about the semantics are relevant beyond the confines of any particular theory. But since the formal analysis is conducted within the framework of Word Grammar (WG; see Hudson 1990), I shall offer a one-paragraph guide to some notable features of the theory. The syntax is based on dependency (asymmetrical relations between pairs of words), and the grammar is monostratal – i.e. there is only one level of representation, so the structure of an utterance is only and entirely the surface structure of the utterance and the meaning thereof. In the approach taken in this article, the monostratality of syntax is carried over into word-formation: so, for example, there is no level of representation at which Bogart's *slap*, quoted above, is not a mediopassive; it has no derivational history. Mediopassive is, like 'noun' and 'verb' a category of words. Words themselves are acts of uttering, and are the basic units of utterances. 'Words' in the sense of lexemes, or entries in the lexicon are themselves, again like 'noun', 'verb' and 'mediopassive', categories of words. Bogart's *slap*, for example, belongs to the categories 'verb', SLAP (the lexeme) and 'mediopassive'. The mediopassive category is contained within the verb category.[3]

The membership of the mediopassive category is open: a verb of any lexeme can be a mediopassive providing that it has the appropriate syntactic structure (see below). This is in contrast to, say, the category of modals; a verb's membership of the modal category must be stated explicitly in the grammar. Actual usage of mediopassives is further constrained by their semantics; mediopassives with meanings that are contrary to what the speaker wishes to express are, of course, unlikely to get uttered. This is the sort of view I understand Pinker (1989) to hold when he says of lexical rules:

> Because a rule takes a semantic structure as input and alters it in particular ways (adding, suppressing or redescribing arguments), the changes it tries to effect can interact with the semantic structure that the verb has to begin with. Some semantic changes, when applied to some verb meanings, may produce a new verb meaning that just doesn't hang together. For such verbs the rule is avoided; that is the equivalent of the rule being constrained by a semantic criterion.

All I would add to this is that the verb meanings in question are not extrasentential but intrasentential – i.e. modified by the referents of the dependents of the verb. Halliday (1967) seems to hold similar views with respect to mediopassives and other alternations in complementation. It is common practice, however, to judge data as if pragmatic anomalies lead to ungrammaticality; this practice I wish to avoid.

It could be the case – though it happens not to be – that the semantic structure of verbs, which is prescribed by the grammar, renders them ineligible to have mediopassive versions; in this case the grammar would generate mediopassives of only a limited class of verbs. This is the view put forward by Levin and Rapoport (1988), who claim, following Hale and Keyser (1987), that mediopassives are grammatical only if the verb's sense is a caused change of state, the crucial part of the claim being that CAUSE must be present in the Lexical-Conceptual Structure of the verb: their grammaticality judgements show *split, cut* and *fry* are in, and *paint, save* and *hit* are out. This claim cannot be right, for it surely predicts that *The book reads well* should be unacceptable.[4]

It is necessary to state the analysis of the syntax of mediopassives that I shall be using for this exegesis of their semantics. Unfortunately, shortage of space allows for only the most cursory mention of the syntactic analysis and for no justification of it whatever. The feature of the syntax that is crucial for the semantics is that the subject of the mediopassive be also either a complement (e.g. an object) of the mediopassive or a complement of a subordinate of the mediopassive (e.g. *dissent* in *It permits of dissent*, where *dissent* is object of a prepositional object (*of*) of the verb). ('Subordinate of X' is defined recursively as a dependent of X or a subordinate of a dependent of X; so in *pictures of her* both *of* and *her* are subordinates of *pictures*, and *her* is also a subordinate of *of*.) All speakers have mediopassives whose subject is also their object; other speakers allow a much wider syntactic range, more like that of passives.[5] (1a–b) give some illustrative dependency graphs (*o* = object, *s* = subject).

(1) ←— o & s —— ‹
a. The book was read quickly.
←— o & s – ‹
b. The book read quickly.
←— s — ‹
c. Sophy read quickly.

In the passive example, (1a), and the mediopassive example, (1b), the category 'subject of *read*' is equated with the category 'object of *read*': *The book* is both the subject and object of *read*. By contrast, in (1c) *Sophy* is only the subject of *read*, and not its object.

These points of syntax are relevant in so far as they serve to explain why *letters* in *Referenced letters file easily* gets understood as if it were the object of *file*: the reason is that *letters* actually is the object. This is explained in section 2. Section 3 looks at the interpretation of the 'demoted' subject, and section 4 at the interpretation of the 'promoted' subject.[6] Section 5 explains why mediopassives usually collocate with adverbs or auxiliaries. Section 6 explains why mediopassives are usually generic and/or stative. Section 7 summarises the (highly parsimonious) grammar of mediopassives.

2 The semantics of subject demotion and promotion

(2a–b) are some of the default semantic rules. The sense of a verb has an *er* argument.[7] The *er* of the sense of word X is the argument of the sense that is usually expressed by the active subject of X when X is active; for most verbs the *er* is an agent. By default the *er* of the sense of word X is the referent of the subject of X.[8]

(2) a. The referent of the subject of every word is the *er* of the sense of that word.
b. The *er* of every sense is the agent of that sense.

To see how this machinery works, consider (3):

(3) Sophy protested.

The grammar tells us that the *er* of the sense of *protest* is the agent of the sense of *protest*. Since the referent of the subject of a word is the *er* of that word's sense, the referent of the subject of *protest* is the agent. And finally, since the subject of *protest* in (3) is *Sophy*, the referent of *Sophy*, i.e. Sophy, is the agent of the sense of *protest*, whose sense therefore is 'protests by Sophy'. The chain of equations is as follows:

agent of sense of X = *er* of sense of X = referent of subject of X

I will explain now how mediopassives (including passives) fit into this picture. First of all, there is the relationship between the *er* and the referent of the subject. In (4a) the pill is the swallowee, but almost certainly not the swallower (*er*) – pills don't swallow themselves. In (4b), Sophy is the scrubbee, but could also be the scrubber (*er*).

(4) a. The pill swallows easily.
b. Sophy scrubbed clean.

What this shows is that the default identification of the *er* (agent) and the subject referent is optional in the case of mediopassives; the *er* of a mediopassive's sense can – but needn't – be the subject referent.[9] (5) expresses this:

(5) Not every *er* of the sense of every mediopassive is the referent of the subject of that mediopassive.

Next to be explained is how the pill and Sophy in (4a–b) get understood to be the swallowee and the scrubee. Taking *Scaffolding dismantles* as an example, the grammar tells us that the patient of the sense of *dismantle* is the referent of the object of *dismantle*. And since here the object is the subject, the referent of the subject is the patient.[10]

It is important to realise that reference to the 'referent of subject of X' can still succeed as a way of identifying an argument of X's sense even if X has no subject. If the grammar equates the category 'referent of subject of X' with some other category, e.g. '*er* of sense of X', then 'referent of subject of X' is simply another way of saying '*er* of sense of X'. In the case of the utterance *Halt!*, addressed to Sophy, Sophy is the *er* (agent, theme or whatever) of the sense of *halt*, and because the *er* (of a non-mediopassive) is equated with the referent of the subject, it follows that Sophy is the referent of any subject of this utterance of *halt*, even though the category 'subject of [this utterance of *halt*]' is empty. This matters for examples like (6a–b) (and for subjectless verbs in general). Here the mediopassive has no subject.

(6) a. *Steering* well while turning corners is this car's strength.
b. *Dismantling* awkwardly is this scaffolding's weakness.

In (6a) the 'referent of the subject' of *turning*, which is equated with the theme of turning, is the 'referent of the subject' of the mediopassive, which, because the subject of the mediopassive is equated with the object of the mediopassive, is equated with the patient. In (6b) the *er* of the sense of *awkwardly* is the 'referent of the subject' of the mediopassive, i.e. the patient.

3 The interpretation of the *er* (the implicit agent)

Levin (1982) claims that the agent in a mediopassive construction is quantified by 'a generic quantifier, Q, which is intended to be read "people in general" or "one" '. She suggests that *This book reads easily* may be paraphrased by *People, in general, read this book easily.* Levin's claim is open to a number of objections. Gillian Brown has pointed out (p.c.) that rather than meaning 'people in general', *one* means 'a category whose prototypical member is the speaker'. And Fellbaum (1985) suggests that an apter paraphrase is *People, in general, can read this book easily.* Unlike Fellbaum's, Levin's paraphrase implies that there are specific occasions on which the book is read easily. While both paraphrases may be appropriate in the right context, the meaning of Fellbaum's is the more common with mediopassives. But the main objection to Levin is that what she (and Fellbaum (1985) and Fagan (1988)) says about the interpretation of the agent is false: the *er* need not be interpreted as generic, arbitrary, non-specific or whatever – it can be specific, as in (7a–b).[11]

(7) a. The car handles smoothly when Sophy drives it.
b. Odes to herself write easily when she's in a narcissistic mood.

It is generally true that unexpressed arguments may be interpreted as non-specific, but equally, they may be interpreted as specific. At any rate, none of this is peculiar to mediopassives. In (8a–c) *kissing* is not a mediopassive: in (8a) the agent of the sense of *kissing* would tend to be understood as non-specific; In (8b) the agent would tend to be understood as specific; in (8c) the agent clearly is specific.

(8) a. Kissing the stone is forbidden.
b. Kissing the stone cured him.
c. Kissing himself cured him.

4 The interpretation of the subject

Unlike (9a), (9b) is not (virtually) synonymous with (9c).

(9) a. The book is read easily.
b. The book reads easily.
c. Someone reads the book easily.

This is because a semantic constraint applies to the referent of the subject of a mediopassive: as Lakoff (1977) has noticed, the referent of the subject must be primarily responsible for the sense of the mediopassive.[12] I shall call this primarily responsible participant the *Archagonist* of the mediopassive's sense. The relevant grammatical rule is (10).

(10) The referent of the subject of a mediopassive is the archagonist of the sense of that mediopassive.

The term archagonist alludes to Talmy's (1985) theory of force dynamics, in which various kinds of causation and related concepts like letting, preventing, trying, failing, succeeding, etc. are analysed in terms of structured interactions between the opposing forces of two participants, the *Agonist* and the *Antagonist*. It is within a framework like Talmy's that the semantic content of the archagonist relation might best be explicated. But here I shall simply point out the difference between an archagonist and a causer. In *Sophy melted the ice* the subject referent is a causer: Sophy's action is a sufficient condition for the ice to melt, but need not be a necessary condition; *Sophy melted the ice* does not entail that had Sophy never existed the ice would not have got melted. In *The book sold well* the subject referent is an archagonist: the properties of the book are a necessary condition for the book to sell well, but need not be (and typically are not) a sufficient condition; if it were not for the properties of the book, it would not sell well, but even though the book has the properties it has it will not sell well unless some other participant (an agent) gets involved in getting the book to sell well.

Van Oosten (1977) suggests that (11a–b) are counterexamples to the claim that the subject referent is archagonist.

(11) a. A: You didn't leave enough of a margin on the bottom of the page.
B: No, it just photocopied too low.
b. You think you understand the difference between the three voices in Greek and how to translate each one but then once in a while you come across a verb that won't translate right.

Clearly the page is not literally responsible for its being photocopied too low, and a Greek verb does not literally determine whether there exists an English one to translate it. But the rhetoric of the examples deliberately suggests otherwise. In both cases the speaker is faced with an adverse circumstance, and seeks, as we do, to blame someone or something (other than themself). The very use of the mediopassive in (11a–b) serves to pass the blame, by imputing archagonism to page and verb.

Lakoff (1977) suggests that primary responsibility is one of the prototypical features of the meaning of subjects, along with such features as volition and control, and he uses this to provide a functional-cognitive explanation for the mediopassive construction: the referent of the subject of a mediopassive is expressed by the subject because it conforms to the semantic prototype for subjects. Van Oosten (1977) argues along the same lines. We might go along with this as a functional-cognitive explanation for why the mediopassive construction exists in the first place, but Lakoff's and van Oosten's proposals do not apply to the formal grammar of mediopassives, for whereas, as (12a–c) show, the subject of a non-mediopassive does not have to have primary responsibility, the referent of the subject of a mediopassive *must* be primarily responsible, but need not be volitional or have any other feature of the subjecthood prototype.

(12) a. Sophy hit the ground, after Arthur pushed her over.
b. The stone dropped.
c. She suffered the tedium.

The mediopassive subject referent is primarily responsible not simply because it is a subject referent but rather because the grammar explicitly says the mediopassive subject referent is primarily responsible.

It is commonly said (e.g. by Lakoff 1977, van Oosten 1977, Fellbaum 1985) that the referent of the subject of a mediopassive must be a Patient. Certainly most mediopassives' subjects' referents are Patients, but this is simply because the subject is an object, and most objects' referents are Patients; there is no requirement that the mediopassive subject referent be a Patient.[13] Usually Patient is treated as one of a set of roles that includes Source, Goal, Location, etc. Vague though the notion of patienthood is, it would usually be assumed not to encompass the referents of the italicised words in (13a–e). These referents are, unlike patients, not typically understood to be affected. Moreover, they all qualify better as Location, Path, Goal, etc. Yet (13a–e) all have mediopassive paraphrases, (14a–e).

(13) a. Sophy hid under *the bed*.
b. Sophy crossed *the bridge*.
c. Sophy approached *London*.
d. Sophy entered *the house*.
e. Sophy forded *the river*.

(14) a. The bed hides under easily.
b. The bridge crosses easily.
c. London approaches easily, when there's not much traffic.

d. The house entered easily, once the barricades were removed.
e. The river fords easily.

For those who think that a word (or its referent) may have only one semantic role, (15a–d) would serve as further evidence that the mediopassive subject referent need not be a Patient. In (15a), *paint* and *the ceiling* must have distinct roles, for otherwise (15b) would not be sylleptically odd. Yet (15c–d), whose subjects must have different roles, both make good mediopassives.

(15) a. Sophy sprayed the paint on the ceiling.
b. !The paint and the ceiling were sprayed.
c. The paint sprayed easily.
d. The ceiling sprayed easily.

While it is possible that some extremely watered-down notion of patient might cover all subjects of mediopassives, it is quite unnecessary to invoke such a notion: the fact that the subject's referent is the object's referent and the archagonist is sufficient to account for the interpretation of mediopassives.[14]

Mediopassives form an acceptability gradient determined by the oddity of construing the subject referent as the archagonist.[15] For example, (16a) is odder than (16b) because whereas the car might reasonably be thought of as being more responsible than the driver for the easy starting, contexts are rare in which the car is more responsible than the seer for the easy seeing.

(16) a. !The car sees easily.
b. The car starts easily.

The same explanation goes for (17a–b) (from Lakoff 1977). (17b) is more normal than (17a) because bean curd is more likely to be archagonist of digestion than of eating, since the digester has less control than the eater.

(17) a. !Bean curd eats easily.
b. Bean curd digests easily.

Our acceptability judgements on (16)–(17) are based on the relative likelihood of there being contexts in which the referents of utterances are plausible. But, of course, with enough imaginative ingenuity a plausible context can be found for any mediopassive. For example, Keith Brown has observed (p.c.) that in contexts such as a rose or wine catalogue, utterances like (18a–b) would be quite likely.

(18) a. This rose prunes easily.
b. This wine drinks well.

In this sort of context, where there is implicit or explicit comparison between roses or wines, the standard of comparison by which the senses of *easily* and *well* are measured changes so that the senses of the (18a–b) mediopassives become 'pruning easily relative to the ease of pruning the average rose' and 'drinking well relative to the drinking of the average wine'. Therefore, although in general a rose is an unlikely archagonist of pruning, it is a very likely archagonist of 'pruning more easily than the average rose'. By this argument, then, (19a–b) should be relatively less odd than (16a) and (17a).

(19) a. Bean curd eats more easily than chicken bones (do).
b. The Victory of Samothrace, at the top of a flight of steps, sees more easily than the Mona Lisa, which is always surrounded by a crowd.

Plausible contexts cannot be found for examples like (20a–b) (after Roberts (1986)).

(20) a. !Tabs keep on Sophy easily.
b. !Our support throws behind liberal candidates easily.

In (20a) the subject is empty of meaning, so the subject referent cannot be the archagonist. As for (20b), *to throw support* means 'to support', and therefore in this idiomatic phrase *throw* and *support* arguably refer to the same thing: in this case, (20b) is claiming that the support is the archagonist of itself, which is impossible. Not only can the subject referents not be archagonists – they also cannot be responsible to any degree. We can see this from (21a–b); the subject referent of a *tough*-movement adjective need not be an archagonist, but it must be partly responsible for the sense of the adjective.

(21) a. !Tabs are easy to keep on Sophy.
b. !Our support is easy to throw behind liberal candidates.

Note that subject referents that make possible but improbable archagonists are OK as subject referents of *tough*-movement adjectives, as in (22a–b); it is relatively less improbable that the subject referents are only partly responsible.

(22) a. The car is easy to see.
b. Bean curd is easy to eat.

For the reasons explained, the vast majority of mediopassives generated by the grammar will be unacceptable, on the grounds of mismatches between the mediopassive's meaning and our understanding of the world. Though the vast majority of all sentences generated by the grammar would of course be unacceptable for the same reason, the fraction of mediopassives that are normal is smaller than the fraction of (say) passives that are normal.

5 The collocational peculiarities of mediopassives

Mediopassives often are complements of an auxiliary verb or have certain adjuncts like *easily* and *slowly* (Dixon 1991 gives a list of these items). The grammar in no way demands the presence of such words; they simply turn up so frequently because the contribution of their meaning to the mediopassive's sense makes it more plausible that a non-*er* is archagonist. Consider *The book read quickly/easily*: that the reader could read the book at all is most likely contingent on properties of the reader, such as literacy, but that reading was quick or easy is relatively more likely to be contingent on properties of the book, such as clarity and liveliness of style.

If there is no adjunct restricting the sense of a mediopassive, the subject referent is archagonist of the unrestricted sense. So whereas (23a) means, roughly, 'she was primarily responsible for the occurrence of a good interview with her', (23b) means (it is mediopassive) 'she was primarily responsible for the occurrence of an interview with her'. Obviously, given the way interviews happen, the former circumstance is more likely than the latter, which is why (23a) would be more frequent and normal than (23b).

(23) a. She interviewed well.
b. She interviewed.

The more newsworthy adjunctless mediopassives are, the less odd they are. (23b) would be more normal if it were an answer to *Did she interview?* The newsworthiness of adjunctless mediopassives is often indicated by emphatic auxiliaries, as in (24a), contrastive stress (as Roberts (1986) notes), as in (24b), and other kinds of prosodic (and syntactic) prominence, as in (24c–d).

(24) a. The car *will* steer, after all.
b. These bureaucrats *bribe*.
c. Boy did that mountain climb!
d. She sure did interview.

These are newsworthy partly because the referent of the mediopassive is contrary to prior expectations, or occurs to a degree in excess of prior expectations. (24a), for example, might be said of a car whose steering mechanism had been believed to be broken; (24c) suggests that more climbing went on than might have been expected, and (24d) might be said of an abnormally cooperative interviewee.

Mediopassives that are complements of negative auxiliaries, as in (25a–e), are common because they are often newsworthy. (25a–e) might plausibly be uttered in contexts in which we expect that wool can be plaited, people consent to be interviewed, constraints can be violated, rulers can be impeached, and cars can be steered.

(25) a. Wet wool doesn't plait.
b. She wouldn't interview.
c. That sort of constraint doesn't violate.
d. Dictators don't impeach.
e. The car won't steer.

While such utterances as (25a–e) may be understood simply as denials of some proposition (e.g. 'It is not the case that the car will steer'), they will tend to be interpreted as if the subject referent is the archagonist of the sense of both the mediopassive and the auxiliary – that is, the subject referent is primarily responsible for the non-occurrence of some situation.[16] This explains why the negative auxiliary is often *won't*, as in (25e): the subject referent of *won't* is often a refuser. If one refuses to do something, one is the archagonist of that something's non-occurrence. Perhaps it is for this reason that (25e), with a mediopassive, is more normal than *The car won't be steered*, with a passive. Note, incidentally, that *refuse* itself may be used: *Her hair refuses to comb*.

Mediopassives not collocated with adjuncts or auxiliaries or prosodically marked can still be normal (as Fellbaum 1985 and Fagan 1988 note), provided they are newsworthy but not contrary to prior expectations. Examples are (26a–c).

(26) a. The object promotes.
b. The tripod packs away.
c. The dress zips up.

For the reasons explained above, *easily*, like many adverbs, tends to make mediopassives less odd, and hence it is something of a convention to use it in examples of mediopassives in linguistic discussion. This practice does carry a risk, though, since if a mediopassive with *easily* as its adjunct is deemed odd, the cause of the oddity may be the adjunct rather than the mediopassive construction itself. This happens with (27a–d), for example, which Keyser and Roeper (1984) say they find inexplicably ungrammatical.[17]

(27) a. '*' French acquires easily.
b. '*' The arguments assume easily.
c. '*' The answer learns easily.
d. '*' The answer knows easily.

To the extent that (27a–d) are odd, their oddity is due in part to the subject referents being less plausible archagonists than the agents (or cognizers) are. For instance, if one feels that it is largely the properties of the acquirer that are a necessary condition for the easy acquisition of French, then one will balk at (27a), which makes French and not the acquirer the archagonist. (28a–d), where the subject referent is not an archagonist, ought to be somewhat more acceptable than (27a–d), and they are.

(28) a. French is easy to acquire.
b. The arguments are easy to assume.
c. The answer is easy to learn.
d. The answer is easy to know (– it's written on every billboard in town).

But there are other problems with (27)–(28) which are not the mediopassives' fault: (29a–d), active versions of (27a–d), are also odd to a lesser or greater extent.

(29) a. !She acquired French easily.
b. !She assumed the arguments easily.
c. !She knew the answer easily.
d. !She learnt the answer easily.

The oddity here is that *easily* implies the possibility of resistance or difficulty, yet we tend to think of acquiring a language, assuming an argument, knowing an answer, and, to a lesser extent, learning an answer as rather spontaneous, unimpeded processes.[18] There is thus a mismatch between the semantics of (27)–(29) and our expectations of how the world is, and as usual this results in oddity. Similar examples are easy to find; (30a) is odd; (30b) is normal only on an interpretation where the splinter is removed.

(30) a. The light glowed easily.
b. The splinter came out easily.

If *easily* in (27a), (28a) and (29a) is replaced, the acceptability should increase; cf. (31a–c).

(31) a. French acquires more rapidly than Esperanto when children are under six.
b. French is pleasant to acquire.
c. She acquired French rapidly.

6 Genericity and dynamicity

Mediopassives usually (or, some claim, always) have 'habitual' aspect: this means that they refer not to an individual event but to a generic event, i.e. some category of events. Reference to a category implies (though doesn't entail) the existence of members of the category: *The five-legged frog is not yet extinct* implies that there are some tokens of a type of frog that has five legs; *Sophy writes poetry* implies that there are some individual events that are tokens of an event type, the category of events of Sophy writing poetry. A category may be linked to another concept either collectively, applying to the category as a whole (I shall notate this *category*^{C}), or distributively, applying to every member of the category[19] (I shall notate this *category*^{D}). In *Sophy jogged for an hour a day for five years*, the *er* of the referent of *for (an hour a day)* is the sense^{D} of *jogs*, so it specifies the duration of each event of jogging, while the *er* of the referent of *for (five years)* is the sense^{C} of *jogs*, so it specifies the duration of the category of Sophy's hour-long jogs. In *congregations that are numerous*, where the sense of *congregations* is a category (specifically, a set) of congregations (which themselves are sets), the *er* of the referent of *numerous* is the sense^{D} of *congregations*, so it means that each congregation is numerous. By contrast, in *numerous congregations* the *er* of the referent of *numerous* can be the sense^{C} of congregations, so it means many congregations. This collective-distributive distinction is the same as Smith's (1975) distinction between class generics and individuated generics. (32a) is a class generic; the category Dodo^{C} is the *er* of extinction. (32b) is an individuated generic; the category Dodo^{D} is the *er* of fig eating.[20]

(32) a. John studies *the dodo*, which is extinct.
b. John studies *the dodo*, which ate figs.

The collective-distributive distinction relates to mediopassives in an interesting way. Consider *The dress zips up*. In a context like (33a) we take the subject referent to be the archagonist of the verb's sense^{D} – i.e. of each event of zipping – so it means 'it is often/regularly the case that the dress is the archagonist of it being zipped up'. But in a context like (33b) we take the subject referent to be the archagonist of the verb's sense^{C} – i.e. of the category of zippings rather than of each zipping – so it means 'the dress is the archagonist of it being potentially the case that the dress is zipped up'.[21]

(33) a. The dress often/regularly zips up.
b. The dress doesn't button up: it zips up.

The collective interpretation given to (33b) is, of course, the more usual. The archagonist of each event of zipping is the agent, not the dress. Rather, as Dixon (1976, 1991), Lakoff (1977), van Oosten (1977) and Fagan (1988) note, the ability of the dress to be zipped up is contingent on properties of the dress, i.e. its having a zip, rather than, say, buttons: the dress is primarily responsible for the existence of a category of zippings up of the dress.

It is not surprising that so many mediopassives are generic. One reason is that if the properties of, for example, some car are such that it permits driving without much effort from the driver, it is likely that these properties are fairly constant, applying generally to any event in which the car is driven. To refer to such a situation we naturally use that form of mediopassive in which the subject referent is archagonist of a generic situation^{C}. A second reason is that it is easier to construe a non-*er* as the archagonist of a generic event^{C} than of an individual event. Consider for example *The silk weaves smoothly*: it is easier to see the silk as archagonist of the category weaving-smoothly^{C}, being therefore primarily responsible for there potentially being an event in which the silk is woven smoothly, than to see the silk as archagonist of each event. There is a gradient of probability here: the silk can be seen as the archagonist of each event of weaving, but this is unlikely, for the weaver is better qualified as an archagonist; or the silk can be seen as the archagonist of each event of weaving smoothly (with the focus on the smoothness), and this is less unlikely; or the silk can be archagonist of the category weaving-smoothly^{C}, and this is most likely. To repeat, the silk is less likely to be seen as the archagonist amid the force dynamics of an individual event, and is more likely to be seen as the archagonist of that type of event being potential. As another (non-mediopassive) example, consider the slogan *Guns don't kill people – people kill people*. In any particular event of murder by gun the archagonist is the person using the gun; the killer can't put the blame on the gun unless it went off spontaneously. But many people agree that the blame for the existence of a category of murders by gun can reasonably be attributed to the existence of guns (and only secondarily to human depravity or whatever).

Although, as I have just explained, the normal workings of pragmatics will tend to lead to mediopassives being generic, if the only reason for the prevalence of genericity with mediopassives is pragmatic we should still expect mediopassives to be able to refer to individual events. In the literature on mediopassives there has developed a consensus that mediopassives referring to events are ungrammatical; see e.g. Keyser and Roeper (1984), Fellbaum (1985), Fagan (1988), and Roberts (1986), who offers a Government-Binding theoretic syntactic explanation for this 'fact'.[22] There are four possibilities for the semantic constraints the grammar imposes on the referent of a mediopassive:

I The referent of a mediopassive needn't be generic and may be dynamic.[23]
II The referent of a mediopassive must be generic but may be dynamic.
III The referent of a mediopassive needn't be generic but mustn't be dynamic.
IV The referent of a mediopassive must be generic and mustn't be dynamic.

Since individual events are (by definition) dynamic and not generic, any lect for which mediopassives referring to individual events are acceptable is of the liberal type I, while lects of types II–IV would reject such mediopassives as those in (34a–l) ((34j–l) from Keyser and Roeper 1984, with their judgements quoted).

(34) a. That curry digested surprisingly easily last night.
b. The Eiffel Tower erected easily.
c. After much bargaining, the haunted house sold.
d. This passage just isn't translating.
e. Now the floor's waxing nicely.
f. Bureaucrats are bribing left right and centre.
g. *Crime and punishment* was reading slowly, as Sophy grew ever more bored.
h. Sophy saw three goals score easily.
i. We filmed that bureaucrat bribing all too easily.
j. '?' Yesterday, the mayor bribed easily, according to the newspaper.
k. '*' The chicken is killing.
l. '*' I saw bureaucrats bribe easily.

Like Keyser and Roeper, Bresnan (1982b) finds progressive mediopassives ungrammatical, but it would be surprising if they genuinely rejected the following convincing examples from Nesfield and Wood (1964).

(35) a. The drums are beating.
b. The book is printing.
c. The film is showing at the Scala.
d. While my baggage was loading. . . [from A. W. Kinglake]
e. In the kitchen dinner was preparing. [from Thomas Hardy]

Although I find (34) and (35) fully acceptable, some speakers, to judge from reports in the literature, apparently do not. It is possible that in some lects the natural tendency for mediopassives to be generic has been grammaticalised (i.e. incorporated into the semantics), so that the referent of a mediopassive is a category rather than an individual, and the subject referent is archagonist of the referent[C.24] It is further possible that since mediopassives tend to be generic, and since generics tend to be non-dynamic, this non-dynamicity has been grammaticalised, so that the referent of a mediopassive must be non-dynamic, but since in general generics can be dynamic, it would be rather surprising if mediopassives could not be dynamic. The verbs in (36a–d) have generic referents; in (36c–d) the verb referents are also dynamic (the referent of a progressive must be dynamic; cf. Žegarac (1989, 1990, 1991, 1992)).

(36) a. She lives in London.
b. She smokes.
c. She is living in London.
d. She is smoking less these days.

Speakers who accept (37a) but reject (37b) must have lects of type III or IV.[25]

(37) a The car handles well.
b. The car is handling better these days.

If lects of type III or IV exist, they can be distinguished by (38a–c), which (it is intended) contain mediopassives whose referents are neither generic nor dynamic. Type III lects could accept them; type IV lects could not.

(38) a. As a pet, my goldfish owns more cheaply than my leopard.
b. He finds that, as his friend, Sophy knows more intimately than Euphrosyne.
c. For Sophy, this political proposition believes with more certainty than that religious one.

I have not come across any speakers of type III or IV. I have found speakers who find (34a–l) odder than clearly generic mediopassives, but at present it is not clear whether they therefore have type II: it remains a possibility, for future investigation, that these speakers simply have trouble construing a non-*er* as the archagonist of anything but a generic category of event.

7 Conclusion

Much discussed though it is, and complex though it superficially appears to be, the mediopassive construction analyses not easily, perhaps, but certainly simply. Mediopassives have just three properties that distinguish them from actives.[26]

I Lect 1: The subject of a mediopassive is the object of the mediopassive.
Lect 2: The subject of a mediopassive is whatever can be the subject of a passive – i.e. the object of the mediopassive or some other subordinate of the mediopassive, determined by principles as yet unknown.

II Not every referent of the subject of a mediopassive is the *er* of the sense of the mediopassive.

III The referent of the subject is the archagonist of the sense of the mediopassive.

Even these properties are not all unique to mediopassives: I also applies partly (for Lect 1) or entirely (for Lect 2) to passives. II also applies to passives.[27] Only III is unique to mediopassives, and it is the workings of this property that, as I have shown, suffice to account for the peculiarities of their collocational behaviour, their interpretation and their tendency to be odd outside a relatively narrow range of contexts. If any verb satisfies requirements I–III, it can have a mediopassive version.

Notes

1. I thank Sid Greenbaum, Dick Hudson, Bas Aarts, Nik Gisborne, Chuck Meyer, Yibin Ni, Itzchak Schlesinger and Vlad Žegarac for helpful discussion and/or comments.
2. See Trask (1993) on the meanings of *middle*; in the terminology of Quirk et al. (1985) *middle verbs* are ones like *lack* that do not passivise. Rarer terms for the mediopassive construction include *passival* (attributed by Trask to Sweet 1898), and *Patient Subject Construction* (van Oosten 1977 and Fellbaum 1985). According to Trask *mediopassive* was current in the nineteenth century and revived by Grady (1965).
3. Since most properties of mediopassives also apply to passives, we might profitably consider that the mediopassive category itself contains the passive category, so all passives are mediopassives. As far as this article is concerned, nothing hinges on this.
4. Levin and Rapoport's judgements are explicable only if their lects surprisingly lack mediopassives altogether. This would explain why *paint, save* and *hit* are out. *Split* and *fry* could be in in their non-causative 'ergative' form. (The 'ergative' class contains verbs that can have a causative form, e.g. *move* – *The chair moved* vs. *She moved the chair*.) Though *cut* is not usually considered to be ergative, on the grounds that its sense (unlike that of undisputed ergatives) entails some causing agent or instrument, there is evidence presented in section 4 that it is ergative.
5. So for all speakers *Paper cups discard easily* is grammatical, and for some but not all speakers *This cup disposes of easily* is grammatical.
6. The terms *demotion* and *promotion* are borrowed from Relational Grammar (see e.g. Blake 1990), but are here used purely for descriptive convenience and do not imply any transformation relating different stages of derivation. The idea is that the active subject is demoted in the passive, and the active object (or whatever) is promoted to passive subject.
7. *Er* is formed from the suffix in e.g. *receiver, runner, striker* and is meant to connote a notion like *primary argument*. (The analysis and terminology are different from Hudson's 1990.)
8. WG holds that virtually all words have a sense and a referent. This includes verbs. So *kiss*, for example, always refers to an event of kissing, irrespective of whether it is a noun or a verb. Generally, the sense of a word incorporates the

referents of its dependents, so the sense of *kiss children* is not just a category of events of kissing, but rather is a category of events of kissing children.

9. In Rosta (1992) I claimed (in effect) that Lakoff's (1970, 1977) *willingly* test for underlying subjects suggested that mediopassives have no *er*. The argument was that, as (i) shows, the *er* of *willingly* (the willing entity) is either the referent of the subject of its head (i.e. Edgar) or the *er* of the sense of its head (i.e. Euphrosyne). But, I claimed, in (ii) only Sophy and not her seducer can be willing, and therefore the mediopassive's sense must not have an *er* (though it still has an agent). (Lakoff (1977) and van Oosten (1977) make the same judgement on pairs like (i)–(ii).) And I also suggested that this would explain why the *by* that refers to the *er* of the sense of a passive can't occur with mediopassives (**He seduced by her*).

   (i) Edgar was seduced willingly by Euphrosyne.
   (ii) Sophy seduces willingly.

   In fact my (1992) observations about (ii) are incorrect: in (ii) the *er* of the sense *willingly* may be the seducer; this is a bit more obvious for the italicised adverbs in (iii):

   (iii) Sophy seduces *rakishly/lustily/manfully* easily.

   As for the restriction on *by*, this is, in Hudson's (1990) analysis, a word that is, by stipulation, only ever an adjunct of passives (or, we might add, of nouns).

10. Note that nothing hinges on the role Patient. If the referent of the object of *dismantle* were an experiencer, then the referent of the subject of mediopassive *dismantle* would be an experiencer.
11. (7a) was suggested by Deirdre Wilson (p.c.). (7b) is adapted from an example in Stroik (1992).
12. And cf. Erades (1950: 156) who says: 'the construction in question is only found when the subject is represented as having certain inherent qualities which promote, hamper or prevent the realisation of the idea expressed by the predicate'.
13. I take the Patient to be a participant that is on the receiving end of transmitted force, much as in the system of Jackendoff (1987, 1990).
14. These arguments apply equally well to Massam's (1987) assertion that the promoted complement must be affected. The evidence given here refutes that view, and the data she seeks to account for (e.g. the badness of *The mountains see easily*) are accounted for by the ramifications of the presence of the archagonist relation, as explained below.
15. They also form another gradient determined by the plausibility of taking the verb to be active rather than mediopassive. So though in *Sophy understands easily* Sophy makes a good archagonist on a mediopassive interpretation (i.e. she is easy to understand), the (equally plausible) active reading (she understands people/things easily) is more salient, doubtless because we encounter actives so much more often than mediopassives.
16. Note that auxiliaries whose complement is not a mediopassive may also be interpreted as if the subject referent is the archagonist of the sense of both the mediopassive and the auxiliary. In (i) the complement of *didn't* is a

mediopassive; in (ii) it isn't. But both (i) and (ii) may be read with the meaning of (iii), with Sophy being primarily responsible for her not being provoked.

(i) Sophy didn't provoke.
(ii) Sophy didn't let herself be provoked.
(iii) Sophy resisted being provoked.

17. '*' indicates a quoted grammaticality judgement.
18. In normal usage, languages are *acquired* by children, but by adults they are, with a great deal of effort and difficulty, *learnt*. Though learning can involve effort and difficulty (e.g. learning multiplication tables), learning an answer, as in (29d), is likely to be spontaneous and unimpeded, being simply the inception of knowing the answer.
19. With distributive linking, properties apply to every member by default, but there may be exceptions: I intend *every* to be understood here as a generic quantifier rather than as a universal quantifier in the strict sense.
20. Cf. e.g. Heyer (1985), Jackendoff (1983), Ni (in preparation), for discussion of related matters.
21. By analogy we might expect *Sophy melts ice* to be ambiguous between a distributive reading, in which Sophy causes each event of melting, and a collective reading, in which Sophy causes the category of events of melting. In fact, only the distributive reading is possible. This must be due to the grammar of causatives rather than to pragmatics, since a collective reading is available for *The deity made birds fly.*
22. Fagan (1988) holds that the mediopassive is used to ascribe properties to the subject referent, and that ascribed properties are stative (i.e. non-dynamic; see next note), as in the case of *Sophy is tall.* But some properties, such as the referents of *nude* and *angry* can be dynamic, as (i) shows. The xcomp (predicative complement) of *see* must have a dynamic referent (which is why (ii)–(iii) are odd; cf. Bolinger 1973, Dowty 1972; see also Aarts, this volume).

›—x—›
←s–‹
(i) She saw him angry/nude.
›————x—›
‹——s——‹
(ii) !She saw the statue nude.
›—x—›
←s–‹
(iii) !She saw him tall.

The nudity and anger referred to in (i) are dynamic because we conceptualise them as temporary, inherently tending to cease.
23. In my view, dynamicity is the defining property of events: a dynamic situation has an inherent tendency to cease, and an expense of energy from some external source is necessary for the situation to continue. Non-dynamic

situations have an inherent tendency to continue, and an expense of energy from some external source is necessary for the situation to cease.

24. An analogue of this grammaticalisation is Žegarac's (1991) finding that for some speakers a few verbs like *know* are semantically specified as non-dynamic, so for these speakers such verbs can therefore never be progressive, and (i)–(ii) violate the grammar, since *know*'s referent cannot be dynamic yet progressives must be. I, among others, find both (i) and (ii) below acceptable, and an example like (ii) is attested; see Žegarac (1991).

    (i) %She is knowing more and more about less and less.
    (ii) %Lock both locks when you're knowing I'm out.

    What has happened for these speakers is that the non-dynamicity of the sense of *know* is treated not as a relatively constant, but overridable, property of knowing, but rather as an inalienable property of the sense of *know*.
25. I have not found anyone who accepts (37a) but rejects (37b). It is because it has been claimed that mediopassives are stative that I am considering the possibility of there being type III and IV lects.
26. As suggested in section 6, some speakers may also add a requirement of genericity, and possibly even of non-dynamicity.
27. II also applies to the infinitival *for*/*to* in *tough*-movement constructions and to recipe imperatives like *Baste and cover with foil* (see Massam 1987, 1992 for further comparisons among these constructions). There is a semantic difference between recipe imperatives and passive or mediopassive imperatives: the addressee of recipe imperatives is the *er* (cf. *Baste, O chef*), but the addressee of passive and mediopassive imperatives is the subject referent (cf. *Baste, O turkey*). This is a fourth grammatical requirement in addition to I–III.

References

Andrews, A. (1982) The representation of case in modern Icelandic. In Bresnan, J. (ed.), *The mental representation of grammatical relations*. Cambridge, MA: MIT Press. 427–503.

Antonopoulou, E. (1991) *Agent-defocusing mechanisms in spoken English: a cognitive explanation of impersonalization*. Athens: Περιοδικο "Παρουσια", Παραρτημα **16**.

Blake, B. (1990) *Relational grammar*. London: Routledge.

Bolinger, D. (1973) Essence and accident: English analogs of Hispanic *ser-estar*. In Kachru, B. B., Lees, R. B., Malkiel, Y., Pietrangeli, A. and Saporta, S. (eds.), *Issues in linguistics: papers in honor of Henry and Renée Kahane*. Urbana, Chicago, London: University of Illinois Press. 58–69.

Bolinger, D. (1974) On the passive in English. *LACUS Forum* **1**. 57–80.

Bresnan, J. (1982a) The passive in lexical theory. In Bresnan, J. (ed.), *The mental representation of grammatical relations*. Cambridge, MA: MIT Press. 3–86.

(1982b) Polyadicity. In Bresnan, J. (ed.), *The mental representation of grammatical relations*. Cambridge, MA: MIT Press. 149–172.

(1982c) Control and complementation. In Bresnan, J. (ed.), *The mental representation of grammatical relations*. Cambridge, MA: MIT Press. 282–390.

Carrier, J. and Randall, J. (1992) The argument structure and syntactic structure of resultatives. *Linguistic Inquiry* **23**: 173–234.

Dixon, R. M. W. (1977) Syntactic orientation as a semantic property. In McCawley, J. (ed.), *Notes from the linguistic underground. Syntax and semantics* **7**. New York: Academic Press. 347–362.

(1991) *A new approach to English grammar on semantic principles*. Oxford: Clarendon Press.

Dowty, D. (1972) Temporally restrictive adjectives. In Kimball, J. (ed.), *Syntax and semantics* **1**. New York: Seminar Press. 51–62.

Erades, P. (1950) Points of modern English syntax XII. *English Studies* **31**: 153–157.

Fagan, S. (1988) The English Middle. *Linguistic Inquiry* **19**: 181–203.

Fellbaum, C. (1985) Adverbs in agentless actives and passives. *Chicago Linguistic Society* **21**. 21–31.

Grady, M. (1965) The mediopassive voice in modern English. *Word* **21**: 270–272.

Hale, K. and Keyser, S. J. (1987) A view from the middle. *MIT Lexicon Project Working Paper* **10**.

Halliday, M. A. K. (1967) Notes on transitivity and theme in English, Part 1. *Journal of Linguistics* **3**: 37–81.

Heyer, G. (1985) Generic descriptions, default reasoning, and typicality. *Theoretical Linguistics* **12**: 33–72.

Hudson, R. (1989) English passives, grammatical relations and default inheritance. *Lingua* **79**: 17–48.

(1990) *English word grammar*. Oxford: Blackwell.

(1992a) So-called 'double objects' and grammatical relations. *Language* **68**: 251–276.

(1992b) *Teaching grammar*. Oxford: Blackwell.

Jackendoff, R. (1983) *Semantics and cognition*. Cambridge, MA: MIT Press.

(1987) The status of thematic relations in linguistic theory. *Linguistic Inquiry* **18**. 369–411.

(1990) *Semantic structures*. Cambridge, MA: MIT Press.

Jespersen, O. (1961) *A modern English grammar on historical principles*. London: Allen and Unwin.

Keyser, S. J. and Roeper, T. (1984) On the middle and ergative constructions in English. *Linguistic Inquiry* **15**. 381–416.

Lakoff, G. (1970) *Adverbs and opacity*. Indiana University Linguistics Club.

(1977) Linguistic Gestalts. *Chicago Linguistic Society* **13**. 236–287.

Levin, B. and Rapoport, T. (1988) Lexical subordination. *Chicago Linguistic Society* **24**. 275–289.

Levin, B. and Rappaport, M. (1989) An approach to unaccusative mismatches. *Proceedings of the North Eastern Linguistics Society* **19**. 314–328.

Levin, B. and Rappaport Hovav, M. (1992a) The lexical semantics of verbs of motion: the perspective from unaccusativity. In Roca I. M. (ed.), *Thematic structure: its role in grammar*. Berlin and New York: Walter de Gruyter. 247–269.

(1992b) A preliminary analysis of (de)causative verbs in English. MS.

Levin, L. (1982) Sluicing: A lexical interpretation procedure. In Bresnan, J. (ed.), *The mental representation of grammatical relations*. Cambridge, MA: MIT Press. 590–654.

Massam, D. (1987) Middles, *tough*, and recipe context constructions in English. *Proceedings of the North Eastern Linguistics Society* **18**. 315–332.
(1992) Null objects and non-thematic subjects. *Journal of linguistics* **28**. 15–137.
McCawley, J. (1988) *The syntactic phenomena of English*. 2 vols. Chicago University Press.
Nesfield (1898) = Nesfield and Wood (1964)
Nesfield, J. C. and Wood, F. T. (1964) *Manual of English grammar and composition*. London: Macmillan.
Ni, Y. (in preparation) Generics in English. University of London Ph.D. thesis.
Oosten, J. van (1977) Subjects and agenthood in English. *Chicago Linguistic Society* **13**. 459–471.
Pinker, S. (1989) *Learnability and cognition: the acquisition of argument structure*. Cambridge, MA: MIT Press.
Quirk, R., Greenbaum, S., Leech, G. and Svartvik, J. (1985) *A comprehensive grammar of the English language*. London: Longman.
Rappaport Hovav, M. and Levin, B. (1992) Classifying single argument verbs. MS.
Roberts, I. (1986) *The representation of implicit and dethematized subjects*. Dordrecht: Foris.
Rosta, A. (1992) English mediopassive. *University College London Working Papers in Linguistics* **4**. 327–351.
Smith, N. V. (1975) On generics. *Transactions of the Philological Society*: 27–48.
Stroik, T. (1992) Middles and movement. *Linguistic Inquiry* **23**. 127–137.
Sweet, H. (1898) *A new English grammar, logical and historical*. Oxford: Clarendon Press.
Talmy, L. (1985) Force dynamics in language and thought. *Chicago Linguistic Society* **21**. 293–337.
Trask, R. L. (1993) *A dictionary of grammatical terms in linguistics*. London: Routledge.
Žegarac, V. (1989) Relevance theory and the meaning of the English progressive. *University College London Working Papers in Linguistics* **1**. 19–31.
(1990) Pragmatics and verbal aspect. *University College London Working Papers in Linguistics* **2**. 113–143.
(1991) Relevance and aspect. University of London Ph.D. thesis.
(1992) Some observations on the pragmatics of the progressive. *Lingua* **90**. 201–220.

8 The expression of Root and Epistemic Possibility in English[1]

JENNIFER COATES

1 The Root/Epistemic distinction

The distinction between Root (or Agent-oriented or Deontic) modality and Epistemic modality has proved enormously useful to those attempting to describe the modal systems obtaining in the world's languages. The analysis of English is no exception (see Coates 1983, Haegeman 1983, Palmer 1990). Moreover, there is general agreement on the definition of these terms. Epistemic modality is concerned with the speaker's assumptions or assessment of possibilities, and in most cases it indicates the speaker's confidence or lack of confidence in the truth of the proposition expressed. Root modality encompasses meanings such as Permission and Obligation, and also Possibility and Necessity. This means that the Root/Epistemic distinction cuts across the necessity/obligation and possibility/permission distinctions (see diagram below). As in many languages, in English the same linguistic forms express both Root and Epistemic meanings. So, for example, *may* can express both Root and Epistemic Possibility; *must* can express both Root and Epistemic Necessity.

As far as the expression of necessity is concerned, this polysemy is unproblematic: the Root/Epistemic distinction remains distinct, as the following examples illustrate. *Must* in (1a) expresses the Root meaning of Obligation,

	Root		Epistemic	
can *may*	Permission ⟵	⟶ Possibility	Possibility	*may*
must *have to*	Obligation ⟵	⟶ Necessity	Necessity	*must* *have to*

Figure 8.1 Meaning and the Root/Epistemic distinction

in (1b) it expresses the (weaker) Root meaning of Necessity, and in (1c) it expresses Epistemic Necessity.

(1)		
	a. You *must* finish this before dinner.	Root
	b. All students *must* obtain the consent of the Dean.	
	c. I *must* have a temperature.	Epistemic

It is my impression, however, that there is some confusion about the Root/Epistemic distinction when it is applied to Possibility. In this chapter I want to re-examine this area of modality, and will argue that: (i) the semantic contrast between Root and Epistemic Possibility is considerably weaker than in other Root/Epistemic pairs; (ii) where the same linguistic form expresses both Root and Epistemic Possibility, instances of *merger* (see Coates 1983: 17) are common (*may*); (iii) where a linguistic form expresses predominantly Root Possibility, Epistemic readings are likely to develop (*can*).

2 Root and Epistemic Possibility

In order to discuss the Root/Epistemic contrast in relation to the expression of possibility in English, I shall make use of the set of properties developed by Heine (1992) in his analysis of the German modals. Heine argues that the following properties are criterial:

a. There is some force F that has an interest in an event either occurring or not occurring (Heine comments that F 'is characterised by some "element of will", to use the wording of Jespersen (1924: 320–321)' (Heine 1992: 16).)
b. That event is to be performed by some agent (A).
c. The event is dynamic (D).
d. The event has not yet taken place at reference time and, if it does take place, it will be at a time later than reference time (L).
e. The event is non-factual, but there is a certain degree of *probability* that it will occur (P).

In an utterance such as *she must go to bed now*, F may refer to the speaker ('I insist that she goes to bed now') or to an absent parent ('her mother insists that she goes to bed at this time') or to any other source of power the speaker may have in mind. The pronoun *she* is the agent (A), the event – *go* – is dynamic (D), the event has not yet taken place at the moment the utterance is produced (L), and there is a high probability (P) that the event referred to will take place.

As Heine (1992: 18) says: 'While prototypical instances of agent-oriented modality are characterised by the presence of the properties (i.e. F, A, D, L and P), prototypical instances of Epistemic modality lack all properties except P.' This means that if fewer of these properties are relevant to differentiating semantically between any two sentences containing a particular modal verb, the semantic contrast between the two interpretations of these sentences will be weaker. If we look at the examples given in (1) above, we can justify the claim that the semantic contrast between Root and Epistemic meaning is strong here by applying Heine's criteria. In (1a) and (1b) *all* of the properties are present, while only P is present in (1c). In other words, examples of Root *must* in English would normally be classified as prototypical examples of agent-oriented modality, while examples of Epistemic *must* would be classified as prototypically Epistemic.

Let's turn to the contrast between Root and Epistemic Possibility. Examples (2) and (3) below are typical instances of the expression of Root Possibility:[2]

(2) well I think there is a place where I *can* get a cheap kettle (S.1.4.62)
(3) I am afraid this is the bank's final word. I tell you so that you *may* make arrangements elsewhere. (W.7.9.37)

Can (see example (2)) is the normal exponent of Root Possibility in English, while *may*, as illustrated in example (3), is the exponent of Root Possibility in more formal contexts (in this case, a letter from a bank manager). Properties A, D, and L are present in both (2) and (3), but F (force) is absent.

In everyday discourse, *can* expressing Root Possibility is most commonly found in examples like (4) and (5) below, general statements of possibilities with impersonal subjects.

(4) certain things *can* be sex-linked to the Y chromosome (S.5b.2.54)
(5) first thing in the morning they come, you *can* hear the whistle (S.1.14A.43)

These two examples display *none* of Heine's properties apart from P. Even more perplexing are archetypal examples of *can* such as (6) below, which Palmer (1990: 152–154) describes as 'existential':

(6) Lions can be dangerous.

Palmer justifies his use of the term 'existential' by claiming that paraphrases involving 'some' (*some lions are dangerous*) or 'sometimes' (*lions are sometimes dangerous*) are more appropriate than paraphrases using 'possible for'. What is intriguing about examples like (6) is that, besides lacking F, A, D, and L (the properties associated with non-Epistemic modality), they also lack P. In other words, some examples of *can* lack all the properties which Heine claims are normally associated with modal meaning.

Although we have seen that examples of Root Possibility vary in the number of properties associated with them (examples (2) and (3) are associated with properties A, D, L and P, examples (4) and (5) are associated only with P, while example (6) is associated with none of the properties), they all share one characteristic: absence of F. In his analysis of German modals, Heine argues that only F is obligatorily connected with Root modality: 'once the use of a modal is characterised by a lack of F then it lacks that "element of will" that Jespersen (1924: 320–321) referred to, and we are dealing with an epistemic rather than an agent-oriented sense' (Heine 1992: 19). On the basis of this argument, (2), (3), (4), (5) and (6) all fail as instances of Root modality.

Let's look now at the expression of Epistemic Possibility in English. Epistemic Possibility has many exponents, notably *maybe, perhaps, I think, possibly, probably* and the modal auxiliaries *may, might* and *could.* Examples are given in (7), (8), (9) and (10) below.

(7) that *may* be yellow fever, I'm not sure (S.4.2.65)
(8) I *may* be a few minutes late, but don't know (S.7.3E.6)
(9) I think it's unlikely actually but he *might* do it today (S.8.1A.18)
(10) The only snag is that it has been raining... and I *could* get held up for anything up to a week. (W.7.2.29)

These examples are not associated with F. However, examples (8), (9) and (10) are associated with L (since they refer to events that are to occur later than reference time), and example (9) is also associated with A and D. Thus, only (7) is prototypically Epistemic in Heine's sense.

A summary of the properties associated with examples given so far is presented in the figure below. This shows that, using Heine's criteria alone, we are unable to distinguish clearly between instances of Root and Epistemic Possibility in English. Figure 8.2 includes examples (1a), (1b) and (1c) to show how clearly Heine's properties distinguish between Root and Epistemic Necessity. But in the case of examples of Root and Epistemic Possibility in English, this table would force us to conclude that there is often no difference (cf. examples (2) and (9) which share four properties; examples (4) and (7) which both have one property, P). While the use of these criteria has helped to demonstrate that the distinction between Root and Epistemic Possibility is weak, it is not the case that examples are indistinguishable. So what distinguishes Root from Epistemic Possibility?

The crucial distinction between forms expressing Root Possibility in English and forms expressing Epistemic Possibility in English is that the latter involve *Subjectivity* (which I shall refer to as S). Forms involving S can be

Example	Properties					Type of modality
	F	A	D	L	P	
(1a)	+	+	+	+	+	Root Obligation
(1b)	+	+	+	+	+	Root Necessity
(1c)	–	–	–	–	+	Epistemic Necessity
(2)/(3)	–	+	+	+	+	Root Possibility
(4)/(5)	–	–	–	–	+	Root Possibility
(6)	–	–	–	–	–	'Existential'
(7)	–	–	–	–	+	Epistemic Possibility
(8)	–	–	–	+	+	Epistemic Possibility
(9)	–	+	+	+	+	Epistemic Possibility

Figure 8.2 Matrix showing presence or absence of Heine's properties

defined as 'devices whereby the speaker, in making an utterance, simultaneously comments upon that utterance and expresses his attitude to what he is saying' (Lyons 1977: 739). As examples (7), (8), (9) and (10) above illustrate, S is an integral component of the expression of Epistemic Possibility. The speakers in (7), (8), and (9) and the letter-writer in (10) are not only making statements but are simultaneously expressing their lack of confidence in the propositions expressed in these utterances. In every case here, speaker's uncertainty is encoded in an accompanying phrase which reinforces the modal: *I'm not sure* in (7), *don't know* in (8), *I think it's unlikely* in (9), and *the only snag is* in (10). (We can compare earlier examples of Root Possibility: *I can get a cheap kettle* (2) and *you can hear the whistle* (5). Both are statements of fact; subjectivity is not involved. The difference between *I can get a kettle* and *I may get a kettle* is that in the latter the speaker's uncertainty is encoded too.)

We therefore need to add S to the matrix to show that this acts as the criterial property where the expression of possibility is concerned (see Figure 8.3).

If we ignore P, which is common to both Root and Epistemic modality (except in unusual cases like (6)), we can see that the reason for the weak-

Example	Properties						Type of modality
	F	A	D	L	P	S	
(1a)	+	+	+	+	+	–	Root Obligation
(1b)	+	+	+	+	+	–	Root Necessity
(2)/(3)	–	+	+	+	+	–	Root Possibility
(4)/(5	–	–	–	–	+	–	Root Possibility
(6)	–	–	–	–	–	–	'Existential'
(1c)	–	–	–	–	+	+	Epistemic Necessity
(7)	–	–	–	–	+	+	Epistemic Possibility
(8)	–	–	–	+	+	+	Epistemic Possibility
(9)	–	+	+	+	+	+	Epistemic Possibility

Figure 8.3 Matrix to show the distinction between Root and Epistemic meanings in English

ness of the Root/Epistemic distinction in the expression of Possibility is the absence, in utterances involving Root Possibility, of properties normally associated with Root meaning. Exponents of Root Necessity (e.g. (1b)) differ from exponents of Epistemic Necessity (e.g. (1c)) on five measures, whereas exponents of Root Possibility (e.g. (2/3)) may differ from exponents of Epistemic Possibility (e.g. (9)) by as little as one property (presence or absence of S).

One of the reasons that the weakness of this distinction has been unproblematic for speakers of English is that Root and Epistemic Possibility are, by and large, expressed by *different* linguistic forms. *May* is the only modal form which regularly expresses both Root and Epistemic Possibility, and when expressing Root Possibility it is restricted to the most formal contexts (as in (3) above). The extent of overlap between the two forms is small, as the statistics given in Table 8.1 show (these record my analysis of a representative sample of 200 cases of *can* and 200 cases of *may*, all examples of spoken British English taken from the Survey of English Usage).

Table 8.1 *The use of* can *and* may *in contemporary spoken English*

can:	Root Possibility	129	*may*:	Epistemic Possibility	147
	Ability	41		Permission	32
	Permission	10		Root Possibility	7
	Undecidable	20		Valediction	1
				Undecidable	13
	TOTAL	200		TOTAL	200

As these figures demonstrate, each linguistic form is overwhelmingly associated with one particular meaning (*can* with Root Possibility, *may* with Epistemic Possibility). The category 'undecidable' refers to those examples which I could not assign unproblematically to one meaning rather than another. Often, this was because there was not enough contextual evidence to permit a definite reading; in the case of *may*, however, some examples exhibit 'merger', that is, the phenomenon whereby utterances containing *may* combine elements of both Root and Epistemic meaning (see 3.1 below).

3 The linguistic consequences of a weak Root/Epistemic contrast

In the previous section, I have demonstrated the weakness of the Root/Epistemic distinction in the expression of Possibility. As I have argued, the blurring of the Root/Epistemic boundary in this semantic area is not often problematic in English, given the use of different linguistic forms. However, there are certain interesting linguistic developments in this area which are a direct result, I would argue, of the weakness of the distinction. One involves the growing instances of merger with *may*. The other is the development of Epistemic readings for *can* in contemporary spoken American English.

3.1 *May* and merger

Merger, as I have explained elsewhere (see Coates 1983; Leech and Coates 1980), refers to instances where two meanings co-exist in a both/and relationship. In other words, two readings are available for a given utterance, but instead of having to choose one meaning and discard the other (as with ambiguous examples), the hearer is able to process *both* meanings.

Merger occurs quite frequently in more formal texts (example 11) and is becoming endemic in academic writing (as example (12) illustrates):

(11) or the pollen *may* be taken from the stamens of one rose and transferred to the stigma of another (W.10.3.27)

(12) . . . the process of *simplification* . . . through which even forms and distinctions present in all the contributory dialects *may* be lost (Trudgill *Dialects in Contact*, 1986: 126)

In both these examples, the only property clearly present is P. Properties associated with Root meaning (F, A, and D) are absent, while S, normally criterial for Epistemic meaning, is not typically associated with this kind of formal style with its passives and inanimate subjects. So instances such as these lack clear markers of either Root or Epistemic meaning. The two meanings merge, and the reader is not required to choose one or the other:[3]

(11')	Root:	'it's possible for the pollen to be taken . . .'
	Epistemic:	'it's possible that the pollen will be taken . . .'
(12')	Root:	'it's possible for forms and distinctions . . . to be lost'
	Epistemic:	'it's possible that forms and distinctions . . . will be lost'

It is significant that such examples of merger come typically from the (formal) written domain. In spoken language, exponents of Root and Epistemic Possibility are normally distinguished prosodically: for example, *may* and *can* do not receive stress when expressing Root Possibility, but *may*, when it expresses Epistemic Possibility, *is* normally stressed. Epistemic *may* is also typically associated with fall-rise intonation (see example (13) below):

(13) I may be wrong (S.1.2.38)

While *writers* can exploit the both/and relationship of Root and Epistemic meanings when talking about possibilities, *speakers* are constrained by prosodic factors to choose one or the other. If a speaker uttered example (11) with a fall-rise nucleus on *may*, for example, the only interpretation available to hearers would be Epistemic.

3.2 The development of Epistemic *can*

Given the historical pattern of Epistemic meanings developing from Root meanings (Bybee and Pagliucca 1985; Traugott 1989), it would not be surprising if *can* were to develop an Epistemic reading. Moreover, the homogeneous picture of *can* given so far in this chapter is not the whole truth: *can* does have some well-established specialised Epistemic uses.

First, it provides the missing negative form in the Epistemic *must* paradigm. The invariant form *can't* (not *cannot* or *can not*) expresses 'it's necessarily the case that . . . not . . .' (nec ¬p) or 'it's not possibly the case that' (¬poss p) in examples such as (14). (Note the stress on *can't* and the fall-rise intonation contour.)

(14) (speaker describes friends arriving early)
I almost phoned them up and said come a bit later and then I thought oh they've probably left by now so I didn't and twelve thirty, now that . . . *can't* be them, and it was (S.2.7.6)

Second, *can* is used in interrogative constructions to express Epistemic Possibility. Example (15) is a cliché of pop music and Hollywood-style films, but it makes the point clear:

(15) Can it be true?
'Is it possible that this is true? that she loves me?'

Such examples have a clear relationship with the use of *can't* discussed above, in that (15) could be glossed 'it can't be true!' ('it must be false'). Example (16) comes from a radio discussion of Government policy on pensions:

(16) Can that be sensible?
'Is it possibly the case that that is sensible?'

The speaker was clearly trying to make the point *That can't be sensible!*

In British English, these are still the only contexts in which a form of *can* is used with Epistemic meaning (though *could* is making headway as an alternative to *might* in the expression of tentativeness – see example (10)). But in American English, *can* is starting to appear in other contexts. The following example occurred during the Symposium on Mood and Modality (held at the University of New Mexico in May 1992) as a participant finished her presentation:

(17) we hope this coding system *can* be useful
[to other linguists working in the field]

This utterance meant something like 'we hope there's a chance that this system *will* be useful'. For British speakers, this utterance is not possible: a British speaker would have to say 'we hope this coding system will be useful', thereby losing the subjective force. As the person who uttered (17) commented to me afterwards, *can* in this utterance is 'a sort of hedge'. American speakers seem to have no problems with utterances of this kind.

So if *can* is developing an Epistemic meaning in the United States but not in Britain, what is different in the linguistic environment in the United States? I would like to suggest three factors:

a. *can* is less commonly used to express Permission in American English; *may* is the normal exponent of Permission (Coates and Leech 1980);
b. the 'bleaching' of Root *can* is further advanced in American English, with the majority of examples not associated with F, A, D or L;
c. *may* is the chief exponent of Epistemic Possibility in British English, but is less common in American English, where *may* has connotations of formality.

More generally, there are many reasons why we would expect *can* to develop Epistemic Possibility readings. First, all the other modal auxiliaries in English express both Root and Epistemic meaning. Second, it seems to be the case that Epistemic meanings derive from earlier, non-Epistemic meanings (Traugott 1989: 52). Third, the evidence from child acquisition research is suggestive: children develop Deontic meaning much earlier than Epistemic meaning (Stephany 1986); Guo (1992) claims that the Mandarin form *neng* (*can*) is starting to be used to express Epistemic Possibility in children's speech. Fourth, the occurrence of merger with examples of *may* (illustrated in section 3.1) illustrates the fuzziness of the Root/Epistemic boundary in the expression of Possibility. Fifth, as this chapter has attempted to demonstrate, Root and Epistemic Possibility are only weakly distinguished.

Given these circumstances, and a historic pattern in the development of *can* from Ability meanings to Permission meanings to Root Possibility meanings (Bybee 1988), I would predict that initially examples of Epistemic *can* will co-occur with syntactic features such as inanimate subject and stative verb, and in contexts where accompanying words support an Epistemic reading. Example (17) is of this type, with an inanimate subject *this coding system*, and the phrase *I hope* introducing Subjectivity to the utterance. However, it is difficult to imagine *can* becoming a serious contender in the expression of Epistemic Possibility unless it can develop a stressed alternative to the usual [kən]; until that happens, utterances like *I can come* will be processed as Root.

4 Conclusions

In this chapter, I have argued that the distinction between Root and Epistemic Possibility is much weaker than that found in other areas of modal meaning. I have demonstrated that the weakness of this distinction arises from the nature of Root Possibility, typical examples of which are not associated with Heine's properties F, A, D and L (normally criterial for Root meaning). As a direct consequence of the weakness of the Root/Epistemic distinction, instances of merger are common (in the case of *may*), and Epistemic readings are beginning to occur in declaratives with *can*. Speakers will exploit the potentialities of the English modal system to say the things they need to say. Whether this means that *can*, like the other English modal auxiliaries, will develop the full range of Epistemic meanings remains to be seen.

Notes

1. I was a participant at the Symposium on Mood and Modality held at the University of New Mexico, Albuquerque, in May 1992, and this chapter originated as a response to papers given at the Symposium. It appears in the volume arising from the symposium: J. Bybee, and S. Fleischmann (eds)., *Modality in grammar and discourse* (Amsterdam and New York: John Benjamins, 1994). I am grateful to John Benjamins and to the editors for giving permission for this chapter to appear in the present volume. I would also like to record my gratitude to Joan Bybee, Suzanne Fleischmann, Talmy Givón and Bernd Heine for their comments on earlier drafts of this chapter.
2. Examples from this point onwards will be taken from the Survey of English Usage, University College, London (prosodic information omitted).
3. *Can* is also beginning to be involved in merger, in contexts where the speaker/writer wishes to hedge what they are saying. A nice example occurs on Inland Revenue (UK) Tax Forms: False statements can result in prosecution.

References

Bybee, J. (1988) Semantic substance versus contrast in the development of grammatical meaning. *Proceedings of the Fourteenth Berkeley Linguistic Society.* 247–279.

Bybee, J. and Pagliucca, W. (1985) Cross-linguistic comparisons and the development of grammatical meaning. In Fisiak, J. (ed.), *Historical semantics and historical word formation.* The Hague: Mouton. 59–84.

Coates, J. (1983) *The semantics of the modal auxiliaries.* London: Croom Helm.

Coates, J. and Leech, G. (1980) The meanings of the modals in modern British and American English. *York Papers in Linguistics* **8**. 23–34.

Guo, J. (1992) The interactional structuring of meaning: children's use and development of the Mandarin modal *neng* (*can*). Paper presented at the Symposium on Mood and Modality, University of New Mexico, Albuquerque. In Bybee, J. and Fleischmann, S. (eds.) (1994), *Modality in grammar and discourse.* Amsterdam and New York: John Benjamins.

Haegeman, L. (1983) *The semantics of* will *in present-day British English.* Verhandelingen van de Koninklijke Academie voor Wetenschappen, Letteren en Schone kunsten van België, klasse letteren. 45.103. Published by John Benjamins.

Heine, B. (1992) Agent-oriented vs. epistemic modality – some observations on German modals. Paper presented at the Symposium on Mood and Modality, University of New Mexico, Albuquerque. In Bybee, J. and Fleischmann S.

(eds.) (1994), *Modality in grammar and discourse*. Amsterdam and New York: John Benjamins.

Jespersen, O. (1924) *The philosophy of grammar*. London: Allen and Unwin.

Leech, G. and Coates, J. (1980) Semantic indeterminacy and the modals. In Greenbaum, S., Leech, G. and Svartvik J. (eds.), *Studies in English Linguistics for Randolph Quirk*. London: Longman. 79–90.

Lyons, J. (1977) *Semantics*. 2 volumes. Cambridge University Press.

Palmer, F. (1990) *Modality and the English modals*. (2nd edition). London: Longman.

Stephany, U. (1986) Modality. In Fletcher, P. and Garman, M. (eds.), *Language acquisition*. (2nd edition). Cambridge University Press. 375–400.

Traugott, E. C. (1989) On the rise of epistemic meanings in English: An example of subjectification in semantic change. *Language* **65**. 31–55.

PART 2

Descriptive approaches to the study of the English verb

9 *Find* and *want* A corpus-based case study in verb complementation

JAN AARTS and FLOR AARTS

1 Introduction

The number of corpus enthusiasts in linguistics is rapidly growing. This in itself is a healthy development where linguistic methodology is concerned; new attention for actual language use was needed after a long period during which linguistics suffered from observational anaemia. Yet every linguist knows that corpus data are in at least two ways inferior to intuitive data, which were regarded as the only reputable source for linguistic research for two or three decades. In the first place, a few minutes of introspection can produce an example of a construction which is infrequent and may only be found after the perusal of millions of words of text. Secondly, a corpus can yield no data about the grammatical–ungrammatical (or, for that matter, acceptable–unacceptable) distinction; the source of data about this distinction can only be the linguist's or his informants' intuitions. So, if corpus data are inferior to linguistic introspection in two respects, they had better have some advantages over introspection. And, of course, they do. The first of these was mentioned by Quirk as early as 1960: corpus data enable the linguist to go for 'total accountability', that is, he can study *all* the linguistic features of a given text as well as the ways in which these features interrelate in context. It is clear that this is a very labour-intensive and time-consuming thing to do. Since corpus data also come in great numbers, it is not very appealing for a linguist to spend much time and energy in the intensive scrutiny of, *a fortiori*, comparatively small pieces of text. If tens of millions of words are clamouring for your attention, it is difficult to summon the patience and the stamina to study only a negligible fraction of this. Therefore we think that 'total accountability' will remain, for the time being, the stuff that linguists' dreams are made of. Another great advantage of corpora is of course that they give access to information about the frequency of occurrence of units and constructions, something that only became possible through the introduction of computational techniques. It is now possible to collect data about the numerical aspects of language use; and the more detailed the linguistic information contained in corpora is, the more sophisticated these data will be. It goes without saying that, as is the case with all numerical data, such data should be used with great circumspection. In particular, however much he may be tempted to draw sweeping conclusions, the linguist should be very careful not to be too hasty in generalising findings based on a limited number of samples from a limited number of language varieties to *the* language as a whole.

We may say, then, that there are two ways of looking at corpora. The first, to which the principle of total accountability belongs, can be called the *microscopic* view of a corpus, which allows the linguist to deal with the details of language use. For some linguists, this seems to be the most appealing feature of corpora; they provide, as Sinclair (1987: 107) put it, 'a refreshing change from the usual unseemly rush of linguists to kick aside the concrete linguistic object in favour of some idealised abstraction'. And the concrete object is often felt to be revealing: '. . . when you delve into authentic text you will often be surprised at what you actually find' (Allén 1992: 1). On the other hand, if the linguist wants to collect numerical data (something which is inherent in the study of language use), he is committed to the *macroscopic* view of a corpus. For the collection of numerical data of any kind beyond the level of the individual word necessarily entails the creation of classes of units at a higher level of abstraction and consequently, loss of individual detail and contextual information. It is difficult to combine the two approaches and steer a middle way between the macroscopic and the microscopic views of a corpus. Still, if one wants to study language use (and what else can one do on the basis of corpus data?) the two approaches have to be combined, for in language use lexis, grammar and context interact. It is therefore necessary to pay attention to individual occurrences of linguistic items and at the same time collect numerical data about types of construction at a higher level of abstraction, in which these items play a role. In this article we try to do this. On the basis of a detailed study of two lexical items, we try to establish links between lexical (and therefore individual) features and grammatical (and therefore more generalised) phenomena. We try to find out not only how these interact, but also how they relate to the nature of the wider context in which they occur. Since the topic of this volume is the verb in English, we have selected two: *find* and *want*. The choice is rather arbitrary, but prompted by the fact that these are two verbs with a varied pattern of complementation; at the same time they are clearly semantically different in that *want* creates opaque contexts, whereas *find* does not. Our study is also an exercise in methodology. We want to find out whether the descriptive tools we employ are appropriate to achieve the aim mentioned above.

Our starting point is entirely syntactic. In sections 2 and 3 we first pay attention to the complementation patterns of the two verbs, where differences between patterns are primarily defined in terms of the functional constituents required by the verbs. We comment on the frequencies of these patterns, investigating to what extent their frequencies are affected by two variables: the categories by which the functional constituents are realised on the one hand and the form of the verb itself, and, where applicable, of the Verb Phrase in which it occurs as the lexical verb on the other. In addition to this, we pay special attention to some questions of language use which can only be answered on the basis of corpus data. First of all, we ask the question whether the patterns we find are semantically conditioned; in other words, are our syntactic findings affected by a particular sense of the verb and/or by particular semantic features of its complement(s)? We also investigate if there are contextual conditions of a more incidental nature that seem to favour the occurrence of particular patterns; or, to put this differently, we want to find out if there are syntactic counterparts of what on the discourse level are called clichés, and on the lexical level, collocations. Finally, we consider the correlation between syntactic and semantic observations: is there a perfect correspondence between the two, or can generalisations more easily be made in either syntactic or in semantic terms? Finally, we summarise our findings and draw some conclusions in section 4.

For our study we have used one million words from the TOSCA corpus.[1] The total number of occurrences of *find* in the one-million-word fragment was 559, that of *want* 868.

2 *Find*

2.1 Forms

The TOSCA corpus contains 559 forms of the word *find*. These include examples of the nouns *find* (three occurrences), *finding* (ten occurrences) and *findings* (thirteen occurrences) as well as 59 forms of the phrasal verb *find out*. In what follows we will deal exclusively with the 474 forms of the verb *find*. They are broken down in Table 9.1.

The most striking thing about the distribution of the forms in Table 9.1 is the fact that the non-finite forms are almost four times as frequent as the finite ones. As we shall see below, this is partly explained by the fact that the verb *find* is frequently accompanied by an auxiliary.

As far as the finite forms of *find* are concerned, what is very striking is the preponderance of present tense forms (88 examples; *find* occurs 63 times and *finds* 25 times) as compared with the past tense form *found* (two examples). It

Table 9.1 *Forms of the verb* find

Find				
Finite forms	Present tense	88		
	Past tense	2		
	Imperative	8		
			TOTAL	98
Non-finite forms	Bare infinitive	186		
	To-infinitive	128		
	Ing-participle	60		
	Ed-participle	2		
			TOTAL	376
			TOTAL	474

would seem that there is a strong tendency for the verb *find* to be used in making timeless statements, as illustrated by the following examples:

(1) But people *find* all kinds of ways of killing themselves, you know.
(2) . . . the law of segregation of hybrids as discovered by Mendel for peas *finds* very general application in the plant kingdom.

Another explanation for the paucity of the past tense form *found* is that in many sentences involving past time reference we find the collocation *could find* instead of the simple past tense *found*. Here are three examples:

(3) . . . though he looked on the floor and felt under the seats, he *could find* nothing to explain it.
(4) If she *could find* one before Christmas, it just might do something to improve Santa's image.
(5) I checked the crew lists but *could find* no record of a Greek sailor.

Among the non-finite forms by far the least frequent one (with only two examples) is the *ed*-participle *found*. One example occurs after *have* in:

(6) I doubt if we'd have *found* what we did find at the scene.

The other occurs in the only passive construction with *find* in the corpus:

(7) 'But one *wasn't found* at the hospital after the fire?', asked Amy.

The virtual absence of passive *find*-constructions in the corpus is very interesting. A possible explanation might be that there is a tendency for the verb *find* to occur in sentences in which the subject has the thematic role of agent rather than patient.

The *ing*-participle form *finding* is chiefly found after prepositions (24 examples), as in:

(8) She was responsible for *finding* this information . . .

and in non-finite clauses (seventeen examples), as in:

(9) Not *finding* it, he looked at me strangely again.

There are no examples in the corpus of the progressive construction *be* + *finding*. This is not surprising, since *find*, at least in its most frequent sense, is a stative rather than a dynamic verb.

The bare infinitive *find* occurs only in combination with auxiliaries, particularly modal auxiliaries. Some modals are very infrequent: there are only three examples of *must find* and two of *shall find*. Other combinations are more frequent. Those that occur more than ten times in the corpus are listed in Table 9.2. The corpus contains 186 examples of the bare infinitive form *find*, preceded by an auxiliary. Combinations of *can/could* + *find* and of *will/'ll/would/'d* + *find* together account for almost 68 per cent.

Table 9.2 *Auxiliaries* + find

can find	18		
could find	38		
		TOTAL	56
will find	19		
'll find	20		
would find	20		
'd find	11		
		TOTAL	70
		TOTAL	126

The most frequent function of the 128 occurrences of *to find* is that of adverbial adjunct. There are 43 examples of this use, which is more than 33.5 per cent. Two meanings can be distinguished, the 'in order to' meaning and the 'resultative' meaning, exemplified, respectively, by:

(10) I came here *to find* you.

and

(11) Later, he awoke *to find* Lex standing over him.

Apart from this adverbial function, *to find* also occurs as postmodifier in Adjective Phrases (31 examples), after verbs that require a *to*-infinitive construction (27 examples) and as postmodifier in Noun Phrases (thirteen examples). These uses are illustrated by the following sentences:

(12) Frederick . . . was amazed *to find* she had changed her mind.
(13) . . . our first resort was to try *to find* a more probable theory.
(14) Ethel made no special effort *to find* him.

It is interesting to observe that in more than half the cases where *to find* functions as postmodifier in an Adjective Phrase, the head is realised by an adjective expressing an emotional state: *distressed, overjoyed, sorry, ashamed, puzzled*, etc.

2.2 Complementation

There are only two examples in the corpus of the use of *find* as an intransitive verb. The first example illustrates a more or less technical use of *find* in the sense defined by the *OED* as 'to discover (game) in hunting':

(15) Hounds would *find* almost at once, their snuffles and whines deep within the trees . . .

In the second example *find* is part of the phrase *find in favour of*:

(16) . . . the Supreme Court took a step backwards by *finding in favour of* a common selling agency . . .

For the remaining 472 examples we can distinguish three patterns:

(a) monotransitive complementation: direct object (O_d)
(b) ditransitive complementation: indirect object (O_i) + O_d
(c) complex transitive complementation: O_d + object complement (C_o)

Each of these can be further subdivided, as illustrated in Table 9.3. The picture that emerges from Table 9.3 is very clear. *Find* is overwhelmingly used as a monotransitive verb, the object in the vast majority of cases being realised by a NP. The next most frequent construction is that in which *find* functions as a complex transitive verb. Of the three possible patterns the one with an AP as complement to the object is clearly favoured. Ditransitive *find* is only represented by eleven examples in the corpus. In sections 2.2.1–2.2.3 we will briefly comment on the complementation patterns listed in Table 9.3.

2.2.1 *Monotransitive complementation*

The subject of monotransitive *find* + NP usually has personal reference. There are only nine examples (out of 279) with a non-personal subject.

Table 9.3 *Types of complementation after* find

Functional type		Realisation		
Monotransitive	O_d	NP		280
		Finite clause	*that*-clause	31
			ϕ-clause	18
			Wh-clause	3
		Non-finite clause	[$_s$ NP + *ing*-participle	23
			[$_s$ NP + *ed*-participle	17
			[$_s$ NP + bare infinitive	1
Total	373			
Ditransitive	O_i + O_d	NP + NP		2
		NP + *for*		9
Total	11			
Complex transitive:	O_d + C_o	NP + AP		67
		NP + NP		7
		NP + PP		14
Total	88			

In the majority of these *find* occurs in more or less fixed collocations, such as *find application in*, *find a parallel in* and *find favour*. Examples:

(17) The pain will *find* you soon enough.
(18) . . . the law of segregation of hybrids . . . *finds general application in* the plant kingdom . . .
(19) The fear that society is being quickly taken over . . . *finds its parallel in* much of the anti-semitic writing of the period . . .
(20) . . . any linguistic unit . . . *finds its own context in* a more complex linguistic unit.
(21) The SI movement argued that SIs could *find* a range of different uses.
(22) The truth, that he was working for Lord Petrefact, was hardly likely to *find favour* . . .

In the 280 examples of monotransitive *find* + NP the most frequently used form is the bare infinitive *find*. It occurs 119 times, always after an auxiliary. There are two very striking patterns. In 47 cases *find* is preceded by *can* or *could* and in 39 cases by one of the forms *will*/*'ll* or *would*/*'d*. Examples:

(23) I *can find* little evidence for Hazel Henderson's assertion . . .
(24) He made as if to scratch his ankle, but *couldn't find* the knife.

(25) Somehow we'll *find* her.
(26) . . . he couldn't be sure he'*d find* matches in the vestry.
(27) . . . one day, when perhaps the war was over, they *would find* a boat to steal . . .

Although monotransitive *find* can be followed by finite and non-finite clausal complements, these constructions are considerably less frequent than the one with an NP object (93 versus 280). The following examples illustrate the various possibilities:

Finite clause:

that-clause:

(28) You may find *that what I say does not fit*.

ϕ-clause:

(29) I walked ten miles to find *they were not at home*.

Wh-clause:

(30) If they never find *who did it* . . . we'd never forgive ourselves.

Non-finite clause:

NP + *ing*-participle:

(31) I do find *myself forgetting things*.

NP + *ed*-participle:

(32) They would find *doors pulled* from their hinges.

NP + bare infinitive:

(33) . . . I would find *strength and tone in the left leg wilt away*.

When followed by a finite clause *find* belongs to what Quirk et al. (1985: 1181) call the 'private type of factual verb', which 'expresses intellectual states such as belief and intellectual acts such as discovery'. The subject invariably has personal reference. The finite clause may be introduced by ϕ or by a Wh-word, but there is a marked preference for the subordinator *that*. *Find* in this pattern appears predominantly in its infinitival form, with eighteen examples of the *to*-infinitive and seventeen of the bare infinitive. The *to*-infinitive examples are divided equally over two constructions:

Adjective + *to find*:

(34) Frederick . . . was *amazed to find* she had changed her mind.

To find as adverbial adjunct:

(35) Ernest came back late from a gig one night *to find* that she had gone away with someone else.

The seventeen bare infinitive forms all appear after auxiliaries, particularly after *will/'ll* and *would/'d*. The most frequent pattern (with nine examples) has *you* as subject:

(36) You*'ll find* you can't make outgoing calls on our phone . . .
(37) You *will find* that the context of reference shifts away . . .

Quirk et al. (1985: 1204) note that the finite clause is preferred to the non-finite construction when the clause following *find* contains a verb other than *be*. This is confirmed by the corpus data: of the 49 clauses introduced by *that* or *φ*, 29 contain a verb other than *be*.

When followed by a non-finite clause, monotransitive *find* allows three patterns, but one of these is only represented by one example in the corpus. This is the NP + bare infinitive construction (not mentioned in Quirk et al. 1985: §16.52 as a possibility for *find*):

(38) . . . I would *find* strength and tone in the left leg wilt away.

The NP + *-ing* pattern is the most frequent of the non-finite constructions (23 out of 41 examples). The subject of *find* has personal reference, except in the following examples:

(39) One week would *find* him lecturing the fleet at Rosyth; another would *find* him explaining the progress of the war to troops at the front . . .
(40) Any one gene can be said to meet another when they *find* themselves sharing a body.

In seven cases (out of 23) the subject of the non-finite clause in this construction is a reflexive pronoun, as in:

(41) I *find* myself reading Hannah Ahrend.

In the NP + *-ed* pattern the subject of *find* has personal reference in all cases. As in the case of the NP + *-ing* construction, there is a tendency for the subject of the non-finite clause to be realised by a reflexive pronoun (four out of seventeen examples):

(42) Yet the reader is likely to *find* himself forced continually to revise his sense of what any particular story is about.

Table 9.4 compares the non-finite clause data in the TOSCA corpus with those in three other corpora: van Ek (1966), Andersson (1985) and Mair (1990). Since Mair is only concerned with *to*-infinitival clauses, there are question

Table 9.4 Find + *non-finite clause in four corpora*

	Tosca Corpus	van Ek (1966)	Andersson (1985)	Mair (1990)
	c. 1 million	1 million	2 million	c. 1 million
NP + *ing*	23 (active)	53 (active) 2 (passive)	90 (active) 2 (passive)	? ?
NP + *ed*	17 (active)	18 (active) 3 (passive)	34 (active)	?
NP + bare inf.	1 (active)	—	—	?
NP + *to*-inf.	—	1 (active) 6 (passive)	10 (active) 25 (passive)	1 (active) 7 (passive)

marks in the last column. In these corpora the participial constructions are considerably more frequent than the infinitival ones. Indeed, there is only one example of the bare infinitive construction. The NP + *-ing* construction is represented by the most examples. On the whole these corpora thus seem to confirm the data of the TOSCA corpus. We have no explanation for the fact that the NP + *-ing* construction is relatively more frequent in the corpora of van Ek and Andersson than in our material.

2.2.2 Ditransitive complementation

The ditransitive construction, with *find* followed by two NPs, occurs only twice:

(43) . . . he could use his influence . . . to *find them work* at the University.
(44) . . . and asked the librarian to *find her a book* on the life-cycle of slugs.

There is a clear preference for the prepositional construction with *for* (nine out of eleven examples):

(45) I don't think I want to *find him for you.*

2.2.3 Complex transitive complementation

Complex transitive *find* can be followed by three complementation patterns: NP + AP, NP + NP and NP + PP. The subject of *find* has personal reference in all examples.

The most frequent pattern is the string NP + AP, with 67 out of 88 examples. Three interesting facts stand out. The first is the relatively large number of finite forms in this pattern. There are 21 examples of finite *find* and eleven examples of *finds*. This means that more than 47 per cent of the forms of *find* in this pattern are finite. This is striking since the forms of monotransitive and ditransitive *find* are overwhelmingly non-finite. Secondly, we find that the NP following *find* is usually a pronoun (46 examples) and that in 22 cases the pronoun is realised by *it*. There is also a tendency for certain adjectives to be used in this pattern: *difficult* occurs six times, *hard*, *easy* and *wrong* occur three times each and we also find adjectives that are negative in meaning, such as *unforgivable, incredible, inadequate, impossible, unacceptable,* and *unintelligible*. Typical examples of this pattern are the following:

(46) We *find it hard* not to laugh.
(47) He *finds it impossible* to take her quite seriously.

Complex transitive *find* can also be followed by two NPs. There are only seven examples in this corpus, in six of which the first NP is realised by a pronoun, as in:

(48) You *find me an interesting case*, I perceive.

In the third pattern, complex transitive *find* is followed by the string NP + PP. Although this pattern is twice as frequent as the previous one, the corpus contains only fourteen examples. In ten cases the NP is realised by a reflexive pronoun. Examples:

(49) He had originally professed bewilderment at *finding himself amid patients*, when, as he said, he himself didn't feel ill.
(50) . . . I *find myself in virtually complete agreement with what he established earlier*.

2.3 Meaning

The various senses of the verb *find* are not always easy to keep apart. Indeed, dictionaries agree neither on the number of different senses nor on what senses can be grouped together (see, for example, *Cobuild*, *Longman Dictionary of Contemporary English* (*LDOCE*) and *Oxford Advanced Learner's Dictionary* (*OALD*)). Nevertheless, it is possible to distinguish five main senses, the first three of which are closely related:

1. to discover or get by searching or effort;
2. to discover accidentally, to come across;
3. to succeed in obtaining or achieving;
4. to discover (by chance or by experience) that something is the case; to become aware of;

5. to regard as, to look upon.

It is interesting to see that it is possible to relate the five senses distinguished above to particular syntactic patterns. Monotransitive *find* + NP is chiefly found in senses 1, 2 and 3. Examples:

Sense 1:

(51) I'd like you to *find Mr Joy.*
(52) Now I'll just *find your essay.*

Sense 2:

(53) He showed not the least surprise in *finding the Richardsons* there.
(54) She says it's so wonderful to *find unspoiled people* these days.

Sense 3:

(55) . . . one hardly knows how to *find the time* for it all.
(56) We are here to *find a solution.*

Ditransitive *find* is invariably used in sense 1, as in:

(57) He could use his influence . . . and *find them work* at the University.

Sense 4 typically correlates with monotransitive *find* followed by a finite or non-finite clause:

(58) I walked ten miles to *find they were not at home.*
(59) Often she would turn and *find him watching her.*
(60) They would *find doors pulled from their hinges.*

However, sense 4 is also found with various complex transitive patterns, as the following examples illustrate:

(61) You'll *find the Turks very hospitable.*
(62) He was surprised to *find his room empty.*
(63) You will *find Mrs Carson in a distraught condition.*

Sense 5 is not easy to distinguish from sense 4. *OALD* and *LDOCE* do not list it as a separate sense, but *Cobuild* (sense 7) does. Sense 5 occurs especially with complex transitive *find*, when followed by NP + NP or by NP + AP, as in:

(64) I *find that quite unforgivable.*
(65) I *find that a rather odd statement.*
(66) You *find me an interesting case*, I perceive.
(67) You know *how upsetting* Papa *finds all this.*

Note that one way of distinguishing between sense 4 and sense 5 is that the latter does not cooccur with forms of the auxiliary *will.*

3 *Want*

3.1 Forms

Non-verbal uses of the word *want* are very infrequent. As a noun, the form *want* occurs only three times; *wanting* as an adjective is found once (in: *The saleswoman on the ground floor assessed and found wanting the cut of Hackett's coat*); the adjective *wanted* has three occurrences. Most frequent of all is the adjective *unwanted*, with ten occurrences; however, six of these come from the same sample, which deals with unwanted pregnancies.

The verb *want* occurs 868 times. A survey of the various forms found is given in Table 9.5. There are 637 occurrences of finite forms, and 231 occurrences of non-finite forms. Expressed in percentages, 73 per cent of the tokens are finite, while 27 per cent are non-finite. This is in striking contrast with the verb *find*, which presents an almost exactly inverse picture: 21 per cent of the occurrences of *find* are finite, 79 per cent are non-finite. It should be pointed out that the distribution of the non-finite forms of *want* is as follows: bare infinitive: 161; *to*-infinitive: 5; *ing*-participle: 27; *ed*-participle: 38. The number of finite Verb Phrases in which *want* is the lexical verb is much larger than the number of single finite forms of this verb. There are 203 complex finite Verb Phrases in which *want* is the lexical verb, so that the number of finite Verb Phrases with *want* reaches a total of 840 (203 + 637), while the number of non-finite Verb Phrases is no larger than 28; in percentages 97 per cent and three per cent respectively. Of the finite forms of *want* the present tense is more frequent than the past, but not dramatically so: there are 364 present tense forms as opposed to 273 past tense forms.

Table 9.5 *Forms of the verb* want

Want				
Finite forms	Present tense	364		
	Past tense	273		
			TOTAL	637
Non-finite forms	Bare infinitive	161		
	To-infinitive	5		
	Ing-participle	27		
	Ed-participle	38		
			TOTAL	231
			TOTAL	868

The large number of bare infinitives (161) occurs in combination with *do* and the modal auxiliaries. The lion's share of these occurrences is accounted for by *do*: 138. Of these, a large majority of 114 are the negative forms *don't*, *didn't* and *doesn't*. The least frequent of the auxiliaries are *might* (two occurrences) and *may* (one occurrence). *Can* does not occur at all, although *cannot* does once.

To-infinitives are preceded by a semi-auxiliary (*seem to*, *turn out to*), and if they stand alone, function either as an extraposed subject or as an extraposed object, as in the following examples:

(68) It is natural . . . *to want* to be free.
(69) . . . we may consider it bad *to want* to have more children . . .

Ing-participles that stand alone show a variety of syntactic functions: postmodifier in a Noun Phrase, adverbial, prepositional complement, subject, object complement. The adverbial function is the most frequent. A participle as subject or as object complement occurs only once. The following are examples of each of these functions:

(70) I was much visited by Dowayos *wanting* to see this wonder.
(71) 'Can't it wait?' Tina said, not *wanting* to come near him.
(72) The difficulty lay in *wanting* to move.
(73) Not *wanting* to see Joanna in the buff vied with a curiosity about how poignant she would look.
(74) Funny how a glorious love-making session the night before always left her *wanting* more the following morning.

3.2 Complementation

There are no occurrences in the corpus of intransitive uses of *want*, although there are some 40 cases where *want* is not accompanied by an explicit complement. All these occurrences can be looked upon as instances of ellipsis of one kind or another. Closest to an intransitive use of *want* are expressions of the type 'if you want'; in other cases the lack of a complement is due to a zero relative in postmodifying clauses with *want*, or ellipsis of a verb is signalled by the infinitive marker *to*. Leaving aside instances where the relative pronoun is omitted, the uses of *want* without an explicit complement follow the following patterns (where the ellipted elements are enclosed in square brackets):

1. *want* [*to* V]
2. *want to* [V]
3. *want* NP *to* [V].

The first pattern is not very frequent (six occurrences) and contextually the most restricted: it only occurs in adverbial clauses of time, condition or manner. These are introduced by *if*, *when*, *as long as*, *as* or *the way*. Some examples are:

(75) You can wait outside if you *want*.
(76) . . . I think you'd both be very wise to let Mosson produce it the way he *wants*.
(77) . . . the process of exploration has continued as long as he *needs or wants* . . .

The second pattern is not only more frequent (fifteen occurrences) but its distribution does not seem subject to any contextual restrictions, although adverbial clauses with *if* appear to favour the construction (eight instances):

(78) . . . if she *wants to*, she can get in touch with you.
(79) 'May I call you, Edna?' he said hoarsely. 'Oh. Well yes, if you *want to*, Sam.'
(80) Is it only because he cannot that he *wants to* so much?
(81) He would start work next year, and didn't know whether he *wanted to* or not.
(82) 'Did he go back with you?' 'No. I offered but he didn't seem *to want to*.'

Pattern 3 is the least frequent (three occurrences). In all instances the NP in the pattern is a pronoun:

(83) . . . even his eyeballs wouldn't move though he *wanted them to*.
(84) 'I can't leave it!' 'I don't *want you to*.'

Finally, in postmodifying clauses the zero relative may be either the object of *want* or a raised object of the ellipted verb complementing *want*:

(85) . . . they made sure that I couldn't get to the people I *wanted* . . .
(86) It was common knowledge that I was capable of understanding anything I really *wanted to*.

A description in terms of the syntactic functions of the complements of *want* yields only two types: *want* is either followed by a single direct object or by a direct object together with an object complement. In other words, *want* is used either as a monotransitive or as a complex transitive verb. But within these two functional types there is much variation in the categorial constituents that can fill these functions. We start by giving a survey of the various ways in which the complementation of *want* can be realised by categorial constituents in Table 9.6, giving absolute frequencies for both functional and categorial types (for ease of reference the types are numbered).

Table 9.6 *Types of complementation after* want

Functional type		Realisation	
1 Monotransitive:	O_d	1.1 NP	280
		1.2 Wh-clause	1
		1.3 [$_s$ *to*-infinitive	482
		1.4 [$_s$ NP + *to*-inf	96
		1.5 [$_s$ NP + *ing*-participle	5
		1.6 [$_s$ NP + *ed*-participle	14
Total	838		
2 Complex transitive:	$O_d + C_o$	2.1 NP + AdvP	15
		2.2 NP + PP	12
		2.3 NP + AP	2
		2.4 NP + *Wh*-clause	1
Total	30		

3.2.1 Monotransitive complementation

It is clear that we could have presented the categorial constituents realising the object function at a higher level of abstraction; if we disregard the one occurrence of a Wh-clause, we could have said that the complement of monotransitive *want* is either a NP or a non-finite clause and that this clause may or may not have a subject of its own. It is also clear, however, that this would not have done justice to the frequencies found, which are very unevenly distributed over the various patterns. Obviously, there are only two complementation patterns with a really high frequency: the one where the object is realised by a Noun Phrase, the other in which the object is a non-finite infinitive clause whose subject is the same as that of the matrix clause. And even between these high-frequency patterns there is a big difference, for pattern 1.3 is almost twice as frequent as pattern 1.1. With respect to the latter pattern it can be observed that in twenty per cent of the occurrences the object-NP has a human referent, while in 34 per cent of the cases it is a Wh-word. A striking fact in pattern 1.3 is that in no less than eight per cent of the total number the infinitive is *to know.*

We give one example of each of the six monotransitive patterns:

(87) Employees *want a greater say* at work.

(88) . . . a man who *wanted what was being offered.*

(89) You *want to know if my honour is still bloody loyalty*?

(90) He . . . moved his head to show that he *wanted us to get going.*

(91) We don't *want skeletons this size tumbling out of cupboards* at this stage, thank you very much.
(92) Many of their members will not *want these organizations nationalized.*

3.2.2 Complex transitive complementation

In this type of complementation, the realisation of the O_d is always a simple Noun Phrase, often a pronoun or a proper name. We first illustrate each of the patterns (2.1–2.4) mentioned in Table 9.6:

AdvP:

(93) I *want them all out*.

PP:

(94) . . . she *wanted Susan at home* to look after her.

AP:

(95) But if he *wanted Berowne dead* . . .

Wh-clause:

(96) I *want Stinnes where he can be protected.*

When the C_o function is realised by an adverb, this is usually a particle-like one. We recorded the following adverbs: *along*, *back*, *here*, *home*, *off*, *over*, and *out*. With six occurrences, *back* is by far the most frequent one. *Off* comes second with three occurrences. Prepositional Phrases as C_o are almost without exception indications of place (*in the house*, *on my doorstep*, *all over the floor*, *up her innards*). In one example we find a phrase introduced by *as*: *as commander.* There are only two occurrences of an adjective; in both cases this is the adjective *dead.*

Semantically, the complex transitive pattern expresses a situation resulting from an implied action (which is very often 'come' or 'go', as the above examples show). The pattern might therefore be said to carry the feature 'perfective'. This feature is also inherent in another complementation pattern which, however (owing to the syntactic nature of our classificatory scheme based as it is on syntactic functions and categories realising these functions), we have been compelled to put under the monotransitive use of *want*. This is the pattern in which the O_d is realised by a non-finite clause containing an *ed*-participle, as in the following examples:[2]

(97) . . . *wanting no impressions of the journey imprinted on his mind.*
(98) . . . they *wanted whips abolished* . . .
(99) . . . municipal workers . . . who *want their incomes maintained.*

The only difference between this pattern and the complex transitive ones without a verb seems to be that the *ed*-participle makes explicit the action leading to the situation desired. Conceptually speaking, therefore, this pattern naturally seems to classify with the complex transitive examples discussed above. Perhaps superfluously, it should be pointed out that what has been said about the patterns with an *ed*-participle does not apply to monotransitive patterns with a present participle; on the contrary, if we assign the feature 'perfective' to the former pattern, the latter should receive the feature 'imperfective':[3]

(100) I didn't *want some squad of Special Branch detectives creeping up to grab Ted* . . .

3.2.3 Special patterns

Brief mention should be made of one or two syntactically 'marked' sentence patterns in which *want* occurs. The most important of these are sentences or clauses introduced by a Wh-word. This is in the vast majority of cases the word *what*; of a total number of 76 occurrences of this pattern, only six are introduced by different Wh-words (*where*, *whatever*, *when* and *how*).

Of this total number, 56 are straightforward cases of Wh-fronting, while the remaining number involve object-raising. These latter cases correspond either to pattern 1.3 in Table 9.6 or to pattern 1.4. Fifteen simple sentences with Wh-fronting are direct questions which have either of the following two forms:

(101) What do you *want*?
(102) What you *want*?

The latter form is not at all infrequent; it occurs six times. The pattern *what pronoun want* would seem to be a rather fixed pattern which is neutral between interrogative and non-interrogative contexts. In an interrogative context it can function as a simple direct question, while in non-interrogative contexts it occurs as sub-clause in a variety of functions. In the latter function it has a variant which is syntactically rather different: *all pronoun want*. In spite of its different syntactic structure, however, this pattern has exactly the same contextual distribution as *what pronoun want*.

Sub-clauses introduced by a Wh-word can realise various functions: subject (this includes pseudocleft patterns), object and subject complement. These are the most frequent functions, with thirteen, eighteen and thirteen occurrences respectively. Other functions are much less frequent. They include: object complement, prepositional complement, adjectival complement and adverbial.

As is apparent from the use of *what pronoun want* as a question, *want* is prone to be used in elliptic sentence patterns. Ellipsis usually involves the auxiliary *do* and sometimes the subject as well:

(103) You *want* to see?
(104) You *want* to help me?
(105) *Want* to bet?

Needless to say, such elliptic patterns only occur in the dialogue passages of fiction texts.

3.3 Meaning

A comparison of three dictionaries (*OALD*, *LDOCE* and *Cobuild*) shows that, roughly, three meanings of *want* can be distinguished. The first is usually paraphrased as 'desire', the second as 'require' or 'need' (as in 'the house wants painting') and the third as 'lack' or 'fall short by' (as in 'you shall never want' or 'it wants one inch of the regulation length'). We can be brief about the third meaning – it does not occur in our material. It is also a meaning that is not recorded in *Cobuild*, the most recent of the three dictionaries.

Of the two other meanings we shall call the 'desire' meaning the 'volitional' sense, and the 'need/require' meaning the 'non-volitional' sense, for it is clearly the presence or absence of volition that distinguishes between the two senses. The complement for both senses always indicates some sort of state or activity that is 'desired' or 'required'. This is always true, even when the complement is only realised by a Noun Phrase. In the latter case, the Noun Phrase either refers directly to a state or activity, as in:

(106) I loved and missed my mother, *wanted her comfort* . . .

or the state or activity is contextually or stereotypically associated with the referent of the Noun Phrase, as in the following example, where sexual activity is stereotypically implied:

(107) . . . he *wanted a woman* badly.

while in the following occurrence the predicate 'drink' is contextually implied:

(108) He put the phone down and went back to the bar. 'I *want something strong and odourless*,' he told the bartender.

In all but seventeen of the 868 occurrences of *want* in our material, the subject of the verb is human. This correlates with an almost total preponderance of the volitional sense of the verb.[4] In eight of these seventeen cases, the subject refers to an institution or a body (e.g. 'the Institute for Physical Research',

'Congress', 'the armed forces'). Even with such subjects, however, we find the volitional sense rather than the non-volitional sense; the same is true if the subject refers to a group of people ('a cosmopolitan crowd', 'the group'). In most of the remaining cases, the pressure of the volitional meaning is so strong that the subject Noun Phrase undergoes personification, as in:

(109) The earth wasn't generous in giving breath, because it *wanted* all people walking about to be under its soil and feeding it.

The same happens to subjects like 'divinity' and 'the Law'. In two occurrences – both from non-fiction, but not from the same sample – the writer indicates that he is aware of this process of personification by putting *want* between quotation marks:

(110) Albino genes do not really '*want*' to survive or to help other albino genes.

(111) We aren't, of course suggesting that clays '*want*' to go on existing.

There is only one clear case of the non-volitional sense of *want* in the corpus:

(112) . . . reduction in expenditure becomes difficult because monopoly capital *wants* social investment to be maintained if profits are to be assured . . .

In this connection it should be pointed out that a complementation type which is most strongly associated with the non-volitional sense does not occur in our material. This is the monotransitive complementation pattern realised by the *ing*-form of a verb. All three dictionaries give examples of this complementation pattern to illustrate *want* in the sense of 'need/require':

OALD	'Your hair *wants* cutting'
LDOCE	'The house *wants* painting'; 'This job *wants* doing'
Cobuild	'. . . jobs that *want* doing in the garden'

Finally, a use of *want* that is recorded in *Cobuild* (where it is paraphrased as 'advise') and in *LDOCE* (paraphrased as 'ought'), but not in the *OALD*, expresses what might be called 'projected volition'; the speaker projects his volition onto his interlocutor. It occurs only once:

(113) 'You don't *want* to study too near an exam,' Willy had said. 'It addles the brain.'

4 Summary and conclusions

This section does not repeat the detailed information about the complementation patterns of *find* and *want* and the numerical data presented in the previous sections. Instead, we want to select some of the more general aspects of our findings for some further comment.

The verb *find* in this corpus is almost exclusively used as a transitive verb. As such it mainly occurs in the monotransitive pattern, followed by a NP, but the object may also be realised by a finite or non-finite clause. Ditransitive and complex transitive *find* occur far less frequently. In the vast majority of cases the subject of *find* has human reference. What is very striking is the preponderance of non-finite forms (almost four times as frequent as the finite ones) and the frequency with which the bare infinitive cooccurs with auxiliaries, particularly with *can/could* and *will/want*. The pattern 'Human subject + auxiliary + *find* + NP' occurs in 119 out of 472 examples, that is more than 25 per cent.

Find can be used in five main senses, which correlate in interesting ways with the syntactic patterns in which this verb can occur. Ditransitive *find* always means 'discover by searching'. Monotransitive *find* + NP can also have that sense, but, in addition, can mean 'discover by chance' and 'succeed in obtaining or achieving'. However, when followed by a clause (finite or non-finite), monotransitive *find* means 'discover that something is the case'. This sense is also found in some complex transitive patterns, but not in all. Complex transitive *find*, when followed by NP + NP or by NP + AP, can also mean 'regard as, look upon'. In that case it does not cooccur with forms of the auxiliary *will*.

About the verb *want* we can say, first of all, that it occurs with three senses in our corpus material: the volitional sense ('desire'), the non-volitional one ('need/require'), and a sense that we have called 'projected volition' and which can be paraphrased as 'ought' or 'I advise you'. The frequency of occurrence of the latter two senses is negligible compared with the first. The projected volition sense occurs only once, while the non-volitional one is, expressed in percentages, not quite two per cent of the total number of occurrences of *want*. A comparison with *OALD*, *LDOCE* and *Cobuild* shows that one of them (*OALD*) does not record the projected volition sense, and that one sense of *want* recorded in *OALD* and *LDOCE* ('lack' or 'fall short by') does not occur in the corpus material – a finding that is corroborated by *Cobuild* which does not record this sense either.

Regarding the interaction between syntactic pattern and the selection of one of the senses of *want*, we can say that in contrast to what we found in the case of *find*, there does not seem to be an interaction between the sense of the verb and its complementation pattern. The one pattern that might condition the non-volitional sense of the verb, namely a monotransitive pattern in which the O_d is realised by the *ing*-form of a verb ('your hair wants cutting') does not occur in our material. However, if no interdependence is found between the complementation of the verb and its sense, we do observe a clear interaction between sense and subject. Whenever the subject is marked with the feature 'human' the cooccurrent verb sense is volitional, whereas a non-human subject favours the non-volitional sense.

It is very likely, in fact, that there is a strong correlation between various of our findings. In the first place, the heavy preponderance of volitional senses correlates with an equally large predominance of human subjects. This, in its turn, seems to explain the fact that more than two-thirds of the total number of occurrences of *want* is found in the fiction texts of the corpus; after all, human subjects are more likely to occur in narrative prose than in other genres. Finally, as has also been manifest in the examples given throughout this chapter, the verb *want* tends to occur especially in dialogue passages of fictional texts; this in its turn can explain why this verb is comparatively frequently found in elliptic sentence patterns, which are employed in fictional dialogue to mimic spontaneous speech.

Finally, we think that on the basis of our study some more general conclusions can be drawn with respect to some descriptive principles in the study of corpus data. We have seen that a description in terms of syntactic functions – like O_d, O_i and C_o – and their corresponding syntactic features of verbs like monotransitive, ditransitive and complex transitive, is useful if one wants to make large generalisations. But we have also seen that, in order to get a real insight into what is usual and what is less usual in actual language use, this functional description has to be supplemented by a detailed description in terms of the categories that realise the syntactic functions in question, for there may be very great differences in the frequency of occurrence of the various realisation patterns for one and the same functional constituent. And even then, these two types of description can give an unnatural bias to the way in which one classifies one's findings. As we have seen, this appeared to be the case with *want* if in its monotransitive complementation pattern an *ed*-participle clause was involved; a 'natural' conceptual grouping was prevented by a syntactic function/category classification (see the discussion on pp. 175 f.). This drawback of a function/category description can, however, be remedied by the introduction of conceptually based features. These may be either purely semantic in nature, like the features 'human'–'non-human', or syntactico-semantic, like the 'perfective'–'imperfective' distinction in the case of *want*. Such features can be assigned to the function/category classes arrived at by means of the syntactic description. We think we have shown that by means of the three descriptive tools mentioned (a classification in terms of syntactic functions, one in terms of syntactic categories and, where relevant, the assignment of conceptually based features), it is possible not only to present a fairly complete syntactic description of the phenomenon studied, in which cooccurrence tendencies on the lexical, syntactic or semantic levels and their interaction can be accounted for, but that it is also possible on the basis of this description to make observations about the distribution of the phenomena described across genres (such as narrative vs. non-narrative) as well as within genres (such as dialogue vs. non-dialogue).

Appendix

Genres included in the one-million-word sample from the TOSCA corpus:

Fiction:	general fiction, novel
	general fiction, short story
	psychological novel
	love and romance
	humour
	science fiction and fantasy
	crime and mystery
	horror
	thriller and adventure
Non-fiction:	(auto)biography
	education
	history
	language and linguistics
	literary criticism
	philosophy
	sociology and anthropology
	women's studies
	mysticism and the occult
	politics
	travel
	biology
	economics
	geography
	health and medicine
	psychology and psychiatry

The genres are distinguished on the basis of the publishers' classification system.

Notes

1. The TOSCA corpus was compiled by the TOSCA Research Group for Corpus Linguistics at the University of Nijmegen. It numbers 1.5 million words of post-1985 printed English. The samples making up the corpus have a length of 20,000 words. A full account of its compilation and the principles underlying it is given in Oostdijk (1988a and b). The genres included in the one-million-word fragment used for this study are given in the appendix.
2. In our material it is especially the non-fiction samples that seem to favour this construction; only three out of a total of fourteen occurrences come from fiction texts.
3. In contrast with the occurrences with an *ed*-participle, the ones with a present participle are all found in fiction texts.
4. This probably also accounts for the fact that well over two-thirds of the total number occurs in the fiction samples, for it may be assumed that human subjects are more likely to occur in narrative prose than in other genres.

References

Allén, S. (1992) Opening Address. In Svartvik, J. (ed.), *Directions in corpus linguistics*. Proceedings of Nobel Symposium 82. Stockholm 4–8 August 1991. Berlin: Mouton de Gruyter. 1–3.

Andersson, E. (1985) *On verb complementation in written English*. Lund: CWK Gleerup.

Ek, J. A. van (1966) *Four complementary structures of predication in contemporary English*. Groningen: Wolters.

Mair, C. (1990) *Infinitival complement clauses in English: a study of syntax in discourse*. Cambridge University Press.

Oostdijk, N. (1988a) A corpus for studying linguistic variation. *ICAME Journal* **12**. 3–14.

(1988b) A corpus linguistic approach to linguistic variation. *Literary and Linguistic Computing* **3**. 12–25.

Quirk, R. (1968) Chapter 7 in *Essays on the English language: medieval and modern*. London: Longman.

Quirk, R., Greenbaum, S., Leech, G. and Svartvik, J. (1985) *A comprehensive grammar of the English language*. London: Longman.

Sinclair, J. (1987) *Looking up. An account of the COBUILD project in lexical computing*. London: Collins.

10 Indeterminacy between Noun Phrases and Adjective Phrases as complements of the English verb[1]

GEOFFREY LEECH and LU LI

1 Introduction

Complements of the verb (both subject complements and object complements) are a neglected area of English grammar. This study uses the resources of syntactically analysed corpus data to try to show that there is much of interest to explore in the relations between verb and complement. We will particularly focus on the phenomenon of grammatical indeterminacy (Quirk et al. 1985: 90–91) and more particularly on indeterminacy between nominal and adjectival complements.

The data on which this study was based consisted of the four corpora in table 10.1, three of which were syntactically analysed by a method known as *skeleton parsing*.[2] That is, the corpora had been annotated not only with grammatical word tags, but with a constituent structure bracketing, so that constituents such as Noun Phrase objects and complements could be identified. The remaining corpus, the Lancaster–Oslo–Bergen (LOB) Corpus, had been grammatically tagged but not skeleton-parsed.

Table 10.1 *Corpora used in the study*

	No. of words (approximately)	Annotations	Variety of English
APC	1,000,000	skeleton parsed	American
Hansard	750,000	skeleton parsed	Canadian
SEC	50,000	skeleton parsed	British
LOB	1,000,000	word tagged	British

Brief details of the corpora are as follows:[3]

The APC (Associated Press Corpus) we used was a treebank consisting of about a million words of Associated Press newswire, i.e. a set of news stories in American English, dating from the period 1979–1980.

The Hansard (Canadian Hansard) corpus was a collection of transcripts, dating from the 1980s, from the proceedings of the Canadian Houses of Parliament.

The SEC (IBM/Lancaster Spoken English Corpus) was a small corpus of prepared (usually scripted) British English speech, sampled from the mid 1980s, containing such material as BBC broadcasts.

The LOB (Lancaster–Oslo–Bergen) Corpus of British English was a million-word corpus sampled from writings published in the UK in 1961.

Altogether, the amount of corpus data searched amounted to *c.* 2,800,000 words. Although this was gratifyingly large, it was far from an ideal collection of data in terms of variety and spread: it just happened to be a large set of data that had been grammatically annotated at Lancaster, much of it in connection with another project.[4] In fact, the data consisted very largely of written English. Its value for the present study was that it could be used for syntactically defined, as well as lexically defined automatic searches by a concordance program.

We should explain that for this topic there was a particular advantage in using treebanks, or syntactically annotated corpora. Unless the data had been syntactically analysed, there would have been no way in which the full range of occurrences of subject complements or object complements could be searched for, without undertaking the massive and impracticable task of reading through the whole corpus. It would have been possible to undertake multiple searches, looking for individual verbs such as *be, become, make,* etc. But it would not have been possible to look for the Verb + Complement pattern itself, so that examples of verbs not included in a predetermined list of verbs would not have been found. Therefore, one of the advantages of using treebanks is that we can find examples with verbs such as *write, walk,* and *act*, which are not normally found in lists of verbs taking a subject complement:

(1) . . . a trouser-press and a pen that *writes wet* with dry ink. (LOB)
(2) My son is dead, and his killer is *walking free*. (SEC)
(3) . . . O'Neill said he would have '*acted* a lot *tougher*' with both Iran and U.S. allies. (APC)

Another advantage, a highly practical one, is that we can retrieve from the corpus examples of Verb + Complement constructions, without having to look laboriously through thousands of examples of (say) *have* in order to discover the relatively few examples which occur with object complements.

Having said this, we cannot claim to have found all examples of Verb + Complement in the corpora, because of the rather limited type of syntactic analysis we had to deal with in the first three corpora, and because, in the case of LOB, we had to undertake searches purely on the basis of words and their grammatical tags. All that is claimed is that every reasonable effort was made to find relevant examples, and that the use of annotated corpora saved enormous time and effort in locating what we were looking for. We were therefore able to search a far larger collection of corpus data than would otherwise have been possible. While few claims about frequency can be made in this chapter, the study has thrown into relief many features which are common in the use of phrasal complements of the verb.

Our study pursues an interest in both subject complements and object complements, and particularly in the relation between nominal and adjectival complements. Therefore the four types of construction examined were:

(a) Verb + AdjC (copular verb followed by adjectival subject complement)
(b) Verb + NomC (copular verb followed by nominal subject complement)
(c) Verb + O + AdjC (complex transitive verb followed by object and adjectival object complement)
(d) Verb + O + NomC (complex transitive verb followed by object and nominal object complement)

and the special focus of the study is on the relation between (a) and (b), and between (c) and (d). Examples are:

Verb + AdjC: You just *remain calm* . . . (APC)
Verb + NomC: Rockefeller *became chairman of the bank* . . . (APC)
Verb + O + AdjC: This *leaves patients susceptible to other diseases* . . . (APC)
Verb + O + NomC: . . . he *found Anglesey a strong, energetic man* . . . (LOB)

(In these and subsequent corpus examples, we show the omission of irrelevant parts of the sentence by '. . .', and the corpus from which the example is taken by 'APC', 'Hans', 'SEC', or 'LOB'.)

2 The adjectival qualities of NPs as subject complements

It is well known that Noun Phrases (henceforward NPs) in the position of complement are often similar to Adjective Phrases (henceforward APs) in terms of meaning: they 'characterise' the referent of the subject rather than refer to it. Therefore, typically at least, a complement NP is non-referring, and in this respect unlike most NPs in subject or object roles. What has not been fully explored is the extent to which complement NPs resemble Adjective Phrases not only in meaning, but also in their formal characteristics.

Three formal aspects of complement NPs may be immediately cited as pointing to their uncharacteristic qualities. First, there is the tendency for NPs to be of more restricted occurrence in complement function than APs, in that complement NPs, except with the copula *be* itself, occur less than readily with the full range of copular verbs, especially in American English (see Quirk et al. 1985: 1173). Other constructions are frequently employed as preferred 'substitute' constructions:

(4) Daley added the issue *appeared to be a dead horse.* (LOB)
(rather than: . . . *appeared a dead horse.*)

(5) My boss *seemed like a very nice man.* (APC)
(rather than: . . . *seemed a very nice man.*)

(6) A promise to increase pensions *appears as altruism* to some . . . (LOB)
(rather than: . . . *appears altruism to some* . . .)

Second, there is a tendency to omit the article initiating an NP, a characteristic which (we argue below) gives the NP a more adjectival quality. This omission of the article occurs not only in the well-known case of NPs defining a 'unique role or status' of the subject referent, as in *remain chairman, become secretary,* but in other cases such as *turn traitor, fall prey to* . . ., which are more widespread than can be easily explained as idiomatic anomalies (see further 2.1 and 4.1 below).

Third, there is the facility with which NPs can be coordinated to APs as complements, as if to underline their equivalence to APs in semantic function:

(7) . . . the neighbour whom I've already referred to who had been found murdered and whose house *was still unoccupied and a ruin.*

The NP *a ruin* here is not a typical NP semantically, since it is (like most APs) gradable: for example, it could be expanded into *an utter ruin* (see further below). In the following examples, the gradability of the NP complement is made overt in the intensifying phrases *very much* and *too much*:

(8) Michael stood for a moment *feeling useless and very much the passer-by.* (LOB)

(9) . . . the whole may be *too peripheral and too much of a gamble* for either of the other parties. (LOB)

Although NPs are not usually associated with gradability, the gradable nature of some types of NPs has been discussed, for example, by Bolinger (1972: 58ff, 84), also by Fillmore (1968: 84).

Having given initial plausibility to the proposal that NPs in complement position take on a quasi-adjectival quality, we will now illustrate this point more fully, with reference to four different phenomena which characterise the quasi-adjectival quality of NPs as subject complement. (Later the same characteristics will be illustrated with NPs functioning as object complement.)

2.1 Singular count NPs without an article

Returning firstly to the well-known phenomenon of *become secretary* above, we discover this phenomenon to be more widespread than is usually supposed, and this leads us into a broader consideration of NP-AP indeterminacy. It is typically supposed (e.g. in Quirk et al. 1985: 276) that the zero article with singular count nouns in complement position is restricted to (a) cases where the NP identifies a unique role or status, and (b) a very few idiomatic combinations such as *turn traitor.*

The occurrence of the zero article should, however, be seen in the context of a wider range of data. For example, we observe from corpus data that there are not infrequently cases of indeterminacy between count and non-count nouns (*it seems fair comment . . . , it also remains federal policy . . .*). Compare, for instance, the parallel use of *a reality* and *reality* in:

(10) That agreement . . . will, as I say, allow those aspirations of British Columbians to *become a reality.* (Hans)

(11) I therefore hope that the words of the minister *will become reality* . . . (Hans)

In the second case, it is difficult to decide whether the noun is being used purely in its non-count use, or whether it is moving diachronically in the direction of noun-to-adjective conversion. The latter process, which itself testifies to the tendency for Noun Phrase complements to gravitate towards adjectival use, is illustrated in its fullest form by the adjectival use of *fun* both predicatively and attributively (as in *The event was fun* and *It was a fun event*). However, one suspects that in cases such as the following, the slippage towards adjectival status is at least incipient:

(12) Gasohol – the mixture of gasoline and a substance similar to vodka – *is becoming big business* as Americans seek a way out of their reliance on imported oil. (APC)

(13) The lower half of the door was unlatched to admit him into a room which *seemed half church, half office.* (LOB)

(14) A promise to increase pensions appears as altruism to some; to others it *seems rank bribery.* (LOB)

The next example, with *turn*, will lead us on to the question of idiomatic examples with the verbs *turn* and *fall*:

(15) Father Harry was a pro, brother Phil *turned pro* on the same date as Denny . . . (APC)

The interest here lies in the fact that *pro* in its first occurrence is definitely a noun, whereas *pro* in its second occurrence could well be an adjective – if we acknowledge that *pro* in its sporting sense has undergone conversion to an adjective. However, another interpretation is that *pro*, like *traitor*, is capable of occurring after *turn* as a noun. This second interpretation appears more likely in the light of evidence elsewhere that *turn* is not restricted to one or two fixed expressions such as *turn traitor*:

(16) I find good ideas that tend to *turn comic book*. (APC)

The same point can be made about *fall*, which is attested not only with the familiar idioms *fall victim*, *fall prey (to)*, but also more productively in:

(17) . . . more than nine hundred *fell captive* to the Spaniards. (LOB)

and in the curtailed version of *falling prey to* in:

(18) 'When a useful means of redress runs the risk of being thwarted . . . the commission must act to avoid *falling prey*,' Statler said. (APC)

The most important point to consider here, however, is whether it is justified to consider the case of zero article for 'unique role or status' as a zero *definite* article, as the term 'unique' implies. It is observable that the same NP, or similar NPs, may occur with or without the definite article, when the reference is decidedly unique:

(19) . . . Churchill *remained the Air Minister* . . . (LOB)
(20) Her father, Theodore Roosevelt, *became president* in 1901 . . . (APC)

It was beyond the scope of the research reported here to determine what factors influenced the choice of *the* or zero.[5] However, we did note that the zero article did not appear to be limited to cases of uniqueness. This is not unexpected with examples of *turn* + NP:

(21) Ireland's Sean Mannion, 147, of Galway, *turned slugger* and stopped Pat Maloney, 145, of New York. (APC)

But examples such as the following, where the paraphrase of *a sergeant* is easily more acceptable than *the sergeant*, break the assumed restriction to uniqueness in non-idiomatic cases:

(22) You *became sergeant* the very next day . . . (LOB)

The NP does not need to define an institutional role:

(23) . . . Ellen might well recoil from *becoming stepmother* to girls of her own age and a gang of young boys. (LOB)

On the other hand, no corpus evidence was found to justify extending the use of 'zero definite article' to clauses with inanimate subjects; e.g. *the* is apparently not omissible in (24):

(24) He is a fervent supporter of a total division of Belgium into two independent states with Brussels *becoming the capital of a United States of Europe*. (APC)

All in all, however, the evidence of the corpora (although too limited for definite conclusions) is that the zero article occurs with singular count nouns in complement position rather more widely than is standardly assumed: a point giving some support to our thesis of the adjectival tendencies of complement NPs.

2.2 Gradable nouns as head of the complement NPs

The initial point to make about gradable nouns in complement function is that they perform a function similar to that of an adjective: describing the extent to which a property holds of the referent of the subject. This is graphically illustrated by examples from the corpora in which a complement noun could be replaced, without apparent change of meaning, by an adjective:

(25) But his trip to the U.S. Consulate *proved a disappointment*. (APC) (. . . *proved disappointing*)

(26) . . . it is just beginning to see that rampant inflation *has already become a disaster* for millions of Canadians. (Hans) (. . . *become disastrous*)

Sometimes the combination of adjective + noun switches easily to adverb + adjective:

(27) Fascism *remained a possible peril* to 'progressives' till the Fascist leaders were defeated and destroyed. (LOB) (. . . *possibly perilous*)

(28) The STOL program, which is being developed rapidly, has *become a real success.* (Hans) (. . . *really successful*)

It is characteristic of gradable abstract nouns of quality (such as *disappointment, disaster, peril,* and *success*) that they can be accompanied by degree modifications such as *rather a, more of a, too much of a,* etc. Such modifications, however, apply to a wider range of gradable nouns in complement position, as is illustrated by (29)–(35):

(29) A night club sounds *rather a come-down.* (LOB)
(30) Getting it through to some parents that earlier puberty is now a fact is proving *quite a headache to doctors and teachers.* (LOB)
(31) 'It seems *such a waste.*' (LOB)
(32) He was *too much of a dreamer ever to do any good.* (LOB)
(33) I've not been *much of a mother to you*, Helen. (LOB)
(34) I know *how much of a drag* it can be . . . (LOB)
(35) Last winter was *more of a panic than anything else* . . . (APC)

It is evident from the corpora that such NPs occur more frequently in complement function than in other functions.

2.3 The 'dummy noun' phenomenon

The next quasi-adjectival characteristic to be considered may be conveniently called the 'dummy noun' phenomenon. It is noteworthy that an exceptional number of complement NPs contain adjectives preceding the noun, and that these adjectives often carry the major functional load of the phrase, so that the noun is reduced to a non-communicative 'dummy' status. This situation arises most obviously in examples where the head of the NP is the substitute pronoun *one* or *ones*:

(36) . . . the question would seem to *be a legitimate one* . . . (APC)
(37) The Administration decided to take the risk, which indeed did not appear to *be a large one*. (LOB)
(38) The waste disposal problem . . . has *become a serious one* for Connecticut industry. (APC)
(39) 'They *are fine ones*, Jimmy.' (LOB)
(40) . . . they *were* only *little ones.*

The substitute pronoun refers back, in such examples, to the subject of the clause or to its antecedent, and could be omitted without substantial change of effect, the NP complement being replaced by an AP; e.g.:

(41) . . . the question would seem to *be legitimate* . . .

The head of the NP in (36)–(40) appears to have a 'dummy' status, acting as little more than a device for converting an AP into an NP. The accompanying modification can also be a postmodifier such as a Prepositional Phrase:

(42) Thus, the main point of dispute arising from the Garnett ruling has *become one of scope.* (APC)

although in this case, the pronoun *one* could not be omitted. Equally vacuous seem NP complements whose head repeats the head of the subject:

(43) . . . university people seem, perhaps, to laymen outside, *rather odd people*. (LOB)

In other cases, the complement NP's head is a general noun, whose range of meaning adds little or nothing to that of the subject's head:

(44) He *looked a mournful man* and his handshake was loose . . . (LOB)
(45) '. . . I *became a political being* for the first time in my life,' she said. (APC)
(46) But the traditional high-school memory book in recent years *has become very much a thing of the present*. (APC)

To emphasise the tendency for the head noun to add little to the adjective, we add here two pairs of examples which show the parallelism of function between the NP and AP as complement, where the same adjective is used:

(47) It *sounded a good idea* . . . (LOB)
(48) That *sounded pretty good* . . . (Hans)
(49) . . . the Lebanese Republic *became an independent sovereign state* on November 27th, 1941. (LOB)
(50) St. Lucia (pop. 120,000) *became independent* earlier this year. (APC)

The frequency of the 'dummy noun' phenomenon indicates that the role of NP complements is often almost indistinguishable from that of AP complements. In that case, one might ask, why does a writer prefer to use a longer NP, with a vacuous noun as head? – a question to which we have no answer, and which invites further investigation.

2.4 Subject-complement discord

We use the term 'discord' in contrast to the term 'concord', which is often (e.g. in Quirk et al. 1985: 767) used for agreement of number, not only between subject and verb, but also between subject and complement. Thus, the normal assumed rule is that if the subject of a copular verb is singular, the complement NP will also be singular; and similarly for the plural. The lack of such concord ('discord') in certain cases has also been noted often enough, though little researched.

Since subject complement discord describes a relation between two NPs, it appears at first glance to have little relevance to our present topic, the relation between NP and AP as complements of the verb. However, Table 10.2 will help to establish this relevance. It shows the observed frequency of the occurrence of two opposite types of discord: *Plur–sing discord* is the type where a plural subject is followed by a singular subject complement, and

Table 10.2 *Frequencies of discord occurrences*[6]

	SEC	LOB	APC	Hans	TOTAL
plur–sing	16	112	145	125	398
sing–plur	10	73	89	56	228
TOTAL	26	185	234	181	626

sing–plur discord is the type where a singular subject is followed by a plural subject complement. The figures show that plur–sing discord is substantially more common than sing–plur discord in all four corpora: a disparity which begs explanation.

Our explanation is as follows. If we accept that the NP complement in many cases has a quasi-adjectival role, then one of the features to be associated with this adjectival tendency is a lack of number contrast between singular and plural. The singular form of the noun is in general morphologically unmarked (having no *-s* morpheme), and singular number is also syntactically unmarked in certain respects (e.g. the form of the verb following a subordinate clause as subject is singular: *How old you look* IS *less important than how old you feel*).[7] It can thus be supposed that APs in English, lacking number contrast, are singular by default. And hence complement NPs, to the extent that they resemble APs, will show a preference for singular number rather than plural.[8]

The repercussions of this generalisation in plur–sing discord can be most easily seen in examples such as (51):

(51) . . . they *fell victim* to a lovers' quarrel . . . (APC)

where the idiomatic combination of verb and complement does not allow variation between singular and plural: **they fell victims* is not attested. More generally, we can identify five categories of singular NP complement which occur with a plural subject. These categories are listed and described below, but are not always as distinct as the headings make them appear. They make up a spectrum, rather than a set of clearly demarcated classes. Although we will focus on cases of plur–sing discord, the same classes of complement also frequently occur, naturally enough, with singular subject NPs, where no problem of explaining discord arises.

2.4.1 Collective nouns as complement head

The class of plur–sing discord where the complement is a singular collective noun is the least surprising, since it is well known that plur–sing discord between subject and verb can take place in similar circumstances (see Quirk et al. (1985: 758) for this so-called *notional concord*):

(52) . . . *we*'re *an improved club* . . . (APC)
(53) . . . *they* are *a team used to working together* . . . (LOB)
(54) *The Hungarians* are *a lively people,* with a sense of humour very much like ours. (LOB)

2.4.2 *Abstract non-count nouns as complement head*

These nouns are extremely common as heads of a subject complement: they resemble adjectives in being (in the relevant sense) invariable for number, and also in expressing a property or attribute predicated of the subject:

(55) *The successes of the Labour Party at the polls*, particularly in the 1920's, are *good evidence of this*. (LOB)
(56) I suggest to the hon. member that such questions are not questions: *they* are *debate*. (Hans)

As further testimony to this attribute-bearing role, we note that the abstract NP as complement can be matched to a concrete NP as subject, leading to a double 'discord' both of number and of animacy:

(57) . . . *these coins* are *legal tender in Canada* . . . (Hans)
(58) *Shirts* are *his business.* (LOB)
(59) . . . *'abominable snowmen'* are just *'myth or legend'.* (APC)

2.4.3 *Generic terms as complement head*

A generic term may act as head of the complement NP, showing a link between plur–sing discord and the topic of 'dummy nouns' in 2.3 above: since the subject head is a hyponym of the complement head, the complement head adds little information to that conveyed by the adjective:

(60) Moreover *mushrooms* are *a very risky crop.* (LOB)

2.4.4 *Partitive nouns as complement head*

Another important category of nouns occurring as head of the complement NP consists of nouns whose semantic function is to partition, in quantity or amount, the substance referred to by another noun, often overtly connected to the partitive noun by *of*:

(61) *Small businesses* are *a unique form of enterprise*. (Hans)
(62) *These people* are not *the kind who demonstrate*: they just suffer. (Hans)

(63) *Farm service supply needs* are now *a major item of paperwork*. (Hans)

The noun *part* itself is particularly frequent in this function, and provides a link to the topic of zero article in 2.1 above:

(64) . . . Greg Norman's outstanding achievements were just *part of a magnificent year for Australian sport*. (SEC)

Part occurs either with or without the article, except that when *it* is premodified, either an article or some other determiner must precede it:

(65) *We* are *an integral part* of the vibrant city of Edmonton. (Hans)
(not: *We* are integral part . . .)

Like the preceding category, that of partitive nouns brings out the abstractness of the complement NP, as constrasted with the often more specific and concrete subject NP.

2.4.5 Relational nouns as complement head

Relational nouns are nouns whose function is to act as a kind of textual pivot, carrying the discourse forward (the term 'carrier noun' is used by Ivanic (1991), in discussing a similar range of phenomena). Their meanings, like those of the noun categories discussed in 2.4.3 and 2.4.4 above, are relational, abstract, and often very general, so that they are more than usually chameleonlike in taking on meaning from their context. *Example* is a case in point:

(66) . . . *our shipyards* are *an example* of the prosperity of the Canadian industry . . . (Hans)

Relational nouns are commonly deverbal:

(67) *All jokes* were *a reshuffle* of the same old lot . . . (LOB)
(68) *They* are now *a threat* to world economic stability. (Hans)
(69) . . . such occupations are *a violation* of human rights . . . (APC)

or de-adjectival:

(70) *The fears of some* became *a reality* Thursday when three new tremors were felt. (APC)
(71) *The rice fields and the town's public garden* were *the pride of the residents*. (APC)

They can be ambivalent in concord, as the following pairs of examples indicate:

(72) . . . *they* were *a fake*. (LOB)

(73) . . . *some of the so-called Tudor windows incorporated in rebuilding operations* were *fakes.* (LOB)
(74) . . . *the questions raised by Statler* are *a major concern* of the commission . . . (APC)
(75) He added that *nutritional programs for the elderly* . . . would be *top concerns* of his administration. (APC)

And can sometimes be metaphorical:

(76) *These people* are *the backbone of society.* (Hans)
(77) *The Olympics* were *a dream of mine* since I was a child . . . (APC)

3 Further issues relating to discord

Looking at the whole range of noun-types occurring as complement in 2.4.1–2.4.5 above, we can observe that they share one major characteristic: they are all, in their various ways, more abstract and more general than the subject head, or (in the case of personal pronouns) the head of the Noun Phrase to which the subject co-refers. In fact, the complement head in many cases has little meaning in its own right, but takes meaning from the context in which it occurs. Being abstract and general, the complement is also adjective-like in losing its variability for number. These are the circumstances which provide a natural explanation for the use of a singular complement head, even where the subject is plural.

This generalisation is not restricted to those cases which may be distinguished as *ascriptive* rather than *identificational* uses of the complement NP. Where the copular verb is equivalent to an identity-relation (=), we would expect the complement NP to be more of a full-blooded NP, often having a referring function:

(78) These principles are *the very foundation of our country.* (Hans)
(79) Town meetings are *the traditional New England way of doing things* . . . (APC)
(80) Animals are *our hope of survival* if we will learn from them. (APC)

These sentences exemplifying plur–sing discord can in principle be reversed, and turned into cases of sing–plur discord, e.g. *Our hope . . . is animals* . . . , and of course this opposite kind of discord does occur with identificational sentences:

(81) My subject is *the universities* . . . (LOB)

Nevertheless, the predominant pattern is plur–sing discord, and the tendency to prefer the more general and abstract concept in complement position is confirmed by the three examples above, all illustrating the use of abstract relational nouns (*foundation, way, hope*) as the complement head.

We cannot leave the topic of subject–complement discord without commenting on the view (see Rensky 1981, Jacobsson 1990, and Allerton 1991) that the roles of subject and complement are at least in some degree reversible, so that when *My subject is the universities* is transformed into *The universities is/are my subject*, the ordering is no longer Subject–Verb–Complement but Complement–Verb–Subject. This issue must be addressed in this context, since it might be advanced that the predominance of plur–sing discord is merely based on a erroneous parsing of the sentence: that in fact the occurrence of a Noun Phrase in first position should not lead us to classify it necessarily as subject, nor should the occurrence of a Noun Phrase following the copular verb lead us to classify it as a complement.

Much of the argument on this issue has centred around the occurrence of ambivalent subject–verb concord in pseudocleft sentences:

(82) . . . what you need *are* high-speed drills . . . (LOB)

(83) I sat down to figure out what they couldn't use for war, and what I came up with *was* birds. (LOB)

As we see from the above two sentences, the concord can be controlled either by the plurality of the following NP, or by an assumed singular number of the preceding *wh*-clause (see 2.4 above on unmarked singular number). But it would be rash to assume that the plurality of *high-speed drills* in the first example signals its subject status.[9] A count of all examples that could be found in the APC demonstrated, in cases of subject–complement discord, an overwhelming preference for subject–verb concord with the preceding NP (234 cases of agreement with the first NP, and only 16 cases of agreement with the second NP). In other words, the first NP, which we have assumed to be the subject, is the NP which has the dominant controlling influence on the number of the verb. The postverbal NP, which we have assumed to be the complement, has only a weak controlling influence on the verb, and may (as we have seen) in any case be ambivalent as regards number. All in all, the issue of subject–complement reversability can be ignored, as an interesting side-issue, in considering the findings of this study, and we may continue to regard the evidence of concord as backing our assumption that the dominating order is Subject–Verb–Complement.

4 Indeterminacy between Adjective Phrases and Noun Phrases as object complements

So far we have restricted our illustrations of the NP–AP indeterminacy to the Subject–Verb–Subject Complement (SVC) pattern. The argument now focusses on object complements, and we will aim to show that the same quasi-adjectival features of NPs are also observed in the Subject–Verb–Object–Object Complement (SVOC) pattern. We will simply run through the same categories as were observed for subject complements in 2.1–2.4 with brief explanation:

4.1 Singular count NPs without an article

We notice, as with examples such as *turn traitor*, that idiomatic combinations of verb and object complement (such as *hold NP hostage*) are not so fixed and unproductive as might be supposed: the examples *hold NP hostage, hold NP captive*, and *hold NP prisoner* all occur in the corpora. Moreover, it is clear from the following passive example that no 'uniqueness' is implied by the zero article in such cases:

(84) A U.S. marine . . . says he was tortured and sentenced to death while he *was held hostage* at the U.S. Embassy in Tehran . . . (APC)

In fact, many U.S. personnel were 'held hostage' in this incident.

A more productive category where the object complement defines a unique role, task or status, is that associated with verbs such as *elect* and *appoint* (where, incidentally, the vast majority of cases are in the passive):

(85) Choi *was elected president* by an electoral college Dec. 6 as originally scheduled. (APC)

(86) He entered the foreign service the next year and *was appointed first secretary in the Paris embassy.* (APC)

(87) Woody Allen *was voted best director* for 'Manhatten' . . . (APC)

(88) Melvyn Douglas *was chosen best supporting actor* for 'Being There'. (APC)

There are many more examples like these in the APC, and the uniqueness of the office in question is rarely in doubt, as is indicated particularly clearly by the use of the superlative *best* in the last two examples above.

However, as with subject complements, it is apparent that the uniqueness rule is not always upheld:

(89) Mr Brian James Bond . . . *has been appointed tutor in the Department of History at Exeter University.* (LOB)

(90) He *was named instructor in anatomy* at the Medical College of Virginia in 1954 . . . (APC)

Presumably the subject referents of the above sentences were not the sole holders of the offices of tutor and instructor respectively.

4.2 Gradable nouns as head of the object complement NP

The adjective-like characteristic of gradability is common with object complements, as is illustrated by (91)–(93):

(91) Mrs. Tyler is *finding* it *a bit of a strain* looking after her on deck. (LOB)
(92) We *made* it *quite a session*. (LOB)
(93) . . . the environment of an enthusiastic society *makes* it *much more of a pleasure*. (LOB)

4.3 The 'dummy noun' phenomenon

In examples such as the following, we observe the occurrence of a 'dummy noun' or substitute pronoun, with little information value, as head of an object complement:

(94) They have found the area a desirable *place* . . . (Hans)
(95) The East Berlin government rejected his accusations and labeled the pastor 'an abnormal *person*'. (APC)
(96) 'We shall have to come here for our holiday next year and make it a proper *one*,' she added, smiling wanly. (LOB)

4.4 Subject/object–object complement discord

Parallel to the phenomenon of subject–complement discord with copular verbs is the occurrence of plur–sing discord between object and object complement with complex transitive verbs such as *judge*. However, it happens that very many examples in the corpora are passive, so that the following are representative:

(97) . . . and the constant passage of heavy and rapidly increasing traffic had *made them a danger* to the community. (LOB)
(98) In China, for instance, *dried rats* are *esteemed a delicacy*. (LOB)
(99) *Manpower and employment services* must be *judged a failure* when considered from the standpoint of the needs of those with low incomes. (Hans)

All in all, we see that the 'adjectival' qualities found in NPs as subject complements are found also in object complements. This conclusion confirms that a common pattern of adjectival symptoms applies to complement NPs in general, and adds force to the overall argument that complement NPs show marked adjectival tendencies.

5 Conclusion: some more theoretical remarks

In 1973 John Robert Ross published an article with the intriguing title 'A fake NP squish' (Ross 1973), in which he argued that not all constituents which have NP characteristics are 'copperclad, brass-bottomed NP's', but that to varying degrees, different kinds of NP may lack some NP characteristics. We consider that the data and observations presented in this chapter confirm this view, showing a somewhat similar 'NP squish' to that noted by Ross. However, we see 'our' squish as specifically relating NP complements in different ways and to different degrees to AP complements, and would argue that the squish is genuine rather than fake! To characterise the phenomena of indeterminacy which arise when linguistic categories are found to have blurred edges, other scalar concepts, such as those termed *gradient* (Bolinger 1961) and *cline* (Halliday 1961), have also been used.

Although there is little difference between the models implicit in the varied terminology applied to grammatical indeterminacy, we find that the concept of *prototype* (Rosch and Mervis 1975, Rosch 1976, etc.) fits most happily with our investigation of quasi-adjectival NPs as complement. Prototype theory, arising from experimental studies in cognitive psychology, proposes that categories are identified by reference to a best, most typifying instance, or prototype. This then forms the definitional core of a category, and less prototypical instances form a periphery of progressively diminishing similarity to the prototype. Applying this to NPs, we see a prototype, 'brass-bottomed' NP as (a) being a referring expression, (b) beginning with a determiner, and (c) containing a head which is a noun variable for number, and so on. Arguably (especially viewing NPs from a developmental viewpoint), an NP prototype is also (d) a concrete Noun Phrase, referring to some physical entity or entities. The NPs we have focussed on in this chapter have characteristics which have been 'borrowed', so to speak, from the prototypical AP: e.g. they are (a) property-ascribing, rather than referring expressions; they are (b) abstract, rather than concrete; they are (c) gradable, rather than non-gradable, and they are (d) invariable, rather than variable for number. Some of the adjectival characteristics are derived largely from the noun which forms the head of the NP, but it is the whole NP, rather than simply the head, that is being characterised by degrees of prototypicality. Our case is not that all complement NPs share characteristics of APs, but rather that the complement function is particularly favourable to those less prototypical characteristics of NPs which NPs may share with APs.

As a final point, we may argue that whereas *countability* is another aspect of the prototype NP, non-count nouns resemble adjectives, as the following examples suggest:

(100) Manufacturing the block and planting it *is very little more trouble than normal potting* . . . (LOB)
(101) Mr Macmillan said we could *be more help to the Commonwealth* through the strength we would gain in the Common Market than by isolation. (LOB)

Here the comparative adverb of degree *more* fits comfortably with *trouble* and *help* as non-count nouns, whereas if these nouns had been treated as count, their status of heads of NPs would have become evident through the use of a preposition and an article (*of a*):

(102) . . . *very much more of a trouble* . . .
(103) . . . *more of a help to the Commonwealth* . . .

As it is, examples (100) and (101) illustrate something close to the limit of the NP category in their non-prototypicality and their resemblance to typical APs. This is seen by the fact that only one step is necessary to make the head nouns purely adjectival: the addition of the adjectival suffix *-some* or *-ful*:

(104) . . . *very much more troublesome* . . .
(105) . . . *more helpful to the Commonwealth* . . .

The three sets of examples above show the NP–AP indeterminacy in a nutshell: the intermediate cases (100) and (101) relate on the one hand to the clearly nominal forms of (102) and (103), and to the purely adjectival forms of (104) and (105) on the other.

Notes

1. This chapter is based on research undertaken by the second author under the supervision of the first author, and reported in an unpublished PhD thesis: Lu Li, Copular and complex-transitive constructions in modern written English: a corpus-based study (Lancaster University, 1992). It gives us great pleasure, in the present context, to acknowledge our debt to Sidney Greenbaum, who acted as external examiner for the thesis.
2. Skeleton parsing is an assignment of labelled bracketing to each sentence in a corpus (see Garside and Leech 1991, Black et al. 1993: 52–56). In addition to word-tagging, constituents internal to sentence structure (such as phrases and clauses) are marked off by labelled brackets. The term skeleton parsing is used

because much detail is omitted: e.g. some brackets are left unlabelled, and functional labels (such as subject, object and complement) are not applied. A sample skeleton-parsed sentence is:

> [S&[N The_AT book_NN1 N][V is_VBZ [N a_AT1 short_
> J Jone _NN1 N]V]S&] ,_, but_ CCB [S+[N it_PPH1 N][V
> was_VBDZ [P by_II [N any_DD standards_NN2 N]P][N a_AT1
> remarkable_JJ feat_NN1 [P of_IO [N literary_JJ activity_NN1
> N]P]N]V] ,_, and_CC [[P for_IF [N a_AT1 sick_JJ man_NN1
> N]P][J quite_RG astonishing_JJ J]]S+] ._.

3. The AP Corpus and the Hansard Corpus were part of a large body of electronic corpus material made available to us under the terms of a research programme (between 1986 and 1992) in collaboration with, and funded by, the IBM T. J. Watson Research Center, Yorktown Heights, New York, whose support we gratefully acknowledge.
4. The project in question, part of the research programme referred to in note 3 above, was in collaboration with the Continuous Speech Recognition Group, led by Fred Jelinek, at IBM T. J. Watson Research Center (see Black et al. 1993).
5. One pattern observed was that in such zero-article structures, there was a tendency for the British English corpora to use initial capitals, where in American English lower-case letters were preferred. Compare for example:

> I have warned the country again and again of this since I became *Chancellor*. (LOB)
> Sir Joseph Latham joined the Board in August, and since that date he has become *Director of Finance*. (LOB)

with:

> Her father, Theodore Roosevelt, became *president* in 1901 . . . (APC)
> Augustine became *archbishop* in 597 . . . (APC)

6. Because of the limitations of the search method with available software, and with corpus annotation restricted to skeleton parsing and grammatical tagging, the frequencies are limited to sentences with the copula *be*.
7. Arguments in favour of treating the singular as the syntactically unmarked number are strengthened by the tendency for the singular verb to occur in informal English after existential *there,* where clearly *there* as surface subject determines the number agreement of the verb rather than a following plural Noun Phrase as underlying subject: e.g. *There's too many people in the waiting room* (see Quirk et al. 1985: 1405).
8. There are, of course, exceptions to this: in examples such as *My best suit was hearts* (in a card game), or the slang *She's nuts on these video games*, the number of the complement is invariably plural, rather than singular.
9. A possible explanation of the use of *are* here is that the subject of a pseudocleft sentence, being a nominal relative clause, is in many respects like a NP rather than a nominal clause: e.g. it can refer to concrete entities, and even to persons, in addition to abstractions. It can therefore switch between singular

or plural agreement according to the semantics of the context (see Quirk et al. 1985: 1056). Thus *What you need are high-speed drills* can be paraphrased *The things that you need are high-speed drills.* Plurality, in other words, is present in the subject as well as in the complement.

References

Allerton, D. J. (1991) Points on Modern English syntax. *English Studies* **72**. 267–270.

Black, E., Garside. R., and Leech, G. (eds.) (1993) *Statistically-driven computer grammars of English: the IBM/Lancaster approach.* Amsterdam: Rodopi.

Bolinger, D. (1961) *Generality, gradience and the all-or-none.* The Hague: Mouton.

(1972) *Degree words.* The Hague: Mouton.

Quirk, R., Greenbaum, S., Leech, G. and Svartvik, J. (1985) *A comprehensive grammar of the English language.* London: Longman.

Fillmore, C. F. (1968) The case for case. In Bach, E. and Harms, R. T. (eds.), *Universals in linguistic theory.* New York: Holt, Rinehart and Winston. 1–90.

Halliday, M. A. K. (1961) Categories of the theory of grammar. *Word* **17**. 241–292.

Ivanic, R. (1991) Nouns in search of a context: a study of nouns with both open-class and closed-system characteristics. *IRAL* **29**. 93–114.

Jacobsson, B. (1990) Subject-verb concord in equative sentences in English. *Studia Linguistica* **44**. 30–58.

Leech, G. and Garside, G. (1991) Running a grammar factory: the production of syntactically analysed corpora or 'treebanks'. In Johansson, S. and Stenström, A.-B. (eds.), *English computer corpora: selected papers and research guide.* Berlin and New York: Mouton de Gruyter. 15–32.

Rensky, M. (1981) The subject/complement in English copulative clauses. In Esser, J. and Hubler, A. (eds.), *Forms and functions: papers in general, English and applied linguistics presented to Vilem Fried on the occasion of his 65th birthday.* Tübingen: Narr. 137–141.

Rosch, E. (1976) Classification of real-world objects: origins and representations in cognition. In Ehrlich, S. and Tulving, E. (eds.), *La memoire semantique.* Paris: Bulletin de Psychologie. Reprinted in Johnson-Laird, P. N. and Wason, P. C. (eds.) (1977), *Thinking: readings in cognitive psychology.* Cambridge University Press. 212–222.

Rosch, E. and Mervis, C. B. (1975) Family resemblances: studies in the internal structure of categories. *Cognitive Psychology* **7**. 573–605.

Ross, J. R. (1973) A fake NP squish. In Bailey, C.-J. N. and Shuy, R. W. (eds.), *New ways of analyzing variation in English.* Washington, D. C.: Georgetown University Press. 96–140.

11 Having a look at the expanded predicate[1]

JOHN ALGEO

1 Verbs and nouns in grammar and lexis

Language, it is said, is a system in which 'tout se tient'. Nevertheless, there are oppositions in the midst of the self-contained system of language, in which things push apart rather than hold together. One of those oppositions is a contrast between grammar and lexis with respect to the part of speech that is central to each.

It is generally acknowledged that the verb is the centre of sentence grammar. Much of the rest of a sentence – objects, complements, certain kinds of adverbials, tense-aspect options, voice – are dependent on the type of verb in the clause. Efficient grammatical descriptions will therefore privilege the verb.

It is otherwise in lexis. There are more nouns than any other part of speech. New words entering the language are overwhelmingly nouns. Moreover, the semantic burden of the sentence is carried disproportionately by its nouns. The vocabulary is noun-centred.

The consequence of such observations is that English is a verbal language grammatically, but a nominal language lexically. And that generalisation may be true of many if not all languages. There are, as it were, two magnetic poles in linguistic systems: a grammatically verbal one and a lexically nominal one. Together they are the yang and yin of language.

2 The expanded predicate

Somewhere near the middle of the magnetic field of language, however, where grammar and lexis meet, the pull of the two poles in opposite directions results in an intermingling of their characteristics. One such case is the grammatical/lexical construction *have a look*, an approximate synonym of the verb *look*. There is no generally accepted term for this construction;

here it is called the *expanded predicate*.[2] This term is not perspicuous, but at least it has the virtues of brevity (in comparison with a more descriptive term like *predicate consisting of a semantically general verb and an eventive object*) and appropriateness (since a predicate like *have a look* is a longer or expanded correlate of simple *look*).

The expanded predicate is an idiomatic verb-object construction in which the verb (e.g. *do, give, have, make*, or *take*) is semantically general and the object is semantically specific (such as *somersault, nod, rest, promise,* or *walk*). Such verb-object combinations are the semantic equivalents of verbs to which the noun objects are morphologically related: *do a dive* = *dive*, *give an answer* = *answer*, *have a bath* = *bathe*, *make a discovery* = *discover*, *take a walk* = *walk*.

The object in the expanded-predicate construction has been called an *eventive object* since it is deverbal and is the exponent of the meaning of its verbal correlate (Quirk et al. 1985: 750). The effect of the expanded-predicate construction is to transfer the semantic focus of the clause from the verb to the eventive noun object while leaving a semantically less specific verb in the syntactically central position.

The expanded predicate is janus-like, looking in two directions simultaneously. It is a syntactic construction at the core of the grammar of the clause. But it is also a lexical unit that requires entry in a dictionary. Because it is not exclusively either grammatical or lexical, it is likely to be treated inadequately in both grammars and dictionaries.

The construction, however, has not been ignored. It has been dealt with in reference grammars like those of Jespersen (1942: 117–118) and Poutsma (1926: 394–400). It has been studied as part of a larger class of complementation with words implying events (Olsson 1961, Renský 1964), and varieties of the construction have been noted (Live 1973). A limited variety (*have a* . . .) has been studied as an exponent of ten semantic formulas (Wierzbicka 1982). Semantic and syntactic differences have been traced between *have, take*, and *give* in a corpus of fiction (Stein and Quirk 1991), and semantic distinctions between expanded predicates and their corresponding specific verbs have been detailed (Stein 1991). Efforts have been made to describe the construction in terms of transformational-generative grammar (Nickel 1968 and Prince 1972).

Expanded-predicate constructions are found in other languages, but 'nowhere else is their inventory so rich nor their frequency so high as in English' (Renský 1964: 292). Although they appear to be increasing in present-day use (Nickel 1968: 2), expanded predicates are of ancient lineage in English. Increase in their use was doubtless fostered by the loss of inflections marking parts of speech in Old English and to a lesser extent in Middle English, thus permitting the freer conversion of verbs into nouns. However, they existed even in Anglo-Saxon days. Thus, a verb like *læðan* 'to hate' (as in *Gif hwelc cymiþ to me and ne lædes fæder his*, 'If anyone comes to me and does not hate his father' cited in Bosworth and Toller, s.v. *læðan*) was matched by an expanded predicate like *læððe habban to* 'to have hate for' (as in *Ðæt ærest is ðæt man to oðrum læððe hæbbe*, 'The first [sort of murder] is that a person have hate for another', cited in Bosworth and Toller, s.v. *hæbban*).

3 Rhetoric of the expanded predicate

An increase in the use of expanded predicates may be due partly to grammatical changes in English, but it is also rhetorically or stylistically motivated. Quirk et al. (1985) point to a number of uses of the expanded-predicate construction. The construction focusses items that otherwise would not be in the natural focus of a sentence. For example, the ditransitive expanded predicate focusses on the activity, rather than on the participant affected by it (Quirk et al. 1985: 1396): *He gave Helen a nudge* versus *He nudged Helen.*

The monotransitive expanded predicate is a way of avoiding a simple unmodified SV clause, which is not favoured in English. *My friend cooked* sounds incomplete (Quirk et al. 1985: 1401) – truncated or brusk – so the expanded predicate is an option to make such sentences more acceptable: *My friend did the cooking.*

It is likely that such rhetorical motives were a factor in the choice of expanded predicates over simple semantically specific verbs even in Old English. The subsequent loss of inflectional endings made conversion of parts of speech easier and therefore facilitated the invention of new expanded predicates. But the motive for choosing the expanded construction was doubtless always rhetorical.

4 Variations on the expanded predicate

The expanded predicate has several subvarieties and related constructions. In its simplest and purest form, the eventive noun is a formally unaltered functional shift of the verb: *try* = *have a try* (in which the noun is historically derived from the verb) or *party* = *have a party* (in which the verb is derived from the noun). What Bloomfield (1933: 163–164) called modulation (change of prosodic phonemes) and phonetic modification (change of segmental phonemes) may differentiate the verb/noun pair: *protést* = *make a prótest*; *breathe* = *take a breath*. Or affixation may play a part: *compare* = *make a comparison*; *conceive* = *have a conception*; *prefer* = *have a preference*.

In addition to such formal variation, for some related constructions there is a flaw in correspondence between the expanded predicate and a corresponding simple verb. Some have no parallel single-word verb in ordinary present-day use: *do homework, do linguistics, have a game, have a haircut, have mercy, make an effort, make fun, make peace*. Others have a noncognate single-word verb equivalent: *have sex* = *copulate* (or various popular vulgarisms), *take cover* = *hide*, *do a favour for* = *help*.

In some cases, the eventive noun is morphologically related to a simple verb, but the expanded predicate differs semantically from that verb: *make love (to/with)* ≠ *to love, have a bite* 'eat a little' ≠ *bite*, *take a chance* ≠ *to chance*. In other cases, the expanded predicate may correspond to a passive rather than an active simple verb: *have a bath (the baby will . . .)* = *be bathed, have a fright* = *be frightened, take a beating* = *be beaten, take offence at* = *be offended by*.

The choice of verb in the expanded-predicate construction also distinguishes one type from another. Typically, the verb is semantically general: *have, take, make,* etc. Semantic generality or specificity is, to be sure, a continuum. Yet it is possible to recognise degrees along that cline.

Semantically specific verbs are those with a more limited sense and therefore typically shorter dictionary entries. In expanded-predicate constructions, they typically collocate with a restricted number of eventive objects.

> ask a question; breathe a sigh; effect an alteration; find a solution; go for a walk; grant permission; heave a sigh; hold interest for; offer an apology, one's resignation, a suggestion; pick a quarrel; reach an agreement; submit an application; tender one's apologies; utter a curse, a sigh

Semantically general verbs are those used in an idiomatic (nonpredictable) meaning, which typically have long dictionary entries because defining them requires the specification of many different senses, according to the verbal context. In expanded-predicate constructions, they typically have a large number of different eventive objects.

> *be* a challenge, an embarrassment, in need of
>
> *come* to an agreement, a stop, an understanding
>
> *do* some cleaning, some cooking, a dance, a dive, some drawing, a drawing, some homework, an investigation, a jig, a job, a journey, some knitting, a painting, some repairing, a report, some sewing, a shriek, a sketch, a somersault, some thinking, a translation, a turn, some work, some writing
>
> *get* a glance, a look, a shot, a view

give some advice, an answer, one's assent, a blessing, a cheer, some consideration, a cough, a cry, a definition, a description, some encouragement, an explanation, a gulp, some help, a jump, a kick, a kiss, a look, a nod, a nudge, a performance, one's permission, a pinch, a press, a prod, a push, a reply, a shout, a shriek, a sigh, a smile, a thought, a wash, a wave, a yawn

have an argument, a bash, a bath, a bite, a chat, a chew, a cough, a cry, a cuddle, a dance, one's dinner, a dream, a drink, an effect, a feel, a fight, a fright, a game, a gossip, a guess, a haircut, a holiday, an influence, a job, a journey, a kick, a kiss, some knowledge, a laugh, a lick, a lie-down, a life, a listen, a look, some love, a meeting, a nap, some need, a nibble, a quarrel, a read, a rest, a ride, a run, a seat, a see, a shampoo, a shave, a shower, a shriek, a sip, a sleep, a smell, a smoke, a sneeze, a sniff, a suck, a swim, a talk, a taste, a think, a throw, a try, a walk, a yawn

make an accusation, an agreement, an allowance, an apology, an application, an approach, an arrangement, an attack, an attempt, a bargain, a bow, a call, a choice, a comment, a confession, contact, a contribution, a copy, a correction, a criticism, one's debut, a decision, a detour, a difference, a disclaimer, a discovery, a dive, an effort, an entrance, an entry, an escape, fun, a fuss, a get-away, a gift, a guess, an impression, an improvement, an inquiry, an investigation, a joke, a journey, love, a mistake, a move, a movement, a note, an objection, an observation, an offer, a payment, peace, a promise, a proposal, a recommendation, a reduction, a reference, a reply, a report, a request, a sale, a start, a suggestion, a turn, use, a vow, war, one's way

pay attention, a call, a visit

put emphasis on, an end to, a question, a stop to

take a bath, a beating, a bite, a breath, care, one's choice, into consideration, a decision, one's departure, a dislike, a dive, a drink, one's ease, a fall, a glance, a guess, a journey, one's leave, a look, a nap, a note, notice, a photograph, one's pick, pity, one's place, a rest, its rise, a risk, a seat, one's seat, a shave, a shower, a sleep, a smoke, a step, a stroll, a swim, trouble, a vacation, a walk, a wash

5 The core expanded predicate

A core subset of the general construction consists of expressions that satisfy the following conditions.

First of all, the verb of the expanded predicate is one of the four most frequent semantically general verbs: *give, have, make, take*. The Appendix shows the relative frequencies of these verbs in the Brown and LOB (Lancaster–Oslo–Bergen) corpora (Francis and Kučera 1979; Johansson, Leech, and Goodluck 1978). Thus *give a sigh* belongs to the core, but *breathe/heave/whisper a sigh* do not. The latter verbs are semantically heavier than *give* in relation to *sigh*, indicating the manner in which the action is done.

Similarly, *sigh a sigh* is excluded, as are all other instances in which the verb and eventive object are morphological cognates. This option is literary, high-style, and archaic in effect. An unmodified cognate object is acceptable only rarely: *Your old men will dream dreams*. Modification improves acceptability: *Tigger smiled his happiest smile*, but in some cases even with modification the combination of cognate verb and object is marginal or unacceptable: *?*They answered a long answer* (versus *They gave a long answer*).

Although the four verbs *give, have, make, take* are semantically general in relation to their following eventive objects, they are not semantically empty (Stein 1991). In some cases, the choice among them is a matter of collocation with the object: *have a chat* but **give/make/take a chat*. In other cases, more than one general verb is possible with little difference of referential meaning: *have a nap* or *take a nap*. In a few cases, however, the choice of general verb disambiguates some meanings covered by the simple verb: *give a scream* (involuntarily) versus *have a scream* (for one's own benefit), both = *scream*; *give a high-pitched laugh* (on a particular occasion), *have a high-pitched laugh* (as a rule), both = *laugh with a high pitch*.

Second, the eventive object is morphologically identical with a simple verb to which it is semantically related. This condition eliminates correspondences of the type *take account of* = *allow for*, in which there is no morphological similarity, as well as *do an investigation* = *investigate*, in which there is morphological relation but not identity, and *have a bash at* = *try* but ≠ *bash* 'strike, attack', in which there is morphological identity but not semantic relationship (or at least no predictable relationship of meaning).

Third, the eventive object is an indefinite noun. This condition eliminates constructions like *I'll do the answering. Do the V-ing* is widely available as an alternative for simple verbs and thus seems to be a more purely grammatical rather than lexical construction. It also eliminates a construction like *take one's pick*, although it allows the marginal *take a pick*.

Finally, constructions that meet some but not all of the foregoing requirements are *pseudo expanded predicates*. They are particularly those whose object is not eventive or does not correspond to a semantically specific verb.

6 British and American expanded predicates

There are national differences between British and American English in the particular items that are exponents of the construction. Here the emphasis is on those that are characteristically British. These differences are of several types.

First, the differences are often statistical rather than categorical. That is, both options are used in both varieties, but with different probabilities of occurrence. In the discussion that follows, 'British' and 'American' may thus mean either of two things:

Found in the variety named and not at all in the other – the extreme and relatively rare case of categorical difference. Some British eventive objects do not exist in American. In the following example, the semantically specific verb (*cock up*) does not exist in American either:

> In the article on the delights of Sardinia...David Wickers *made a bit of a cockup*. (21 February 1993, *The Sunday Times*, sec. 2, p. 7/2 (letter to editor))

Found in both varieties, but more frequently and characteristically in the variety named and with limitations on its occurrence or uncharacteristically in the other variety:

> Let me just *have a little look* at my diary. (S8.2.1209)[3]

There is nothing categorically un-American about *have a look* (although *take a look* would be somewhat more likely). However, the short sentence above has several stylistic Briticisms in it that mark it clearly as British and not American. The latter would be likely to be *Let me look quickly at my calendar*.

The label 'British' or 'American' thus usually does not mean that an item so labelled is unique to that variety. Rather it is a signal of some type of unequal distribution of the item between the two varieties, ranging from unique to varying frequencies. A few of the collocations occur with relatively high frequency in either or both of the national varieties, but many do not, being infrequent although acceptable combinations. For the latter, statistical comparisons of British and American English are not meaningful, and speaker intuition is the only feasible way of distinguishing them nationally.

Lexically, the differences are of the following types, in which the exemplified form is British and the gloss American:

(1) The object is a Briticism in a pseudo expanded predicate:

> *come a cropper* 'fail utterly': 'Predictably, it all *came a cropper*,' says Cheetham today. (7 February 1993, *The Sunday Times*, sec. 6, p. 9/1)

go a bomb on 'be a great success with': Franco detested the Basques, never forgiving them for their staunch republicanism during the Civil War. They didn't *go a bomb on* him either (other than literally). (10 February 1993, *The Evening Standard*, p. 27/3)

take the mick 'satirise, ridicule' (usually transitive as *take the mickey out of*; here perhaps punning headlinese): Jagger *takes the mick* with tv Camilla sketch/ Mick Jagger poked fun at the Royal Family on a U.S. comedy show [Saturday Night Live] – by dressing as Camilla Parker Bowles' butler and delivering a special gift from Prince Charles. (12 February 1993, *The Sun*, p. 17/2–4 (heading and article))

(2) The object is a Briticism in a core expanded predicate:

give (something) a look-over 'look over (something)': He had a mind to let his cousin, who was a heavy woollen manufacturer, *give it a look-over*. (W16.4.40)

give a miss 'skip, do without'; related to the Briticism *miss (something) out*: 'I like the skirty look, so that's quite me,' said violinist Catherine Morgan, 22. 'But the hats I could *give a miss*.' (4 February 1993, *The Daily Telegraph*, p. 13/3)

have a holiday 'take a vacation'; related to the Briticism *to holiday*, as in: The General could not resist *holidaying* regularly in San Sebastian, a seaside resort that survives today as elegant and eloquent testimony to the belle epoque. (10 February 1993, *The Evening Standard*, p. 27/3)

(3) Different general verbs are favoured in British and American in a pseudo expanded predicate:

do a course 'take a course': Having *done a short course*, which costs about £800, a graduate with a qualification to teach English as a foreign language can cross the Channel for a subsistence wage. (13 February 1993, *The Spectator*, p. 21/2)

One of the most frequent Briticisms of this category is *take a decision*, for which American normally has *make a decision*, although the British general verb has begun to appear in American use, chiefly in governmental and military contexts.

(4) Different general verbs are favoured in British and American also in some core expanded predicates:

give a lead 'take the lead': What we do say at this moment as the opposition is this: for heaven's sake, *give a lead* and try and break down this dreadful suicidal wall where no one will yield an inch. (S5.4.67) *give a look* 'take a look': Barrington *giving a look* round the field. (S10.1.1)

have a look 'take a look': Well I was just thinking that if the questioner went to the Tate Museum in London and *had a look* at the portraits of the kings and queens of England you can see a wonderful example of inheritance of eye colour within these portraits because your brown and non-brown eyes are inherited. (S5.2.101)

Parfitt *having a look* at the field walking away from his crease. (S10.1.45)

Quirk et al. (1985: 752) observe that, when the eventive object collates with both *have* and *take*, *have* is typically the British option, and *take* the American: *have/take a guess*. For the most part there is agreement in choice of general verb for the expanded predicate in British and American, as sampled in the Brown and LOB corpora (see Appendix). In those corpora, both varieties have *have an appeal, a chat, a drink, a fight, a glimpse, a glow, a hope, an impact, an influence, a regard, a respect, a row, a smell, a talk, a wish*; both have *take a glance, a shower, a sip, a stand, a step*; and both have either *have* or *take a look, a view, a walk* (though not necessarily with equal frequency). However, British *have a seat* balances American *take a seat*. British has either *have* or *take a bath*, whereas American prefers *take a shower*. American has either *have* or *take a nap*, whereas British prefers *have a sleep*; and whereas British has either *have* or *take an approach*, American prefers *take an approach*. The difference is not strong, but it is clear. Even within corpora of the limited size of Brown and LOB, where there is a slant in preference, British lists *have*; American *take*.

There are examples where, although the object is eventive, the expanded predicate does not correspond to the sense of the morphologically related verb, and the collocation does not occur in American.

give (someone) a go 'give (someone) a chance': I was ready to *give* Fiona Armstrong *a go* until I heard her simpering on about only putting on a stone or something while pregnant. (17 February 1993, *The Times*, p. 13/8)

have a go 'make an attempt': We were on the ferry and he played the fruit machine, and every time he won, he gave me the money, and let me *have a go*. (1989, Ruth Rendell, *The Bridesmaid*, 234)

put paid to 'end': Looking fondly at Sheryl, Gazza, 25, *put paid to* press reports that they had split up. (12 February 1993, *The Sun*, p. 12/3) *take a punt* 'take a chance or gamble' (presumably from the chance involved in punting in soccer): Given the dullness of this administration, I really would *take a punt* on Lord Archer of Weston-super-Mare to do the job for a three-year stint, up until the election. (2 February 1993, *The Evening Standard*, p. 13/1)

There are also examples where, although both the general verb and the eventive noun are found also in American and the semantic relationship is predictable, their collocation is a Briticism. American does not use the expanded predicate:

have a moult 'moult': They seem to be permanently losing a feather or two, instead of *having a good moult*, getting it over and then looking smart again, bright of eye and comb. (13 February 1993, *The Spectator*, p. 7/1)

have a peck 'peck; could peck': Water is supplied on an upturned dustbin lid. 'I can't use a bird table,' he says, 'because we're so exposed to the westerlies. It would be blown off before the birds *had a peck*.' (13 February 1993, *The Weekend Telegraph*, p. 2/3)

have a rant and rave 'rant and rave': Every Sunday more than 17 million fans watch actor Richard Wilson, left, play flat-capped moaning groaner Meldrew, who is never happier than when he is *having a good rant and rave*. (12 February 1993, *The Sun*, p. 11/2–3)

have a shave 'shave (oneself)': I *had a* bath and *shave* every day. (February 1993, *The Woman's Journal*, p. 39/2)

make a loss 'lose; fail to make a profit': 34 per cent of Welsh farms *made a net loss* in 1990/91. (3–10 February 1993, *Time Out*, p. 12/2)

make savings 'save, achieve savings': And the clinching argument is the £100,000-a-day cost of the operation when defence chiefs are under pressure to *make savings* after Wednesday's announcement that four famous Army regiments will not be axed. (5 February 1993, *The Daily Express*, p. 10/2)

In some instances the expanded predicate is found normally in both varieties, but with some difference in its complementation:

I *had a long talk to* her about two weeks ago. (S.5.8.99)

American English includes both *talk to* and *talk with* someone, but only *have a talk with*.

A comparison of the expanded predicates in the Brown and LOB corpora shows that the construction is at home in both national varieties, though not equally so. The Brown Corpus has 199 tokens (instances), representing

133 types (different verb and eventive object combinations) compared with the LOB Corpus' 245 tokens and 149 types. Brown Corpus types are used an average of 1.50 times each; LOB Corpus types are used an average of 1.64 times each. To the extent that these two corpora are representative of their national varieties, we can say that, although the expanded predicate is a shared construction, British English uses it somewhat more than American.

A more striking difference, however, is in the particular verbs used in expanded predicates. Lists of expanded predicates with the general verbs *do, give, have, make* and *take* in the Brown and LOB corpora are in the Appendix to this chapter. Because of difficulties in deciding what to count as an expanded predicate, those lists are not definitive, but they were compiled in the same way and are thus roughly representative of the two corpora. The lists show that the difference between British and American is minor for all verbs except *have*. British uses *have* as the verb of an expanded predicate nearly twice as often as American does and in about one and three-quarters as many different constructions. *Have* is the British verb of preference, accounting for 41 per cent of both types and tokens of expanded predicates, whereas in American it accounts for only 28 per cent of tokens and 26 per cent of types. The British preference for *have* casts a different light on the *have/take* difference noted above. The difference is not that American favours *take* but that British favours *have*.

Differences between British and American expanded-predicate constructions may also reflect other differences between the two varieties. For example, both varieties use *have/take a bath*. But, although *bath* is cognate with the older verb *bathe*, common to both varieties, only British English has shifted the noun to a verb:

> You can *bath* in it, drink it, spill it down your dress and it won't leave a mark. (LOB, P22: 7)

This intransitive verbal use of *to bath* makes *have/take a bath* a core expanded predicate in British use, whereas it is only a pseudo expanded predicate in American, cognate with *to bathe*.

7 Conclusion

The expanded predicate is a noteworthy construction for several reasons.

First, it is at the boundary between grammar and lexis, partaking of some of the characteristics of each, such as the verb-centrality of syntax and the noun-centrality of vocabulary.

Second, because of its janus-like nature, it challenges the assumption of a hermetic seal between grammar and lexis, and also the prejudice widely held among linguists in favour of syntax over the lexicon as an object of study.

Third, it is important stylistically, since its appropriate use varies according to register and functional variety.

Fourth, as a *tertium quid*, it has been inadequately treated in both grammars and dictionaries, and therefore has been underanalysed syntactically, lexically, and stylistically.

Fifth, it is an important area of difference between the two extensively standardised varieties of English: British and American.

Sixth, although its history has not been sufficiently studied to permit firm conclusions, it appears to be a construction that has been increasing in scope and importance during recent times.

Seventh, it is a matter of importance to non-native learners of the language, being both abundant and important for normal idiomatic usage.

It has certainly not been feasible to study the expanded predicate here with the detail and scope required to address any of these reasons adequately. It has not been possible to deal with a number of interesting aspects of this construction. For example, with the general verb *have*, adjectival *good* modifying the eventive object does not correspond to adverbial *well* modifying the corresponding specific verb. *To have a good cry* is not *to cry well*, but rather *to cry much and with satisfactory results*. The implication is that the action of the eventive object is to the benefit of the subject.

Appendix

Expanded predicates in the Brown and LOB corpora

Summary Tokens/Types

	Brown	LOB
do	4/4	0
give	40/30	40/29
have	55/35	100/61
make	59/44	67/39
take	41/20	38/20

do

Brown: 4 tokens, 4 types (a kick up, a pirouette, a study, a work)

LOB: None

give

Brown: 40 tokens, 30 types (an account, an answer, a divorce, an echo, a grin, a gulp, a hug, a laugh, a lecture, a look, a lurch, a name, a pat, a picture, a pout, a pull, a push, a report, a ride, a sigh, a sign, a signal, a smile, a snort, a thought, a thrust, a tip, a wave, a whack, a yell)

LOB: 40 tokens, 29 types (an account, an answer, a bow, a cackle, a chuckle, a cough, a cry, a display, a finish, a groan, a hop, a jolt, a laugh, a mumble, an order, an outline, a picture, a rebuff, a scream, a shiver, a shout, a shrug, a sigh, a smile, a snort, a sob, an undertaking, a view, a whistle)

have

Brown: 55 tokens, 35 types (an answer, an appeal, a ballot, a bounce, a chat, a cough, a crackle, a dislike, a dread, a drink, a fear, a fight, a glimpse, a glow, a grasp, a hope, an impact, an influence, a joke, a look, a nap, a range, a regard, a respect, a row, a run-up, a scrimmage, a smell, a study, a talk, a taste, a tour, a view, a walk, a wish)

LOB: 100 tokens, 61 types (an appeal, an approach, an average, a bath, a blow (of wind), a change, a chat, a control, a desire, a distrust, a dream, a drink, an escape, an experience, a fancy, a feed, a fight, a function, a glimpse, a glow, a hold, a holiday, a hope, an impact, an influence, an interest, a journey, a list (slant), a look, a love, a lunch, a need, a practice, a quarrel, a quiver, a regard, a respect, a return, a ride, a ring, a row, a save, a search, a seat, a sense, a sleep, a slope, a smell, a squint, a start, a swear, a swim, a talk, a taper, a try, a view, a visit, a walk, a war, a wish, a yield)

make

Brown: 59 tokens, 44 types (an advance, an appeal, an assault, an attack, an attempt, a bend, a break, a break-away, a canvass, a change, a charge, a claim, a compromise, a dash, a deal, a debut, a dive, a gesture, a guess, a hit, an inventory, a leap, a list, a motion, a note, a pirouette, a pop, a profit, a promise, a raid, a remark, a report, a rush, a shift, a sign, a stand, a start, a study, a survey, a throw, a trek, a turn, a visit, a wish)

LOB: 67 tokens, 39 types: (an approach, an attempt, a bargain, a bid, a break, a broadcast, a change, a check, a circle, a comment, a debut, an entry, an exit, a fight, a gesture, an impact, an imprint, a journey, a list, a move, a note, an offer, an order, an outlay, a profit, a race, a report, a return, a rule, a sacrifice, a search, a sound, a stand, a start, a study, a survey, a test, a tour, a turn)

take

Brown: 41 tokens, 20 types (an approach, a fall, a glance, a gulp, a hop, a lead, a look, a nap, a poll, a seat, a shower, a sip, a stand, a step, a swallow, a swig, a swipe, a tour, a view, a walk)

LOB: 38 tokens, 20 types (an aim, an approach, a bath, a chance, a glance, an inventory, a look, a nibble, a paseo, a pose, a ride, a risk, a share, a shower, a sip, a stand, a step, a turn, a view, a walk)

Notes

1 I am grateful to Carmen Acevedo Butcher for gathering citational evidence on which this chapter is based, to Robert Ilson for discussions of the subject, and to Adele S. Algeo for her critical eye.

2 This term was suggested by the expression *expanded construction* in Quirk et al. (1985: 752, note b): 'The verbs *vacation* ⟨esp AmE⟩ and *holiday* ⟨esp BrE⟩ are less usual than the expanded constructions.' Alternative possibilities are *extended predicate*, suggested by 'This Eventive object...is semantically an extension of the verb and bears a major part of the meaning' (Quirk et al. 1985: 750), or *stretched predicate*, suggested by 'Other means have therefore had to be devised for "stretching" the predicate into a multi-word structure' (Quirk et al. 1985: 1401).

3 This number identifies the quotation in the corpus of the Survey of English Usage. S = spoken corpus, W = written corpus.

References

Bosworth, J. and Toller, T. N. (1898) *An Anglo-Saxon dictionary.* London: Oxford University Press.

Francis, W. N. and Kučera, H. (1979) *Manual of information to accompany a standard sample of present-day edited American English for use with digital computers.* Revised edition. Providence, RI: Department of Linguistics, Brown University, original edition 1964.

Jespersen, O. (1942) *A Modern English grammar on historical principles.* Volume 6: *Morphology.* London: Allen and Unwin.

Johansson, S., Leech, G. and Goodluck, H. (1978) *Manual of information to accompany the Lancaster–Oslo–Bergen corpus of British English, for use with digital computers.* Oslo: Department of English, University of Oslo.

Live, A. H. (1973) The take-have phrasal in English. *Linguistics* **95**. 31–50.

Nickel, G. (1968) Complex verbal structures in English. *International Review of Applied Linguistics* **6**. 1–21.

Olsson, Y. (1961) On the syntax of the English verb with special reference to 'have a look' and similar complex structures. *Gothenburg Studies in English* **12**. Stockholm: Almqvist and Wiksell.

Poutsma, H. (1926) *A grammar of late Modern English*. Part II, Section II. The verb and the particles. Groningen: Noordhoff.

Prince, E. F. (1972) A note on aspect in English: the take-a-walk construction. In Plötz, S. (ed.), *Transformationelle Analyse*. Frankfurt am Main: Athenäum. 409–420.

Quirk, R., Greenbaum, S., Leech, G., and Svartvik, J. (1985) *A comprehensive grammar of the English language*. London: Longman.

Renský, M. (1964) English verbo-nominal phrases: some structural and stylistic aspects. *Travaux Linguistiques de Prague* **1**. 289–299.

Stein, G. (1991) The phrasal verb type 'to have a look' in Modern English. *International Review of Applied Linguistics* **29**. 1–29.

Stein, G. and Quirk. R. (1991) On having a look in a corpus. In Aijmer, K. and Altenberg, B. (eds.), *English corpus linguistics: studies in honour of Jan Svartvik*. 197–203.

Wierzbicka, A. (1982) Why can you have a drink when you can't *have an eat? *Language* **58**. 753–799.

12 'This scheme is badly needed': some aspects of verb-adverb combinations

STIG JOHANSSON

1 Introduction

In a book on verb-intensifier collocations Sidney Greenbaum suggests that '[t]he lexicon should contain for each degree intensifier a specification of the collocational range of verbs' (Greenbaum 1970: 87). Collocational tendencies could be established through corpus studies and through elicitation tests like those presented in Greenbaum's book.

This chapter starts by looking briefly at verb-adverb combinations in general, based on a study of the tagged Lancaster–Oslo–Bergen (LOB) Corpus.[1] The general survey is followed by a closer look at combinations of the intensifier *badly* with verbs in three corpora of present-day English texts and in the quotations of the *Oxford English Dictionary*. In conclusion, there is some discussion of the form of a distributional lexicon.

2 Combinability of adverbs

A study of tag combinations in the LOB Corpus shows that the grammatical context of adverbs is far more varied than that of the other word classes (see Johansson and Hofland 1989). Compare the percentages accounted for by the three most common tags preceding and following singular nouns (NN), base forms of verbs (VB), adjectives (JJ), and adverbs (RB):[2]

–NN 54.16	–VB 62.87	–JJ 43.71	–RB 22.81
NN– 53.40	VB– 30.82	JJ– 69.09	RB– 33.33

Note that there may be great differences in the figures for left and right contexts. A lower figure indicates a lower degree of uniformity of the grammatical context. Adverbs show low figures both for left and right contexts, because they are characteristically more mobile than the other word classes and because they form a very heterogeneous group (the heterogeneity of verbs with respect to complementation patterns presumably accounts for the very low figure for the right context of VB). To quote Quirk et al. (1985: 438), 'it is tempting to say . . . that the adverb is an item that does not fit the definitions for other word classes'. The heterogeneity makes it difficult to establish generalisations on the behaviour of the adverb class as a whole.

3 Verb adjacency

The degree of attraction of adverbs to verbs is shown by the following figures from the tagged LOB Corpus (again derived from Johansson and Hofland 1989). The first figure gives the absolute frequency of the combination, the second the percentage of the combination as compared with the total number of adverbs:[3]

VB + RB	1070	3.03%	RB + VB	1621	4.58%
VBD + RB	1484	4.20%	RB + VBD	1346	3.81%
VBG + RB	578	1.63%	RB + VBG	646	1.83%
VBN + RB	1022	2.89%	RB + VBN	3222	9.11%
VBZ + RB	350	0.99%	RB + VBZ	553	1.56%
TOTAL	4504	12.74%		7388	20.89%

In other words, adverbs appear more characteristically immediately before than immediately after verbs (note, in particular, the figures for adverbs preceding VBN, i.e. past participles). But only about a third of all adverbs in the LOB Corpus are placed in a position adjacent to a lexical verb.

The degree of verb adjacency varies greatly with the individual adverb, as shown in the last column of the lists in the Appendix.[4] Among adverbs with a low percentage for verb adjacency, there is one group consisting of adverbs which are predominantly found as modifiers of adjectives: *extremely, comparatively, relatively, purely,* etc. Others are adverbs which typically function as conjuncts or disjuncts (not shown in the Appendix): *however*, *moreover*, *nevertheless*, *surely, maybe*, *perhaps*, etc. Adverbs with a high percentage for verb adjacency form two distinct groups, depending upon whether they tend to occur before or after the lexical verb; see the last two lists in the Appendix. In the former group we mostly find frequency, time, and degree adjuncts (and some sentence adverbials), in the latter process and place adjuncts.

The tendencies revealed in our tables are certainly not new discoveries, but rather confirm what has long been known about the position of adverbs. The tables suggest, however, how one might exploit information derived from a tagged corpus to construct a distributional lexicon, i.e. a lexicon which specifies the combinatory potential of each item. I shall come back to this question at the end of the chapter.

4 Verb-adverb collocations

A distributional lexicon should specify the combinatory potential of words not only with reference to grammatical context but also in terms of collocational links, as suggested by Greenbaum in the passage quoted at the beginning of this chapter. To reveal such links we need an extremely large corpus (Greenbaum 1970: 81). As the LOB Corpus is insufficiently large for a proper collocational study, I turned to two additional corpora and to the vast treasury of the *Oxford English Dictionary*, in a study of collocations of *badly* + verb.

5 Greenbaum's observations on *badly*

Badly is one of the adverbs included in Greenbaum's (1970) elicitation experiment, where informants were asked to complete sentences for which the opening words were provided. The two principal collocates after *I badly* were *need* and *want*, with over 90 per cent of the responses. Here the meaning is clearly one of degree, i.e. 'much, greatly'. Less frequent collocates were some verbs of injuring and judging (and a small 'miscellaneous' group which need not concern us here): *hurt*, *injure*, *sprain*, *pain*; *judge*, *misjudge*, *miscalculate*.

With verbs of injuring the meaning of *badly* is a mixture of degree and manner: '. . . we are saying something about the extent of the wounding and at the same time referring to its unpleasant consequences' (Greenbaum 1970: 63). Commenting on the comparative rarity of these combinations in his material, Greenbaum suggests that *badly* may collocate more normally with verbs of injuring when it is in post-verb position (he points out later, however, that preferences are different before the past participle).

With respect to verbs of judging, Greenbaum notes that combinations with *miscalculate* and *misjudge* are like those with verbs of injuring in expressing a blend of manner and degree: 'We may suppose that *badly* is in these cases in part reinforcing the sense of the prefix *mis-*' (Greenbaum 1970: 66f.). On the other hand, *badly* is only a manner adjunct in combinations with *judge* (and is far less acceptable in pre-verb position).

6 *Badly* + verb in the LOB, Brown, and London–Lund corpora

All examples of *badly* were retrieved from the LOB, Brown, and London–Lund corpora.[5] There were in all 102 occurrences, 94 of which were found in combinations with verbs; see Table 12.1. As the number of occurrences in each corpus was limited (LOB Corpus: 44, Brown Corpus: 34, London–Lund Corpus: 24), no attempt will be made to identify differences between the corpora, but all examples will be attributed to the relevant corpus.[6]

6.1 Transitive verb + *badly*

Among the examples where *badly* follows an active transitive verb (column 1 in Table 12.1) we find instances where the meaning is manner and degree as well as a blend of the two:

(1) In prison he was described as an unhappy creature who had started life badly . . . (LOB H09: 8)
(2) Woodruff wanted this political windfall very badly . . . (Brown G52: 40)
(3) . . . you're misjudging me badly. (LOB N02: 79)

The manner meaning occurred with the following verbs: *do, fit, start, take*. The pure degree meaning was only found with *need* and *want*. A blend of manner and degree was more common and was found with: *cut, fear, hold up, misjudge, neglect, slop*. All of these verbs include a negative element in their semantic make-up, a matter which we will return to below.

The few examples where *badly* precedes an active transitive verb (column 4 in Table 12.1) only exhibit the pure degree meaning (3 examples with *need/want*) and the blend of manner and degree (1 example):

(4) She looked slim and tiny and he badly wanted to protect her. (LOB P10: 183)
(5) The dogs followed her and she killed three and badly wounded Old John. (Brown F36: 60)

The lack of the manner type was expected, as adjuncts of manner are known to prefer final position in the clause. The blend of manner and degree is found predominantly in post-verb position in our material of transitive constructions; the single example of pre-verb placement (5) is probably motivated by the congruent distribution of information in the last two of the

Table 12.1 Badly *in the corpus material: survey of verbs (trans = transitive verb, intrans = intransitive verb, past ptc = past participle)*

	trans +*badly*	intrans +*badly*	passive +*badly*	*badly*+ trans	*badly*+ intrans	*badly*+ past ptc	Other	Total
affect						1		1
attend						1		1
baptise						1		1
behave		1				2		3
blunder		1						1
bother						1		1
burn						1		1
come out		1						1
curtain						1		1
cut	1							1
cut up			1					1
damage						2		2
deteriorate		1						1
disillusion						1		1
distort						1		1
disturb						1		1
do	1	5					1	7
dress						1		1
educate						1		1
fare		3						3
fear	1							1
feel		2						2
fit	1							1
garble						1		1
go		2						2
handicap						1		1
head away						1		1
hold up	1							1
hurt			1					1
injure						2		2
jump/wave around		1						1
limp		1						1
mark			1					1
misjudge	2							2

ble 12.1 Badly *in the corpus material: survey of verbs (trans = transitive verb, intrans = intransitive verb, st ptc = past participle* (contd.)

	trans +*badly*	intrans +*badly*	passive +*badly*	*badly*+ trans	*badly*+ intrans	*badly*+ past ptc	Other	Total
ed	1			2		2		5
glect	1							1
int						1		1
y						2		2
ace						2		2
ay						1		1
ll		1						1
coil		1						1
ng		1						1
e						1		1
p	1							1
mp		1						1
ell						1		1
it							1	1
ck						1		1
rt	1	1						2
te			1					1
ell						1		1
e	1							1
r						1		1
nk		1						1
ow						1		1
vel		1						1
at						2		2
e							1	1
nt	4			1				5
sh			1					1
ar		1				1		2
und				1		2	1	4
TAL	16	26	5	4	0	39	4	94

coordinated clauses, with the focus on the final direct object rather than on the degree/manner of the action.

6.2 Intransitive verb + *badly*

The first thing to note is the complete dominance of post-verb position in our material (see columns 2 and 5 in Table 12.1). Examples of intransitive verb + *badly* are divided between those expressing manner and manner/degree:

(6) . . . Lindsay started badly and fell back in a spin. (LOB E16: 59)
(7) Whether he sang well or badly had nothing to do with it. (Brown L12: 130)
(8) This part of the city had worn badly. (LOB K24: 132)
(9) In Cuba, the US had blundered badly and created the impression of impotency against Communist penetration even on its own doorstep. (Brown A34: 49)

The manner meaning was found with the following verbs: *behave*, *come out*, *do*, *fare*, *feel*, *go*, *poll*, *sing*, *start*, *think*, *travel*. These verbs allow questions with *how* and a contrast between *well* and *badly*, both indications of the manner meaning. Note the following examples:

(10) 'I travel badly,' he tells us, 'and I speak French and Italian atrociously.' (LOB G13: 79)
(11) . . . the new party which had polled badly and lost all parliamentary representation. (LOB J56: 33)

The meanings are 'I am a bad traveller' and 'achieved bad results at the election', respectively. The examples may not fit quite comfortably in the manner category, but they are clearly distinct from the manner/degree type.

A blend of manner and degree was found with the following verbs: *blunder*, *deteriorate*, *limp*, *recoil*, *slump*, *wear*. These are all verbs with a negative meaning component; cf. 6.1 and the discussion further below. The following example requires special comment:

(12) The figures on the worksheet paper in front of her were jumping and waving around so badly it was all she could do to make them out clearly enough to copy them with the typewriter. (Brown L10: 108)

The verbs in *jumping and waving around* do not themselves include a negative element, but *badly* certainly indicates manner/degree and colours the interpretation of the verbs.

6.3 Passive and past participle constructions

We note, first of all, the low number of passive constructions with *badly* in post-verb position (see column 3 in Table 12.1). The examples are so few that they can all be given here:

(13) . . . can often result in a candidate being marked badly. . . (LOB E13: 37)
(14) Ordinary politeness may have militated against this opinion being stated so badly . . . (Brown E29: 3)
(15) Before the fight was over, the Harlem boy had a concussion and Trig was cut up badly. (Brown K03: 28)
(16) . . . he was hurt so badly he did not seem for long in this world. (Brown K09: 64)
(17) 'The road's washed badly,' said Dill, 'but there's a trail you can get over with a horse.' (Brown N07: 102)

The first two examples exhibit the manner reading, the others a blend of manner and degree. The verbs in (15) and (16) agree well with those we have found earlier to combine with the manner/degree meaning (cf. 6.1 and 6.2). The verb in (17) is not negative in general, but in this context the meaning is 'wash away, destroy', and the example is therefore in agreement with the general pattern found with blends of manner and degree.

We are now getting to the most frequent pattern, viz. *badly* + past participle (see column 6 in Table 12.1). This includes finite passive constructions as well as nonfinite participle constructions (generally occurring as pre- or post-modifiers of nouns). Examples:

(18) We record this week that a cricket pitch at Penhill was badly damaged on Friday night by hooligans, . . . (LOB B25: 84)
(19) There was nothing much to see except that the left one was badly swollen. (LOB F31: 14)
(20) . . . the language sounds like badly garbled Swedish, to a Swede. (LOB N15: 100)
(21) Others, badly wounded, gripped hands in manes, knees in bellies, held on as long as possible . . . (Brown N04: 162)

These examples illustrate a blend of manner and degree. The blend is again found with verbs containing a negative element in their semantic make-up: *bother*, *burn*, *damage*, *disillusion*, *distort*, *disturb*, *garble*, *handicap*, *injure*, *swell*, *tear*, *wear*, *wound*. There is also a negative element in the following examples, which contain verbs which are not generally negative in meaning:

(22) . . . her husband's horse fell and he was badly thrown. His arm was broken . . . (LOB A09: 10)

(23) The novelist who has been badly baptized in psychoanalysis often gives us the impression that since all men must have an Oedipus complex all men must have the same . . . (Brown G26: 50)

In addition to the blend of manner and degree, we find examples of pure manner and pure degree:

(24) It would appear that teachers today are not really badly paid . . . (LOB B27: 62)
(25) His untidy, dirty, badly spelled and careless paper does not indicate . . . (LOB J26: 3)
(26) Letch had returned from his debacle unrepentant and more badly behaved than before. (Brown R03: 73)
(27) I welcome this scheme for it is badly needed. (LOB F43: 5)
(28) Georgia's mental health program received a badly needed boost from the General Assembly . . . (Brown B01: 47)

While the degree meaning was only found with *need*, the manner meaning was registered with a range of verbs: *affect*, *attend*, *behave*, *curtain*, *dress*, *educate*, *head away*, *paint*, *pay*, *place*, *play*, *site*, *spell*, *stack*, *treat*.

The *badly* + past participle constructions do not form a homogeneous group. Some of them are ordinary passives with a straightforward active counterpart, e.g. (18) and (27). In other cases, an active counterpart seems unlikely, e.g. in (20) and (23). Statal passives (cf. Quirk et al. 1985: 170) occur, as in:[7]

(29) Fabrics that are badly distorted in their unlaundered state due to faulty finishing may give deceptive dimensional change results when laundered by any procedure. (Brown J77: 57)

A couple of past participle constructions are not passive at all, but rather correspond to constructions with intransitive verbs, e.g. (19) and (26). There are also cases where we may be in doubt whether to analyse the *-ed* form as deverbal or denominal:

(30) Some of those dangers were ugly and badly sited buildings . . . (LOB F20: 3)
(31) . . . caught by a trick of light from a badly curtained window . . . (LOB L17: 58)

To conclude, the most frequent pattern we have found with *badly* presents a varied picture, in spite of the superficial similarity. The uses of *badly* + past participle range from clearly verbal to more adjective-like constructions. This brings us to our next point.

6.4 Other combinations with *badly*

As indicated in Table 12.1, there were some cases of *badly* + verb which did not fit into the categories taken up above:

(32) The state will keep them going however badly they do . . . (LOB G62: 53)

(33) . . . it doesn't matter how badly a story is typed; if it has real merit it will sell. (LOB K25: 114)

(34) '. . . He was wounded in a brush with the Apaches last night.' The girl stood very still. She said: 'Badly?' (LOB N20: 71)

(35) Split badly during the recent presidential election into almost equally divided camps of party loyalists and independents, the Democratic party in Mississippi is . . . (Brown A08: 49)

Apart from the order difference compared with our previous categories, there is nothing remarkable about these examples. The first two are examples of manner, the last two of manner/degree (both with 'negative' verbs).

In a few instances *badly* was found in combinations which are clearly non-verbal. As the focus of this chapter is on verb-adverb combinations, I will give these examples in abbreviated form:

very badly wrong. . . not badly wrong (LLC 12.3: 383–384)
had gone badly awry (Brown N05: 164)
badly out [tennis] (LLC 10.10: 865)
badly out of focus (LOB E10: 56)
badly in need of repairs (Brown N05: 161)
go badly at sea (LLC 1.1: 580)
go out of focus very badly (LLC 1.8: 673–674)

In other words, *badly* may combine with adjectives, adverbs, and Prepositional Phrases. The meaning is degree or manner/degree. The conditioning appears to be much the same as with verb constructions, i.e. degree with *in need of* and degree/manner with the rest, all of which have a negative meaning component.

6.5 Conclusions from the corpus study

There are three favoured patterns: active transitive constructions + *badly*, intransitive verb + *badly*, and *badly* + past participle constructions. The dominant meanings are manner and manner/degree; see Table 12.2.

Both are found with a variety of verbs, while pure degree only occurs with *need* and *want* (altogether 10 instances in the material). The manner/degree meaning combines most typically with forms that have a negative meaning

Table 12.2 Badly *in the corpus material: survey of meanings (trans = transitive verb, intrans = intransitive verb, past ptc = past participle)*

	trans +*badly*	intrans +*badly*	passive +*badly*	*badly*+ trans	*badly*+ intrans	*badly*+ past ptc	Other	Total
manner	4	19	2	0	0	19	2	46
degree	5	0	0	3	0	2	0	10
manner/ degree	7	7	3	1	0	18	2	38
TOTAL	16	26	5	4	0	39	4	94

component. This applies both to verb-adverb combinations and to the limited number of instances where *badly* was found to combine with forms other than verbs.

From these results we may conclude that collocational patterns are sensitive to the meaning of the verb and to the individual verb form. The most striking result is the high frequency of past participle constructions. What does this say about *badly*-constructions? To explore this matter further, let us turn to the material of the *Oxford English Dictionary*.

7 *Badly* + verb in the *Oxford English Dictionary* (*OED2*)

The entry for *badly* in *OED2* is brief and includes just a handful of examples illustrating the meanings of manner, degree, and degree/manner (as well as the use of *badly* as an adjective).[8] There is little information on collocational patterns beyond a reference to the link between *need/want* and the meaning of degree 'much, greatly'. Using the search facilities of the CD-ROM version, it was possible to extract some 450 examples of *badly* from the whole body of *OED2* quotations, the great majority found in combinations with verbs. These are the basis of the following observations.

7.1 Manner

The manner meaning is found in a great number of the examples in the *OED2* material. These are some of the verbs used with *badly* in a fairly straightforward manner sense:

> *act, adjust, advise, agree, apply, arrange, behave, bind (together), bowl, build, camouflage, chew, clothe, coil, come (down/off/out), command, construct, deliver, design, do, draw, dress,*

drive, end, engrave, execute, fit, flavour, fly, form, frame, function, guide, imitate, jump, learn, locate, lodge, make (up), manage, manufacture etc.

Prototypical cases of manner have an agent subject and a verb of action.

Often the focus of *badly* + verb is on results or consequences rather than the process of an action:

(36) 1880 *Illustrated Sporting and Dramat. News* 4 December 278/3: The withdrawal of the subsidy augurs badly for the annual grant of £2,000 usually given towards the added money for the Grand Prix.

(37) 1874 L. Tollemache in *Fortn. Rev.* February 231: The inveterate habit of ending stories badly, with pessimism aforethought.

(38) 1852 C. M. Yonge, *Cameos* II. xxxiii. 342: The French must have been very badly officered.

(39) 1598 W. Phillips, *Linschoten* in Arb. *Garner* III. 423: There grew a great noise and murmuring in the ship, that cursed the Captain and Officers, because the ship was badly provided.

The notion of result is naturally coupled with some patient. Who is adversely affected? Against this background we may understand the frequent use of *badly* in passive or passive-like constructions (cf. 6.3).

Non-agent subjects are not uncommon with intransitive verbs, e.g. *fare* and *feel*. Note also examples like:

(40) 1858 *Jrnl. R. Agric. Soc.* XIX. i. 75: Potatoes so grown . . . dress badly.

(41) 1898 *Daily News* 4 October 9/3: The Arun continues to fish badly.

(42) 1852 *Beck's Florist* December 271: They do not . . . make good plants for exhibition, as they travel badly.

Here the verb + *badly* combination singles out a characteristic of the subject referent with respect to some action; cf. similar examples with *well* and *easily*: *sell well*, *wash easily*, etc. See also Rosta (this volume). There is no focus on a process, and no agent is mentioned or implied.

7.2 Blends of manner and degree

Although the manner group turns out to be less straightforward than one might have thought at first, the examples above are similar in allowing questions with *how* and a contrast between *well* and *badly*. In our next group *badly* contrasts with a degree adverb, as in:

(43) 1868 *Rep. U.S. Commiss. Agric.* (1869) 415: The wheat rusted badly on the blade and slightly on the stalk.

Corresponding questions are introduced by *how much*, *how seriously*, or the like.

What do we mean by a blend of manner and degree? So far, we have been using this notion rather vaguely to indicate that *badly* retains part of its original meaning at the same time as it has acquired the meaning of degree. After examining our material, we shall raise the question whether 'manner' is the best way of characterising the component of meaning that is beyond degree in these constructions.

The manner/degree category is very frequent in the *OED2* material. In the most typical examples the focus is on results or consequences rather than on a process. There is characteristically a patient suffering the effects of some action. Cf. the remarks on similar examples in 7.1.

As in the LOB Corpus material, the great majority of the verbs contain a negative element as part of their meaning. These are some examples from the *OED2* material, broken up into groups of verbs which are somewhat related:

bleed, burn, get the fever, hurt, infect, injure, maul, nettle, scald, scar, scour (= have diarrhoea), scratch, shoot (up), suffer, wound, wrick (his back)

bore, get on her tits, have the jitters, miff, rattle, scrub (= reprimand severely)

lame, limp, stagger

attack, batter, beat, hit, scoop (= defeat), worst (= defeat)

break, buckle, chafe, crack, crush, cut, damage, dent, distort, smash up, split, tear

blot, stain

frost, winter-kill

date, erode, fade, rust, sag, shank (= decay), warp, wear

ice up, obstruct, snarl (the trawls), twist

bungle, clutter, fail, falter, fluff, let down, miscue, misjudge, mistime, muff (his lines), slip up

Verbs of injuring are frequent, as are those indicating some physical damage or change. Note the verbs containing the negative prefix *mis-* in the last group. Other examples of prefixes with a negative implication are found in: *badly overstepped the mark, badly undertimed, badly undernourished, badly under-rehearsed, came badly undone*.

It can be debated whether some of the verbs above do indeed contain a negative element, or whether they are just coloured by the addition of *badly*.[9] There are examples of verbs which have no negative meaning in general, but still combine with *badly* (cf. similar examples in the LOB Corpus, given in 6.3):

(44) 1971 C. Bonington, *Annapurna South Face* x. 117: The rope behind Martin was dragging badly because of the friction caused by its passage through the tunnel and various piton runners.

(45) 1891 *Daily News* 21 November 3/5: He was badly thrown. . . . It is feared that his condition is serious.

(46) 1935 H. Davis Honey, in *Horn* xviii. 305: A man run down by a bunch of sharpshod horses has a tendency to scatter around badly.

(47) 1923 *Land and Sea* 182: That wind's funnelling badly in the valley.

The verbs in the first two examples have contextual meanings which we can easily associate with one of our groups above (*drag* with verbs indicating some sort of obstacle, *throw* with verbs of injuring). The last two examples might possibly be interpreted as pure manner, but it seems more natural to place them in the manner/degree category; note that a contrast with *well* seems very unlikely.

We are now ready to reconsider our manner/degree category. In combinations with verbs that have a negative meaning (injuring, defeating, obstructing, deteriorating, failing, etc.) *badly* serves to reinforce the negative element; cf. the comment by Greenbaum on *miscalculate* and *misjudge* in section 5.[10] It does not indicate that the injuring, failing, etc. proceeds in a particular manner. Rather than speaking about a blend of manner and degree we should perhaps say that there is a blend of (high) degree and negative evaluation, from the point of view of some implied or overtly expressed patient.[11]

With verbs that are not negative in the sense we have been referring to in this chapter, *badly* is normally used in a manner sense and contrasts with *well* rather than *slightly*. On occasion it may, however, colour the meaning of the verb and express (high) degree as well as negative evaluation.

7.3 Degree

As is well known, there are degree adverbs expressing negative evaluation plus degree which have become pure degree adverbs (*awfully, terribly*, etc.), and it should therefore be no surprise that we find the same development with *badly*. What is perhaps a bit surprising is the limited use of *badly* as a pure degree adverb.[12] It is said expressly in *OED2* (as well as in the original *OED*) that the meaning 'much, greatly' is found in colloquial use with *need* and *want*, though it is only supported by an unattributed example:

(48) Mod. I wanted to see you very badly.

A search in the whole body of quotations, however, revealed 18 examples of *badly* + *need* (the earliest from 1899) and 6 examples of *badly* + *want* (the earliest from 1889):

(49) 1899 Spencer and Gillon, *Native Tribes Cent. Austral.* vi. 170: It sometimes happens that the members of the totem, such as . . .the rain or water totem, will hold their Intichiuma when there has been a long drought and water is badly needed.

(50) 1889 R. Kipling, *Willie Winkie* 72: British Regiments were wanted – badly wanted – at the Front.

The examples in the *OED2* material are evenly distributed among the three patterns we found for these verbs in the corpus study: 8 examples of active verb + *badly*, 8 examples of *badly* + active verb, 8 examples of *badly* + past participle.

Why is the pure degree meaning found with these particular verbs? Greenbaum (1970: 62) notes that the '[i]nformation [in the *OED*] that *badly* is restricted to colloquial usage may help to explain why it does not collocate with verbs that occur with similar meaning in more formal usage, e.g. *require, desire*, and *wish*'. We shall look at another possible explanation why the pure degree meaning is found with, and apparently restricted to, *need* and *want*.

If we examine the *OED2* material closely, we do indeed find some related examples:

(51) 1881 *Daily News* 9 July 2 (Cricket): When the Harrow crack had made 90, he was badly missed at mid-off.

(52) 1963 *Times* 12 January 11/3: The sound is all too full and forward, and badly lacking in aural perspective.

These are much like the type discussed in 7.2, with a blend of (high) degree and negative evaluation. Both *need* and *want* are close in meaning to *miss/lack*; hence, combinations with *badly* are not unexpected. But they also have the more positive meanings 'require' and 'desire', which have presumably developed by implication from *miss/lack*. What appears to have happened is that *badly* has spilled over to, and become conventionalised with, these meanings and at the same time lost the element of negative evaluation.

7.4 *Badly* in combinations with non-verbs

The few combinations of *badly* with forms other than verbs in the *OED2* material are generally in accordance with the patterns dealt with above. *Badly* was found with:

adverbs:	*awry, off* (in the idiom *badly off*)
adjectives:	*eccentric, plonked, hipped on* (= 'fond of', 'bitten with'), *short of*
compound participles:	*light-struck, Planet-struck, rope-burned, worm-eaten*

Prepositional Phrases: *at outs* (= 'at variance or enmity'), *in need of*, *out of trim*

With one exception, these forms were immediately preceded by *badly*:

(53) 1928 A. Waugh, *Nor Many Waters* ii. 84: We were at outs pretty badly about that time. And when you're at outs it doesn't take much to send you off.

Note also the unusual combination of *badly* in a manner sense plus adjective in:

(54) 1602 Warner, *Alb. Eng.* ix, xlvi. 218: Labouring their Mischiefes farre and neere, Whilst Eccho and Narcissus are more badly busie heere.

8 Concluding remarks on combinations with *badly*

In the concluding section of his study of verb-intensifier collocations Greenbaum (1970: 87) proposes that collocational patterns for adverbs could be stated in some cases in terms of the semantic features of the groups of verbs they cooccur with. He notes, however, that 'there will also be cases, e.g. *badly*, where individual verbs must be listed, since no generalisations can be made' (ibid.). Our study of combinations with *badly* suggests that there is a great deal of uniformity in these combinations, and generalisations can indeed be made. There is good agreement between the corpus material and the quotations from the *Oxford English Dictionary*, in spite of the difference in the age of the material. In other words, collocational patterns appear to be remarkably stable.

One of the main findings of this chapter is that it is not sufficient to establish links between verbs and adverbs in general. Collocational links may be sensitive to the individual verb form, as shown by the particular association between *badly* and past participle forms. This must be taken into account in the structuring of a distributional lexicon.

9 Towards a distributional lexicon

What should a distributional lexicon for adverbs look like? If we turn to published dictionaries of word combinations, we find very little information on adverbs. Kozlowska and Dzierzanowska (1988) focus on combinations with nouns and do not include adverbs at all. Benson et al. (1986) do not list adverbs as head words, though they may be included in entries for adjectives and verbs (e.g. *badly*, *desperately* and *sorely* are listed in combinations with the verb *need*). Adverbs are also only marginally considered in the lists of word combinations in Johansson and Hofland (1989).

To find more systematic surveys of adverb combinations, we must turn to studies focussing on adverbs. Even before Greenbaum's study of verb-intensifier collocations Sven Jacobson compiled a dictionary of adverb placement, as part of his study of adverbial positions in English (Jacobson 1964: 203–363). This is a pure positional description, however, and does not include collocations. A couple of years after the publication of Greenbaum's study Ulf Bäcklund (1973) presented his thesis on the collocation of adverbs of degree in English, with a detailed discussion of collocational patterns of individual adverbs, based on a corpus of newspapers, magazines, novels, and plays. The book includes a dictionary section giving the combinations found for each individual adverb, sorted by six categories of head (adjectives, adverbs, comparatives, *too* + adjectives and adverbs, Prepositional Phrases, and superlatives)[13] and, under each grammatical context, by text type.

Ideally, we would like to have a distributional lexicon which, for each item, gives information on grammatical context as well as collocation (and perhaps also on text type). To derive significant generalisations, we need to go beyond the manual techniques of Jacobson and Bäcklund to computational studies based on large text corpora. Beale (1987) provides a beginning, by considering how a distributional lexicon might be derived from the tagged LOB Corpus, though he is aware that the corpus is insufficiently large. Jacobson (1964: 366) foresees a time when:

> [i]n their well-equipped laboratories these [future] linguists will have at their disposal fast-working electronic computers capable of counting, analysing and storing linguistic material on a scale which far surpasses the capacity of scholars working with index-card systems.

Given that we now have the vast corpora needed for collocational studies and appropriate computational tools, the time seems ripe to compile a large-scale distributional lexicon for English adverbs.[14]

Appendix

The distribution of adverbs in the LOB Corpus

The following lists are based on a study of forms tagged RB in the LOB Corpus. Forms which occur 30 times or more are included. The total frequency of occurrence is shown as well as occurrence in the following contexts (raw frequency and percentage of the total frequency):

-J*	before an adjective
-R*	before an adverb
-VB*	before a verb form
VB*-	after a verb form
VB*	before or after a verb form

The asterisk is used to define a group of related tags, e.g. J* equals all tags beginning with J. For a definition of the tags, see Johansson et al. (1986). Forms which only occur in ditto-tagged sequences (*a little*, *at all*, etc.) are excluded.

1 Alphabetical list (beginning only)

	total	-J*		-RB*		-VB*		VB*-		VB*	
about	437	3	0.7	6	1.4	3	0.7	71	16.2	74	16.9
abroad	55	0	0.0	1	1.8	1	1.8	17	30.9	18	32.7
absolutely	39	28	71.8	0	0.0	7	17.9	3	7.7	10	25.6
actually	114	2	1.8	4	3.5	71	62.3	1	0.9	72	63.2
afterwards	77	0	0.0	0	0.0	8	10.4	15	19.5	23	29.9
again	660	2	0.3	12	1.8	44	6.7	157	23.8	201	30.5
ago	270	2	0.7	1	0.4	5	1.9	0	0.0	5	1.9
ahead	92	0	0.0	4	4.3	5	5.4	38	41.3	43	46.7
all	289	10	3.5	134	46.6	12	4.2	38	13.1	50	17.3
almost	464	110	23.7	114	24.6	61	13.1	53	11.4	114	24.6
alone	69	0	0.0	1	1.4	8	11.6	0	0.0	8	11.6
already	362	31	8.6	13	3.6	166	45.9	13	3.6	179	49.4
also	994	64	6.4	35	3.5	400	40.2	46	4.6	446	44.9
altogether	54	7	13.0	2	3.7	3	5.6	6	11.1	9	16.7
always	515	53	10.3	18	3.5	200	38.8	2	0.4	202	39.2
any	52	6	11.5	41	78.8	0	0.0	13	25.0	13	25.0
anyway	58	0	0.0	0	0.0	0	0.0	4	6.9	4	6.9
anywhere	41	1	2.4	6	14.6	0	0.0	12	29.3	12	29.3
apparently	76	15	19.7	6	7.9	16	21.1	2	2.6	18	23.7
approximately	49	6	12.2	0	0.0	0	0.0	6	12.2	6	12.2

2 List sorted by percentage of occurrence in context -J* (above 40%)

	total	-J*		-RB*		-VB*		VB*-		VB*	
extremely	58	54	93.1	4	6.9	0	0.0	4	6.9	4	6.9
comparatively	31	27	87.1	2	6.5	0	0.0	1	3.2	1	3.2
highly	99	79	79.8	1	1.0	16	16.2	8	8.1	24	24.2
relatively	81	64	79.0	8	9.9	0	0.0	7	8.6	7	8.6
purely	41	32	78.0	0	0.0	0	0.0	0	0.0	0	0.0
somewhat	58	42	72.4	8	13.8	4	6.9	5	8.6	9	15.5
increasingly	32	23	71.9	1	3.1	4	12.5	12	37.5	16	50.0
absolutely	39	28	71.8	0	0.0	7	17.9	3	7.7	10	25.6
pretty	57	40	70.2	17	29.8	0	0.0	12	21.1	12	21.1
perfectly	60	42	70.0	9	15.0	0	0.0	9	15.0	9	15.0
equally	89	61	68.5	4	4.5	6	6.7	5	5.6	11	12.4
fairly	83	55	66.3	17	20.5	6	7.2	9	10.8	15	18.1
quite	394	220	55.8	77	19.5	36	9.1	55	14.0	91	23.1
sufficiently	60	29	48.3	3	5.0	9	15.0	10	16.7	19	31.7
reasonably	50	23	46.0	5	10.0	14	28.0	5	10.0	19	38.0
virtually	40	17	42.5	1	2.5	9	22.5	5	12.5	14	35.0
slightly	105	44	41.9	9	8.6	9	8.6	33	31.4	42	40.0
thoroughly	30	12	40.0	0	0.0	10	33.3	5	16.7	15	50.0

3 List sorted by percentage of occurrence in context -RB* (above 40%)

	total	-J*		-RB*		-VB*		VB*-		VB*	
any	52	6	11.5	41	78.8	0	0.0	13	25.0	13	25.0
no	188	21	11.2	146	77.7	6	3.2	14	7.4	20	10.6
all	289	10	3.5	134	46.4	12	4.2	38	13.1	50	17.3

4 List sorted by percentage of occurrence in context -VB* (above 40%)

	total	-J*		-RB*		-VB*		VB*-		VB*	
originally	41	1	2.4	0	0.0	28	68.3	2	4.9	30	73.2
greatly	52	6	11.5	1	1.9	34	65.4	11	21.2	45	86.5
actually	114	2	1.8	4	3.5	71	62.3	1	0.9	72	63.2
fully	111	22	19.8	2	1.8	64	57.7	7	6.3	71	64.0
never	689	20	2.9	52	7.5	396	57.5	6	0.9	402	58.3
specially	35	9	25.7	0	0.0	20	57.1	3	8.6	23	65.7
rarely	44	3	6.8	0	0.0	25	56.8	0	0.0	25	56.8
successfully	36	0	0.0	0	0.0	20	55.6	5	13.9	25	69.4
inevitably	45	0	0.0	2	4.4	24	53.3	3	6.7	27	60.0
gradually	41	1	2.4	0	0.0	21	51.2	5	12.2	26	63.4
widely	59	8	13.6	1	1.7	30	50.8	12	20.3	42	71.2
ever	336	12	3.6	19	5.7	166	49.4	10	3.0	176	52.4
closely	74	3	4.1	2	2.7	36	48.6	12	16.2	48	64.9
readily	44	7	15.9	0	0.0	21	47.7	3	6.8	24	54.5
often	415	32	7.7	17	4.1	198	47.7	5	1.2	203	48.9
easily	128	15	11.7	0	0.0	61	47.7	14	10.9	75	58.6
properly	45	3	6.7	3	6.7	21	46.7	7	15.6	28	62.2
deliberately	45	8	17.8	1	2.2	21	46.7	1	2.2	22	48.9
usually	239	24	10.0	9	3.8	111	46.4	2	0.8	113	47.3
already	362	31	8.6	13	3.6	166	45.9	13	3.6	179	49.4
previously	63	4	6.3	0	0.0	28	44.4	1	1.6	29	46.0
hardly	139	20	14.4	7	5.0	61	43.9	4	2.9	65	46.8
regularly	32	0	0.0	1	3.1	14	43.7	7	21.9	21	65.6
undoubtedly	46	2	4.3	0	0.0	20	43.5	1	2.2	21	45.7
half	61	12	19.7	9	14.8	26	42.6	5	8.2	31	50.8
seldom	33	2	6.1	2	6.1	14	42.4	0	0.0	14	42.4
normally	59	7	11.9	3	5.1	25	42.4	4	6.8	29	49.2
finally	166	2	1.2	1	0.6	70	42.2	2	1.2	72	43.4
evidently	29	1	3.4	0	0.0	12	41.4	0	0.0	12	41.4
really	313	62	19.8	12	3.8	129	41.2	6	1.9	135	43.1
suddenly	173	15	8.7	3	1.7	71	41.0	24	13.9	95	54.9
swiftly	22	0	0.0	5	22.7	9	40.9	5	22.7	14	63.6
first	260	1	0.4	1	0.4	106	40.8	30	11.5	136	52.3
recently	127	6	4.7	2	1.6	51	40.2	8	6.3	59	46.5
also	994	64	6.4	35	3.5	400	40.2	46	4.6	446	44.9

5 List sorted by percentage of occurrence in context VB*- (above 40%)

	total	-J*		-RB*		-VB*		VB*-		VB*	
forward	173	2	1.2	9	5.2	1	0.6	136	78.6	137	79.2
straight	65	0	0.0	23	35.4	1	1.5	47	72.3	48	73.8
quietly	66	4	6.1	1	1.5		9.1	36	54.5	42	63.6
considerably	41	11	26.8	4	9.8	7	17.1	21	51.2	28	68.3
hard	67	0	0.0	3	4.5	2	3.0	34	50.7	36	53.7
steadily	37	1	2.7	2	5.4	11	29.7	18	48.6	29	78.4
sharply	46	2	4.3	4	8.7	4	8.7	19	41.3	23	50.0
ahead	92	0	0.0	4	4.3	5	5.4	38	41.2	43	46.7
high	34	0	0.0	8	23.5	0	0.0	14	41.2	14	41.2
rapidly	77	11	14.3	2	2.6	14	18.2	31	40.3	45	58.4

Notes

1. For a description of the LOB Corpus, see Johansson et al. (1986).
2. For a definition of the tags, see Johansson et al. (1986). Note, in particular, that a number of common degree adverbs (including *very*) have a special tag and are therefore excluded from the comparison. As regards adverb tags in the LOB Corpus, see Johansson et al. (1986: 68ff.).
3. Explanation of the tags: VB = base form of verb, VBD = past tense, VBG *ing*-form, VBN = past participle, VBZ = third person singular form of the present tense. All these tags apply to lexical verbs only. Again, the survey only includes the main adverb tag RB.
4. I am grateful to Knut Hofland, Norwegian Computing Centre for the Humanities, for providing me with the material for these lists.
5. As regards the Brown and London–Lund corpora, see Francis and Kučera (1979) and Svartvik (1990), respectively.
6. References to the Brown and LOB corpora give the identification of the text (letter plus two digits) followed by the sentence number (as given in the WordCruncher version of the ICAME CD-ROM). References to the London–Lund Corpus give the text identification plus tone-unit number. Grammatical tags and prosodic information have been removed in quotations from the LOB and London–Lund corpora.
7. Bolinger (1972: 168) makes the point that combinations consisting of intensifier + passive may be ambiguous and indicate action or result (in the latter case, they are statal passives). When the intensifier does not precede the participle, we have true passives. The order difference is claimed to mark a contrast between action and result in: *How badly were they wronged by him?* (action) vs. *How badly wronged were they by him?* (result) (ibid.: 172).
8. The entry for *badly* is divided into seven senses, the first four of which are of the manner type. The fifth corresponds to our manner/degree category: 'So as

to cause pain, danger, disgrace or harm of any kind; cruelly, unkindly, dangerously, noxiously, disagreeably, etc.' The sixth is the degree sense 'Much, greatly' and the seventh the use of *badly* as a 'quasi-adj'.

9. 'Negative element' is used rather loosely. One way of making it more precise would be to make a close analysis of definitions of such verbs. A search in *OED2* revealed a considerable number of definitions containing the word *badly*, but it was not possible to explore the matter further within the scope of this chapter.
10. Note also Bolinger's (1972: 246ff.) discussion of the semantic redundancy of intensifiers. There is a match between the adverb and the intensifiable feature of the verb.
11. The evaluation we are speaking of here concerns the consequences for the patient and is different from the evaluation of a disjunct like *sadly*, which evaluates an event or state of affairs from the point of view of the speaker/writer. Compare: *She was badly injured* (it had bad consequences for her) vs. *She was sadly inefficient* (I think it is sad).
12. This is presumably why Bolinger (1972: 175) places *badly* among his 'relatively ungrammaticized' intensifiers, though he later refers to *badly* as a 'rather more grammaticized intensifier among the relatively ungrammaticized ones' (1972: 249).
13. Note that combinations with verbs are excluded (with a couple of exceptions), though they are dealt with in the main body of the thesis. Other grammatical contexts are included in some cases.
14. Unfortunately, the new book by Kozlowska (1991) came to my attention too late to be taken into account in the writing of this paper.

References

Bäcklund, U. (1973) *The collocation of adverbs of degree in English. Studia Anglistica Upsaliensia* **13**. Uppsala.

Beale, A. (1987) Towards a distributional lexicon. In Garside, R., Leech, G. and Sampson, G. (eds.), *The computational analysis of English: a corpus-based approach*. London and New York: Longman. 149–164.

Benson, M., Benson, E. and Ilson, R. (1986) *The BBI combinatory dictionary of English: a guide to word combinations*. Amsterdam/Philadelphia: John Benjamins Publishing Company.

Bolinger, D. (1972) *Degree words*. The Hague and Paris: Mouton.

Francis, W. N. and Kučera, H. (1979) *Manual of information to accompany a standard corpus of present-day edited American English, for use with digital computers*. Revised edition, Providence, RI: Department of Linguistics, Brown University.

Greenbaum, S. (1970) *Verb-intensifier collocations in English*. The Hague and Paris: Mouton.

ICAME collection of English language corpora (1991) CD-ROM. Distributed by the Norwegian Computing Centre for the Humanities, Bergen.

Jacobson, S. (1964) *Adverbial positions in English*. Stockholm: Department of English, University of Stockholm. (Earlier: AB Studentbok.)

Johansson, S., Atwell, E., Garside, R. and Leech, G. (1986) *The tagged Lancaster–Oslo–Bergen corpus: users' manual.* Bergen: Norwegian Computing Centre for the Humanities.

Johansson, S. and Hofland, K. (1989) *Frequency analysis of English vocabulary and grammar, based on the LOB corpus.* Volume 2. Oxford: Clarendon Press.

Koslowska, C. D. (1991) *English adverbial collocations.* Warsaw: Panstwowe Wydawnistwo Naukowe.

Kozlowska, C. D. and Dzierzanowska, H. (1988) *Selected English collocations.* Revised and enlarged edition. Warsaw: Panstwowe Wydawnictwo Naukowe.

Oxford English Dictionary (1992) 2nd edition. CD-ROM. Oxford University Press.

Quirk, R., Greenbaum, S., Leech, G. and Svartvik, S. (1985) *A comprehensive grammar of the English language*. London: Longman.

Svartvik, J. (ed.) (1990) *The London–Lund corpus of spoken English: description and research. Lund Studies in English* **82**. Lund University Press.

13 *That* and zero complementisers in Late Modern English: exploring ARCHER from 1650–1990

EDWARD FINEGAN and DOUGLAS BIBER

1 Introduction

In certain theoretical and descriptive frameworks, the study of grammar in the past few decades has drawn on intuitions about grammaticality and acceptability as the principal source of data for analysis. During the same period other grammarians have developed corpora of natural language texts to facilitate the investigation of language structures of all kinds, and large-scale computerised corpora have proven especially useful in the investigation of phenomena that do not lend themselves readily to intuitive analyses.[1] Now a thriving enterprise, corpus linguistics has been particularly valuable in the investigation of variable grammatical phenomena and, with sufficiently large corpora, lexical patterns. Computerised corpora first compiled during the 1960s and 1970s have enabled researchers to investigate not only the patterns of occurrence of various grammatical structures in different registers or genres, but also the discourse conditions favouring the appearance of one structure over another.

1.2 Synchronic studies of *that* and zero

Among the structures that have been investigated in corpora are noun clauses serving as direct objects of verbs such as *hear*, *hope*, *know*, *think*, *say* and *tell*. Sometimes called *object clauses* or *nominal* that-*clauses*, they can be marked by *that*, as in the sentences of (1), or left unmarked, as in those of (2).

(1) a. I was sorry to hear *that you are now without a cello.*
b. I hope *that becoming a catholic will give you peace of mind.*
c. I feel *that a great deal of my weakness is caused by worry.*
d. He said *that, unless we permit the strong to flourish, we won't be in a position to help the weak.*
e. It is gratifying to see *that 82 per cent are in sinus rhythm.*

(2) a. I told him *I had a letter from you.*

b. I hope *you'll do it soon.*
c. I think *they will do very well.*
d. I know *he is an ingenious person.*

Among the early investigators whose analyses predated the advent of computers, Fries (1940: 228–231) found in a corpus of handwritten American letters that the ratio of *that* to zero in object clauses such as those in (1) and (2) was 84:16 (N=302).[2] Bryant (1962: 209), another early investigator, reports several studies. In one, a single issue of a mass-circulation magazine displayed an overall preference for *that* over zero by a ratio of 58:42 (N=811), although in dialogue zero predominated by a ratio of 67:33 (N=278). Bryant also reports that a taped interview showed a pattern favouring *that* by a ratio of 61:39 (N=94). In all, Bryant reports, five verbs (*think*, *know*, *say*, *hope* and *tell*) accounted for about half the zero examples but only a sixth of those with *that*. She concludes that *that* appears most often in formal writing, zero most often in informal speech, with relatively formal speech falling in between.

About the same time, McDavid (1964) explored a corpus of well-edited American nonfiction written after 1950. Of the wide variety of structures taking *that* or zero complementisers in her investigation, clauses with single-object verbs (e.g. *hope*, *know*, and *say*, but not *give* or *tell*) were the most numerous. Sentences having a single-object verb and a *that*-clause serving as object accounted for 38 per cent of her 650 examples. Of these, only 14 per cent occurred with zero, more commonly when the subject of the object clause was a personal pronoun.

1.2.1 Discourse conditions promoting that *and zero*

In a related study, narrower than McDavid's in scope, Elsness (1984) explored *that* and zero complementisers in four genres of the Brown Corpus, a computerised corpus of American writing published in 1961. In his 128,000-word subcorpus, Elsness examined conditioning factors for the occurrence of *that* and zero in object clauses in active sentences such as those in (1) and (2) above. The genres of Press Reportage and Fiction showed a slight preference for zero, while Belles Lettres and Learned and Scientific Writing showed strong preferences for *that* (zero occurred only once among 79 object clauses in Learned and Scientific Writing). Among the factors Elsness identified as influencing the choice of connective in his 671 object clauses were situational informality (which promotes zero), structural complexity of the subject of the object clause (with complexity favouring *that*), and adverbials intervening between the matrix verb and the subject of the object clause (with adverbials promoting *that*). Most importantly, he observed that zero 'marks a closer link' between the matrix clause and the object clause, citing as evidence his findings that zero connectives are more frequent: 1) for object clauses with a pronominal subject that is coreferential with the subject of the matrix clause; 2) when the subject of the object clause is definite and, presumably, anaphoric; 3) when the subject of the matrix clause or the subject of the object clause is a first or second person pronoun.

The discourse conditions influencing the choice of *that* or zero have also been studied by Thompson and Mulac (1991). Using a 240,000-word corpus of conversation among American college students, they found several factors favouring zero (among them: a first or second person subject in the matrix clause and the matrix verbs *think* and *guess*) and others favouring *that* (among them: the appearance in the matrix clause of an auxiliary verb, an indirect object, or an adverbial; and, as subject of the complement clause, a noun rather than a pronoun). As a unified explanation for these seemingly disparate influences, Thompson and Mulac (1991: 237) observe that 'certain combinations of main clause subjects and verbs in English (such as *I think*) are being reanalysed as unitary epistemic phrases'. They claim that '[a]s this happens, the distinction between "main" and "complement" clauses is being eroded, with the omission of *that* a strong concomitant'. From their analysis, Thompson and Mulac (1991: 250) conclude that the choice between *that* and zero has 'exclusively to do with such discourse and interactional parameters as expression of epistemicity and topic' and that their findings support a 'view of grammar as discourse-dependent in the strongest possible way'.

1.3 Diachronic studies of *that* and zero

Besides their utilisation in synchronic studies, corpora have also been used to examine the historical development of *that* and zero complementisers. Exploiting the rich resources of the computerised Helsinki Diachronic Corpus, Rissanen (1991) describes the history of *that* and zero as object clause links in Late Middle and Early Modern English. Aiming to illustrate the value of a large computerised corpus in the investigation of historical syntax, he shows that the relative frequency of zero 'increases rapidly' in Late Middle English and continues throughout Early Modern English. Focussing on object clauses occurring after four particular verbs in about a dozen registers, Rissanen reports a gradual increase of zero links from 14 per cent (in the period 1350–1420) to 70 per cent (in the period 1640–1710). According to his analysis, zero linking advances through three linguistic environments: when the object clause has a pronominal subject, when the object clause directly follows the matrix verb without intervening elements, and when texts 'have a fairly close relationship to speech'.[3]

1.4 Exploration of ARCHER

The present study continues the diachronic analysis of *that* and zero complementisers by tracing their development in three registers of British English between 1650 and 1990, a period that has not previously been studied in its entirety. Relying on data from ARCHER (A Representative Corpus of Historical English Registers), we examine letters, sermons, and medical articles in seven continuous half-century periods.

1.4.1 A proviso concerning corpus size

At the outset, it should be noted that the compilation of computerised *diachronic* corpora is a relatively new undertaking and that both the Helsinki Diachronic Corpus (at about 1.6 million words) and ARCHER (at about 1.7 million), though larger than the earliest synchronic corpora, are quite small by current standards for synchronic corpora. Given recent advances in computer technology in both commercial publishing and text-based research, corpora of present-day English (and of certain other languages) are today very much larger than early corpora such as Brown, LOB (Lancaster–Oslo–Bergen), and London–Lund.

The compilation of computerised historical corpora is challenging and expensive, and the resulting limited corpora are dwarfed by the mammoth corpora available today for lexicographical and grammatical analysis. It is generally recognised that smaller corpora have more to contribute in the arenas of morphological and grammatical analysis than in lexical analysis, where their use is circumscribed by the nature of lexical distributions. Consequently, the findings reported here concerning distributional patterns of *that* and zero after particular verbs are tentative, pending the compilation and exploration of much larger diachronic corpora. That proviso granted, we offer an exploration of some of ARCHER's resources.

2 Methods

2.1 ARCHER: The corpus

ARCHER is a computerised corpus of texts representing a wide variety of speech-based and written English over the past 340 years. In its approximately 1.7 million words, ARCHER incorporates texts from ten registers, including fiction and fictional conversation, drama, newspaper articles, legal opinions, sermons, letters, and diaries. ARCHER's texts are organised into seven periods of half a century each, the first period covering 1650–1699, the last 1950–1990. Most texts are British, but ARCHER also contains parallel groupings of American texts for three periods (1750–1799, 1850–1899, and 1950–1990). The structure of the corpus and its contents are described in detail elsewhere (Biber et al. 1994).

2.1.1 Registers used in the present study

The present study relies on three ARCHER registers: Letters, Sermons, and Medicine (i.e. medical journal articles), and we examine texts of British English only. Letters were chosen to represent relatively colloquial language intended for a relatively familiar audience; Sermons to represent formal, planned speaking intended for a general audience; and Medicine to represent specialised writing for a professional audience. Table 13.1 gives the number of words examined in each register for the seven periods analysed.[4] While no register is represented by fewer than 5,000 words in any one period, most cells contain several times that many words for each register in each period.

Table 13.1 *Number of words analysed per period for three ARCHER registers*

	1650–1699	1700–1749	1750–1799	1800–1849	1850–1899	1900–1949	1950–1990	Total
Ser	5,245	5,246	5,245	5,245	5,245	5,245	5,245	36,716
Med	8,014	17,234	7,110	26,639	32,558	20,807	18,890	131,252
Let	13,332	18,693	13,378	15,307	12,032	13,463	12,709	98,914

2.2 Structures used in the analysis

Using a KWIC concordance, ARCHER's Letters, Sermons, and Medicine were searched for structures combining a matrix verb and an embedded clause introduced by *that* or zero. The goal was to identify all instances of sentences such as those illustrated in (1) and (2) above. In addition, clauses occurring as subject complements (or predicate nominals) were included, such as those illustrated in (3).

(3) a. The worst that can be said of this artful disguise is *that it is a needless pomp.*
  b. All that I can say for myself is *that I was directed to take notice of that circumstance by Mr. Addison.*

The KWIC concordance was examined for entries that fell within the definitions of *that* and zero complementation exemplified in (1), (2) and (3). All other related structures were excluded, among them those exemplified in (4).

(4)
a. Preposed clauses: *That such is the case,* any one can convince himself by looking at the advertising columns . . .
b. Subject clauses: *That this country has escaped so well* is indeed surprising, when one considers how enormous is the traffic.
c. Extraposed clauses: It seems to me *that the explanation is to be found in the unsatisfactory condition of the endometrium.*
d. Result clauses: It is only by dissecting the body again and again *that an intimate and lasting acquaintance with its structure can be achieved.*

3 Findings

3.1 Verbs

The number of different verbs occurring with *that* and zero complementisers differs across the three registers examined. Table 13.2 shows the number of different verbs appearing in each register with a *that* or zero complementiser. Because ARCHER's registers are of different sizes, Table 13.2 also provides a normalised number for a text length of 100,000 words. Here again we should note that, while normalised counts give some measure of comparability, lexical diversity is not a linear function of sample size. Consequently, normalised frequencies, especially where the actual counts are relatively small (as in the case of Sermons), should be regarded cautiously. On the other hand, the counts of Table 13.2 do suggest that Sermons and Letters exhibit a relatively larger number of different verbs taking *that* and zero complementisers than does Medicine.

Table 13.2 *Number of different verbs taking* that *or zero in three ARCHER registers (1650–1990) and normalised per 100,000 words*

		Per 100,000 words
Sermons	53	144
Medicine	86	66
Letters	105[5]	106

Of the particular verbs that occur in ARCHER's texts, no single verb occurs in all three registers in all seven periods, although *say* and *tell*, both of which appear in Letters of all periods, also occur in Medicine and Sermons in six periods. The verb *know* occurs in Letters and Sermons in all periods, but in Medicine in only two periods. Three additional verbs occur in two of the three registers in six periods: *find* and *believe* (in Letters and Medicine) and *be* (in Letters and Sermons).

Each register exhibits one or more verbs appearing in every period. In Letters of all periods are *be*, *hear*, *hope*, *know*, *say*, *suppose*, *tell*, *think* and *wish*; in Medicine, *believe* and *find*. Curiously, in Sermons, only the verb *know* occurs in every period. Table 13.3 lists all verbs that occur with *that* or zero complementisers in six periods or (as marked by an asterisk) seven periods for each register.

Table 13.3 *Verbs occurring at least once in six or *seven ARCHER periods*

Sermons	*be, *know, say, tell*
Medicine	**believe, *find, inform, observe, say, tell*
Letters	**be, believe, fear, find, *hear, *hope, *know, *say, see, *suppose, *tell, *think, *wish*

3.2 Patterns for *that* and zero complementisers

Turning now to the distributional patterns of *that* and zero complementisers, we see in Table 13.4 that during the last three and a half centuries Sermons and Medicine have shown a very strong preference for *that*. Overall, since 1650, *that* marks 89 per cent of the relevant complement clauses in Sermons and 83 per cent of those in Medicine. Even Letters, the most informal and colloquial of the three registers, show a slight overall preference for *that*.

Table 13.4 *Percentages of* that *and zero complementisers in three ARCHER registers: 1650–1990*

	that	zero
Sermons	89%	11%
Medicine	83%	17%
Letters	53%	47%

The finding of a preference for *that* over zero in the past 340 years can be compared with various analyses of present-day English, both spoken and written. Most notably, our findings for Sermons, Medicine and Letters contrast with the very strong preference (86 per cent) for zero linkage that Thompson and Mulac (1991) found in the conversation of college students. Our findings also differ from those of Elsness (1984: 521), who observed a slight preference for zero in Press Reportage (52 per cent) and a somewhat stronger preference in Fiction (58 per cent), although his registers of Belles Lettres and of Learned and Scientific Writing (like ARCHER's Sermons and Medicine) strongly favour *that* over zero. Also consonant with our findings are those of McDavid (1964), whose study of well-edited nonfiction uncovered an 86 per cent preference for *that* (a figure matched, surprisingly, by the 84 per cent preference that Fries found in handwritten letters of a somewhat earlier period).

Rissanen (1991: 285), in addition to a detailed analysis of texts through 1710, inspected several registers of British writing published in 1961 as represented in the LOB Corpus; he found a 64 per cent preference for *that* after *say* but, after *think*, an even larger (79 per cent) preference for zero. From his analysis he concludes that 'the rapid increase of zero in Early Modern English', which is the principal focus of his study, 'came to a halt some time in later Modern English'. In section 3.3 below, we address the 'halt' in the rapid increase of zero, as it is represented in three registers of ARCHER.

3.3 History of *that* and zero complementisers since 1650

In this section we examine the course of development of *that* and zero complementisers since 1650. Table 13.5 gives the percentages of *that* and zero for three registers in each of seven periods.

Table 13.5 *Percentages of* that *and zero for three ARCHER registers (N given in parenthesis): 1650–1990*

	1650–1699			1700–1749			1750–1799		
	that	Ø		*that*	Ø		*that*	Ø	
Ser	76%	24%	(29)	95%	5%	(20)	87%	13%	(23)
Med	60	40	(20)	74	26	(46)	73	27	(22)
Let	32	68	(114)	42	58	(165)	65	35	(106)

	1800–1849			1850–1899			1900–1949			1950–1990		
	that	Ø		*that*	Ø		*that*	Ø		*that*	Ø	
Ser	100%	0%	(22)	96%	4%	(26)	89%	11%	(19)	84%	16%	(32)
Med	81	19	(73)	87	13	(109)	89	11	(70)	98	2	(40)
Let	74	26	(99)	73	27	(75)	42	58	(110)	60	40	(98)

3.3.1 Medicine

Since 1650, Medicine shows a consistent preference for *that* over zero, with present-day English being the most marked and with only the earliest period having a preference rate (60 per cent–40 per cent) lower than about 3:1. Insofar as the complementiser *that* tends to cooccur with features representing more 'literate' forms of expression (in contrast to zero, which is more 'oral') and is typically found in more 'involved' and less 'informational' registers (Biber 1988)[6], the increase in *that*-complementisers in Medicine is indicative of a pattern whereby Medicine bucks the more general evolutionary trend among English registers toward more 'oral' characterisations, as judged by a wide range of features (Biber and Finegan 1989; 1992). In this regard, however, Medicine does follow a trend occurring in other professional and specialist registers (such as Legal Opinions and Science), which have become increasingly less 'oral' and more 'literate' since the eighteenth century (Biber et al. 1994).

3.3.2 Sermons

Since 1650, Sermons too show a consistent preference for *that*, indeed even stronger than the preference shown in Medicine; only the first period Sermons (76 per cent–24 per cent) fall below an 84 per cent preference for *that*. To judge again by this one feature, Sermons, like Medicine, have followed the trend of other professional registers in becoming increasingly 'literate' in expression.

3.3.3 Letters

Only three of the twenty-one cells in Table 13.5 show a preference for zero over *that* connectives, and all three occur in Letters. In the earliest periods (1650–1699 and 1700–1749), the preference that ARCHER's Letters show for zero confirms Rissanen's (1991) finding of more zero in the Helsinki Corpus Letters in 1570–1640 and 1640–1710, and extends the preference for zero into the eighteenth century.[7] After 1749, however, Letters join the overall march to an increasing preference for *that*, as in Sermons and Medicine.

Why only the first half of the twentieth century should break the pattern with its preference for zero is somewhat perplexing; and it may be noteworthy that this exception contradicts the pattern favouring *that* in the same period in the much larger sample of letters analysed by Fries (1940). One likely explanation is that letters are not so well defined a register as sermons and medical articles and that, as a consequence, they represent more variability among writers and periods, highly dependent as well on topic and other situational parameters.

3.4 Connectives after four verbs

Partly because they represent speech act verbs and private verbs and partly because of their relative frequency, four verbs have received detailed attention in study of the historical evolution of *that* and zero complementisers. As noted above, the study of lexical items should be based on much larger samples of text than are available at present for historical studies. Consequently, our analysis of the distribution of *that* and zero after particular verbs, and our comparisons with the Helsinki Corpus, should be viewed as tentative. With that proviso, Table 13.6 presents the proportion of *that* and zero complementisers following the verbs *say*, *tell*, *know* and *think* during the 340-year period represented in ARCHER.

Table 13.6 *Percentages of* that *and zero for four verbs in three ARCHER registers: 1650–1990*

	Sermons		Medicine		Letters		Total		
	that	Ø	*that*	Ø	*that*	Ø	*that*	Ø	N
say	88%	12%	66%	34%	58%	42%	63%	37%	(90 52)
tell	92	8	88	12	86	14	87	13	(76 11)
know	87	13	100	0	52	48	62	38	(45 28)
think	56	44	34	66	14	86	21	79	(32 121)

Ten of twelve cells in Table 13.6 exhibit a preference for *that* connectives. For the verb *think*, however, both Medicine and Letters show a strong preference for zero, although Sermons do not. Given in Table 13.7 for reference are the frequency counts for the four verbs for each register in each period, and from Table 13.7 it can be seen that relatively few tokens of *think* appear in Sermons of any period. Further, the fact that only nine instances of *think* appear in Sermons over the 340 years of our analysis suggests caution in accepting and interpreting this exception. Thus, leaving aside occurrences of *think* in Sermons, the verbs *say*, *tell* and *know* show strong preferences for *that* connectives in our three registers, whereas *think* shows a distinct preference for zero, at least in Medicine and Letters. This finding is consonant with the interpretation of the role played by *think* in the claims of Thompson and Mulac (1991).

Table 13.7 *Number of* that *and zero complementisers for four verbs in ARCHER Letters, Sermons and Medicine (counts based on samples of different sizes; cf. Table 13.1)*

	1650–99		1700–49		1750–99		1800–49		1850–99		1900–49		1950–90	
	that	Ø	*that*	Ø	*that*	Ø	*that*	Ø	*that*	Ø	*that*	Ø	*that*	Ø
say														
Ser	0	0	2	0	1	0	4	0	0	1	2	1	6	0
Med	1	2	1	1	1	1	3	2	9	3	4	1	0	0
Let	2	4	8	9	10	5	11	5	7	1	8	14	10	2
tell														
Ser	0	1	2	0	2	0	2	0	4	0	0	0	1	0
Med	1	0	3	0	2	1	2	0	3	0	3	1	0	0
Let	4	3	14	3	7	1	8	0	7	0	7	1	4	0
know														
Ser	4	1	2	0	3	1	1	0	1	0	1	0	1	0
Med	0	0	0	0	0	0	0	0	3	0	1	0	0	0
Let	1	5	2	6	5	5	10	2	4	1	0	3	6	4
think														
Ser	3	0	0	0	0	1	2	0	0	0	0	1	0	2
Med	0	0	1	3	1	3	3	9	4	5	3	3	0	0
Let	1	16	1	14	1	6	1	6	4	5	4	27	3	20

3.5 Comparing ARCHER and Helsinki Corpus findings: 1650–1700

The Helsinki Corpus and ARCHER partly overlap chronologically, as well as in their representation of registers. The final period represented in the Helsinki Corpus (1640–1710) encompasses the first ARCHER period (1650–1699), and among the registers represented in both corpora are Letters and Sermons. Table 13.8 compares the frequency counts for *that* and zero in Letters and Sermons of ARCHER and of the Helsinki Corpus.

Where frequency counts are as low as indicated in Table 13.8 for some verbs in some periods, direct comparisons between the two corpora can only be heuristic. Moreover, the ARCHER frequency counts for Sermons are based on a sample less than half the size of the Helsinki Corpus sample. It is noteworthy, nonetheless, that the ratios of *that* and zero complementisers in ARCHER and the Helsinki Corpus are comparable in most cells having higher frequencies.

The fact that ARCHER and the Helsinki Corpus are structured differently may help explain the discrepancies between the frequency counts in some

Table 13.8 *Number of* that *and zero complementisers for four verbs in two registers of ARCHER (1650–1699) and the Helsinki Corpus (1640–1710)*

	say		*tell*		*know*		*think*	
	that	Ø	*that*	Ø	*that*	Ø	*that*	Ø
ARCHER letters	2	4	4	3	1	5	1	16 (13,322 words)
Helsinki letters	6	11	4	3	2	2	0	9 (12,740 words)
ARCHER sermons	0	0	0	1	4	1	3	0 (5,245 words)
Helsinki sermons	0	1	5	1	1	0	0	1 (12,470 words)

cells. For example, while in this period the Sermons in the Helsinki Corpus contain more words than those in ARCHER[8] and favour entire sermons over the extracts that ARCHER includes, the Helsinki Corpus contains sermons by only two preachers (Taylor and Tillotson)[9] compared to ARCHER's five (Barrow, Baxter, Bunyan, Howe, and Tillotson) for the comparable period. Thus, although the number of words representing any one preacher is fewer in ARCHER than in the Helsinki Corpus, a wider range of speakers is represented and the possibility of stylistic skewing by a single speaker is thereby reduced.

One possible effect of the difference between the two corpora can be seen in the fact that in the Helsinki Corpus Sermons the verb *tell* occurs six times with a *that* or zero complementiser, whereas among the samples from ARCHER's five preachers *tell* occurs only once. Even normalising the count of ARCHER's *tell* to match the size of the sermons in the Helsinki Corpus, we would reach only 2.4 occurrences, not the six that the Helsinki Corpus actually contains. One possible explanation of the difference is that one or both of the preachers in the Helsinki Corpus in this period exercised a (personal) stylistic preference for the verb *tell*.

As it happens, in the sermons of Tillotson (who is represented in both ARCHER and the Helsinki Corpus) *tell* occurs twelve times (not all with complement clauses) in the Helsinki Corpus selection. By contrast, the Helsinki Corpus selection from Taylor shows *tell* only three times in a comparable stretch of text. It appears that with respect to lexical items a single author can sometimes affect frequency counts, especially when fewer authors represented by proportionately larger samples of text are analysed. In the approximately 2,200 words in ARCHER for each of its five preachers in the first period, the verb *tell* ranges in frequency from zero to six, a sobering diversity. To further underscore the difficulties of generalising about lexical matters on the basis of small samples, we can note that ARCHER's selection from Tillotson (about one third the length of that in the Helsinki Corpus) represents the verb *tell* at only half the rate of the Helsinki Corpus sample. Thus, Tillotson's use of *tell* appears to have been determined in part by factors such as topic or purpose, as well as by personal style. Given that topic and purpose can vary from one part of a sermon to another (and indeed across subsections of any register) and given that lexical choices may vary accordingly, lexical generalisations must be made with caution when they are based on small text samples.

3.6 Discourse factors promoting *that* and zero complementisers

Referring once again to Table 13.6 and Table 13.7, we can see that in ARCHER's Letters the verb *know* occurs with a *that* connective 28 times and with zero 26 times (52 per cent–48 per cent). This roughly equal balance between occurrences of *that* and zero makes the set of sentences represented in this cell a useful one for investigating discourse features surrounding the choice of connective.

As Table 13.9 shows, in 26/28 instances with a *that* connective, the subject of the matrix verb is a first or second person pronoun (and a third person pronoun in the two remaining instances). In the complement clause itself, first or second person pronouns account for 13/28 subjects, while 'full' Noun Phrases account for eleven more (third person pronouns accounting for the remaining four instances).

For the complement clauses with zero, 22/26 exhibit personal pronouns as subjects, while only two exhibit 'full' Noun Phrases, one of which is a vocative (*Your Lordshippe*).[10]

An examination of the 54 sentences in Letters in which *know* takes *that* (N=28) or zero (N=26) gives a distinct sense as to how the two sets of sentences differ. Despite a few instances of parallel structures (*You know that I am not . . . /You know I have been . . .*), generally the sentences with *that*-connectives are structurally more complex by virtue of having one or more of the characteristics illustrated in (5)[11] and tabulated in Table 13.9:

(5) a. 'Full' Noun Phrase (rather than pronoun) as subject of the complement clause: *I know that my three talks every year . . . ; I know that our deceased friends . . .*

b. Adverbial or other structure intervening between the matrix verb and the subject of the complement clause: *I knew, when I was in London . . ., that I had left . . . ; you will know by this time, by the letter . . . I enclosed to you, that the whole trouble . . .*

c. Negative matrix verb: *I do not know that I should . . . ; I don't know that you ought to have shown . . .*

Table 13.9 *Subjects of matrix and complement clauses for* that *and zero complementisers after* know *in ARCHER Letters 1650–1990 (N given in parenthesis)*

	that	zero
Subject of matrix verb	(28)	(26)
1st person pronoun	16	18
2nd person pronoun	10	4
3rd person pronoun	2	2
Relative pronoun	0	2
Noun Phrase	0	0
Form of matrix clause	(28)	(26)
Infinitive	7	3
With negative	4	1
With auxiliary	5	0
With intervening element	7	0
Other	5	22
Subject of complement clause	(28)	(26)
1st person pronoun	9	5
2nd person pronoun	4	11
3rd person pronoun	4	6
Existential *there*	0	2
Noun Phrase	11	2

d. Infinitival matrix verb (including bare infinitives): *I am delighted to know that you have found a place . . .*; *of leting* [sic] *me know that you got home safe . . .*

Thus, in ARCHER's Letters, among the sentences with a *that*-complementiser, 11/28 have 'full' Noun Phrase subjects in the complement clause, compared with only 2/26 in the sentences with zero complementisers (and both the latter contain a possessive pronoun: *Your Lordshippe; His majesty*). Among the sentences with a *that*-complementiser, 7/28 have intervening elements between the matrix verb and the subject of the complement clause, and 7/28 (25 per cent) have infinitival matrix verbs. By contrast, among the sentences with zero, not a single one has *any* element intervening between the matrix verb and the complement clause subject, while only 3/26 (11.5 per cent) have an infinitival matrix verb. In addition, 4/28 matrix clauses with *that*-connectives are negative, and 5/28 matrix verbs have an auxiliary, as compared to one negative and not a single auxiliary with zero.

Elsness has noted for several registers of present-day English that coreferentiality between the subjects of the matrix clause and the complement clause tends to promote zero. ARCHER's Letters do not fall under that generalisation, for sentences with *that* (4/28=14 per cent) and sentences with zero (3/26=11.5 per cent) show comparable frequencies of coreferentiality.

4 Discussion and conclusions

We have shown that studies of *that* and zero complementisers have a considerable history in corpus linguistics, both preceding and following the advent of computers. Included among such investigations are synchronic analyses for early and late twentieth-century English and diachronic analyses from Old English through the Early Modern English periods. In the present study, we have provided a diachronic analysis of three registers of English between 1650 and 1990. For the second half of the seventeenth century, we have also compared our findings for ARCHER's Letters and Sermons with related findings based on the Helsinki Corpus.

The texts of ARCHER show that the trend in late Middle and early Modern English toward an increasing preference for zero, as reported by Rissanen (1991), has been reversed in some registers. As Rissanen's inspection of the London–Lund and LOB corpora demonstrated, some mid-twentieth-century registers show a distinct preference for *that*, at least after some verbs, thus indicating a 'halt' to the trend he described for the periods preceding 1710. The present study has shown that Sermons and Medicine have strongly and consistently preferred *that* over zero complementisers since 1650. Letters, on the other hand, continued to prefer zero until 1750, when a preference for *that* becomes manifest.

Besides the distributional patterns of complementisers in three of ARCHER's registers, we have examined all the Letters as to the factors influencing the choice of complementiser. We found that the same kinds of discourse factors identified by other investigators as influencing the choice between *that* and zero complementisers in present-day English (and in some cases in early Modern English) have been influential between 1650 and the present.

Finally, we have indicated certain potential pitfalls of making comparisons across corpora and have underscored the tentative nature of inferences that may be drawn about lexical patterns based on relatively small samples of text.

Notes

1. Aarts (1991) and chapters 7 and 8 of Greenbaum (1988) contain useful discussions about the relationship between intuition-based and corpus-based

grammatical studies. For a discussion of the state of the art in corpus linguistics, see Leech (1991).

2. The figures reported here are those among Fries's highest ranking social group (speakers of 'Standard English'); among writers in the lowest ranking social group (speakers of 'Vulgar English') the ratio was 44:56 (N=232).
3. Traugott (1993), likewise using the Helsinki Corpus, traces the development of *that*-complement structures from Old English to Middle English, though she does not address zero complementisers. In her conclusion, she stresses that 'it is important to consider discourse factors and gradience in approaching the phenomena of syntactic change . . .'
4. For Sermons, ARCHER actually contains about twice as many words in each period as is indicated in Table 13.1, but for practical reasons the present study was limited in its exploitation of this register.
5. Coincidentally, the *Collins COBUILD English grammar* lists 105 verbs that take *that* or zero complementisers.
6. Quirk et al. (1985: 1046, 1049) report that '[a]s with other *that*-clauses, the conjunction *that* is frequently omitted from the reported clause in less formal indirect speech' and that *that* is 'frequently omitted except in formal use'.
7. In ARCHER's Letters of other periods, the preference for *that* connectives reaches a high water mark of 74 per cent in the first half of the nineteenth century and tends to decline after that.
8. ARCHER contains about 11,000 words for Sermons in the period 1650–1699, while the Helsinki Corpus contains 12,470 words for its period 1640–1710. As indicated in note 4, however, the present study utilises only about half the available words in this register.
9. Kytö (1993) reports details of the Helsinki Corpus and its composition.
10. The other contains a possessive pronoun (*His majesty*).
11. Here, as elsewhere thrughout the chapter, all examples are taken from ARCHER.

References

Aarts, J. (1991) Intuition-based and observation-based grammars. In Aijmer, K. and Altenberg, B. (eds.), *English corpus linguistics*. London: Longman. 44–62.

Biber, D. (1988) *Variation across speech and writing*. Cambridge University Press.

Biber, D. and Finegan, E. (1989) Drift and the evolution of English style: a history of three genres. *Language* **65**. 487–517.

(1992) The linguistic evolution of five written and speech based English genres from the 17th to the 20th centuries. In Rissanen, M., Ihalainen, O., Nevalainen, T. and Taavitsainen, I. (eds.), *History of Englishes: new methods and interpretations in historical linguistics*. Berlin and New York: Mouton de Gruyter. 688–704.

Biber, D., Finegan, E. and Atkinson, D. (1994) ARCHER and its challenges: compiling and exploring a representative corpus of English historical registers. In Fries, U., Tottie, G. and Schneider, P. (eds.), *Creating and using English Language corpora*. Amsterdam: Rodopi. 1–13.

Bryant, M. M. (1962) *Current American usage*. New York: Funk and Wagnalls.

Collins COBUILD English grammar (1990) London: Collins.

Elsness, J. (1984) *That* or zero? a look at the choice of object clause connective in a corpus of American English. *English Studies* **65**. 519–533.

Fries, C. C. (1940) *American English grammar*. (National Council of Teachers of English: English Monograph No. 10) New York: Appleton-Century-Crofts.

Greenbaum, S. (1988) *Good English and the grammarian*. London: Longman.

Kytö, M. (1993) *Manual to the diachronic part of The Helsinki Corpus of English Texts: coding conventions and lists of source texts*. 2nd edition. Department of English, University of Helsinki.

Leech, G. (1991) The state of the art in corpus linguistics. In Aijmer, K. and Altenberg, B. (eds.), *English corpus linguistics*. London: Longman. 8–29.

McDavid, V. (1964) The alternation of *that* and zero in noun clauses. *American Speech* **39**. 102–113.

Quirk, R., Greenbaum, S., Leech, G. and Svartvik, J. (1985) *A comprehensive grammar of the English language*. London: Longman.

Rissanen, M. (1991) On the history of *that*/zero as object clause links in English. In Aijmer, K. and Altenberg, B. (eds.), *English corpus linguistics*. London: Longman. 272–289.

Thompson, S. A. and Mulac, A. (1991) The discourse conditions for the use of the complementizer *that* in conversational English. *Journal of Pragmatics* **15**. 237–251.

Traugott, E. C. (1993) The development of English *that*-complements revisited. Paper presented at the annual meeting of the Linguistic Society of America. Los Angeles.

14 Changing patterns of complementation, and concomitant grammaticalisation, of the verb *help* in present-day British English

CHRISTIAN MAIR

1 Introduction

In this chapter I will apply the corpus-linguistic method to the study of a problem of grammatical change in Modern (British) English. Of the two points I will be making, one is uncontroversial. I will demonstrate that the way the verb *help* is used in two comparable samples of British newspaper English dating from 1961 and 1991 is significantly different. Beyond that, I will interpret this change as an example of grammaticalisation, that is of 'the dynamic, unidirectional historical process whereby lexical items in the course of time acquire a new status as grammatical, morpho-syntactic forms, and in the process come to code relations that either were not coded before or were coded differently' (Traugott and König 1991: 189; on the history and state of the art of the currently thriving study of grammaticalisation see Lehmann 1985, Traugott and Heine 1991 and Hopper and Traugott 1993).

2 Grammatical changes in British English

Change in present-day English is a fascinating topic on which the available information is of uneven quality. We know rather a lot about changes which have occurred in the pronunciation of standard English since Daniel Jones' days (e.g. Ramsaran 1990), or about changing norms of sociolinguistic propriety (Michaels and Ricks 1980, Ricks and Michaels 1990). Neologisms are being recorded as they emerge by rival dictionary publishing houses,[1] with lexicographers' ingenuity and hunting instincts often benefitting corpus linguists as well – such as when David Barnhart or Fred Shapiro manage to turn the Lexis and Nexis information banks into the biggest linguistic monitor corpora available (cf. e.g. Shapiro 1983, 1986).

Little is known, however, about grammatical changes taking place in standard British English today. It seems that the most widely used method of data gathering, namely anecdotal observation, is not very well suited to the study of the problem. Grammatical change is certainly less noticeable than lexical innovation and possibly also slower than phonetic change, but surely what Sidney Greenbaum (1986: 67) noticed after fifteen years' absence from Britain cannot have been all:

> Two years ago I returned to London after spending fifteen years in the United States . . . What about grammatical changes in those fifteen years? The only one that I have noticed affects an individual word: the word *nonsense*. I repeatedly heard it being used with the indefinite article: *That's a nonsense*, whereas I could only say *That's nonsense* . . .

As far as current grammatical changes are concerned, received wisdom is still largely as enshrined in a list first published in Barber (1964). According to Barber (1964: 130–144), there is:

- less use of the inflected form *whom*;
- a tendency to regularise irregular morphology;
- a tendency to prefer analytical to synthetic comparatives and superlatives;
- spread of the *s*-genitive to non-human nouns;
- a partial revival of the subjunctive;
- elimination of *shall* as a future marker in the first person;
- downgrading of some full verbs (*get, want, go*) to auxiliary status in some of their uses;
- wide acceptance of *due to* used as a preposition, and of *like* and *same as* used as conjunctions;
- a tendency to omit the subordinator *that*, thus increasing the proportion of unintroduced relative clauses and turning *so* into a subordinator;
- omission of the definite article in certain environments;
- increase in the number and types of multi-word verbs (phrasal verbs, *have/take/give a* + noun) (see also Algeo, this volume);
- placement of frequency adverbs before auxiliary verbs (even if no emphasis is intended);
- use of 'American' *do you have* instead of established British *have you got*.

In addition, Barber senses certain developments on the borderline between syntax and style which, incidentally, are eminently suitable for study in corpora (e.g. decrease in average sentence length in the written language, a loss of feel for the value of non-restrictive relative clauses as a rhetorical device). It is with some trepidation that one reads his apocalyptic conclusion:

> We may well be on the eve of a change in which the large-scale formal structure of the language, now largely preserved in writing, will be broken down and replaced by smaller syntactic units loosely connected. (1964: 1444)

Barber's list has not been expanded greatly since. The only important development which he failed to note is the increasing frequency and acceptance of 'singular' *they*. Others not mentioned by him but discussed elsewhere are either unsystematic experiments at the interface of grammar and the lexicon (such as, for example, the above-mentioned reclassification of *nonsense* as a count-noun) or developments that do not take place within the standard language narrowly defined (e.g. uninflected manner adverbs in expressions such as *treat her good, real good*).

3 Corpus-based study of language change

As more than thirty years have elapsed since the compilation of the Brown and LOB (Lancaster–Oslo–Bergen) corpora, I decided to compile a corpus matching the original LOB as closely as possible in every respect except that the new texts date from 1991. The press material (categories A, B and C; 176,000 words) is available for pilot investigations at the moment. Even when completed, the corpus will be too small for most lexicographical searches, but in conjunction with the old LOB it will be a valuable resource for two purposes:

1 the testing of existing hypotheses on grammatical changes taking place in British English (such as, for example, those found in Barber), and
2 the documentation of developments which have gone unnoticed so far, for example because they have not aroused the wrath of prescriptivists.

The corpus-based approach to language change will correct several distortions evident in the existing literature on the topic. It will be possible to separate the usual and normal from the exceptional. Unlike the observer recording the one instance of a new construction while failing to register the masses of evidence for the persistence of the old one, the corpus analyst will be able to describe statistical trends precisely. Also, grammatical innovations generally do not sweep the language across the board but are first established in specific textual genres, registers or functional niches. Corpora, as records of authentic performance, will make it easier to study these types of constraints.

The big drawback of the project is, of course, that it does not deal with spontaneous speech, thereby excluding from consideration one important source of innovation in language. Another possible objection is that at a time when corpora are measured in tens of millions of words and masses of machine-readable material are available from other sources, it may seem pointless to laboriously compile another LOB-style collection of text samples. Could not the questions to be investigated with the help of the new LOB Corpus be tackled as well by using existing resources, for example the British component of the International Corpus of English (ICE; see Greenbaum 1992)? I do not think so. Comparing LOB and ICE will certainly be useful for certain purposes, but the two corpora are too dissimilar for the type of systematic and exhaustive comparative analysis envisaged here. For example, ICE–GB contains much less material from the press than LOB, and material that was collected following different criteria. As I will show below, comparisons with other corpora may usefully complement work with the old and new LOB in the study of specific problems and low-frequency phenomena, but only after the opportunities afforded by a systematic and rigorous comparison of the two matching corpora have been exhausted.

4 *Help*

In the current exploratory phase of the project, the complementation of the verb *help* with either a *to*-infinitive or a bare infinitive has proved interesting to study. This verb is a corpus linguist's delight because its distribution in texts is so clearly influenced by stylistic, contextual, semantic and structural constraints, few of which are categorical in the sense that one variant form can be definitively excluded in a specific environment.[2]

4.1 Earlier accounts

Generally speaking, *help* followed by the bare infinitive (or by an object Noun Phrase and the bare infinitive) is felt to be predominantly, but not exclusively, American (see, for example, Quirk et al. 1985: 1206) – an intuition borne out by Kjellmer's (1985) and Algeo's (1988: 22) comparisons of the Brown and LOB corpora. Within British English, the bare infinitive is considered more colloquial (see, for example, OED Supplement, s.v. *help*) – a judgement which has proved difficult to corroborate empirically (Lind 1983, Kjellmer 1985).

Alongside such sociolinguistic and stylistic accounts for the distribution of the two variant patterns of complementation are others which argue that the distribution of the competing patterns of complementation is due to semantic considerations. An early example is Wood:

> *Help* followed by an infinitive without *to* ('I helped him mend his bicycle,' 'Help me lift this box'), once condemned as an Americanism, is now accepted in British English; but the *to* cannot always be omitted.

> We could scarcely say 'These tablets will help you sleep', or 'Writing out a poem will help you learn it'. It is never wrong to insert *to*; it can be omitted only when the 'helper' does some of the work, or shares in the activity jointly with the person that is helped. (1962: 107)

A look at the relevant material from LOB would suggest that this claim was broadly true for written British English in 1961.[3] However, I invite the reader to have an advance look at examples (1), (2), (3), (11) and (12) from the 1991 material which will be discussed below. They present clear counter-evidence to Wood's claim: (1)–(3) because helper or persons helped (or both) are not named, and (11) and (12) because understanding is an activity which cannot be shared in.

Christophersen and Sandved (1969: 149) have argued that if *help* has the extended meaning of 'be instrumental in', 'contribute to', this makes the bare infinitive unlikely, a position which Lind (1983: 272–273) seems to subscribe to and even extends to cases of *help* followed by an object and infinitive.[4]

A more recent advocate of a semantic explanation of the distribution of complementation patterns is Duffley (1992):

> The impression that comes through constantly with the use of *to* is that the infinitive event is depicted as a consequence or result of the action of helping. The helping is represented therefore as a prior condition or circumstance which enables someone to realize the action denoted by the infinitive . . . The bare infinitive, in contrast, represents its event as an object of co-operation between the helper and the helpee: even though this close co-operation does not always involve the helper actually doing part of the helpee's activity for him it seems to imply a view of the helper as instrumental in the realization of the infinitive's event. This excludes a relationship of 'before' to 'after' between the helping and the event which is realized thanks to the help, and explains the occurrence of the bare form of the infinitive. (1992: 29)

As a general statement, this rather abstract generalisation is valid, although Duffley wisely cautions elsewhere that 'there is a broad grey area between the two poles' (1992: 27). Applied to specific instances of the construction encountered in corpora, however, it proves difficult to test, as the reasoning quickly tends to become circular: many authentic examples are from the grey area, and we may end up with the presence or absence of *to* as the only clue in the choice between a 'consecutive' or 'simultaneous' reading of the *help*-construction.

These and similar semantic constraints should probably not be considered narrowly, i.e. with the intention only of accounting for the distribution of the various patterns of complementation found with the verb *help*. Rather, they are specific instantiations of a more general principle of iconicity in syntactic coding which could be roughly formulated as follows: direct acts of causation and assistance seem to allow a syntactically more reduced type of complement clause than indirect ones, in which assistance is rather like advice and in which enabling condition/cause and resultant state are easy to keep apart. This argument was first put forward with ample cross-linguistic documentation in a seminal paper by Givón (1980) and has recently been taken up again in Dixon's semantic grammar of English (1991). To make his point, Dixon constructs the sentence *John helped Mary (to) eat the pudding* and argues that with the *to* it is more likely to mean that John supported a presumably invalid Mary by, for example, guiding the spoon to her mouth, whereas in the version without the *to* the likeliest inference is that John ate part of the pudding himself, at the same time as Mary did (1991: 199; cf. also 230).

But again, analyses which are convincing in cross-linguistic, typological terms and broad in scope are not necessarily better suited to account for individual examples in corpora (which is, to permit an analogy from pragmatics, similar to the role played by Grice's maxims, which are as uncontroversial as general principles as they are difficult to substantiate on the basis of actual conversational transcripts). Note that Dixon is careful to couch his analysis in probabilistic terms, and note also that such fine minimal pairs will hardly ever occur in context.

The structural factor most often invoked to explain bare infinitives is the presence of an infinitival *to* before the verb *help* itself. Considerations of style and euphony are supposed to work against sentences such as *I sold my car in order to help to pay off my family's debts* or the marginally more felicitous *To help to pay off my family's debts I sold my car*. But again, the pattern *to help* + *to*-infinitive, rare though it may be, remains possible (van Ek 1966: 93–94). Its distribution in the three corpora analysed here can be gleaned from section II of Table 14.1 below. The absence of *to help (NP) to* from Brown must be regarded as fortuitous because of the small size of the corpus. As was the case with the sociolinguistic, stylistic, and semantic explanations, so it is with the structural one. There are strong tendencies, but there is also a considerable range of permissible variation.

4.2 The diachronic factor: grammaticalisation

If each of the four explanations contains part of the truth, one might argue that a complete picture will emerge on combining them all. However, this is not the case as there is a fundamental flaw shared by all four of them. The analyses are all framed in strictly synchronic terms. The central concern of the present chapter, by contrast, is a diachronic phenomenon: the clear shift in usage that has occurred in British English over the last thirty years, and hence the need to insert a historical, diachronic factor into the argument.

In the mid-sixties, van Ek (1966: 91–94) critically and comprehensively reviewed the literature on *help* available at the time. This review and his own analysis of a large corpus suggest that – with the possible exception of casual speech – the infinitive with *to* was indeed the dominant variant in British English then. Table 14.1 below shows that this is no longer so. The figures for LOB and Brown are based on the press sections of these corpora (categories A–C, 88 samples of *c.* 2,000 words each, i.e. a total of *c.* 176,000 words per corpus). They can be directly compared with the more recent FLOB[5] material collected in 1991. Part I of the table gives the figures for all forms of *help* (i.e. *help, helps, helped, helping*), whereas part II separately lists instances of *to help* followed by infinitival complements.

Table 14.1 Help *and infinitival complement clauses in three corpora*

		FLOB	Brown	LOB
I	***help* + infinitive: all occurences**			
	help + bare infinitive	21	9	4
	help + object + bare infinitive	8	10	1
	help + *to*-infinitive	6	5	14
	help + object + *to*-infinitive	7	4	3
	help/all bare infinitives	29	19	5
	help/all *to*-infinitives	13	9	17
	help/all infinitives	42	28	22
II	***to help* + infinitive: all occurences**			
	to help + bare infinitive	10	6	2
	to help + object + bare infinitive	4	6	1
	to help + *to*-infinitive	1	—	4
	to help + object + *to*-infinitive	4	—	1
	to help/all bare infinitives	14	12	3
	to help/all *to*-infinitives	5	—	5
	to help/all infinitives	19	12	8

Whereas in 1961 the *to*-infinitive was the dominant structure of nonfinite complementation (17 out of 22 possible cases), it is now the bare infinitive (29 out of 42). The figures also show that the overall frequency of *help* (with infinitival complement) has increased significantly (from 22 to 42), and that this increase is largely due to the spread of bare infinitive complements. It is worth looking at some typical examples from the FLOB material:

(1) A plan to help 60,000 jobless youngsters find work each year will be rejected by the TUC conference today. (FLOB A 06/245f.)

(2) The theatre's emergency Phoenix fund will help back the cost of some repairs. (FLOB A 34/96f.)

(3) This [additional money] is used to help pay the clergy and bills like heating and lighting. (FLOB A 40/49f.)

None of these examples expresses the idea prototypically associated with 'helping', namely that one animate agent supports another one in the performance of a task. The original LOB corpus contains one lone example of this kind:

(4) No doubt legislation could fix a suitable scale of fines to help finance National Defence . . . (LOB B 27/6f.)

Note that what is emerging at this point in the analysis is a picture rather typical of the early stages to be observed when lexical items are grammaticalised, when – to mention a process richly attested in the history of English – a fossilising verbal form is gradually being reshaped as a semi-auxiliary or catenative verb, or even as a preposition or a conjunction. There is:

1 a noticeable shift in the textual frequency of a construction, and
2 an extension of the narrow literal meaning of the lexical item, providing the starting point of the development, a process frequently referred to as 'bleaching' or 'desemanticisation' in the literature on grammaticalisation.[6]

A 'plan to help youngsters find jobs' is nothing more specific than a 'plan *for* them to find jobs'; and money used to 'help pay' for something is just money used *for* paying something. The specific contribution made by the verb is to express the idea that the expenditure or other effort involved are in partial rather than complete fulfilment of a task. This is the only justification for the presence of the otherwise omissible verb *help* in examples (2) and (3). In other words, the meaning conveyed by *help* (in such uses) has become so general that it is difficult to describe it in lexical terms. It has moved some way towards the grammatical end of the lexico-grammatical cline.

This diachronic trend – the incipient (but of course not necessarily successful) process of grammaticalisation – is a factor which must be considered in addition to the ones usually discussed in the literature on *help* if one wants to understand the changing frequencies and distributions of the competing patterns of complementation found with this verb. In some instances, awareness of the ongoing development towards grammaticalisation may even help (to) correct misperceptions. For example, the allegedly informal character of *help* with bare infinitive may just be due to the fact that grammaticalisation proceeds unhindered in the spoken language, whereas the use of a new construction is discouraged by the conservative norms of writing. Seeing the current distribution of *help* as the synchronic reflection of a gradual and slow diachronic re-shaping of a small part of the grammar of the language is also consistent with the wide range of permissible variation and the many grey areas to be observed in current usage. It seems that many things have yet to be sorted out as new norms of usage are emerging.

It may seem premature to build the case for the grammaticalisation of *help* – from lexical verb to catenative/semi-auxiliary (when finite) or to a type of verb-derived complex preposition/infinitival conjunction (when non-finite) – on a comparison of 176,000 words each of 1960s and 1990s British newspaper prose, were it not for the fact that *help* fits rather easily into an array of similar cases. Gìer Rohdenburg (1990: 146–148) has recently described a general trend towards the creation of new, semantically differentiated grammatical functors from nonfinite verbs in present-day English, offering the following list of verbs which may function as quasi-prepositions when used in the infinitive in certain contexts:

> *accompany, admit, be, become, carry, celebrate, cover, deal with, describe, do, encompass, express, fit, form, get, give, handle, hold, honour, include, join, last, make, mark, match, mean, meet, produce, reach, refer to, replace, see, separate, serve, shield, suborn, support, suit*

Rohdenburg reports the following authentic citations to illustrate the phenomenon:

(5) David McCreary is coming on *to replace* Tommy Jackson. [. . . coming on *for*/*instead of* Tommy Jackson]

(6) He converted the penalty *to make* it three all. [. . . convert the penalty *into* a goal]

(7) *To fit* size 16 (bust 38). . . [*for* size 16 . . .]

Formally, we have adverbial infinitives here, but we would not want to argue that the corresponding semantic notions of purpose ('in order to') or consequence ('so that') are prominent. As the bracketed paraphrases make clear, the infinitives convey the meaning of prepositions. Thereby, the meaning of *to replace* as used in (5) is, of course, more specific than that of the multi-purpose preposition *for*, but not necessarily narrower than that of the complex preposition *instead of*. Questions relating to the normal uses of the verb *replace*, such as whether it denotes an activity or a state ('take the place of' as against 'be in the place of') are obviously irrelevant in (5).

The major difference between Rohdenburg's examples (5)–(7) and the *help*-case is that *help* does not govern a following Noun Phrase but a nonfinite verb construction, namely a bare infinitive complement. *Help* in the new use is thus similar to complex infinitival conjunctions like *in order to* or *so as to*.

Let us now return to Table 14.1 and compare the two British corpora to the 1961 American Brown corpus. It is impossible to say that the figures merely reflect convergence in the sense that British English has moved closer to American English. Rather, it seems that both British and American English are moving towards a new and as yet not fully defined norm, and if there is a difference between the two varieties it is in the slightly different speed of the parallel movement.[7] At any rate, the significant increase in frequency of the bare infinitival construction without intervening object (line 1 in sections I and II of the table) is a genuinely new development in the FLOB material.

The type of 'desemanticised' use of *help* + bare infinitive that provides the input for the grammaticalisation process studied here is attested in the Brown material – more frequently in fact than in LOB – but to judge from the evidence it was still far from common in the 1960s. Compare (8) below, or (9) and (10), where within a few lines of one and the same text, the literal idea of helping is expressed by means of the *to*-infinitival construction, and the more abstract one (with the inanimate subject Noun Phrase) by means of the bare infinitive:

(8) . . . a $500,000 loan to help defray the cost . . . (Brown B 06/30f.)

(9) Good for Mr. Trimmer. Maybe he will help to turn our fair city into a 'ghost town'. (Brown B 19/6f.)

(10) The trucks today help pay for this highway. (Brown B 19/13f.)

The conclusions that have been drawn from Table 14.1 show that the rigorous and systematic comparison of matching databases has its uses. On the other hand, more than 176,000 words of text is often needed to ask further interesting questions. Consider, for example, the following cases from FLOB, in which *help* is followed by *understand*:

(11) The European Business Information Centre is helping many Gloucestershire companies understand the implications of the Single Market on their business. (FLOB B 24/85 ff.)

(12) . . . of authoritarian kitsch in downtown Baghdad, the cast victory arch of crossed swords, held aloft by gigantic bronze casts of the dictator's very own arm. But it also helps us understand how and why a tyrant manages to pluck victory – his own survival – from the jaws of military catastrophe. (FLOB B 15/140ff.)

(13) It was her beautiful hat, not her thoughtful face, which drew me to her; but luckily she turned out to be a professor of literature. 'They will help us to understand democracy,' she said. 'They will see the new challenge, and help us to meet it'. (FLOB B 7/5 ff.)

(14) . . . all of this should help us to understand a particularly grim aspect of the current massacre in the mountains. (FLOB B 15/170ff.).

No clear pattern emerges. Twice *understand* is used as a bare infinitive, and twice it occurs with preceding *to*. Pseudo-human and human subjects combine both with the bare and the *to*-infinitives (e.g. (11) and (13)), and so do inanimate ones (cf. (12) and (14)). As so often with *help*, all combinations are possible, but the more important question is what is normal and frequent.

Here, the unordered masses of text increasingly available on CD-ROM can be very helpful. The following supporting evidence is from *The Guardian on CD-ROM* for the year 1991.[8] A combined search for *help/helps/helping/helped* and *understand*, specifying an interval of between zero and three words between the two, yielded the required data. *Help* + object + bare infinitive and *help* + object + *to*-infinitive were attested 20 and 15 times respectively, the preponderance of the former construction being entirely due to the fact that it occurred in 7 of the 9 instances in which *help* itself was realised as a *to*-infinitive.[9]

How should these facts be interpreted in the light of the most common explanatory parameters invoked to account for the distribution of the constructions studied here? *The Guardian* being a British database, it is impossible to make sociolinguistic comparisons between British and American English (although such comparisons could in principle easily be made with other material). As to the stylistic factor – *help* with the bare infinitive being informal and colloquial in a British context – there is a result: *The Guardian* is a quality daily, and if the construction with the bare infinitive is the more frequent one even in such a corpus, it can safely be said to have lost the informal ring formerly associated with it. The semantic contrast between the two patterns of complementation – whatever its status may have been at the time Woods or Christophersen and Sandved wrote – seems to be only potentially operative today. Dixon and Duffley have shown that semantic minimal pairs involving *to*- and bare infinitives after *help* can be constructed, but specific verbs and/or contexts seem to be required for the contrast to be teased out. As far as the four examples with *understand* – (11) to (14) above – are concerned, *to* can be dropped where present, and inserted where absent, and no change in meaning ensues. Of continuing relevance, however, is the structural factor: where *help* itself is in the infinitive,[10] the bare infinitive is indeed more likely to follow. This, incidentally, is indirect support for the grammaticalisation hypothesis advocated here, as the most likely verbal forms to fossilise are in fact nonfinite ones.

In order to find evidence on the objectless construction (*help* + bare infinitival complement), which was not sufficiently attested among the *understand*-examples, I looked for further combinations of *help* with frequent verbs. The combined search for *help pay*, with no intervening material, yielded 51 relevant examples. Interestingly, in 39 of them the bare infinitive of *pay* again follows the *to*-infinitive of *help*. Compare:

(15) Earlier Kevin had to borrow money against his house to help pay off more than £9,000 debts outstanding when his small business went under. (*The Guardian* 31/12/91, Home, p. 2)

(15) is one of those examples in which the insertion of *to* leads to a small shift in meaning, back to the basic concept of helping. As it stands, the example says that the money borrowed from the bank will 'partially cover' the outstanding debt. With the *to*, the first reading is that Kevin 'will work together (with unnamed third parties)' to pay off the debt. Note, incidentally, that such examples cast doubt on Wood's traditional advice, quoted above, that 'after *help* the *to*-infinitive is always correct', and that Duffley in his recent study is right to emphasise the fact that in a few instances it is the bare infinitive which is the only contextually plausible option (1992: 24, 26–27). In the framework of the present argument, I would argue that the insertion of the infinitival particle yields questionable results in those examples in which the combined processes of fossilisation and grammaticalisation have proceeded furthest. Compare:

(16) But Bournemouth, his previous club, were owed £17,500 on the deal and the rest went to help pay off the bank overdraft. (*The Guardian* 16/12/91, Sports, p. 16)

The meaning of *help* here is prepositional ('. . . went towards paying . . .'). It is interesting to note that semantic bleaching and grammaticalisation can also be observed in a good many cases in which the helpers are active agents, such as human beings or political institutions:

(17) The Government also regularly incurs debt to help pay for its public spending. (*The Guardian* 3/12/91, Educational, p. e2)

(18) It is thinking of finding adoptive 'parents' for them, companies and institutions who will help pay to preserve any of the 200 [statues from Antiquity] that sit outdoors. (*The Guardian* 10/5/91, Euro, p. 25)

(19) Its main plank has been Bonn's decision to overturn general election pledges and raise taxes to help pay for German unity. (*The Guardian* 20/4/91, Foreign, p. 8)

(20) To help pay for the deal, Northern plans a one-for-four extra share issue to raise £227 million. (*The Guardian* 21/11/91, City, p. 13)

Note that (18) would have to read 'will pay to help (to) preserve' if *help* had its literal meaning.

5 Conclusion

To conclude, the present chapter has demonstrated that a development that may end in the grammaticalisation of *(to) help* preceding bare infinitival complements has got under way in British newspaper language over the past thirty years. In the absence of a suitable array of corpora, it will require other methods of investigation to find out whether the innovation is spreading in general spoken and written usage as well.

My immediate aim in this contribution has been to present and discuss new empirical evidence on the use of *help* in present-day British English. Beyond that, I would like the present study to promote corpus-based work, both of the statistical-quantitative and the textlinguistic-qualitative kind, in the study of grammatical change in progress. In particular, I think that available machine-readable corpora – of English and other languages – provide a useful testing ground for two important claims put forward in recent work on grammaticalisation, namely that there is no strict dividing line between the lexicon and grammar of a language, and that textual frequencies and patterns of distribution are important in the emergence and definition of grammatical categories.

Notes

1. In addition to the supplements of the *Oxford English Dictionary (OED)*, compare, for example, S. Tulloch (ed.), *The Oxford dictionary of new words* (Oxford University Press, 1991); K. Barnhart et al. (eds.), *Third Barnhart dictionary of new English* (1990), with its quarterly updates published by Springer as *Barnhart dictionary companion*; H. LeMay, S. Lerner and M. Taylor, *The facts on file dictionary of new words* (New York/Oxford: *Facts on file*, 1988), or J. Ayto (ed.), *The Longman register of new words* (London: Longman, 1990).
2. One rare such instance is that negated infinitives cannot be bare (hence *This helped me not to lose my temper* but not **This helped me not lose my temper*). However, this has nothing to do with the verb *help* itself but is a reflection of general properties of bare infinitive constructions: cf. *This caused me (not) to leave soon* against *This made me (*not) leave soon*. The constraint is relaxed for some uses of *let*.
3. There is, however, one counter-example, discussed as (4) below.
4. Again, the interested reader may note that paraphrases with 'be instrumental in' or 'contribute to' are not at all strange for many of the more recent examples of bare infinitive complements discussed below. Thus, (3) easily translates into '[This money] is used to contribute to paying the clergy and bills'.
5. FLOB is short for Freiburg–Lancaster–Oslo–Bergen. The reader familiar with British slang will forgive the unwanted association.

6. Heine, Claudi and Hünnemeyer (1991: 149, 155–156) contains some useful comments on terminological problems in the emerging subdiscipline.
7. Of course, no entirely convincing conclusions can be drawn as long as there is no sample of 1990s American newspaper language available for systematic comparison. A 1990s replica of the Brown corpus is being compiled at the University of Freiburg for this purpose.
8. Numerous other British national dailies are published and distributed by Chadwyck-Healey.
9. The construction without the intervening object occurred only once, so that no conclusions are possible concerning this type. The material contained one further superficially similar structure in which the infinitival clause followed impersonal *it* and hence had to be analysed as an extraposed subject clause.
10. The *to*-infinitive, to be precise. The combination of *help* as bare infinitive with a bare infinitival complement, though theoretically possible, seems to be extremely rare in actual practice.

References

Algeo, J. (1988) British-American grammatical differences. *Journal of Lexicography* **1**. 1–31.

Barber, C. (1964) *Linguistic change in present-day English*. Edinburgh and London: Oliver and Boyd.

Christophersen, P. and Sandved, A. (1969) *An advanced English grammar*. London: Macmillan.

Dixon, R. M. W. (1991) *A new approach to English grammar on semantic principles*. Oxford University Press.

Duffley, P. J. (1992) *The English infinitive*. London: Longman.

Ek, J. A. van, (1966) *Four complementary structures of predication in contemporary British English*. Groningen: Wolters.

Givón, T. (1980) The binding hierarchy and the typology of complements. *Studies in Language* **4**. 333–377.

Greenbaum, S. (1986) The grammar of contemporary English and The comprehensive grammar of the English language. In Leitner, G. (ed.), *The English reference grammar*. Tübingen: Niemeyer. 6–14.

(1992) A new corpus of English: ICE. In Svartvik, J. (ed.), *Directions in corpus linguistics*. Berlin: Mouton de Gruyter. 171–179.

Heine, B., Claudi, U. and Hünnemeyer, F. (1991) From cognition to grammar: evidence from African languages. In Traugott, E. C. and Heine, B. (eds.), *Approaches to grammaticalization*. Volume I. Amsterdam: John Benjamins. 149–187.

Hopper, P. and Traugott, E. C. (1993) *Grammaticalization*. Cambridge University Press.

Lehmann, C. (1985) Grammaticalization: synchronic variation and diachronic change. *Lingua e Stile* **20**. 303–318.

Lind, A. (1983) The variant forms *Help to/Help ø*. *English Studies* **64**. 263–273.

Kjellmer, G. (1985) *Help to/Help ø revisited*. *English Studies* **66**. 156–161.

Michaels, L. and Ricks, C. (eds.) (1980) *The state of the language*. Berkeley: University of California Press.

Quirk, R., Greenbaum, S., Leech, G. and Svartvik, J. (1985) *A comprehensive grammar of the English language*. London: Longman.

Ramsaran, S. (ed.) (1990). *Studies in the pronunciation of English*. London: Routledge.

Ricks, C. and Michaels, L. (eds.) (1990) *The state of the language*. London: Faber and Faber.

Rohdenburg, G. (1990) Aspekte einer vergleichenden Typologie des Englischen und Deutschen: kritische Anmerkungen zu einem Buch von John A. Hawkins. In Gnutzmann, C. (ed.), *Kontrastive Linguistik*. Frankfurt: Lang. 133–152.

Shapiro, F. R. (1983) Legal data bases and historical lexicography. *Legal Reference Services Quarterly* **3**. 85–87.

(1986) Yuppies, yumpies, yaps, and computer-assisted lexicology. *American Speech* **61**. 139–146.

Traugott, E. C., and Heine, B. (eds.) (1991) *Approaches to grammaticalization*. 2 vols. Amsterdam: John Benjamins.

Traugott, E. C. and König, E. (1991) The semantics-pragmatics of grammaticalization revisited. In Traugott, E. C. and Heine, B. (eds.), *Approaches to grammaticalization*. Volume I. Amsterdam: John Benjamins. 189–218.

Wood, F. T. (1962) *Current English usage*. London: Macmillan.

15 Verbs in public and private speaking

JAN SVARTVIK and OLOF EKEDAHL

1 Public and private speaking

Delegates at international conferences commonly complain about the poor quality of the papers, but the complaint seems to be about oral delivery rather than content. Yet when prompted to explain what in particular makes such public speaking performances poor, they tend to focus on features like the following (for papers delivered in English which, as it happens, now seems to be the near-universal academic conference language): non-native speakers are unable to produce certain English sounds or mispronounce individual words or have an un-English intonation; native speakers speak too fast, slovenly etc., unmindful of the fact that their audience is largely made up of non-native speakers of English. A fairly general complaint is that many speakers do not in fact 'speak' but 'read' their papers, often at tremendous speed, which is understandable considering that the time allotted to papers (sometimes no more than fifteen minutes, including discussion) is found inadequate.

A reason for the failure of public speakers is not necessarily that their papers are read from a manuscript, but that some aspect of the linguistic form of their papers (prosody, lexis, grammar or textual organisation) is not suited to oral presentation. Since this chapter is written for a volume on the verb, we will focus on verbs, but also say something about other word classes in both speech and writing, as well as the place of prosody in spoken discourse.

While we want to focus on speaking, both private and public, it will also be relevant to consider here the basic differences between speaking and writing. On this distinction, Halliday has this to say:

> The written language presents a *synoptic* view. It defines its universe as product rather than as process . . . The spoken language presents a *dynamic* view. It defines the universe primarily as process, encoding it not as structure but as constructing or demolishing. In the spoken

> language, phenomena do not exist; they *happen*. They are seen as coming into being, changing, moving in and out of focus, and as interacting in a continuous onward flow. . . It is not because a written text is itself a fixed and static object that it represents things in this way; even if we never saw the text, and only heard it read aloud, it would still have the effect of a piece of written language. Similarly, spoken language is spoken language even if it is presented to us in the form of a transcription, as text in writing. (1985: 97)

> Spoken language favours the clause, where processes take place, whereas written language favours the nominal group, the locus of the constitution of things. (1985: 99)

'Spoken language' here refers, not to public, but to private speaking, i.e. interpersonal, interactive conversation, which is by far the most widely used, and important, form of speech. Public speaking – which we will use as a general term subsuming the reading of conference papers, lecturing, newscasts etc. – may be seen as a cross-breed between spontaneous, interactive spoken language and written language. It is therefore of interest to compare data from both speech and writing, as we will do in this chapter.

2 Spoken English corpora

This chapter is largely based on research on English corpus data carried out at the Department of English, Lund University.[1] For spoken data we will refer to the London–Lund Corpus of spoken British English (henceforth LLC) as representing interactive and private speaking, and to the Lancaster/IBM Spoken English Corpus (henceforth SEC) as representing public speaking. The material of special interest to a study of public speaking should typically consist of recordings of monologues (rather than dialogues, as in conversation); the speakers may or may not use a script, but a general feature is that their performances have been planned in advance (which cannot be done for interactive discourse); a third feature is that the speakers are typically professionals: correspondents reporting from around the world to a BBC news programme, lecturers broadcasting for the Open University etc.; finally, the texts are usually informative rather than imaginative (as in novels) or interpersonal (as in conversation).

While LLC has been used for a long time in numerous studies (as is apparent from the bibliographic listings in Greenbaum and Svartvik 1990, Altenberg 1991), SEC may need some introduction. Our public speaking material was produced at Lancaster University in collaboration with the Speech Research Group at IBM UK Scientific Centre. The first aim of the

Lancaster project was to collect samples of natural spoken British English to be used as a database for prosodic research (see, for example, Wichmann 1991, Knowles 1993, Knowles and Alderson 1994). With a size of approximately 50,000 words (as compared with 500,000 in LLC) SEC is really too small for lexical and grammatical research, but has the advantage of being available in (a) high-quality audio recordings, (b) professional transcriptions, and (c) machine-readable form (with or without word-class tags). The dominant number of SEC texts that we have used are commentary, news broadcasts, lectures, magazine-style reporting, propaganda etc. They will be labelled *informative* as opposed to the *imaginative* texts consisting of readings of fiction. Here is an example of an informative text type, the opening of a Reith Lecture on economics by David Henderson, broadcast in 1985 on the BBC (SEC text C01):

> Last week I showed my hand as the price mechanist that I am, and I argued, with the help of my fictional colleague Mr MacQuedy that individual willingness to pay should be the main test of how resources are used. You may recall that we made fun of a number of soap-opera notions of do-it-yourself economics (DIYE). In this lecture I want to enlarge on the contrast between DIYE and economic orthodoxy. I want to consider first an aspect of DIYE which I call *unreflecting centralism*. It has two mutually supporting elements. One is the disposition to assume that outcomes have to be planned and decided by governments. The second is the tendency to think of governments and states as the principal or even the only actors on the economic scene, and to attribute to them roles and functions which aren't necessarily theirs.

For comparisons with writing, we will refer to the Lancaster–Oslo–Bergen Corpus (LOB) for written British English and to the Brown University Corpus (Brown) for written American English (see Francis and Kučera 1982, Hofland and Johansson 1982, Johansson and Hofland 1989).

3 Word classes

Before focussing on verbs we want to see how frequent verbs are in relation to other word classes (cf. Halliday above). Table 15.1 shows the frequencies for four broad text collections: LLC for private speaking (c, conversation), SEC for public speaking, and LOB and Brown for writing. The last three corpora have been subdivided into informative (f) and imaginative (m).

The system of word-class tags is adapted from Francis and Kučera (1982) for the Brown Corpus and from Johansson and Hofland (1989) for the LOB Corpus. The tags for LOB and SEC are identical, and the Brown tags almost identical. However, the LLC classification is a little different because of the

Table 15.1 *Word-class frequencies (percentages)*

Word class	LLC:c	SEC:f	SEC:m	LOB:f	LOB:m	Brown:f	Brown:m
Verbs	20.1	16.2	22.9	16.4	21.9	17.0	21.7
Pronouns	17.3	4.5	13.8	5.0	13.1	4.8	11.9
Nouns	14.3	28.0	18.1	26.9	20.0	28.5	21.8
Prepositions	9.2	12.9	8.8	13.1	9.6	12.8	9.9
Adverbs	9.0	6.5	9.6	5.9	8.6	5.5	8.1
Determiners	7.9	16.3	12.4	15.2	11.4	14.9	12.1
Adjectives	6.0	6.9	5.4	7.8	5.7	7.6	5.4
Conjunctions	6.3	5.2	4.9	5.5	5.4	5.9	5.9
Other	9.9	3.3	3.7	4.3	4.4	3.0	3.3

special tagging system used for this spoken corpus. The most notable difference is the category of discourse items (such as *you know, you see* and *I mean*). Being a typical feature of informal speech (see Stenström 1990, and this volume), they have been tagged in LLC as units instead of separate word classes. Since discourse items often contain pronouns and verbs (*you* + *know* etc.), it should be noted that, for LLC, such pronouns and verbs are not included separately in those classes but as collocations in 'other', a class which they dominate with a total of 9.4 percent. Searches of SEC, LOB and Brown gave an approximate total of 50 of these discourse items per corpus. For LLC, the 'other' class also includes some other categories (predeterminers, *wh*-words, infinitival *to* and interjections), but they are so few that they can be ignored for the present purpose. The LLC list is based on approximately 50,000 words of conversation and is taken from Altenberg (1990: 185).

The word-class distributions for the informative (f) sections of SEC, LOB and Brown are very similar. The small differences that occur are hard to explain at this level of analysis, and could well be statistically insignificant. As for the imaginative sections, the differences are slightly greater, but could still be insignificant. However, the differences between the informative and the imaginative sections are much greater. It is interesting to see that, here, the spoken/written distinction has little importance. We have to keep in mind that the imaginative prose texts probably all originate in writing. (It is not clear from the SEC manual exactly where all the texts come from, nor whether they are written to be read.)

The LLC conversations are the odd man out in this company. They show the same tendencies as the imaginative parts, only in a more pronounced way: in particular, fewer nouns and determiners but more pronouns. The large proportion of adverbs is another feature that is shared with the imaginative prose sections of both spoken and written texts.

To see these general trends more clearly, we reduce the table by conflating the major classes and leaving out less frequent word classes. Figure 15.1 shows the three categories Nominal, including nouns, determiners and prepositions (which are chiefly associated with Noun Phrases); Verbal, including verbs and adverbs (which chiefly modify verbs); and Pronominal, including pronouns.

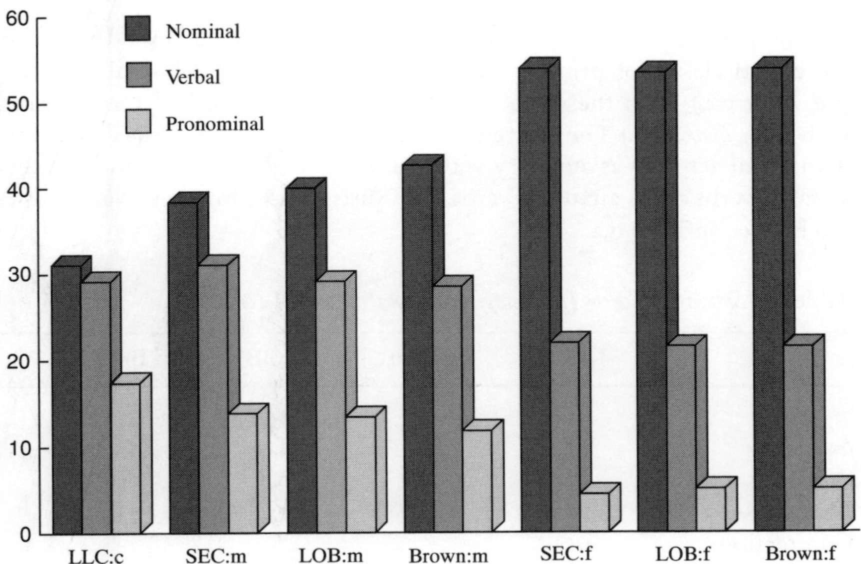

Figure 15.1 *Conflated word classes*

Two major text groups appear clearly in Figure 15.1: in one, remarkably homogeneous, group we find the informative texts of SEC, LOB and Brown, with Nominal featuring very high, Verbal rather low and Pronominal very low; in the other group are the imaginative texts of SEC, LOB and Brown, but also LLC, which are characterised by lower Nominal and higher Verbal and Pronominal bars. However, this second group is less homogeneous than the first, particularly with LLC showing the most extreme tendencies, as compared with writing.

4 Subclasses of verbs

Having established the frequency of verbs in relation to other word classes we now want to take a closer look at different subclasses of verbs, and focus on their use in two major types of spoken discourse: private speaking (conversations in LLC) and public speaking (in SEC). We will leave out the imaginative texts of SEC, since they constitute only a small part of the corpus and, in particular, are atypical of public speaking. LOB and Brown, without textual subdivisions, will be referred to chiefly for comparisons of spoken with written English.

Following the verb classification in Quirk et al. (1985: 96ff) we distinguish the closed classes of primary verbs (*be*, *have*, *do*) and modal auxiliary verbs (*will*, *might* etc.) from the open class of full verbs (also called lexical verbs, such as *say*, *think*, *begin*). The full verbs can act only as main verbs, the modal auxiliaries can act only as auxiliary verbs, and the primary verbs can act either as main verbs or as auxiliary verbs. The distribution for these verb classes can be seen in Table 15.2.

Table 15.2 *Subclasses of verbs (percentages of the total number of words*[2]*)*

	LLC:c	SEC:f	LOB	Brown
be	4.3	4.3	4.9	3.9
have	1.7	1.4	1.4	1.2
do	1.4	0.2	0.4	0.4
Modals	1.7	1.2	1.4	1.4
Contractions	2.1			
Full verbs	9.1	9.2	10.0	11.6
TOTAL	20.3	16.3	18.1	18.5

The distribution is similar for all four corpora. Full verbs make up about one half of all verbs (with percentages varying from 9.1 in LLC to 11.6 in Brown). The textual proportions in the other half are rather alike for *be*, *have* and modals, but the frequency of *do* is somewhat higher in conversation than in the other genres.

There is a larger proportion of auxiliary verbs (both primary and modal) in LLC than in the other corpora. By conflating the primary and modal auxiliaries and comparing their percentages with those of full verbs, we get the distribution in Figure 15.2.

Table 15.3 shows the percentages of the different modal auxiliaries in the four corpora.

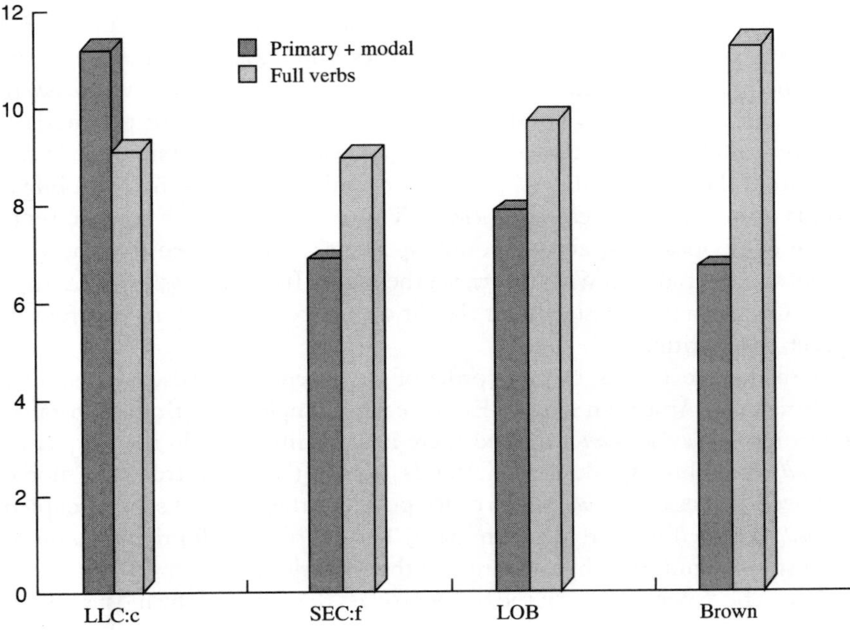

Figure 15.2 *Primary and modal auxiliaries conflated and compared to full verbs*

Table 15.3 *Modal auxiliaries (percentages of the total number of modal auxiliaries)*

	LLC	SEC	LOB	Brown	TOTAL
will	16	29	19	19	21
would	25	17	21	22	21
can	24	18	15	16	18
could	14	10	12	13	12
may	4.1	6.8	9.1	9.4	7.4
should	6.1	7.7	8.8	6.1	7.2
must	6.3	3.9	7.8	7.3	6.3
might	4.4	4.6	5.3	4.7	4.8
shall	2.5	1.4	2.4	1.9	2.0
ought	2.1	0.5	0.7	0.5	1.0
TOTAL	100	100	100	100	100

Will, would, can and *could* form a dominant quartet, together accounting for almost three quarters of all modal auxiliaries. In Dixon's classification (1991: 168), their central meanings are prediction (*will, would*) and ability (*can, could*). In the middle frequency band, totalling about one quarter of the modals, we find *should* (obligation), *must* (necessity), *may* and *might* (possibility). At the bottom of the rank list are *shall* (prediction) and *ought*, indicating that obligation is dominantly expressed by *should*. (This may explain why *ought* presents a case of divided and, among young speakers, perhaps even disappearing usage; see Svartvik and Wright 1977; yet the higher figure for *ought* in LLC supports Collins' 1991: 152 statement that 'it occurs considerably more often in speech than writing'.)

In the four text types, the rank order of the different modals is very similar in British and American written English: for example, in both the top-ranking order is *would-will-can-could*, and there is little difference in the frequency of *shall*. In public speaking, *will* stands out as the most frequent modal (followed by *can-would-could*). In private speaking, the top ranks are occupied by *would* and *can* (followed by *will* and *could*). The distribution for the other modals in speech conforms, by and large, to that of writing.

As can be expected, it is in the full-verb class that we find the most striking differences in verb use among the corpora. The most frequent full-verb lexemes are listed in rank order for each corpus in Table 15.4.

The LOB and Brown corpora are remarkably similar in full-verb frequencies. Of the 45 different verbs that occur more than 400 times per one million words in either LOB or Brown, 22 fall into the same frequency band. Corresponding figures for LOB and LLC are 5 out of 47, for LOB and SEC 10 out of 51, and for LLC and SEC 4 out of 52.

LLC is quite different from the other corpora in that a few extremely common verbs dominate. The 40 most common verbs account for 7.6 per cent of all words in LLC, compared to 3.3 per cent in SEC, 3.6 per cent in LOB, and 3.5 per cent in Brown. Astonishingly, the seven most common verbs in LLC add up to 4.6 per cent of all words.

While the number of verb types is almost identical for the four corpora (between 37 and 40), LLC alone has verbs with (normalised) frequencies over 5,000: *know* 9,000, *think* 7,900, *get* 7,300, *go* 6,200, *say* 6,100. Three of these verbs (*get, go, say*) rank high in all corpora, but the top two LLC verbs, *know* and *think*, are much further down the list in the written corpora, and *mean* only appears at the end of one rank list (LOB). Clearly the common function of these verbs in discourse items – in particular in clauses such as *you know, you see, I mean, I think* – explains their high frequency in interactive discourse. Extrapolation from the figures in Altenberg (1990) gives the following frequencies (per million words) of four common discourse items including verbs: *you know* 4,240, *you see* 2,380, *I mean* 2,040, *thank you* 340. Without these

Table 15.4 *Frequency bands of full verbs*[3]

	LLC	SEC	LOB	Brown
> 5,000	know think get go say			
> 2,000	mean see come	say	say make go	say make
> 1,000	want make take look tell read give find work use	go take make come see get call give	take know see come give get find think look	go take come see get know give find use
> 900	put suppose feel try teach	think find write win know use	use seem tell	think look seem
> 700	write start talk leave call seem	look help pay want seem	show become leave feel ask want put	become tell leave feel show want call ask

Continued over the page

Table 15.4 *Frequency bands of full verbs*[3] (contd.)

	LLC	SEC	LOB	Brown
>500	happen hear live meet ask	lead begin follow turn show provide leave put expect	bring turn keep call	begin turn write follow keep put hold
>400	keep bring let	hold describe work tell include walk try ask add	hold try begin write stand meet mean hear follow live appear	work bring provide let live try stand move hear run need

verb tokens, the percentage for the 40 most common verbs in LLC drops from 7.6 per cent to 6.7 per cent, i.e. almost three quarters of all full verbs. The seven most common verbs in LLC make up 3.7 per cent (i.e. roughly two fifths of all full verbs), which is still more than the 40 most common verbs in any other corpus.

While we have noted these striking differences in verb frequencies between conversation and non-conversation, Table 15.4 shows that the verb types are rather stable, especially for the frequency bands over 700. Of course, the type of discourse covered by the corpora is reflected in the semantic groups: high frequencies in LLC (but no occurrence in the other corpora) of *read, work, teach* cannot be taken to mean that these verbs are typical of conversation in general, but rather of academic conversation, which is over-represented in LLC. Yet the fact that the same verb types occur very largely in all four corpora indicates that there is a fairly small number of English core verbs, which occur with high frequency in all (or most) types of discourse, spoken or written.

5 Semantic verb types

To get an idea of what meanings the verbs represented, we next selected the most common verbs occurring in all four corpora and placed them together in broad semantic groups based on Dixon's (1991) classification system. Ours is of course a rough and superficial analysis which does not do justice to Dixon's refined system of semantic verb classification. This would require a much more detailed study, including the different uses of the verbs in their contexts, and constitute a study of its own.

Table 15.5 shows eight semantic groups (accounting for the majority of the verbs in Table 15.4).

Table 15.5 *Semantic grouping of core verbs*

MOTION	SPEAKING	ATTENTION
bring	ask	find
come	call	hear
go	say	look
meet	speak	see
run	tell	show
take	write	
turn		
walk		
REST	WANTING	BEGINNING
leave	expect	begin
live	mean	start
put	need	keep
set	want	
THINKING	GIVING	
know	give	
think	pay	

The largest groups are as follows: MOTION (8 full verb lexemes), SPEAKING (6), ATTENTION (5), REST (4), WANTING (4), BEGINNING (3), THINKING (2), GIVING (2). The common motion verbs are very vague (e.g. *bring, come, go, take*), and are not necessarily motion verbs. They are all common as parts of phrasal verbs and other expressions where they lack the component of motion, e.g. *go mad, go on, take care, take a picture* (see Algeo, this volume).

Since Dixon lists some 30 main semantic types, our results indicate that, at this level, less than one third of the semantic verb types dominate among the verbs in Table 15.4. Table 15.6 gives the rank order of the semantic types in all four corpora. Again, the written corpora present a rather similar picture.

Table 15.6 *Rank order of the semantic types in four corpora*

LLC	SEC	LOB	Brown
THINKING	SPEAKING	MOTION	MOTION
MOTION	MOTION	SPEAKING	SPEAKING
SPEAKING	ATTENTION	ATTENTION	ATTENTION
ATTENTION	GIVING	THINKING	REST
WANTING	THINKING	REST	THINKING
REST	REST	WANTING	GIVING
GIVING	WANTING	GIVING	BEGINNING
BEGINNING	BEGINNING	BEGINNING	WANTING

Table 15.7 shows a comparison of the dominant verb lexemes in the spoken corpora. The table should be read as follows: Among ATTENTION verbs, *find, hear, look* and *see* are more frequent in LLC than in SEC; only *show* is more frequent in SEC than in LLC. This is an attempt to investigate possible differences in the choice of verbs 'to express the same thing' in different situations. However, the number of verbs is really too small to make any conclusions possible. Yet, we can see, for example, that only verbs of GIVING are more frequent in SEC than LLC; in LLC verbs of THINKING, ATTENTION and SPEAKING dominate.

The semantic analysis here is rough and superficial. Yet we hope that it might give someone the impulse to carry out, in different corpora, a broader semantic investigation of the use of verbs in actual context.

6 Conclusion

To sum up some of the results of our study, word-class distributions were similar for the informative text types in the SEC, LOB and Brown corpora, but with slightly greater variations among their imaginative sections. A more drastic difference was found between informative and imaginative text types. LLC conversations showed up a very different word-class distribution. This indicates that conversation is a distinctly verbal text type, as

Table 15.7 *Comparison of dominant verb lexemes in spoken corpora*

	LLC	SEC
THINKING VERBS	know suppose teach think	
ATTENTION VERBS	find hear look see	show
SPEAKING VERBS	read ask say talk tell	call describe write
MOTION VERBS	bring come go meet	follow lead turn walk
GIVING VERBS		pay provide

opposed to the predominantly nominal character of the other corpora. The patterning suggests that, in terms of word-class distributions, conversation and informative writing are the extreme text types with imaginative writing taking up an intermediate position.

This word-class patterning confirms Biber's results: 'Nouns are the primary bearers of referential meaning in a text, and a high frequency of nouns thus indicates great density of information' (1988: 104). It also endorses Halliday's statement that 'spoken language favours the clause, where processes take place, whereas written language favours the nominal group, the locus of the constitution of things' (1985: 99). However, in view of the different patterns of the Pronominal and Nominal categories in the conflated classification (Figure 15.1), we would like to rephrase the statement so as to separate pronouns (which are typical of spoken discourse) from nominal groups with nouns as heads (which are typical of written discourse).

Among major verb classes, the main difference was the proportionally greater use in LLC of primary and auxiliary verbs as compared with full verbs. Within the modal auxiliaries, we noted the pervasive dominance of the quartet made up of *will, would, can* and *could,* accounting for almost three quarters of all modal auxiliaries. Two verbs, *shall* and *ought*, are little used in all text types.

The most striking difference in the subcategories of verbs was found in the class of full verbs. The seven most common verbs in LLC made up 3.7 per cent of all words, which is a higher ratio than for the 40 most common verbs in any other corpus.

The conversations were further characterised by very high frequencies of one group of verbs: *know, think, get, go, say, mean.* Some, but not all, of these differences can be attributed to the use of certain verbs in 'discourse items' (*you know, I mean* etc.).

The semantic analysis showed that there was a small number of verb types (MOTION, SPEAKING, ATTENTION, REST, WANTING, BEGINNING, THINKING and GIVING) which accounted for the vast majority of commonly used verbs. Most of these 'core verbs' occurred in all four corpora. However, in conversation there was a high frequency of 'private verbs', i.e. verbs that express private attitudes, thoughts and emotions, and in our classification correspond to such categories as verbs of THINKING (*know, think* etc.), WANTING (*mean, need* etc.) and ATTENTION (*see, look* etc.). This result agrees with Biber's statement that private verbs (and also present tense forms) are among the features with largest weights on the factor 'indicating a verbal, as opposed to nominal, style' (1988: 105).

Returning to the observation about speaker performance, made at the outset of this chapter, what can our study tell us about speaking, in public and private, and its relation to written discourse? In general, the differences we have noted are greater between private speaking and public speaking than between public speaking and writing. Whereas private speaking has several characteristic features, we found no single verb feature that we can claim to be distinctly typical of public speaking. Rather, we want to suggest that it is features other than those studied in this chapter, such as textual organisation and oral performance, which constitute the main contrasts between good and bad public speaking.

An essential part of oral performance is prosodic chunking, the division of sentences into smaller bits of information (tone units or information units) with appropriate pauses and pitch movements on nuclear syllables. Here is a prosodic transcription of the beginning of the SEC passage given in section 2 which gives some indication of how the lecture was delivered in oral form:

Lǎst week|
I showed my **hánd**|

as the **prĭce** mechanist |
that I **àm** | - - -
and I **árgued** | - - -
with the help of my fictional colleague Mr **MacQuĕdy** | - - -
that individual willingness to **páy** |
should be the **măin** test |
of how resources are **ùsed** | - - -

This transcription is a simplified version of the original SEC extract, but shows what we believe to be the key prosodic features of public speaking: tone units, nuclei, tones and pauses. The basic information units (i.e. tone units, which are not all co-terminous with sentences or clauses) are separated by vertical bars and printed on individual lines. The most prosodically prominent words in each tone unit (nuclei) are printed in bold face. The nuclear syllable is indicated by a falling tone (e.g. **ùsed**), a rising tone (e.g. **hánd**), or a falling-rising tone (e.g. **măin**). Pauses are marked with three dashes (- - -).

Our word-class data, however limited in this study, indicate that public speaking is much closer to writing than to conversation. Yet, we think that a fine balance between the requirements of writing and speaking, encapsulated in Halliday's synoptic/dynamic view (1985: 87) and Biber's informational/involved production (1988: 107), is what makes or, rather, helps to make a good speaker. Biber mentions two separate communicative parameters: the primary purpose of the writer/speaker and the production circumstances. On both parameters, public speaking is more like writing than like conversation in being 'informational' rather than 'interactive, affective, and involved'; and in offering 'careful editing possibilities, enabling precision in lexical choice and an integrated textual structure, versus circumstances dictated by real-time constraints, resulting in generalised lexical choice and a generally fragmented presentation of information' (ibid.). Yet, a conference audience may feel that a lecture is better when unscripted than scripted. While this may be true for the lecturer who can handle this mode of presentation, it is not reading *per se* that spoils a lecture. More important for a lecture to be successful than can be captured by any one word-class feature is, we believe, the combination of a text organisation which includes an element of involvement and an oral delivery suited to auditory reception.

Notes

1. We want to acknowledge support to the research project Public Speaking by the Swedish Council for Research in the Humanities and Social Sciences. We also want to thank Bengt Altenberg, Bryan Mosey and the editors of this volume for helpful comments on a draft of this chapter.

2. The figure for full verbs in LLC has been extrapolated from the total verb percentage in Table 15.1, with the other types subtracted. 'Contractions' stands for 'indeterminate non-full verbs' in LLC, where contracted verb forms have not been subdivided and placed under their respective full forms in the word lists, as in the other corpora, but are kept as contractions in the word list: *he's*, *I'll* etc. However, in this table the only included contracted forms are those that follow personal pronouns (e.g. *she's*, *they'd*), *that* (e.g. *that's*) and *there* (e.g. *there's*). It would be very difficult to find all contracted forms without having access to word-class tags. For the contractions *'d* or *'s* it is impossible to determine, from the contracted verb alone, what the verb is. It is, however, certain that it is not a full verb. By far the most common form is *it's*, accounting for almost half of the tokens (1102 tokens). The figures for LOB and Brown are as follows:

Contraction	LOB	Brown
's = has	89	65
's = is	1051	893
'd = would	233	214
'd = had	302	176

3. Table 15.4 shows the most common verb-lexemes in the four corpora. For easier comparison with LOB and Brown, the figures for SEC and LLC have been normalised, i.e. adjusted so as to show frequencies per one million words. (The size of the spoken subcorpora used in this study is 34,000 words for SEC, 175,000 words for the LLC verb lexeme count and 50,000 words for the LLC word-class count.) The frequency bands should be read as follows: '> 5,000' = 'frequency of over 5,000 verb lexemes per one million words' etc. The table includes verbs with a frequency higher than 400 verbs per one million words.

References

Altenberg, B. (1990) Spoken English and the dictionary. In Svartvik, J. (ed.), *The London–Lund Corpus of spoken English: description and research.* Lund University Press. 177–191.

(1991) A bibliography of publications relating to English computer corpora. In Johansson, S. and Stenström, A.-B. (eds.), *English computer corpora: selected papers and research guide*. Berlin and New York: Mouton de Gruyter. 355–396.

Biber, D. (1988) *Variation across speech and writing.* Cambridge University Press.

Collins, P. (1991) The modals of obligation and necessity in Australian English. In Aijmer, K. and Altenberg, B. (eds.), *English corpus linguistics: studies in honour of Jan Svartvik*. Longman: London. 145–165.

Dixon, R. M. W. (1991) *A new approach to English grammar, on semantic principles*. Oxford: Clarendon Press.

Francis, W. N. and Kučera, H. (1982) *Frequency analysis of English usage: lexicon and grammar.* Boston: Houghton Mifflin.

Greenbaum, S. and Svartvik, J. (1990) The London–Lund Corpus of Spoken English. In Svartvik, J. (ed.), *The London–Lund Corpus of Spoken English: description and research*. Lund University Press. 11–59.

Halliday, M. A. K. (1985) *Spoken and written language*. Deakin University Press.

Hofland, K. and Johansson, S. (1982) *Word frequencies in British and American English*. Bergen: The Norwegian Computing Centre for the Humanities.

Johansson, S. and Hofland, K. (1989) *Frequency analysis of English vocabulary and grammar.* Oxford University Press.

Knowles, G. (1993) From text to waveform. In Souter, C. and Atwell, E. (eds.), *Corpus-based computational linguistics*. Amsterdam: Rodopi. 47–58.

Knowles, G. and Alderson, P. R. (1994) *Working with speech*. London: Longman.

Quirk, R., Greenbaum, S., Leech, G. and Svartvik, J. (1985) *A comprehensive grammar of the English language*. London: Longman.

Stenström, A. -B. (1990) Lexical items peculiar to spoken discourse. In Svartvik, J. (ed.), *The London–Lund Corpus of Spoken English: description and research*. Lund University Press. 136–175.

Svartvik, J. and Wright, D. (1977) The use of *ought* in teenage English. In Greenbaum, S. (ed.), *Acceptability in language*. The Hague: Mouton. 179–201.

Wichmann, A. (1991) Beginnings, middles and ends: a study of initiality and finality in the Spoken English Corpus. Unpublished PhD dissertation. Department of Linguistics and Modern English Language, Lancaster University.

16 Some remarks on comment clauses[1]

ANNA-BRITA STENSTRÖM

1 Introduction

The verbs *think*, *mean*, *know* and *see* have the following syntactic, semantic and pragmatic features in common: they all take a direct object in the form of a nominal *that*-clause, they all belong to the 'private' type of factual verbs, and they are all used in *comment clauses* (*I think*, *I mean*, *you know* and *you see*) with discourse-specific functions (see e.g. Quirk et al. 1985: 1049, 1112, 1481–1483).

Comment clauses realised by *I think*, *I mean*, *you know* and *you see*, which are used more frequently and for more purposes than any other comment clause, are notoriously difficult to describe in grammatical and semantic terms alone, simply because they depend on the context for their interpretation.

This chapter begins with a brief characterisation of comment clauses in general and the use of *I think*, *I mean*, *you know* and *you see* in particular, as observed in the London–Lund Corpus of Spoken English (LLC) (see Svartvik and Quirk 1980, Svartvik 1990). It goes on to query the status of so-called *type 1 comment clauses*[2] (Quirk et al. 1985: 1113–1115) and certain aspects of the current description, focussing on the interplay between syntax, semantics and pragmatics for an adequate description of their functions.

Considering that *know*, *think*, *mean* and *see* have roles in speech that they do not have in writing, it should come as no surprise that they rank as high as 15, 25, 44 and 45 respectively in the surreptitiously recorded conversations of the London–Lund Corpus, but do not figure at all in the written Lancaster–Oslo–Bergen and Brown corpora in the ranking list comparing the 100 most frequent words in spoken and written language (see Svartvik 1990: 66–68, and Svartvik and Ekedahl, this volume).

In spoken language, *mean*, *know*, *see*, and (less commonly) *think* are typically used in comment clauses:

(1) you've said ALR\EADY **I TH/INK#** that you went to the family UNIV\/ERSITY# (6.4: 599–600) (For a key to prosodic symbols, see Appendix)

In written language, except maybe in dialogues, verbs like *mean, know* and *see* are mainly used as ordinary transitive verbs followed by an object, often in the form of a nominal *that*-clause, as in the following example from LLC:

(2) **I think** that we mustn't worry too much AB\OUT TH/IS# (1.1: 133)

2 General characteristics

Clauses referred to in this chapter as comment clauses have also been termed *softeners* (Crystal and Davy 1975), *fumbles* (Edmondson 1981), *discourse markers* (Schiffrin 1986), *pragmatic expressions* (Erman 1987), and *discourse signals* (Stenström 1989).

Quirk et al. (1985: 1112) define comment clauses as *parenthetical disjuncts*, either content disjuncts expressing the speaker's comment on what s/he says in the matrix clause, or style disjuncts conveying the speaker's view on the way s/he is speaking. *I think, you know* and *you see* are listed as examples of content disjuncts. *I mean*, on the other hand, is not mentioned as a disjunct, but as a device used for *mistake editing* (1985: 1313). However, if we accept Quirk et al.'s definition of comment clauses, *I mean* seems to share enough features with *I think, you know* and *you see* to qualify with them as a type 1 comment clause (1985: 1112ff). The main characteristics of comment clauses are the following:

- they contain a transitive verb
- they resemble matrix clauses but lack complementation
- they are generally syntactically dependent
- they tend to be stereotyped
- they have a number of 'semantic' functions

Like disjuncts in general, comment clauses can occur in initial, medial and final *sentence and/or turn position*:[3]

(3) A: ***you know** I I** I'm I'm just constantly. bowled /\OVER# by your VERS\ATILITY# (2.11: 1260–1261)

(4) A: @:m . you've said ALR\EADY **I TH/INK#** that you went to the family UNIV\/ERSITY# . (6.4: 599–600)

(5) A: because she felt this was not the moment for votes for W\OMEN# or something of TH\AT sort **you S/EE#** (6.4: 723–724)

Unlike disjuncts in general, the same clause can occur in more than one position in the same sentence/turn:

(6) A: . . . because ((**I mean**)) you mustn't take him **I mean** you mustn't . take him too S\/ERIOUSLY **I mean**#
B: \M# (7.2: 572–573)

The statement that comment clauses generally occur in a separate tone unit (see Quirk et al. 1985: 1112) is undoubtedly true for the large majority of comment clauses but not for *I think* and *I mean*, which often have no tone at all. A study of the first 60 instances of *I think*, *I mean*, *you know* and *you see* in the London–Lund Corpus produced the results in Table 16.1. (The first column shows for each clause the percentage carrying a tone, either on the pronoun or the verb, and the second column gives the percentage of tone-carrying clauses occurring in a separate tone unit.)

Table 16.1 *Percentage of comment clauses marked for tonicity and separate tone*

Comment clause	+ tone	+ separate tone unit
you see	84%	74%
you know	75%	67%
I think	43%	50%
I mean	16%	78%

The study shows that *you see, you know* and *I mean*, but not *I think,* generally had a separate tone unit in case they were marked for tonicity, which partly supports the statement in Quirk et al. (1985). Admittedly, this is a small-scale study, but nevertheless the results are not unlikely to reflect the tendency in the larger corpus.

There appears to be a clear difference between '*I*-oriented' and '*you*-oriented' comment clauses with regard to tonicity. Only 16 per cent of the instances of *I mean* had a tone marker, and *I think* was marked for tonicity in less than half of the cases, whereas both *you see* and *you know* are high up the scale. This not only reflects a tendency on the part of the speaker to minimise attention to the self in favour of the listener, but is also the direct result of the diverse *discourse roles* of these comment clauses (see Quirk et al. 1985: 1481–1483, Stenström 1994). As regards occurrence in a separate tone unit, *I think* was found to be the one clause type that was pronounced in a 'compound' tone unit (see Crystal 1975: 26) as often as in a separate tone unit:

(7) A: I've \ALSO **I TH/INK#** managed to {G\ET them} at L\AST# (1.1: 956–957)

I think, *I mean*, *you know* and *you see* might be regarded as the *core set* of candidates for type 1 comment clauses, since they outnumber by far their nearest competitors, according to a count of all occurrences in LLC (see Table 16.2).

Table 16.2 *The overall frequency of potential type 1 comment clauses in LLC*

Clause	Frequency
you know	1985
I think	1966
I mean	1425
you see	701
I suppose	257
I believe	83
I imagine	20

In theory, they can all serve *either* as comment clauses *or* as matrix clauses, as illustrated in (1) and (2). However, the likelihood for these clauses to serve as comment clauses varies. A comparison of the 20 first occurrences of each type of clause in the corpus (to match the number of occurrences of *I imagine*; see Table 16.2) showed that there is a considerable difference in this respect between *you see*, *you know* and *I mean* on the one hand, and *I think*, *I suppose*, *I imagine* and *I believe* on the other. This is shown in Table 16.3.

Table 16.3 *Percentage used as comment clauses*

Clause realisation	Comment clause function
you see	100%
you know	90%
I mean	85%
I think	30%
I suppose	25%
I imagine	25%
I believe	10%

A complementary survey of occurrences in the larger corpus indicated that the figures in Table 16.3 could probably be taken as a rough reflection of the overall tendency in conversation in general.

You see was almost exclusively used as a comment clause. It was sometimes found as part of a longer clause introduced by a conjunction but with a similar function (*if you S/EE what I mean#*). It also occurred in the matrix clause of an interrogative utterance (*do you S/EE what I mean#*).

A similar pattern could be observed for *you know,* which, like *you see*, was sometimes introduced by a conjunction (*as you KN\OW#*) and, somewhat more often than *you see*, appeared in questions (*do you know anything definite AB/OUT him#*).

I think, by contrast, was far less often used as a comment clause than as a matrix clause followed by a *that*-clause.

The grammatical status of *I mean* is not always obvious. There were straightforward cases like *what I mean /IS#*, where *mean* acts as a transitive verb in a pseudo-cleft sentence, and slightly doubtful cases like (8):

(8) I don't KN/OW# **I mean** I haven't B\EEN in# - - the academic world - L\ONG enough# - (1.3: 1181–1183)

where *mean* could possibly be analysed as a transitive verb followed by a nominal *that*-clause with deleted *that*, but more convincingly as a syntactically deletable, but situationally required, comment clause.

The pragmatic function of *I think*, *I mean*, *you know* and *you see* in spoken interaction is influenced, first, by the inherent semantic content of the verbs, while the pronouns involved govern their orientation; second, by position in the sentence (and/or turn) and prosody (see e.g. Stenström 1990, 1994); and third, by the entire context of situation (see Brown and Yule 1983, chapter 2).

Generally speaking, Schiffrin's neat summary of the functions of *you know* (*y'know*) and *I mean* can perfectly well also take care of *you see* and *I think* (see Schiffrin 1986: 267):

Influenced by literal meanings
- *you know* and *you see* mark transitions in information state, relevant for participation frameworks
- *I mean* and *I think* mark speaker orientation toward own talk, i.e. modification of ideas and intentions

Less direct relation to literal meanings
- *you know* and *you see* gain attention from hearer
- *I mean* and *I think* maintain attention on speaker

And one might add:

Minimal relation to literal meanings
- they all act as stallers indicating ongoing planning
- they all act as connectives adding to text cohesion

More specifically, *I think* can be used as a hedge, expressing tentativeness (see e.g. Quirk et al. 1985: 1113). *I mean*, the meaning of which is 'extraordinarily difficult to define' (Crystal and Davy 1975: 97), can be used as a mistake editor (Quirk et al. 1985: 1313) and as a device for introducing clarifications, explanations and additional information (Crystal and Davy 1975: 97f, Erman 1987: 175). *You know* can be used to indicate shared knowledge (c.f. Östman 1981, Stenström 1984, Schiffrin 1986, Erman 1987), and *you see* can be used as a 'request for sympathetic hearing' (Crystal and Davy 1975: 96).

Combinations of *I think, I mean, you know* and *you see* are frequent:

(9) **I mean you know** he'll suddenly out of the blue suddenly say . . . (2.11: 199)
(10) **I think . you know**. really. you you can't blame the individual in this C/ASE# (5.1: 94)
(11) it's C\ERTAINLY# **you KN/OW#** WORTHWH\/ILE# **\/I think#** (71: 1052–1055)
(12) but **I TH\INK# you see I mean** having had the EXP\ERIENCE of# @:m being married BEF\ORE# ... (5.10: 82–83)

Together, they serve as stallers, but taken one by one they are not doing the same thing. Schiffrin (1986: 267) concludes that *y'know* and *I mean* are complementary and socially sanctioned. The same goes for *I think* and *you see*.

As regards function in relation to position, compare *you know* in three different places in (13)–(15). Notice also the typically reduced vowel quality of *you* in (13):

(13) A: oh this is **y'KN/OW#** this just isn't \/ON# (6.8: 928–929)
(14) B: I mean the ((@ @)) the way that Mallet PRES\ENTED them# with every (possib) ***you KN=OW#** when Mallet gets the* bit between
A: *((/\OH# this is just 2 to 3 sylls))*
B: his . T\EETH# he brings in every argument from every field of activity under the S\UN# (1.2: 686–691)
(15) A: well it's a long P\ERIOD# **you KN/OW#** (1.2: 1196–1197)

According to Crystal and Davy (1975: 92f), sentence-initial *you know* is 'an informal way of attracting attention or softening the force of what follows', while sentence-medial *you know* 'introduces a fresh attempt to get a meaning across', and sentence-final *you know* usually invites agreement. Consider, for instance, (16) where the appealing force is reinforced by a fall-rise, while the clause-initial *Y\OU know*, with an atypical fall on *you*, urges the listener to accept the message.

(16) the V=ASE# H\OVERED# . hovered and I thought it was going to CR\ASH# . **you KN\/OW#** but **Y\OU know#** this this is the TR/UTH# (11.3: 973–978)

3 The status of comment clauses

In their discussion of the semantic roles of adverbial clauses, Quirk et al. (1985: 1113f) point out that there is a correspondence between sentences containing type 1 comment clauses, i.e. clauses that 'generally contain a transitive verb or adjective which elsewhere requires a nominal *that*-clause as object', and sentences containing indirect statements. This is illustrated by sentences (17) and (18):

(17) It belongs to me, *you know.*
(18) *You know* that it belongs to me.

The reasoning goes as follows. If the subordinate clause in (18) (*that it belongs to me*) is made into the matrix clause in (17), and the matrix clause in (18) (*you know*) is made into the comment clause in (17), the result is a reversal of syntactic roles, notably 'the relationship of subordination between the two clauses' (Quirk et al. 1985: 1113).

This gives rise to the following query: Can type 1 comment clauses, defined as disjuncts, which are described as not integrated within, but only loosely attached to, the clause in which they have no constituent function (1985: 613), really be said to be subordinate, i.e. embedded, and serve as a constituent in the main clause (1985: 44, 858)? There is evidently a clash here.

Judging by the tendency in LLC, reflected in Table 16.4, the likelihood for

Table 16.4 *Percentage of* that *and of nominal* that-*clauses per clause*

Clause	% *that*	% nominal *that*-clause
I think	7%	6%
I mean	2%	0.8%
you know	2%	0.5%
you see	2%	0.1%

the clauses discussed in this chapter to act as matrix clauses followed by a nominal *that*-clause, as in (18), is minimal. *I think* is an exception.

The first column shows the percentage of the element *that* following *I think, I mean, you know* and *you see,* i.e. including demonstrative *that*, relative *that*, the determiner *that* and the subordinating conjunction *that*, but excluding zero *that*. The second column gives the percentage of nominal *that*-clauses following *I think, I mean, you know* and *you see*.

It appears that only *I think* acted as a matrix clause to any extent worth mentioning (to be compared with *I imagine* 10 per cent, *I believe* 7 per cent and *I suppose* 3 per cent). In reality, however, the percentage is indubitably much higher, since *that* is most certainly more often deleted than expressed (see also Finegan and Biber, this volume). *I mean, you know* and *you see*, on the other hand, which serve almost exclusively as comment clauses (see Table 16.2), are rarely followed by *that* at all, let alone the conjunction *that*.

Two questions are of particular interest in this connection. The first is related to *clause realisation*, the second to the *position* of the comment clause in the sentence.

With the comment clause as a starting-point (contrary to the previous discussion exemplified by (17) and (18)), the question is whether conversion of a comment clause structure into a matrix plus *that*-clause structure would be equally acceptable regardless of clause realisation. Consider (19)–(22):

(19) a. it's too ELL\IPTIC **I TH/INK#** - (6.3: 853)
b. **I think** that it's too elliptic
(20) a. it's difficult to know - you KN/OW **I mean#** (7.2: 551)
b. **I mean** that it's difficult to know - you know
(21) a. I'm more AM\USED **you KN/OW#** (1.1: 813)
b. **you know** that I'm more amused
(22) a. this is the trouble in SCH\OOLS# **you S/EE#** (1.2: 1287–1288)
b. **you see** that this is the trouble in schools

The answer is 'no', except from a purely syntactic point of view, according to which all the (b) sentences are equally acceptable. From a semantic/pragmatic point of view, (21b) and (22b) are definitely less acceptable than (19b) and (20b), which suggests that it is more natural for *I*-oriented than for *you*-oriented clauses to be converted. The reason is obviously that we do not generally go around telling the person we are talking to that he or she knows or sees something.

To make allowance for such awkward cases, Quirk et al. (1985: 1113) argue that 'the verb in the comment clause may have only one of the meanings possible for the verb in the matrix clause', so that, for instance, *you know* in the matrix clause means 'you know that', while *you know* in the comment clause means 'I want you to know that'. On the same lines, it would be possible to say that *you see* means 'you realise that', if it occurs in the matrix clause, and 'I want you to realise that', if it occurs in the comment clause. However, none of the inherent meanings of *know* or *see* have got anything to do with 'want', so it seems that the interpretation is rather a matter of pragmatics than semantics.

The second question is whether conversion is perhaps less natural for sentence-medial than for sentence-final comment clauses. Consider (23)–(26):

(23) a. I've \ALSO **I TH/INK#** managed to {G\ET them} at L\AST# (1.1: 956–957)
b. **I think that** I've also managed to get them at last

(24) a. there is one SN\AG **I mean#** that has (ko . @) or rather a (ko) COMPLIC=ATION# (8.2: 640–641)
b. **I mean that** there is one snag that has . . .

(25) a. now that he's finished his EXAMIN\ATIONS# **you KN/OW#** you'll be S\EEING him# (1.1: 567–569)
b. **you know that** now that he's finished . . .

(26) a. in BR\IGHTON **you S/EE#** we ask them for a S\/UMMARY# (1.1: 959–960)
b. **you see that** in Brighton we ask them for a summary

As in the previous case, conversion from sentence-medial position is fully acceptable from a syntactic point of view, but not always from a semantic and seldom, if at all, from a pragmatic point of view.

Summing up, from what has emerged the potentiality for comment clauses to be converted into matrix clauses followed by a nominal *that*-clause seems to be a scalar matter, mainly depending on the semantic and pragmatic properties of the verb involved in the comment clause.

It appears that, in their capacity as comment clauses, *I mean* tended to occur in initial and mid-sentence position facing forward, and that both *I think* and *you see* tended to occur in sentence-final position facing backward, while *you know* was found as often at the end of the sentence facing backward as in the middle of the sentence facing both ways. In other words, the main difference between sentence-final and sentence-medial comment clauses lies in their scope:

(27) W/\ELL# - **I mean** L\/AST term# she was practically NONEX\ISTENT# . (6.2: 833–834)

(28) but @ really I've got about . THR\EE W/EEKS# less than TH/AT# of hardish W=ORK# spread over those two M\ONTHS# **you S/EE#** (1.1: 155–159)

(29) and @ I don't want to @: **you KN/OW#** run ourselves out of an external EX/AMINER# (1.1: 135–137)

While the entire sentence is within the scope of a sentence-initial or sentence-final comment clause, (27) and (28), the scope of a sentence-medial comment clause, (29), is either what precedes or what comes after or both, depending on the realisation of the clause.

Generalising slightly, we can conclude that in sentence-initial position:

- *I think* is a matrix clause
- *I mean* is possibly a matrix but rather a comment clause
- *you know* is generally a comment clause
- *you see* is always a comment clause

They all act as comment clauses in sentence-medial and sentence-final position.

One crucial question remains, however. Should the comment clauses discussed here, i.e. those realised by *I think, I mean, you know* and *you see*, really be regarded as disjuncts? They differ from other disjuncts in at least the following respects:

- they are extremely frequent and have a highly neutralised meaning
- they serve a different function in a different position
- they are context and situation dependent
- they are person-to-person-oriented and socially required
- they are syntactically deletable but pragmatically required

4 Conclusion

Quirk et al. (1985: 1481–1483) bring up the functions of *I think, I mean, you know* and *you see* again in their last chapter, now under the heading 'Speaker/hearer contact', which emphasises the dual membership of these comment clauses. On the one hand, they are grammatical structures consisting of a subject and a verb that can be interpreted in semantic terms. On the other hand, the way they are typically used in spoken discourse requires a pragmatic interpretation.

Maybe comment clauses of the type discussed in this chapter had better be placed in a specific discourse category together with other discourse phenomena, such as formulae and interjections, instead of being forced into a traditional grammatical category.

Appendix

Key to prosodic symbols

#	tone unit boundary
\	falling tone
/	rising tone
\/	falling-rising tone
/\	rising-falling tone
=	level tone
.	brief silent pause
-	unit silent pause
- -(-)	long silent pause
@(m)	brief voiced pause
@:(m)	unit voiced pause
* *	overlapping speech
{ }	subordinate tone unit

Notes

1. I am grateful to my colleagues Leiv Egil Breivik and Kari E. Haugland for comments on an earlier draft of this chapter.
2. Type 1 comment clauses are distinguished from type 2 comment clauses, which are introduced by the subordinator *as* (*as it happens*) or relative *as* (*as you know*), and type 3 comment clauses, which are nominal relative clauses introduced by *what* (*what's more surprising*) (see Quirk et al. 1985: 115–118).
3. A turn is everything a speaker says before the next speaker takes over.

References

Brown, G. and Yule, G. (1983) *Discourse analysis*. Cambridge University Press.

Coulthard, M. and Montgomery, M. (eds.) (1981) *Studies in discourse analysis*. London: Routledge and Kegan Paul.

Crystal, D. and Davy, D. (1975) *Advanced conversational English*. London: Longman.

Edmondson, W. (1981) *Spoken discourse*. London: Longman.

Erman, B. (1987) *Pragmatic expressions in English: a study of 'you know,' 'you see' and 'I mean' in face-to-face conversation. Stockholm Studies in English* **69**. Stockholm: Almqvist and Wiksell.

Östman, J.-O. (1981) *'You know': a discourse-functional approach*. Amsterdam: John Benjamins.

Quirk, R., Greenbaum, G., Leech, G. and Svartvik, J. (1985) *A comprehensive grammar of the English language*. London: Longman.

Schiffrin, D. (1986) *Discourse markers*. Cambridge University Press.

Stenström, A. -B. (1989) Discourse signals: towards a model of analysis. In Weydt, H. (ed.), *Sprechen mit Partikeln*. Berlin and New York: Walter de Gruyter. 561–574.
(1990) Lexical items peculiar to spoken discourse. In Svartvik, J. (ed.) *The London–Lund Corpus of Spoken English*. Lund University Press. 211–252.
(1994) *An introduction to spoken interaction*. London: Longman.
Svartvik, J. (ed.) (1990) *The London–Lund Corpus of Spoken English*. Lund University Press.
Svartvik, J. and Quirk, R. (eds.) (1980) *A corpus of English conversation. Lund Studies in English* **56**. Lund University Press.

Index of names

Subject index